Discover a Watershed: The Everglades

D1560976

Produced for the South Florida Water Management District by The Watercourse

Principal Authors

Reference section and Activities
George B. Robinson, Technical Advisor to the Director
Sandra C. Robinson, Assistant Director

Activities and Field-Test
Jennie Lane, Curriculum Writer

with The Watercourse Staff

Dennis Nelson, Director
Linda Hveem, Business Manager
Nancy Carrasco, Administrative Support

The Watercourse
201 Culbertson Hall
Montana State University
Bozeman, MT 59717-0057

 Printed on recyled paper.

South Florida Water Management District

3301 Gun Club Road, West Palm Beach, Florida 33406 • (407) 686-8800 • FL WATS 1-800-432-2045

To the Reader,

The Everglades ecosystem is much more than just the sawgrass prairie many people have heard so much about. This ecosystem is defined and connected by water. Its watershed boundaries extend from Orlando to Key West and Ft. Pierce on the Atlantic coast to Ft. Myers on the Gulf of Mexico. We often refer to it as the Kissimmee-Lake Okeechobee-Everglades ecosystem. It is home to more than 5.5 million people.

As you will read, the Everglades ecosystem is unique on this planet and it is endangered. The activities of well-intentioned people during the last 100 years have substantially changed the size and function of the natural system. We cannot turn the clock back a century, but there is hope for what remains of the natural system.

We have a much greater appreciation and understanding of ecological systems than we did just 50 years ago. Most people want to "save the Everglades" but managing water and related resources in southern Florida is a balancing act. Meeting the needs of people for flood control and water supply while protecting the natural environment is a tremendous challenge. By reading this book, we hope you will become more knowledgeable about this global treasure and become motivated to get involved in helping us to restore what is left to its more natural functions.

The South Florida Water Management District is pleased to have had the opportunity to develop this book, *Discover A Watershed: The Everglades* in partnership with The Watercourse. We hope you will find it interesting and valuable reading. Your comments on the book and your suggestions are welcome as we embark on the most ambitious restoration project ever attempted.

About the South Florida Water Management District and the Watercourse

· ·

The South Florida Water Management District

South Florida's subtropical extremes of hurricane, flood, and drought combined with efforts to populate this "new frontier" led the U.S. Congress to adopt legislation creating the Central and Southern Florida Flood Control Project in 1948.

The project's primary goal was to serve the needs of the region's growing agricultural and urban populations and protect and manage water resources. The U.S. Army Corps of Engineers would, over the following decades, design and build a vast 1,400-mile network of levees, canals, and other improved waterways and water control structures—which would help to "tame" the often unpredictable weather extremes of the region.

In 1949, the Florida Legislature created the Central and Southern Florida Flood Control District (FCD) to act as the local sponsor for the project—operating and maintaining the water control network with funding from property taxes levied within District boundaries.

Throughout its history, this regional water resource agency evolved and grew in response primarily to population growth and development and its impact on water resources.

The Florida Water Resources Act of 1972 launched the most significant change in the state's approach to natural resource management. This legislation divided the state into five regional water management districts, greatly expanding the responsibilities of the existing FCD and establishing water management districts throughout the state. This included a greater emphasis on water quality and environmental protection initiatives.

The FCD was renamed the South Florida Water Management District in 1976, and new boundaries were drawn to encompass the region's primary watersheds.

Since 1949, the district has grown into a multifaceted agency responsible for most water resource related issues—from providing flood protection and water supply protection to people living in cities and on farms to restoring and managing natural ecosystems.

The Watercourse

In this decade of change, people are being asked to make important decisions about critical water management issues. Watercourse programs provide opportunities for young people and adults to learn about water resources. The goal of The Watercourse is to promote and facilitate public understanding of atmospheric, surface, and ground water resources and related management issues through publications, instruction, and networking.

The scope of The Watercourse is nationwide, its delivery unbiased, and its mission to build informed leadership in resource decision making. The Watercourse responds to the informational needs of many diverse interest groups. Above all, The Watercourse relies on cooperation with other resource managers, policymakers, water educators, and citizens.

Since its inception in 1989 as a nonprofit organization, The Watercourse has expanded to accommodate the varied interests of water users nationwide. Currently, The Watercourse has two programs: The Watercourse Public Education Program and

· ·

Project WET (Water Education for Teachers).

The Watercourse Public Education Program focuses on contemporary water management issues through the use of materials, training and instruction, and networking. The program staff offers partners over two decades of experience in educational material development and instruction and training. This wealth of experience combined with the program's extensive grassroots network of educators and resource specialists has attracted numerous organizations and agencies to contract for a variety of educational support services. In this capacity, The Watercourse Public Education Program assists local, state, and federal organizations to reach target groups with relevant information.

Project WET (Water Education for Teachers). Project WET is a nonprofit water education program for educators and young people, grades K-12. In 1990, the Western Regional Environmental Education Council (WREEC) became an official cosponsor, in partnership with The Watercourse, of Project WET. The goal of Project WET is to facilitate and promote the awareness, appreciation, knowledge, and stewardship of water resources through the development and dissemination of classroom-ready teaching aids and through the establishment of state- and internationally-sponsored Project WET programs.

In the next decade, through publications, instruction, and networking, The Watercourse and Project WET will reach over a million educators and millions of young people and citizens. Educating people about wetlands, nonpoint source pollution, groundwater, water conservation, and contemporary water issues will insure that water is not only a shared resource, but also a shared responsibility.

Acknowledgements

· ·

Many people contributed to the development and completion of *Discover a Watershed: The Everglades*. The Watercourse and the South Florida Water Management District gratefully acknowledge the participation of all of the individuals involved.

The Technical Advisory Committee reviewed the text and activities for scientific and technical accuracy. Members included:

Ms. Sally Mlecz-Kennedy, Financial Analyst, SFWMD Ecosystem Restoration Office

Mr. Dave Swift, Senior Environmental Scientist, SFWMD Planning Department

Ms. Nancy Urban, Staff Environmental Scientist, SFWMD Research Department, Research Appraisal Division

Ms. Cathy Vogel, Director, Office of Government and Public Affairs, SFWMD

Mr. Paul Whalen, Supervising Professional, SFWMD Regulation Department, Surface Water Management Division

Dr. William B. Robertson, Jr., Research Ecologist, Everglades National Park

Dr. John Ogden, former Wildlife Biologist, Everglades National Park

Ms. Sandy Dayhoff, Supervisory Park Ranger, Environmental Education, Everglades National Park

Dr. Pete Rosendahl, Vice President, Environmental Relations, Flo-Sun, Incorporated

Dr. Bernie Yokel, Florida Audubon Society

Mr. Woody Darden, Regional Director, Florida Game and Fresh Water Fish Commission

Mr. Louis Hornung, U. S. Army Corps of Engineers

Mr. Roy Rogers, Arvida Corporation

Ms. Teresa Woody, Sierra Club

Mr. Art Darling, Florida Dairy Farmers

Mr. Jim Lewis, Florida Department of Environmental Protection

Mr. Estus Whitfield, Governor's Office of Environmental Affairs

The Educational Advisory Committee reviewed the text and activities for educational relevance. Members included:

Mr. Craig Carr, Osceola County Schools

Mr. Bill Hammond, Natural Context

Dr. David LaHart, Florida State University

Mr. David Makepeace, Coral Shores High School, Monroe County

Dr. Tom Marcinkowski, Science Education Department, Florida Institute of Technology

Ms. Georgia Stamp, Oak Ridge Middle School, Collier County

Dr. Mary Ann Davis, University of South Florida

Mr. Neil De Jong, Chief of Interpretation, Everglades National Park

Ms. Helene Nemeth, Environmental Education Coordinator, Dade County Public Schools

Southern Florida educators participated in a workshop and helped to generate the activities in *Discover a Watershed: The Everglades*.

They were:

Pat Althouse
Debbie Butler
Craig Carr
Ruby Daniels
Katie Flannagan
Karen Aubry
Bill Haynes
Sande Haynes
Tom Marcinkowski
Helene Nemeth
Nan Owens
Peggy St. James
Georgia Stamp

· ·

John Wakeman
Marti Yadlowski
Susan Toth-King
Mary Ann Davis
David Makepeace
Roy King

Learning activities were field tested by the following classroom teachers, whose comments and recommendations were helpful in preparing the final versions.

Georgette Treloar
Jim Stark
Susan Weber
Chuck Gibson
Carol Fleck
Carla Bruning
Deborah Vasconi
Pamela J. Shlachtman
Marian Manley
Lynn Sweetay
Irma A. Jarvis
Rosalee Riddle
Wendy Glass
Jamie Prusak
John W. Neth, III
Stephanie Karno
Candace W. Little
Donna Lea Needham
Katie Flannagan
Jan Marriner
Leisha Dyer
Ruby Daniels
Diane Thorpe
Carol Lendermor
Carol Erwin
Nina Campbell
Eric Hoeppner
Steve Karno
Marcia Bisnett
Nadia Le Bohec

Others, whose comments and/or assistance with the text, were helpful in preparing the final manuscript, included:

Sam Poole
Mike Slayton
Sharon Trost

Keith Smith
Kathy Malone
Geoff Shaughnessy
Francois Laroche
Cindy Rezabeck
Magi Terry
Nick Aumen
Ann Weinrich
Eric Swartz
JoAnn Hyres
Ahmad-Poudratchi

Interviews with the following people were helpful in the preparation of *Discover a Watershed: The Everglades.*

Tom MacVicar
Stephen Tiger
Allan Milledge
Lou Toth
Roy King
Bill Laitner
John Ogden
Bill Robertson
Pat Tolle
Pete Rhoads
Marjory Stoneman Douglas
Sam Poole
Jim Webb
Sonny Bass
Randy Jones
Karsten Rist

Montana State University students, Jessica M. Parks and Richard J. Browne assisted with the preparation of the final draft.

The knowledge and editorial expertise of Chuck McCartney of the Broward Edition of *The Miami Herald* were of great value in the final preparation of the manuscript.

The following people assisted in securing permissions for the use of illustrations:

Ms. Susan A. Meyers, National Park Service

Dr. Graig Shaak, Florida Museum of Natural History

Mr. Bill Keegan, Florida Museum of Natural History

Mr. Bob Kauser, Wadsworth Publishing Company

Ms. Jennie Boothe, Pineapple Press

Mr. David M. Cussen, Pineapple Press

Mr. Bob Fuerst, University of Miami Press

Many helpful comments were offered by the co-author's father, Harry B. Robinson.

The authors would like to thank Tom Renison for sharing his intimate knowledge of the watershed. His skill as a pilot added a special dimension to the authors' understanding of the Everglades ecosystem.

We would also like to thank the staff of Falcon Press for their design and production assistance, especially John Grassy, Susan Ferber, Jeff Wincapaw, Kathy Springmeyer and Laurie "gigette" Gould. And, for their editorial assistance, Lee Esbenshade and Beth Judy.

Finally, special thanks are extended to Roy King, Environmental Education Coordinator for the South Florida Water Management District, without whose knowledge of the watershed, sensitivity to the needs of southern Florida educators, and support of The Watercourse staff, this project would not have been possible.

Contents

. . . .

. . . .

Part III
Investigations: Putting the Pieces Together

Interdisciplinary explorations of parts of the watershed puzzle help to put some of the pieces into proper context.

Activity Format

Icon indicates the principal chapter/ topic to which the activity relates.

Grade Level:
Suggests appropriate learning levels: Middle School (6-8) and High School (9-12). Most activities can be adapted for higher and lower grades.

Subject Areas:
Disciplines to which the activity applies.

Duration:
Preparation time:
The approximate time needed to prepare for the activity.
NOTE: Estimates are based on the time needed to set up materials the first time an activity is conducted; because many materials can be used again, preparation times for subsequent uses should be reduced.

Activity time:
The approximate time needed to complete the activity.

Setting:
Suggested site.

Skills:
Identifies skills applied in the activity.

Vocabulary:
Significant terms.

A snappy thought-provoking teaser introduces the activity. This can be presented as an ice breaker.

Summary
A brief description of the concepts, skills, and affective dimensions of the activity.

Objectives
The qualities or skills students should possess after participating in the activity.
NOTE: Learning objectives, rather than behavioral objectives, were established for activities. To measure student achievement, see **Assessment**.

Materials
Supplies needed to conduct the activity. Describes how to prepare materials prior to engaging in the activity.

Making Connections
Describes the relevance of the activity to students and presents the rationale for the activity.

Background
Relevant information about activity concepts.

Procedure
Warm Up
Prepares everyone for the activity and introduces concepts to be addressed. Provides the instructor with preassessment strategies.

The Activity
Provides step-by-step directions to address concepts. The primary component of each step is presented in bold-faced type.
NOTE: Some activities are organized into "parts." This divides extensive activities into logical segments. All or some of the parts may be used, depending on the objectives of instruction. In addition, **Options** consists of alternative methods for conducting an activity.

Wrap Up and Action
Brings closure to the lesson and includes questions and activities to assess student learning.
NOTE: Many activities include an "action" component **Wrap Up and Action**. Action moves learners beyond the classroom and involves friends, family, community, state, national, and/ or international audiences.

Assessment
Presents diverse assessment strategies that relate to the objectives of the activity, noting the part of the activity during which each assessment can occur. Ideas for assessment opportunities that follow the activity are often suggested.

Extensions
Provides additional activities for further investigation of concepts addressed in the activity. Extensions can also be used for further assessment.

Resources
Lists references providing additional background information.

Learning Opportunities

Discover a Watershed: The Everglades is divided into three parts: a reference section that includes the natural and human history of the watershed; contemporary issues and potential solutions; and learning activities. This publication was structured in response to educators' requests for more information to implement activities. Activities provide background information, but they are supplemented with material in the reference section.

Activity ideas were generated by Florida educators during a writing workshop. First drafts of activities were field-tested predominantly by teachers and students from southern Florida, but also from states beyond the watershed. Activities were revised according to recommendations from field-testers and content reviewers.

Who can use *Discover a Watershed: The Everglades*? This publication is useful for both classroom teachers and nonformal educators (parents, environmental educators at nature centers or parks, ranger-naturalists, museum staff, scout leaders) of young people in grades six through twelve.

How can this publication best be used? *Discover a Watershed* was designed to fit the needs of diverse educators. It can provide a six- to eight-week course of study on the watershed with students participating in activities as they are ordered in the guide. (Activities build upon each other and are coordinated with the chapters in the reference section.) Or activities may be used in any order with educators selecting those appropriate for the aspect of the watershed they are studying. Activities cross many disciplines; therefore, the study of the watershed may be integrated into the history and communication arts classroom as well as science and math. Individuals interested in the watershed can benefit from reading the text alone.

Because of the unique challenges that this watershed offers and the unprecedented solutions that are being tested, it is of interest to people both within and beyond the watershed. "What is happening in the Everglades watershed may be a test case for the human ability to achieve balance between needs and desires, and to maintain the ecological integrity of other living things on the planet."

USAGE NOTE:

• Kissimmee-Okeechobee-Everglades is used interchangeably with the abbreviation K-O-E when referring to the watershed and the larger ecosystems.

• The South Florida Water Management District is used interchangeably with the District, the Water Management District, and SFWMD.

• Everglades National Park is used interchangeably with ENP.

Kissimmee-Lake Okeechobee-Everglades Ecosystem

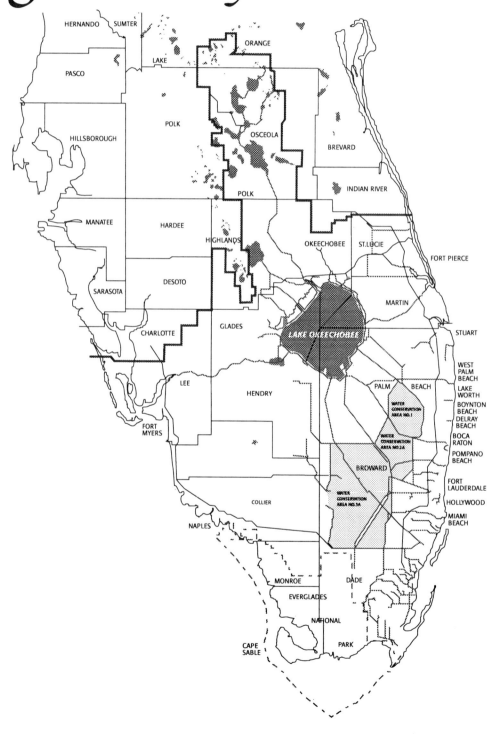

Flatland

In the late nineteenth century, Edwin A. Abbott wrote a fantasy about life in a two-dimensional world, a "flatland." Abbott's world is a place where "the . . . land may have bays, forelands, angles in and out to any number and extent; yet at a distance you see none of these . . . nothing but a grey unbroken line upon the water."

At first glance, the Everglades appears to be a flatland, without height and depth. The place is remarkably flat, but not without dimension. To come to know it, to appreciate its subtle complexities, you must approach with a sense of curiosity and exploration. You must look both from afar and close up at this uncommon world. In other places nature shouts for attention. In the Everglades it speaks in whispers. To hear it you must take time and listen.

Imagine looking down on Florida from a satellite. The peninsula looks like the head of a giant turtle emerging from the shell of the continent; its dark eye, Lake Okeechobee, peers into the tropics; its mouth, the Everglades, opens into the Gulf of Mexico.

From that high perspective, color is the principal dimension, blue the dominant shade. From space, southern Florida—indeed the whole planet—seems the domain

From a high vantage point, the Florida peninsula looks like the head of a giant turtle.

South Florida Water Management District

of water. Water is the vital essence, but this distant view belies the connections of water with rocks, weather, wood storks, and people.

Often the name of a place conjures images of its most popular features. Mention Yellowstone and people picture grizzly bears and geysers, not pocket gophers and volcanic ash. To many people, the wetlands of southern Florida are synonymous with alligators, snakes, and egrets, not with periphyton and copepods. Humans are fascinated by the large or extraordinary rather than the small and commonplace.

There are few other places in the world like the Everglades. Asked to describe this unusual country before seeing it, many people would respond with images from a Hollywood brew of "Gentle Ben," "Tarzan," and "The Creature from the Black Lagoon."

Early descriptions of the region include words like "impenetrable," "poisonous," "miasmic," "dismal," "rotting," "malignant." People created images of endless, foul-smelling swamps overhung by dark trees draped with snakes and Spanish moss. Mysterious, foreboding, and largely unknown—except to the Native Americans who lived there —much of southern Florida is indicated by blank spots on early maps.

Southern Florida is a very different kind of country, but not so mysterious and inhospitable. Here, the broad expanse of earth blends with the constantly changing sea and sky. It is a subtle landscape, periodically flooded and swept by fire, illuminated and warmed by a persistent sun, and animated by bountiful wildlife, some of it quite strange. Only the undulations of ancient beaches and marine terraces and the subtle green topography of trees and shrubs give relief to the undeniably flat land.

The watershed is an ecological drama. Primal elements serve as scenery, props, special effects, lighting, and sound—only they are real, palpable; they are rock and soil, cloud and river, marsh and bay, beach and reef. Plants, animals, and people are the players on the stage. In the greater Everglades ecosystem, there are many roles, and the cast is large and diverse.

Exploration and discovery will draw you closer to the real, not the imagined, Everglades. Unhurried intimacy with a place reveals much about its true character. You will see that it is more than ". . . an unbroken line upon the water." You will discover a watershed.

Part I

The Natural Watershed: Pieces of a Puzzle

. . . .

In the unaltered watershed ecosystem, water, earth, air, fire, and

living organisms fit together like pieces of an ecological puzzle.

Chapter 1

The Vital Essence

The Everglades is a place, a marsh, a region, a watershed, an ecosystem. It is the mirrored glint of sunlight on shallow water that is moving slowly, below a great sweep of saw grass, toward the sea. The Everglades is "a river of grass."

Water is the consistent verity here, but it holds true to what an ancient philosopher observed: one can never step into the same river twice. The moving river is change; gravity is the force, water the instrument. During its life cycle, the protean Everglades is living organisms: cloud, rain, and ground water; lake, stream, and river; wetland and tidal estuary; the open sea. When you look down on the Glades from above, everything stands out in low relief against a glistening backdrop of water. It is a watery place on a watery planet.

Standing knee-deep in a teeming stew of water and periphyton (fibrous mats of blue-green bacteria), your feet held in the mucky grip of bottom marl, you are unaware of the profusion of microscopic organisms swarming about your legs. Millions of tiny

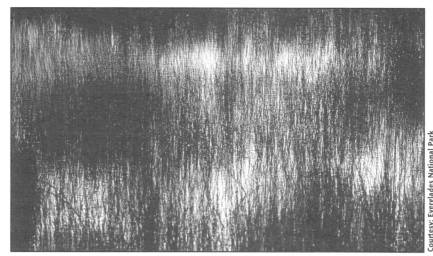

The Everglades is the mirrored glint of sunlight on shallow water below a great sweep of saw grass.

animals and plants stir, suspended in sun-warmed fluid: copepods, fish and insect larvae, diatoms (several million in a single quart of the water), masses of eggs and cysts held protectively in the warm, moist incubators of algal mats. All of them are feeding, or being fed upon.

Above, below, and all about are the children of the river. A gathering of tall birds, standing on spindly legs that seem to grow out of the water, move in slow motion. Dragonflies—gossamer-

winged mosquito hawks—hover, searching their narrow band of sky for food. Here and there, teardrop-shaped clumps of trees and shrubs part the moving water. Periphyton floats everywhere, precipitating, unseen, the mudlike marl that covers the underlying rock. An alligator

Teardrop-shaped tree islands part the moving water.

Everglades is living organisms: cloud, rain, and ground water;

lake, stream, and river; wetland and tidal estuary; the open sea.

Agriculture is one of many water users in southern Florida.

silently cruises a deeper channel, only its eyes and snout visible. Waist-high saw grass seems indivisible from the river. A turtle drifts by, protected by its soft, leathery carapace. Otters play. Responding to maternal instinct, a crocodile gently cares for her newly hatched young on a sheltered beach of Florida Bay.

People too share this place. They harvest sugar cane and rice, tomatoes and grapefruit. They produce dairy products. Like giant water striders, they skim about on airboats, searching for fun and frogs. In distant Florida Bay, an angler's line snaps tight as a sea trout takes the bait, while in the Okeechobee shallows someone else lands a bass. Thousands of vacationers crowd the beaches of the "Sun Coast," while sails fly before the offshore wind like colorful vertical wings. A scientist studies a bird rookery, while another predicts the movements of weather fronts. In the cities, millions of people go about their daily business, often

unaware of the complex and fragile aquatic system that sustains them. This river is alive! And all of its children are connected by the magic of water.

Florida is synonymous with water. The state has more than 2,000 miles of tidal coastline, nearly 7,800 lakes—including the largest lake in the southern United States—and more than 1,700 rivers, streams, fresh- and saltwater marshes, swamps, and deep, free-flowing springs. In the surficial, intermediate, and Floridan aquifers, southern Florida has one of the world's richest supplies of ground water. Around the world, more than 60 percent of the water vapor that may potentially fall as rain circulates in the air above the tropical latitudes; Florida lies within that belt. Florida receives nearly 60 inches of rainfall each year. It also supports one of the highest per capita rates of water use in the country. It is a land shaped by, defined by, and heavily dependent on, water.

Boundaries

On a map, straight lines and angles demarcate the Everglades, making it a seemingly secure wild island. In fact, seen from above, roads, canals, agricultural fields, and housing developments subdivide much of the watershed. Nature also has patterns, but these are not always geometric. Plants and animals do not recognize boundaries drawn on a piece of paper. Surveying, after all, is simply humanity's way of scent-marking the edges of its property. In nature, resources, not the territorial imperatives of people, draw the lines.

The Everglades is much more than the nature preserve at the tip of the peninsula. Three decades ago, a landmark report on the state of research in the national parks concluded that "habitat is not a fixed or stable entity that can be set aside and preserved behind a fence, like a cliff dwelling or a petrified tree . . ." An ecologist once coined the phrase "ghost acreage" to refer to an area beyond established boundaries required to sustain and nurture the populations within those boundaries. This term could apply to the area beyond the boundary of Everglades National Park, an area essential to the park's health and integrity. Conversely, natural environments such as those in the park or in Big Cypress National Preserve, Corkscrew Swamp, or Loxahatchee National Wildlife Refuge could be considered the ghost acreage of agricultural lands and coastal cities.

In hydrologic terms, the Everglades is a watershed: a land area

The landscape is shaped by patterns of human use.

and the Ten Thousand Islands; Florida Bay; and the archipelago of the Florida Keys. A roadside sign placed at the Turkey Lake Service Plaza on the Florida Turnpike near Orlando could appropriately say "Welcome to the Everglades." From Disney World to Key West, from Fort Myers to Fort Pierce, from the angular territories of small villages and towns like Immokalee, Pahokee, Saint Cloud, and Kenansville to coastal urban giants like West Palm Beach, Fort Lauderdale, and Miami, the watershed stretches.

that delivers runoff water, sediment, and dissolved substances to a major river and its tributaries. A watershed includes atmospheric, surface, and subsurface water and the pathways that water follows in its perpetual cycle. The Everglades is unique because the watercouse includes the shallow river of grass with sheet flow.

A watershed also encompasses a confluence of human cultures, traditions, values, beliefs, and resource uses. It has many personas. It is an essential part of the great water engine we call the hydrologic cycle. It defines geographic, political, social, and cultural boundaries—it connects and divides. It is a continuum along which biological, ecological, and hydrological relationships, as well as patterns of human activity, develop and change. It is a route of human travel and exploration, commerce and communication. It is an immigration and migration pathway for other species. The watershed includes diverse habitats and living communities.

It is a conduit for the exchange of energy and nutrients. It shapes and is shaped by the land and patterns of human use. The watershed produces things of value to people. Some of them, like beauty, are intangible. Others can be counted, weighed, and measured. Many of its products are of fundamental ecological or economic value.

The Everglades includes freshwater marshes and swamps, rivers, sloughs and springs, hardwood forests and hammocks, pine flatwoods and rockland, scrub, sandhills, prairies and savannas, mangrove swamps, lagoons, estuaries, and bays. To the north, it encompasses the Upper Chain of Lakes and the Kissimmee River floodplain. At its center lie Lake Okeechobee and its periphery, including the rich soils of the Everglades Agricultural Area. The Everglades encompasses areas south, southeast, and southwest of the lake: the Loxahatchee Slough; the remnant historic Everglades; the Big Cypress country, including Corkscrew Swamp; Chokoloskee

A search for the ecological boundaries of the Everglades would reach at least to the northern shore of Lake Okeechobee, and further, were the pilgrimage made to the true headwaters near Orlando. It would extend into the sky overhead, even as far as air masses marshaling over distant Arctic ice or off the sweltering east coast of Africa. It would reach into the depths of the Caribbean and follow the Gulf Stream snaking around the peninsula.

Historic drainage patterns of southern Florida.

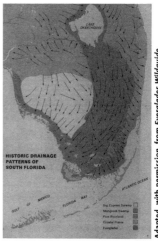

The historic "River Everglade," the 13,000-square-mile sweep of grassy water from Lake Okeechobee to the estuaries of Florida Bay and the Gulf Coast, is ecologically and hydrologically linked with a much larger area through an umbilicus of lakes, sloughs, and rivers—the Kissimmee, Caloosahatchee, and Saint Lucie Rivers, Taylor and Fisheating Creeks, the Big Cypress Basin—with Lake Okeechobee at the heart of the system. It is a watershed draining nearly 18,000 square miles. An extraordinarily long-lived, very lucky, and persistent mosquitofish could travel most of the interconnected watercourses of the watershed with only temporary interruptions at levees and floodgates.

Regrettably, the watershed suffers from what has been called the "tragedy of the commons." The river is shared, used, and sometimes abused by millions of people. Too often, these people have not joined in common cause to ensure the welfare of their common property. It is too easy to assume that someone else will care for it. In the Everglades watershed as in all others, downstream effects result from upstream causes, and those effects are always cumulative.

The remnant Everglades (what remains of the historic River Everglade and lies primarily within the boundaries of Everglades National Park) is at the mouth of the stream. Its residents are the last to drink from a river that begins far to the north. If the headwaters of the Kissimmee River are the faucet, then Florida Bay, Whitewater Bay, and the

Water brings life to this freshwater marsh.

Gulf of Mexico, nearly two hundred miles distant, are the drain.

The river is a beast of burden. Piecemeal, it carries the land back down to the sea. It brings life to slough, marsh, and estuary. It holds the promise of renewal—and the threat of death. The great heart of Okeechobee feeds the river. The lake fills and empties with the ebb and flow of water through its arteries to the north—the Kissimmee River, Taylor Creek, and Nubbin Slough; from the west, Fisheating Creek. Deprived of water, its lifeblood, the river would atrophy and perish.

There are no rapids or cataracts here; just the slow, assertive movement of water drawn to the supplicant marsh. Wider than any river ought to be—historically, 50 miles from edge to edge—the Everglades describes a gentle arc toward the Gulf, mimicking the curvature of the coastal ridge that tilts beneath it.

Unlike the hurried, muddy waters of the Colorado, the dance of this river water is light-footed.

No ancient rock thrusts up to be deeply cut by the river; instead, clear and lazy water touches gently on a land very close to the sea. Through the Grand Canyon, the Colorado drops nearly 2,000 feet in only 277 miles. The "river of grass" falls less than 150 feet in about the same distance.

Elevation, one determinant of stream velocity, is foreign to the Everglades. This is a place of latitude, not altitude. The highest point in the watershed, near the headwaters, is only about 125 feet, and altitude in the upper watershed averages between 25 and 50 feet. South of Lake Okeechobee, most of the Ever-

Waterspouts sometimes form in summer.

glades and Big Cypress Basin are less than 25 feet above sea level.

Beginnings

Like the earth itself, nature is circular. There are no beginnings or endings. There is just process—the continual recycling of elements from place to place within a system of cycles. Still, we look for order and sequence in things. In that sense, the water of the Everglades can be viewed as the offspring of the clouds: conceived through a union of the primal elements, carried in the belly of the sky, and delivered back to the earth and sea as rain. Most summer afternoons, a grand display of sound and light from towering, dark-rimmed clouds announces rain. Other showers come easily, gently. Some storms arrive, full term, from the Caribbean, the Gulf, or the distant Azores, borne in wildly swirling carousels of clouds that bring ten inches or more of rain in a day. Sometimes a dark vortex of air dancing wildly across the land accompanies rainfall. Occasionally a gyrating column of water is drawn up into the clouds from the sea.

Lightning often marks the coming of rain. It may flash more than 2,000 times during one storm, each strike accompanied by a thunderous timpani roll of air, suddenly compressed and just as quickly expanded. More lightning occurs in Florida than in any other place in the country.

These aerial sound-and-light shows bring heavy rain to the southern Florida landscape each year—almost double the annual average for the world. More than 70 percent falls from May to September. Sometimes, more than half of the rain comes in less than two months in late summer.

To the north, nearer the headwaters, less rain falls, but it is more evenly distributed throughout the year. Less than 60 percent of the 50 to 55 inches of precipitation that fall there comes in the summer. In winter, passing storm fronts bring showers to the north that are uncommon in the south.

Water also begins its odyssey through the Everglades as moisture held in the soil, sea, and plants and released into the air by the perpetual workings of the water cycle. Heat from the sun fuels this great water engine. Evaporation and transpiration are the engine's intake manifolds, condensation and precipitation the exhausts. Water vapor rises on unseen currents of warm air.

As the air ascends it expands and cools, causing suspended vapor to condense on tiny airborne particles of dust or salt. These water droplets or ice crystals become visible as clouds. In a land without elevation, clouds are the only mountains. They are mountains of water.

In the agitated inner mist of clouds, particles of water and ice collide, coalesce, and, if they become large and heavy enough, fall from the cloud as rain. The higher the temperature, the more moisture air can hold. In summer, Florida air is as heavy with water as air in the Amazon or Congo Basins during the rainy season.

This enduring cycle completes an exchange of atmospheric moisture about 40 times a year—once every nine days. In this way, nature, the accountant, keeps the

The hydrologic cycle in southern Florida.

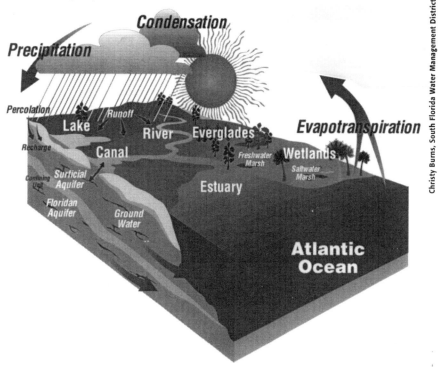

Christy Burns, South Florida Water Management District

water books. On an average day in Florida, 150 billion gallons of rain fall from the sky. Another 25 billion gallons of surface water flow into the state from rivers to the north. On an average day, 100 billion gallons return to the air through surface evaporation or transpiration, and 25 billion gallons enter the ground or move along the surface. The Florida water budget account, it would seem, is in the black. Or is it?

What's It Worth?

On an average day each human being in southern Florida uses 190 gallons of water—twice the national average. Each day, nearly 800 more people become Florida residents, most moving to southern Florida. Southern Florida is home to over 5.2 million people. An estimated 8 million people will live there by the year 2010. In an ecosystem built on water, the needs of so many have enormous significance.

Too often, too easily, we have asked, "of what value is a place like the Everglades unless it is drained?" Wetlands are good for alligators, wood storks, palmetto bugs, and eagles; saw grass, periphyton, and resurrection ferns; snakes, orchids, and shrimp; dolphins, tarpon, and turtle grass. Wetlands are even good for distant, less productive

An estimated 8 million people will live in southern Florida by the year 2010.

Everglades National Park

areas, to which migratory animals carry nutrients. During the life cycle of more than half of the commercial fish and shellfish harvested in the country, wetlands provide a safe harbor at some time. Wetlands are havens for many species nearing extinction. They are incredibly efficient water treatment plants. A single acre of wetland peat can absorb 300,000 gallons of water. Wetlands are buffers against damage by storm, tidal surge, and flood. Wetlands are oxygen factories. They produce protein, assembly-line style.

Economists have estimated that in the myriad ways in which they serve people, wetlands are worth $160,000 an acre. One acre of tidal estuary alone can do the work of a $75,000 water treatment plant, and can generate a commercial and sports fishery worth $8,000. Coastal estuaries and Florida Bay are nurseries for several species of commercial value. In 1989, the spiny lobster harvest in these areas was worth $13 million, the stone crab fishery brought in $8 million, and $40 million worth of

pink shrimp were taken. According to the Florida Department of Environmental Protection Marine Fisheries Information System, in 1992 in Monroe County alone the harvest included more than 4.5 million pounds of spiny lobster ($18,215,064) and nearly 3 million pounds of stone crabs ($7,179,217). Food shrimp landings exceeded 3 million pounds and were valued at close to $10 million.

Economists cannot calculate the value of things that sustain the human spirit. Beauty and wildness nurture us in ways that cannot be measured in dollars. Opportunities to observe timeless processes help us understand the sovereignty of nature; returning to wild places adds perspective to our frenetic lives and times.

Passage

Untroubled by human economics, water continues to cycle. Clouds form as equally heated masses of air, are drawn inward by sea breezes, and converge over the peninsula. They also rise on invisible updrafts of convectively heated air. In those vaporous

Wetlands Prior to Development

Wetlands
1972-74

South Florida Water Management District

A comparison of the extent of wetlands.

pillows there may be molecules of water that were once locked in mile-thick Arctic ice; that passed through the gut of a woolly mammoth; or, that erupted in a column of superheated steam from a distant geyser. These are all reminders of the timeless nature of the water cycle. These cosmopolitan molecules join with others; water drops form and succumb to gravity.

Raindrops fall on the Upper Chain of Lakes near Orlando. Some splash into a small natural basin. Tiny concentric waves spread outward from each entry point, grow larger, touch other circles. The river rises here. The infant stream first stirs as water seeks the outlet of Turkey Lake, a few miles from Kissimmee. The river flows lazily into the Reedy Creek and Shingle Creek Basins, on to Lake Tohopekaliga, and into Cypress Lake. Onward it runs, to Lake Hatchineha, Lake Kissimmee, and through the Kissimmee River into the 730-square-mile shallow basin of Lake Okeechobee.

Historically, Okeechobee—the

Lake Okeechobee is the liquid heart of the watershed.

"big water" of the Seminoles—drained west into the Caloosahatchee River and east through the Saint Lucie River, but had no natural outlet to the south except dendritic streams at high water. Before its modification by engineers, Okeechobee was the gatekeeper. As the lake level periodically rose, water simply washed over the southern rim to bathe the Everglades Basin. Now, there are alternate routes from the lake, all under human control. Water may flow east through the Saint Lucie Canal, or southeast to the Atlantic through the West Palm Beach, Hillsboro, or North New River Canals. It may flow west to the Gulf through the Caloosahatchee Canal, and south through the Miami and North New River Canals and Conservation Area 3 into the heart of Pa-Hay-Okee (the Seminole name for the Everglades).

Sometimes water has been pumped back into Lake Okeechobee from peripheral agricultural lands. Water returned to the lake in this way carries concentrations of chemical nutrients that may cause algal blooms, which deplete dissolved oxygen. If the proliferation of algae goes unchecked, it can hasten the death of the lake through a natural process called eutrophication. Blue-green bacteria would become innocent

The upper watershed showing the Upper Chain of Lakes.

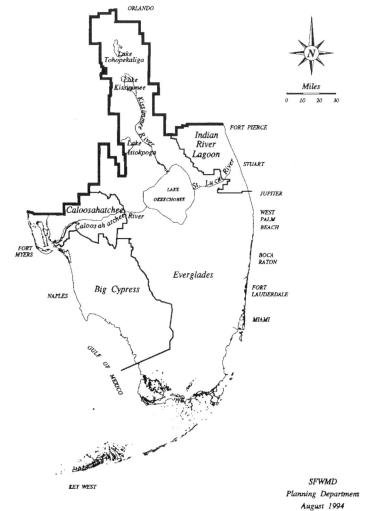

SFWMD
Planning Department
August 1994

A Hydrology Primer

Pulled relentlessly toward the sea by gravity—even on flat land—fallen raindrops join others to form rivulets that merge into larger streams, which then coalesce into rivers. Water evolving in this way from raindrop to river is called runoff. If it travels above the ground, it is said to be surface runoff. If it seeps down into porous rock instead, it is called subsurface runoff.

Surface runoff moving slowly over the ground in thin sheets—like that generated by a rain shower or melting snow—is called overland flow. If surface runoff follows definite pathways or arteries, it is called channel flow.

Subsurface runoff that sinks deep into underlying rock is called ground water. Interflow is subsurface runoff that remains close to the surface and moves horizontally within the soil.

Rainfall—substantial amounts of it—is the principal source of runoff within the southern Florida watershed. But not all rainfall becomes runoff. Much water is lost back to the atmosphere through evaporation and transpiration from plants. The amount of runoff is equal to precipitation minus evapotranspiration (up to 80 or 90 percent within the southern Florida watershed) plus or minus gains or losses in underground storage (ground water and interflow). This relationship is known as the hydrologic equation. While individual factors in the equation vary over time with climatic changes and human withdrawals of the water stored underground, the formula holds true—everywhere, anytime.

Were it not for potential loss factors, the journey of a single raindrop through the watershed could be traced from its impact on a high point on the perimeter of the watershed to the point where the river loses its identity to the sea. The time that the single drop spends in the system is known as the time of concentration. In any watershed, the greater the ratio of channel flow distance to overland flow distance, the shorter the time of concentration and the greater the volume of water that builds up at the mouth of the basin. In an "engineered watershed" that has great lengths of artificial channels, the concentration time is short.

While precipitation is measured in inches over a period of time (usually 1 hour or 24 hours), runoff is measured in units of volume (usually cubic feet per second) moving past a given point. Precipitation is a measure of water entering a hydrologic system (watershed). Runoff, evapotranspiration, and withdrawals from storage are measures of water leaving the system.

Water flowing in channels—such as creeks, sloughs, rivers, canals—is called discharge. Discharge is derived from several sources: rain (called channel precipitation) falling directly into lakes, streams, or other arteries in the watershed; overland flow; interflow (water that enters the soil and moves laterally or downslope more rapidly than it can move downward to become ground water); and ground water flow, which enters streams, rivers, and canals when they intersect the water table. Channel precipitation and overland flow supply water to surface arteries quickly. Interflow and ground water flow feed the hydrologic system much more slowly.

Streamflow is further broken down into storm flow, which occurs during and soon after a storm, comprised mainly of channel precipitation and overland flow; and base flow, the discharge derived from ground water seeping into the channel. Both storm flow and base flow can be augmented by interflow.

Streams and rivers that flow continually are called perennial. During the dry season—even in prolonged drought—their base flow is augmented by inflow from ground water sources. Watercourses that flow only during the wet season are called intermittent, and those that flow only during a storm are called ephemeral.

Waterflow in the Kissimmee Basin has always been perennial. Historically, the Everglades Basin has been what ecologists call a pulse-stabilized system, in which water flow has varied with the swinging pendulum of flood and drought. In Everglades sloughs, estuarine creeks, and rivers, water flow was perennial; in other places, the Glades were intermittently dry. Unfortunately, as a consequence of human modification of natural hydrologic patterns (channelization, flood control, etc.) in recent times, water flow through the Everglades marshes has come perilously close to being ephemeral.

Hydrologists identify three types of human modifications to a watershed. "Pruning" is the cutting back of part of a drainage network by filling natural channels or diverting them to another drainage. This is a practice that is often adopted in urban, suburban, and peripheral agricultural areas where the incentive is strong to claim, or "reclaim," unused ground for development. "Grafting" is the technique of connecting one drainage network with another one beyond its hydrologic boundaries (e.g., with aqueducts, canals, and pumping stations). "Intensification" is the practice of adding artificial channels (canals) to a drainage network to speed the release of overland flow because the water is a nuisance to people and their activities—for example, draining land to facilitate plowing and planting, or, in an urban setting, developing gutters and storm sewers.

Possible results of human development on streamflow include: peak discharges of water resulting in more frequent flooding; water pollution by contaminants (physical sediments, nutrients, pesticides, toxic wastes) from urban and agricultural lands; accelerated channel erosion; and modification of ecological relationships.

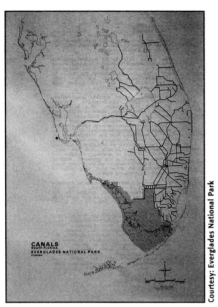

Nearly 1,400 miles of canals channel water through southern Florida.

assassins, with suffocation as their weapon. Ironically, they are the same primitive organisms that form the floating mats of periphyton essential to the life of the Glades. As such, they illustrate what might be called the Law of the Optimum: the right amount in the right place at the right time.

Dikes and floodgates withhold the water of the great lake from the Glades. Three conservation areas (large, shallow impoundments) south of the lake hold excess water from Okeechobee until it is released directly into the sea or the Glades. Nearly 1,400 miles of canals and levees and over 2,000 water control structures serve as evidence that people are the dominant "force" in the watershed. Not until water passes through floodgates on the Tamiami Canal and into Everglades National Park is it released from artificial direction. The past works of engineers are well built and accomplish their mandated purpose, but they have cast a long

shadow over the watershed. While today that shadow is shifting and receding, the "river of grass" is still one of the most highly altered, and intensely managed watersheds in the world.

Once, the only covenant for water rights was consummated through natural processes. Now, there is just the illusion of unlimited quantity. In recent years, minimum flows have been negotiated by water managers instead of by nature. To remain even marginally healthy, the Everglades requires variable minimum water flow levels (measured in acre-feet: enough water to cover one acre to a depth of one foot). Water managers have not consistently met this goal during past decades. Sometimes water levels have been too low in the wet season; at other times levels have been kept abnormally high during the dry season by premature or untimely releases from Conservation Areas, releases which were necessary to minimize flooding in agricultural areas to the north.

Water that once pulsed through the Glades to the rhythm of nature's heartbeat is now metered into the marsh through culverts, levees, and gates. Too often its measure has been too much, too little, too soon, or too late. True to natural laws, the total quantity of water in the system remains unchanged—neither more nor less than 100 years ago—but its distribution has changed. Dr. William B. Robertson, Jr., senior biologist in Everglades National Park, says, "Much water has flowed down the Everglades since the days of Bartram and Audubon, and much that should

have come down has flowed elsewhere." Fortunately, a concerted effort to restore normal sheet flow is now in progress.

Guided by the southwest curve and dip of the pockmarked limestone ridge that underlies the broad river basin of the Glades, water continues its resolute search for the sea. Relentlessly, water drains down the indiscernible slope, barely .2 feet per mile, its route traced by slightly deeper troughs, or sloughs, in the limestone floor. As it nears the coast, its course is set by chance. Some water flows to the Gulf of Mexico through the Shark River Slough. To the east, some follows Taylor Slough into the 850-square-mile shallows of Florida Bay, with its submerged meadows of turtle grass. The tide rolls in, seeking to overtake the land. The river, riding on its gentle but stubborn current, tries to join the sea. The waters mix, and their nutrients enrich the brackish zone. The estuary is neither sea nor river,

Fresh water follows different pathways to the sea.

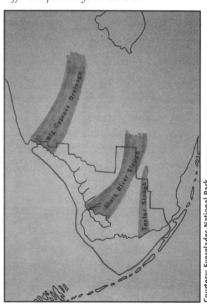

but the constantly shifting edge between the two.

Water for this intricate riverine circulation comes primarily from rainfall. Water records show that 70 percent of local rain returns to the air, and 30 percent collects in wetlands or replenishes underground reservoirs, eventually returning to the sea through springs and rivers.

Water from Rock

The rocky foundation of southern Florida is porous and permeable; water moves easily through it and is stored, at least temporarily, in interstitial spaces in the rock. Rainfall that doesn't collect on the surface or flow off into rivers and streams moves quickly downward into the bedrock until it reaches an impermeable barrier, an aquiclude (or aquitard). When water fills all of the spaces, the rock is said to be saturated—a regular occurrence during a normal rainy season.

The surface of this underground reservoir is called the water table, and the water below it, ground water. Ground water flows laterally and vertically through the rock, its level rising and falling as rainfall comes and goes, and also responding to withdrawals through pumping.

The layers of rock through which this water moves comprise an aquifer, a bearer of water. The spaces or pores between particles of rock hold water. In limestone, larger spongelike spaces are sometimes formed when water joins with carbon dioxide in the air and soil and forms a weak solution of carbonic acid, which dissolves the soft rock.

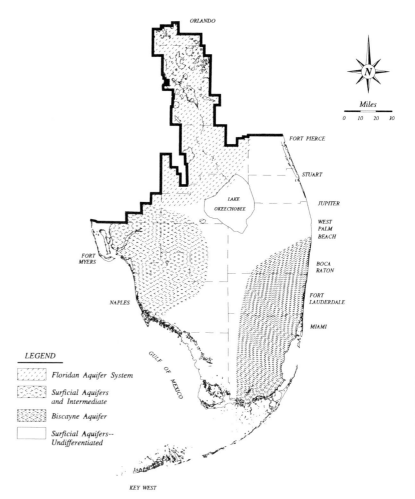

Ground water supply sources.

LEGEND

- Floridan Aquifer System
- Surficial Aquifers and Intermediate
- Biscayne Aquifer
- Surficial Aquifers-- Undifferentiated

South Florida Water Management District

Throughout most of the watershed, the shallow, surficial aquifer intercepts water as it percolates downward. This aquifer is formed of various thicknesses of marine and freshwater sediments covered by a thin surface layer of peat, sand, and other wind- and waterborne material that has not yet hardened into rock.

Just below Earth's surface, under most of the watershed south of Boynton Beach (including Florida Bay and the Keys), the surficial layers are called the Biscayne

Aquifer. A many-layered cake of porous limestone and other sediments, the aquifer rests on a water barrier called the Tamiami Limestone. Thin at its western edge, the aquifer increases, wedge-like, to about two hundred feet in thickness under the coastline. Its upper margin, mostly covered with sand, marl, peat, and other alluvial material, lies only a few feet beneath the surface. This surficial aquifer system—principally the Biscayne Aquifer—is one of the most permeable aquifers in the world, drawing in water over its entire surface.

Beneath the surficial aquifer, older rock layers form the intermediate aquifer system. In places it is absent, removed by erosion during prolonged periods of exposure above the sea. Where it is present, its sediments (impervious clays, silts, and limestones) may form both the lower confining (impermeable) layer of the surficial aquifer and the upper confining layer of the Floridan Aquifer.

Enclosed by impermeable layers, the Floridan Aquifer is an artesian system. Rainwater enters and recharges it where its layers come to the surface near Ocala and all along the Central Florida Ridge. Gravity pulls ground water down the Floridan watercourse. Unable to move up or down through the confining layers of the aquifer, the ground water is under natural (artesian) pressure from the weight of water upstream and from thousands of feet of overburden. In some cases, if a drill taps the aquifer, no pump is needed: water simply flows to the surface. In fact, if the pressure is great enough, water will gush up as in a fountain.

It would be misleading to imply that fresh water percolating through the sandy soils of the Central Florida Ridge finds its way to southern Florida. It doesn't. In southern Florida, water from the artesian system is very salty; fresh rainwater has never flushed it out as in northern and central Florida.

Subterranean water sources meet nearly 90 percent of the human demand for water in Florida.

Nearly 80 percent of the total is supplied by the Biscayne and Floridan aquifers. These waters move quiet, sunless, and unnoticed until a driller's bit pierces the water table, or a streambed or canal cuts it. Surprisingly, these dark, largely anaerobic worlds are not lifeless. Shallow ground water near rivers and lakes supports complex microcommunities of tiny aquatic organisms: insect larvae, blind shrimp, primitive worms. In fact, during times of drought in the watershed, many small creatures may find refuge in the water-filled underground cavities close to the surface (the surficial aquifer).

Worldwide, it is estimated that slightly more than 14 million cubic miles of water are stored underground. Especially in heavily populated coastal southern Florida, the surficial aquifer system supplies enormous quantities of water to people. Some ground water, particularly in deep aquifers like the Floridan, would be brackish and nonpotable unless it were highly processed; it may be thousands of years old, and may move only a

few feet each year. Some believe that water deep beneath the Glades may have seeped into the water table far to the north many centuries ago.

Supply and Demand

Until the last century, the greater Everglades system was one of the largest, most biologically rich and distinctive wetlands in the hemisphere, as productive in some ways as a similar-sized tropical rain forest. Superficially, the system retains much of its primitive character, but the cost of human development and use of this river has been high.

Cities draw heavily on resources from the natural environment. Each day, the average city dweller in the United States uses or consumes 125 gallons of water, 3.3 pounds of food, and 15.6 pounds of fossil fuel. In the same day, the urban resident produces 100 gallons of sewage, 3.3 pounds of solid refuse, and 1.3 pounds of air pollutants. In southern Florida, these figures, especially water consumption, sewage, and solid waste production, may be nearly double.

The greater Everglades system: past and present.

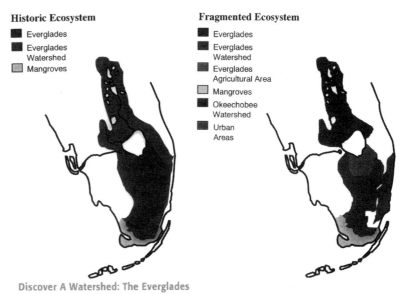

Historic Ecosystem
- Everglades
- Everglades Watershed
- Mangroves

Fragmented Ecosystem
- Everglades
- Everglades Watershed
- Everglades Agricultural Area
- Mangroves
- Okeechobee Watershed
- Urban Areas

South Florida Water Management District

During the past hundred years, natural systems in southern Florida have suffered several losses: fragmentation of critical habitat; drainage of wetlands; saltwater intrusion into aquifers as pumping draws water tables down or canals intersect them; contamination with agricultural pesticides and industrial wastes; nutrient-overloading from sewage and fertilizers; invasion by nonnative species. Losses in biological diversity have been measurable; in beauty and wildness, immeasurable. Only about half of the original 4 million acres of wetland in the historic greater Everglades remains. Approximately one-eighth of the remaining area lies within the relative sanctuary of parks and other preserves known as the Everglades Protection Area. The rest has been substantially altered.

Ebb and Flow

Water is inextricably linked with this southernmost part of the country. Central to life, water is also a subtle but powerful agent of geologic change. The "turtle head" of Florida emerged from a sea that rose and fell (with the retreat and advance of glacial ice) at least five times in the past 100,000 years. Each time, the shape and complexion of the land changed.

From a time beyond human memory, the Everglades marshes have alternated between wet and dry, sometimes fully covered by a sheet of water, at other times thirsty, with water only in the deeper basins and gator holes. Those parts of the watershed on the coast have always been energized by waves, flushed by

lunar tides, and bathed by terrestrial runoff.

That the passage of the seasons here is nearly imperceptible reflects the subtle nature of a place where the only real seasons are wet and dry. At this subtropical latitude, Earth's transit of the sun is marked by the water clock. The rise and fall of water dominates the life of the Everglades. Here, all living things have adapted to the perennial natural flux of water, and any alteration in that flux causes stress.

From October or November through May, there is little rain. The Glades are cooler and drier. From June through September or October, rain falls. There is a great flowering of life. Animals that have suffered the desiccation of winter—and survived— disperse from winter havens of gator holes and sloughs.

The seasons change. The rains come and go. Their return signals

a time of renewal, a magic season of abundant life. In the recurring cycles of nature, neither more nor less water is better; what is right is what is needed, in the quantity in which it is needed, at the time when it is needed. Water may be everywhere, but in no other setting (save perhaps the oceans themselves) does it dominate life more than in wetlands like the Everglades.

The Everglades breathes, sweats, metabolizes. Water shapes the landscape, nourishing pineland, grassland, marsh, and estuary. The surface of the Glades mirrors an abundant past, a troubled present, a hopeful future. Today, 50,000 structures straddle American rivers, so transforming them that some hydrologists no longer call them rivers, but regulated streams. Of late, the "river of grass" has been among them.

The Everglades watershed is a land of edges. It lies at the margin

Mangrove estuaries are flushed by tides and terrestrial runoff.

. . . .

between the temperate north and the subtropical south; between mangrove forest, salt marsh, rocky pineland, and freshwater marsh; between salt water and fresh water; between wet season and dry; even at the boundary of past and present. It is a fragile interface between people and nature, extinction and survival. What remains of the historic watershed is an edge limiting both the inland growth of coastal cities and their need for water. Each evening in the Glades, the eastern sky glows with the cities' light, mirroring their advance on this remnant of primitive southern Florida. And each year, the lights seem to grow brighter.

Here the Ancient Mariner who cried "water, water everywhere and not a drop to drink," might lament differently. In the Everglades there is "water, water, everywhere . . ." but too many living things needing to "drink" from the river. In this ecosystem, water is clearly the vital essence.

Everglades is a fragile interface between people and nature.

Courtesy: Everglades National Park

Chapter 2

Rock from Water

One hundred thousand years ago, the highest point in the heart of the Everglades was under several feet of salt water. Giant sharks and other prehistoric marine organisms flourished in the warm sea. The nearest dry land was far to the north. During the ensuing several thousand years, the outline of southern Florida changed dramatically at least five times. Terraces and the remains of marine creatures left far inland from the present shore mark the changed coast.

Plateau, Peninsula, Pinnacle Rock

Today, the Everglades watershed includes the lower third of a long peninsula that slopes downward as it juts into the sea. Like an iceberg, the peninsula is the tip of a much larger underwater mass of rock called the Floridian Plateau. If the sea dropped just 300 feet (50 fathoms), it would reveal the outer edges of the plateau, nearly 400 miles apart.

From this continental margin, both the Gulf of Mexico and the Atlantic Ocean drop rapidly to much greater depths.

The Everglades lies in a shallow basin, that tilts imperceptibly downwards from northeast to southwest. The highest point, near the headwaters in the Upper Chain of Lakes, rises to an elevation of only about 125 feet. At approximately the midpoint of the watershed, the surface of Lake Okeechobee is only 21 feet above sea level. From there, the rock under the Everglades dips toward Florida Bay and the Gulf of Mexico at the rate of only an inch or so with every mile.

Because its emergence from the sea, in geologic time, is recent, the region has not been pushed up or folded like other landscapes. Elevated above sea level for the last time about 50,000 years ago, the Everglades area is among the lowest, youngest, and most geologically stable parts of the continent.

The unspectacular stuff of geology happened here. Geologic process in the Everglades has been as profound as in rugged mountains, but the difference is measured in inches rather than thousands of feet. In the mountains, changes in elevation bring changes in temperature, moisture, soil, exposure to sunlight, and other conditions; all of these determine which plants and animals can thrive. Also, more elevated and severe topography is subject to accelerated erosion and weathering. Greater vertical relief means more obvious changes.

In the Everglades, the protocols of nature are the same as in other areas, but the scale is different. Imagine tracing a line from a Pacific beach to a mountaintop 10,000 feet high in the Sierra Nevada (or from the Great Plains to the crest of the Rockies), noting

Because its emergence from the sea, in geologic time, is recent, the region has not been pushed up or folded like other landscapes. Elevated above sea level for the last time about 50,000 years ago, the Everglades area is among the lowest, youngest, and most geologically stable parts of the continent.

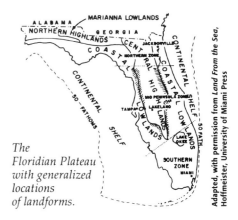

The Floridian Plateau with generalized locations of landforms.

Adapted, with permission from *Land From the Sea*, Hoffmeister, University of Miami Press

the landscape, climate, plants, and animals along the way. Now, do the same from the water's edge in Florida Bay to the center of an Everglades hammock—an island of trees a few feet above the sea. Though less obvious, variations in microclimate and changes in the structure and composition of plant and animal communities would exist along that transect just as they do in the high mountains. But in flat country like this, only the slightly elevated outcroppings of rock that form hammocks, pinelands, and flatwoods vary the topography. In this subtle landscape the mountains are only a few feet high.

The remarkably flat watershed landscape extends with little variation to the horizon. Thin layers of sand, marl, and mucky organic debris cover it and great depths of porous sedimentary rock lie under it—conditions which, coupled with a warm, moisture-rich subtropical climate, favored the development of a huge freshwater marshland ecosystem.

So little vertical relief resulted in few exposures of the kind of geologic strata (layers) found in canyons or on mountainsides. In the Everglades, only canals are analogous to canyons; but rock formations are so thick that canals only expose a single layer, and there is no folding of layers. In most of the watershed, geologic structure must be deduced from the study of drill cores and geophysical logs, or by observing processes now under way in areas believed to be forming in a similar way (e.g., oolite formation on the Great Bahama Bank).

In such places as the Grand Canyon or Yellowstone, geologic alterations are obvious and dramatic; visitors to the Everglades might wonder if anything had ever happened here. But closer examination reveals that over time, a fluctuating sea level, wind, and rain have indeed carved Earth's surface. Marjory Stoneman Douglas describes the rocky landscape of the historic watershed in *The Everglades: River of Grass*:

> *If all the saw grass and the peat was burned away there would be exposed to the sun glare the weirdest country in the world, thousands and hundreds of thousands of acres of fantastic rockwork, whitey gray and yellow, streaked and blackened, pinnacles and domes and warped pyramids and crumbling columns and stalagmites, ridgy arches and half-exposed horizontal caverns, long downward cracks, and a million extraordinary chimney pots. Under the sun glare or the moonlight it would look stranger than a blasted volcano crater, or a landscape of the dead and eroded moon.*

This weird bas-relief was etched into soft stone. Over much of the watershed, cavities so pit and riddle the surface rock that it resembles a sponge. This phenomenon produces a formation called "pinnacle rock," which stands out as one of the few notable geologic features in an otherwise uniform landscape.

A Shifting Sea and Distant Ice

Why is it important to know something about the rock you stand on? Geology controls the development of vegetative communities and associated animal life in an area. Geology controls the movement of water underground, its storage there, and ultimately, its delivery to people. Geology influences surface drainage and contributes to the weather, climate, microclimate, and hydrology of a place. Geology controls environment, and environment controls life. The geologic structure of southern Florida is the foundation on which the living systems of the watershed are built.

Pinnacle rock is one of the few obvious geological features in this uniform landscape.

Courtesy: Everglades National Park

Plate Tectonics

On a global scale, plate tectonics is the massive and continuing displacement and deformation of Earth's crust as it floats on the partially molten rock below. About 300 million years ago, the North American plate began to split away from a giant ancestral continent called Pangaea. The rough outlines of today's North American continent, including the Florida peninsula, began to appear. Today, North America continues to move farther from ancient Africa. As it floats west, the great sheet of rock carries saw grass, alligators, people, and the Everglades with it.

Imagine that the original super-continent Pangaea was a thick layer of ice floating on the surface of a lake. The ice floats because it is less dense than water. As it bobs, it is fractured by internal stress into large, irregular-shaped sheets. These plates of ice are in constant motion due to convection and other currents in the water below. They are always moving away from, into, over, and under one another. At their margins, the sheets constantly build new ice forms. As the sheets pull apart, water rises in the cracks and freezes into new ice; as they come together, they push up into jumbles of folded and broken ice. In places, a plate of ice pushes down under another.

In this metaphor, the sheets of ice represent the continental plates. The lake water is analogous to the molten rock beneath Earth's surface. The features built at the edges of the ice plates show how mountain ranges, mid-ocean ridges, and trenches were formed.

The unusual rock that carpets the Everglades came from the sea. Calcium carbonate precipitated from the water column. The chalky flotsam of marine organisms settled to the bottom of earlier shallow seas along with mud, sand, and silt.

Over the years, the layers of sediment grew deeper and, compressed by their own weight, eventually solidified. The seas receded, exposing the deposits. The deposits dried, completing their transformation into solid rock. Sand, mud, and silt became marl, or sandstone. Calcareous sediments turned into limestone, the most common rock in the region.

Each time the sea receded, wind, rain, tides, and waves eroded the layers of rock, gradually wearing them down and transporting their sediments to lower-lying areas, where the sediments accumulated, adding to the peninsula. Some sediments returned to the sea to begin the cycle anew.

How long does geologic process take to build rock? So long it is difficult for us to comprehend. To measure it, we need to figure in what writer Paul Schullery calls "mountain time." Rocks have life cycles just as alligators and wood storks do; rocks just take longer to complete their life cycles. The time required to form sedimentary rock varies, but coastal embayments, estuaries, and areas over the continental shelf are especially productive. In these shallows, about six feet of sediment can accumulate in a year. Even at a fraction of that rate, a buildup of more than half a mile of sediment would take only

5,000 years. A million years or so of accumulation and compression would result in layers several miles deep.

With little geologic flourish, the sedimentary cycle has shaped the foundation of the Everglades. Over periods of deposition and erosion, sedimentary layers in southern Florida have grown to over three miles thick. The basement rock—the core of volcanic and altered rock on which these layers rest—testifies to an ancestral connection with Africa during the formative years of the continents, a geologically violent time of plate tectonics more than 200 million years ago. Most of the surface rocks in the watershed, however, were formed between 100 thousand and six million years before the present. As rocks go, they are quite young. By comparison, rocks deep in the Grand Canyon date back 1.7 billion years. By the time retreating seas uncovered a youthful southern Florida, geologic processes had already pushed up and worn down the Appalachians.

People often associate sedimentation with deposition in standing or flowing water. But strangely, in this land that is closer to the equator than to the Arctic, ice has been an important agent in the process. In Wyoming, nearly three thousand miles from the sun-warmed coast of Florida, and a mile higher and 20 degrees farther from the equator than the Everglades, winter is bitterly cold. Many inches of ice and snow rime everything in sight; it is easy to imagine an ice age. It is harder to connect ice with the subtropical flatland of Florida.

Yet the landscape here is as much a product of ice as the glacially scoured valleys of Yellowstone National Park in Wyoming. Glaciers are characteristic of the polar regions, high latitudes, and mountaintops, but their influence is global. Although the ice never came closer to Florida than the middle tier of states (e.g., Kansas, Nebraska), most of the rock formations in the Everglades watershed owe their origin to the advance and retreat of ice age glaciers.

The Pleistocene epoch saw five successive glacial advances and four warmer interglacial periods. As massive Arctic ice sheets grew, merged, and advanced on the continent, they absorbed great quantities of water, lowering sea levels enough to empty Florida Bay, and to widen the southern peninsula. Each time the ice sheets melted and withdrew, they released water to the sea again, covering that portion of the peninsula below Lake Okeechobee with rising water.

Sediment that would later become layers of the rocky foundation of the Everglades accumulated throughout warmer periods. For about 14,000 years, we have experienced a warm postglacial (or interglacial) period, with sea levels rising by 1.5 to 5 inches per century. The ice may return and change the shape of Florida. But all the while, the slow process of rock building will continue.

Soft Sediment, Hard Rock

The Everglades watershed includes four of the ten physiographic regions or provinces found in Florida. Each of these subdivides further into areas broadly characterized by surface features such as plains, ridges, valleys, and slopes.

The Upper Kissimmee Basin lies in the Central Lakes physiographic region. Sandhills, lakes, and surface materials composed predominantly of sand, clay, and substantial amounts of organic matter typify this region.

The lower west coast makes up the Southern Flatwoods physiographic region, a low, flat landscape including plateaus, ridges, flatwoods, prairies, rockland and marl plains, and various coastal features. Sand, limestone, and organic deposits predominate in its surface materials.

The upper east coast, another low, flat area, formed as barrier islands and lagoons. It lies in the Eastern Flatwoods physiographic region, characterized by broad expanses of flatwoods, with prairies, ridges, and a variety of coastal features. The surface is mainly sand with large deposits of peat.

The lower east coast—from Lake Okeechobee to the Florida Keys—lies in the Gold Coast-Florida Keys physiographic region. Uniformly low and flat, it is dominated by the Everglades marshes and prairies, the Atlantic Coastal Ridge, mangrove swamps, and the Florida Keys. Surface materials include sand, marl, limestone, and organic matter.

More than a dozen nearly horizontal layers of marine sediment, grouped into distinct formations of differing ages, underlie the watershed. Several of the "youngest" layers date from the "Great Ice Age" (Pleistocene) about 1.6

Glaciation

Ice. The remnants of the last ice age persist. Greenland and Antarctica both retain continent-sized glaciers, giving us a sense of what the broader world was like when the ice flowed widely. The ice has come and gone several times over the last five million years, or so the evidence of the rocks indicates. But in Antarctica there is ice that has remained frozen for half a million years, providing a continuous record of ice hundreds of thousands of years long. The ice is like a vault filled with the fragments of ancient texts, there to be reassembled by anyone with the wit to ferret them out.

—Thomas Levenson, *Ice Time*

Rock's "ancient texts" reveal that Earth has been chilled several times during its lifetime, but the most recent ice age occurred in the Pleistocene epoch. It ended between 10 and 12 thousand years ago, having indelibly marked the topography of southern Florida. During the Pleistocene epoch—"The Great Ice Age"— four successive advances of continental ice each carried ice that was 2 miles thick in places. The first, the Nebraskan glaciation, began about 1.8 million years ago. It was followed by the Kansan, Illinoian, and Wisconsin glaciations, with intervening periods of warming and recession. Glacial ice advanced as far south as northern Missouri, and each glaciation and interglacial period altered sea levels enough to reshape the Florida coastline several times. During the Pleistocene epoch, woolly mammoths roamed the Florida uplands. Fossil evidence of their existence can be observed at the Florida Museum of Natural History in Gainesville, and at the Florida State Museum in Tallahassee.

Sedimentation

How does sedimentation occur? Water, wind, and chemical and biological processes break down rocks on or near Earth's surface and carry the sediments to other locations. Living organisms produce nonliving material that falls to the sea floor or river and lake bottoms. Their calcareous skeletons are deposited there, intermixed with sand, mud, and silt. Over time, these sediments are naturally sorted by gravity. The coarser, heavier particles settle to the bottom first, followed by progressively finer material. To demonstrate the process, try adding different-sized particles of sand to a bottle of water, shaking it, and observing the sequence of deposition—sort of a "time in a bottle" exercise. In the real world, the layers of sediment grow deeper and, over thousands of years, the weight above them compresses and solidifies them. Eventually, they become sedimentary rocks.

The sedimentary rock underlying the Everglades Basin is of both detrital and chemical origin. Detrital sediment is commonly made from clay, silt, and sand. When these materials are compressed, they form sandstone. The principal chemical sediment is calcium carbonate. It comes from the skeletons of animals produced as a metabolic byproduct or is precipitated from seawater. The rock that it forms is limestone.

million years ago; other layers are nearly 65 million years old. Marl and sandstone compose some; others are limestone. The layers of rock read like pages in a book of geological history, and waterborne sediments and organic matter cover the uppermost, geologically youngest page. The rock layers do not occur uniformly throughout the watershed. In some places erosion has removed sediments during long periods of exposure to wind and rain; these are pages torn from the book, and are called "unconformities" in the geologic record.

The most recent deposits form the Pamlico Sand. The sand varies in depth; in places it is 60 feet deep and probably contains many fossils. About 100,000 years old, it is formed of quartz sand from old coastal dunes and beach terraces, some of which have hardened into sandstone. At the beginning of the Wisconsin glacial period, wind and rain scattered the sand irregularly over older deposits. Because it sits inland from the present shoreline, the Pamlico Sand is an indicator of higher sea levels in the past.

The heart of the Everglades lies in the Miami Limestone. Also about

Generalized physiographic map of the lower watershed.

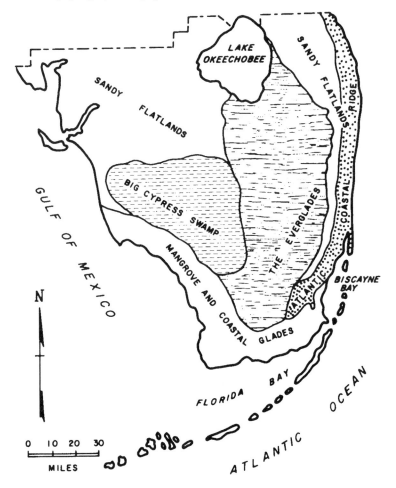

Adapted, with permission, from *Land From the Sea*, Hoffmeister, University of Miami Press

Generalized hydrogeologic column from eastern Palm Beach County.

GEOLOGIC UNIT	AGE OR PERIOD	APPROXI-MATE THICKNESS (FT)	GENERAL LITHOLOGY		HYDRAULIC CHARACTERISTICS
PAMLICO FM. (Qp)	Late Pleistocene	0 – 50	Quartz sand with shelly or silty intervals.	Qp	SURFICIAL AQUIFER SYSTEM
ANASTASIA FM. (Qa)	Pleistocene	0 – 200+	Ranges from sand and shell to well–cemented biogenic limestone.	Qa Qft Solutioned Zone	BISCAYNE AQUIFER Extremely Permeable Solutioned Limestone
FORT THOMPSON FM. (Qa)		0 – 40+	Ranges from shelly marl to biogenic limestone.	Qc	
CALOOSA-HATCHEE FM. (Qc)	Plio-Pleistocene	0 – 50?	Shell and marl with sand and limestone intervals.	Pt?	Unconfined aquifer Permeability ranges over 3 orders of magnitude. May be semiconfined locally.
TAMIAMI FM. (Pt)	Pliocene	0 – 100+	Reefal limestone and talus deposits. Some sandy limestone.		
HAWTHORN GROUP (Mh)	Miocene	500 – 700	Sandy silt grading into dense, green clay with beds of limestone, sandy shell or dolomite. phosphate common. Limestone and marl common in basal unit.	Mh Os?	INTERMEDIATE CONFINING UNIT Extremely low permeability sediments
SUWANNEE FM. (Os)	Oligocene	0 – 100?	Silty to clean, pale orange limestone. Not reliably described in study area.	Eo	Main Producing Interval in Study Area
OCALA GROUP (Eo)		0 – 500	Highly fossiliferous pale orange lime-stone. Commonly fractured and solutioned.		FLORIDAN AQUIFER SYSTEM
AVON PARK FM. (Ea)	Eocene	500 – 700	Fossiliferous, chalky to granular lime-stone with dolomitic beds.	Ea	
LAKE CITY FM. (El)		> 1500 ?	Chalky, fossiliferous limestone and dense brown dolmite.	El	Major Intra-Aquifer Conf-ining Unit
OLDSMAR FM. (Eol)		700 – 900	Biogenic, limestone grading downward into solutioned, crystalline dolomite.	Eol	
CEDAR KEYS FM. (Pc)	Paleocene	> 500	Cavernous grey to brown dolomite with intervals of creamy white limestone. Anhydrite common in lower section.	Pc	Disposal Zone ("Boulder Zone")
LAWSON FM. (Kl)	Late Cretaceous	?	Interbedded dolomite anhydrite and limestone.	Kl	SUBFLORIDAN CONFINING UNIT

South Florida Water Management District

100,000 years old, and up to 40 feet thick near the eastern coast, the Miami Limestone thins to a feather edge at its western margin. It forms the southern part of the Atlantic Coastal Ridge, dipping under Florida Bay and the southern Glades to emerge again as islands such as Big Pine Key and others near Key West.

The coastal areas east and west of Lake Okeechobee are composed mostly of Pleistocene-age sediments called the Anastasia Formation. Coquina shell fragments, sand, calcareous sandstone, and shell marl make up the bulk of the formation, which is over 100,000 years old and up to 120 feet thick. Where sediments outcrop to the southeast of the lake, they grade into the northern limit of the Miami Limestone.

The Fort Thompson Formation underlies and almost completely surrounds Lake Okeechobee itself, extending south through the Glades until it meets the Miami Limestone on the surface. Composed of marine and freshwater marls, limestone, and sandstones of Pleistocene age, the formation measures up to 150 feet in thickness.

The Key Largo Formation makes up the Florida Keys. In contrast to the Miami Limestone, which was formed through precipitation, limestone in the Key Largo Formation was created by fossilized skeletal remains of ancient coral reefs up to two hundred feet thick. The Key Largo Formation also dates from the Pleistocene epoch.

The Caloosahatchee Marl, composed of sandy marl, clay, silt, and sand, is also more than 100,000 years old. With a maxi-

mum thickness of 25 feet, it lies in a rough crescent extending northeast to southwest around the western margin of Lake Okeechobee.

Of the late Pliocene epoch—about 2 million years ago—the Cypresshead Formation occurs only in the northern watershed (Highlands County). It is composed entirely of quartz sands and gravels in a matrix of clay.

The oldest rocks exposed in the lower watershed form the Tamiami Limestone. From the early Pliocene—more than 5 million years ago—it measures up to 100 feet thick. Formed from marl, silt, and shell sands, it surfaces mainly along the west coast and in the Big Cypress Basin.

Other formations underlie the younger rocks exposed on the surface. These formations vary in age from approximately 5 million years old (Miocene) to 65 million years old (Paleocene). Carbonates mix with clay, silt, and quartz sand to form them. Some of them occur beyond the boundaries of the Everglades watershed, but they provide important conduits for (and sometimes barriers to) the movement of underground water within the watershed.

The Hawthorne Group (composed of the upper Peace River Formation and the lower Arcadia Formation) underlies the western margin of the watershed, and dates from the Miocene epoch, between 5 and 25 million years ago. The Suwanee Limestone Formation is of Oligocene age—between 25 and 38 million years old—and occurs in the southwest. The highly permeable Ocala Limestone is exposed in the

central peninsula, beyond the watershed boundaries, but it helps recharge the deep aquifer underlying southern Florida. The Ocala Formation is from the late Eocene epoch. The oldest rock outcrops in Florida belong to the Avon Park Formation—from between 38 and 55 million years ago (Eocene)—and lie in the west central peninsula. The Oldsmar Limestone dates from the early Eocene, and occurs throughout the state. The Cedar Keys Formation, deposited during the Paleocene epoch (between 55 and 65 million years ago), marks the base of the series of formations through which water moves deep below the watershed.

One of the most extensive and unusual rocks in the watershed, the Miami Limestone, merits a closer look. Most of it formed in the third interglacial period. Sea level was close to 25 feet higher than it is now. At that time, the Pamlico Sea, a shallow arm of the Atlantic, covered much of southern Florida. A remnant of the old shoreline known as the Pamlico Terrace is still visible. Its southern extremity lies north of Lake Okeechobee, clearly indicating that most of the area we call southern Florida was underwater.

The Miami Formation is made of both detrital and chemical sediments, largely in the form of tiny egg-shaped structures called ooids, sometimes called oolites (rhymes with zoo lights). These ooids consist of small nuclei of rock fragments, or any bits of material suspended in the water, around which successive layers of calcium carbonate form. Also present in the Miami Limestone are the fossilized shells of small,

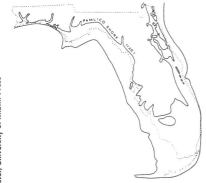

Adapted, with permission, from *Land From the Sea*, Hoffmeister, University of Miami Press

Shoreline of the Pamlico Sea when the sea level was 25 feet higher than at present.

colonial marine invertebrates, or bryozoans, that encrusted grass growing on the floor of the prehistoric sea. If you look closely at an outcropping of pinnacle rock, you can easily see both ooids and bryozoan shells.

As much as 70 percent of the rock volume in the Everglades Basin is of bryozoan origin, but nearly 20 percent of rock volume there consists of calcareous worm tubes, the protective secretions of marine worms. The latter form conspicuous outcroppings at Singer Island's Ocean Reef Park (Palm Beach County), at Blowing Rocks Preserve (Martin County), and at Hutchinson Island (Martin County). A sample core drilled through the Miami Limestone near the coast would reveal an upper 30 feet of oolite overlying 10 feet of bryozoans in a matrix of oolites and pellets. Pellets are tiny, elliptical, calcareous grains thought to have been excreted by marine worms.

The upper layer of the Miami Formation is called the oolitic layer—or "facies" in the jargon of geology; the lower part is the bryozoan layer (facies). The bryozoan facies, covering about 2,000 square miles of southern

Florida, comprises one of the most extensive bryozoan limestones in the United States.

By observing processes now under way about 50 miles east across the Straits of Florida, geologists can infer what must have happened when the Miami Limestone formed in southern Florida. Oolites similar to those in the Miami Formation are now forming in a large underwater sand bar called the Great Bahama Bank.

As water from the deeper Gulf Stream moves north over the shallow Great Bahama Bank, its salinity and temperature increase; this decreases the solubility of calcium carbonate held in suspension. Like wind passing over the upper surface of a wing, the velocity of the water also increases as it passes over the shallow bank. The faster the water moves, the more turbulent it becomes, which further reduces the solubility of calcium carbonate by driving off carbon dioxide.

Because it is not deep, the water moving across the bank is also subject to increased evaporation. All of these conditions cause the precipitation of calcium carbonate, which forms like a shell over any available suspended particle, and begins the development of ooids.

Geologists believe that the Miami Limestone began to form when layer upon layer of loose, unconsolidated particles of calcareous sand settled on the bottom of the shallow sea covering the lower peninsula. Currents then shaped these layers into an underwater ridge similar to the Great Bahama Bank. Bryozoans flourished in the deeper water over the continental shelf to the west, where salinity and water temperatures probably resembled those of today.

When the sea level dropped, it exposed the ridge, which began to dry. Rainwater mixed with carbon dioxide in the air. The resulting weak solution of carbonic acid dissolved some of the

Southeastern Florida and the northwestern section of the Great Bahama Bank. This shows the mirror-image relationship between the chief topographic and stratigraphic features of southern Florida and their recent Bahamian counterparts.

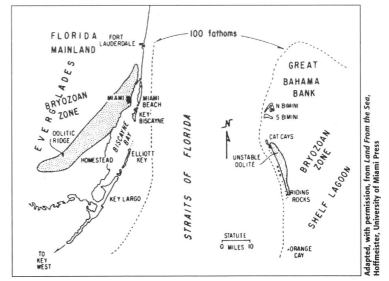

Adapted, with permission, from *Land From the Sea*, Hoffmeister, University of Miami Press

calcium carbonate and redeposited it around other particles as a limey cement, gradually forming the drying sediment into the hardened rocks of the Miami Limestone.

Further evidence that the Miami Limestone began as an underwater bar is found in several depressions that cut across the Atlantic Coastal Ridge. These depressions, with flat bottoms a few feet lower than the ridge (known locally as "transverse glades"), are believed to be channels that tides cut in the unconsolidated submarine ridge.

That portion of the Coastal Ridge formed by the Miami Limestone extends from near Fort Lauderdale south through Miami, curving west to terminate in Everglades National Park at Long Pine Key. From southern Palm Beach County north, the Anastasia Formation forms the ridge. In Miami, the Coastal Ridge, or Rock Ridge as it is sometimes called, rises about 20 feet above sea level, but to the west it is less than 2 feet high. Much of the ridge is barren or covered only by a thin layer of sand.

The ridge is the oldest dry land in southern Florida; parts of it have stood above advancing seas for tens of thousands of years. A few stands of pine cling to the rocky surface of the ridge, the remnants of a larger forest. Exposures of rough pinnacle rock throughout the pinelands reveal the oolitic limestone of the Rock Ridge. It can also be seen in open wet prairies when water levels drop. The high ground of the ridge is also the foundation of the state's east coast cities (Fort Pierce to Homestead and Florida City). The

Anastasia Formation is naturally exposed in scattered locations from near Boca Raton north to Fort Pierce. Along the northern coast it is a major source of ground water.

Limestone is highly susceptible to chemical breakdown—a quality of singular importance in the hydrology of southern Florida. Through a process called "carbonation weathering," ground water combined with carbon dioxide in organic soils dissolves and carries away the calcium carbonate that makes up over 90 percent of the limestone. This process creates the pinnacle rock and the deep cavities called "solution holes" that are characteristic of the Miami Limestone.

Sometimes, thick accumulations of muck cover the bottoms of large, weathered solution holes, and they fill with water. They become miniature worlds, harboring all sorts of aquatic plants and animals, and they can trap unwary critters. Anyone who walks cross-country in the Everglades gains new respect for

the ability of deer to deftly navigate the pitted surface on their delicate, spindly legs without falling into solution holes.

Limestone Factories

The shallow bays and sounds bordering the coast on the east and south of the watershed are basin-shaped. The bottoms are covered by layers of various soft sediments—quartz sand carried in on currents from the north, freshwater mud from the mainland, and fibrous organic matter—and the ebbing tide exposes these as mudflats. Walking on exposed mud is difficult, like trying to walk across deep soft snow. Some naturalists in Everglades National Park use incongruous gear—snowshoes—to walk out into the tidal zone. There, digging down through the thick layers of bottom material, they find the same Miami Limestone that underlies much of the watershed.

Geologists believe the bays formed as a lagoon between the living reef of the Keys and the

Shallow bays and sounds border eastern and southern coasts.

Ken DeYonge

· ·

Ken DeYonge

A honeycomb of mudbanks, some supporting mangroves and other plants, shapes the topography of Florida Bay.

unconsolidated sedimentary mound that would become the Miami Limestone. The formation of the bays and sounds—Biscayne Bay, Card, Barnes, and Blackwater Sounds—dates to about 100,000 years ago, when water levels were at least 25 feet higher. During a glacial period, the floor of the ancient lagoon was exposed. It dried and consolidated into hard rock.

Surface streams flowed to the lowered sea cut channels in the exposed surface. Remnants of some of these ancient streambeds are still visible on the bottoms. Numerous solution holes, similar to those that pock the surface of the Miami oolite in the Everglades, provide further evidence that the lagoon bottom was exposed. The presence of freshwater sediments also indicates a period of emergence, stream erosion, and sedimentation.

The presence of peat indicates a later submergence, and the growth of coastal mangroves. The climate during the interglacial period was probably similar to today's, as it was conducive to the growth of corals on the eroded surface.

Florida Bay covers about 850 square miles at an average depth of less than three feet, reaching eight to nine feet at a few points. A honeycomb of mudbanks shapes the topography of the bay bottom. Low tide often exposes the banks, revealing a series of deeper bodies of water or lakes that average four to six feet in depth. Mangroves and other plants tolerant of brackish water have established a foothold on many of the banks.

On the bay bottom, the unconsolidated calcareous mud (about 90 percent of the sediment is calcium carbonate) is on average 3 feet deep over the banks, and 6 inches deep in the intervening lakes. Along the Gulf Coast near Cape Sable, the mud is as much as 10 to 12 feet thick. Geologically, the sediments are very young—less than 4,000 years old.

Because Florida Bay is so large, and deep sediment blankets its floor, it produces great quantities of limestone. In fact, the waters of coastal southern Florida produce more limestone than any other place in the country. Because limestone is among the world's principal oil-bearing rocks, geologists interested in learning more about petroleum have studied the area extensively.

The fine-grained nature of most sediments in the bay has led researchers to suggest formation either by precipitation by bacteria or by the disintegration of shelled organisms. Shelled animals living in the bay are primarily gastropods (a group of mollusks that includes snails and limpets), and foraminifera (various single-celled animals). One hundred forty species of mollusks are known to inhabit Florida Bay. These shell-producing animals have no doubt contributed to the wealth of sediment. However, the fact that the mud is so fine-grained suggests that extensive beds of calcareous green algae, commonly called seaweed, are the main producers of sediment.

Some algae secrete delicate skeletons ("shells") of aragonite crystals that disintegrate when the plants die. Aragonite is a form of calcium carbonate. Geologists have calculated that at the present rate of production, algae could have contributed at least one-third of the calcareous mud to the bay bottom. Several genera of algae, such as *Halimeda*, live in Florida Bay. They all produce calcareous external skeletons, and together could have built up a lot of sediment in Florida Bay.

During the Ice Age, sea levels were drawn down as water froze into glaciers and ice fields far to the north. The mainland, including Florida, and the Keys came to be as much as 100 feet above sea level. The emergent landscape then dried and hardened into the Miami Formation. In ensuing years, streams drained the lower peninsula and lightly, but nonetheless extensively, eroded the Miami Limestone.

Following this period, sea levels gradually began to rise. At one time, what is now Florida Bay looked very much like the Glades, and extended south as far as the Keys. A low-profile landscape, it sloped gradually southward. Vegetation typical of the Everglades covered it, lakes dotted it, and it was veined with sloughs and smaller streams.

About 4,000 years ago, the most recent rise in sea level reached the lowest parts of the landscape. The topography of Florida Bay today results from the slow encroachment of seawater into an ancient Everglades landscape that extended much farther south. As water moved inland, various marine animals and plants invaded newly submerged habitat. Among them were mollusks, calcareous algae, and mangroves.

A Coastal Rampart

Thousands of islands, large and small, encircle the tip of the Florida peninsula. They can be grouped as follows: the barrier islands—elongated sedimentary islands on the east and west coasts (e.g., Palm Beach, Miami Beach, Key Biscayne, Sanibel, Captiva); the Ten Thousand Islands on the

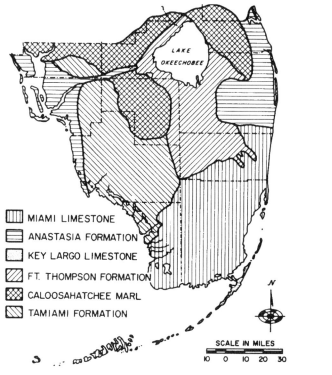

MIAMI LIMESTONE
ANASTASIA FORMATION
KEY LARGO LIMESTONE
FT. THOMPSON FORMATION
CALOOSAHATCHEE MARL
TAMIAMI FORMATION

SCALE IN MILES
10   0   10   20   30

Adapted, with permission, from *Land From the Sea*, Hoffmeister, University of Miami Press

Geologic map of the lower watershed showing location and surface area of each formation.

Gulf Coast (including Marco Island); and the Florida Keys.

The bryozoan layer of the Miami Limestone forms most of the southwestern coast. To the north (above the mouth of Shark River), the Tamiami Formation is the predominant surface rock. The entire coastal area slopes gradually toward the Gulf of Mexico. The Anastasia Formation and the oolitic layer of the Miami Formation rim the eastern coast.

Sediments overlying the rock of the Gulf Coast vary in depth from 12 to 15 feet, and are composed of calcium carbonate, silica, and organic material. Southern coastal sediments are mainly calcareous. Where silica is found, longshore currents probably carried it there. For example, small amounts of quartz in sediments on the west

coast probably came from the Cape Romano area above the Ten Thousand Islands, which is composed almost entirely of silica sand.

Unconsolidated sediment, where heavy growths of mangroves and associated plants live, composes most of the southern coast of Florida. The prop roots of red mangroves trap detritus, which gradually accumulates and builds new soil. Mangroves have helped add nearly 2,000 acres to the southern Florida coastline in the past 50 years. They contribute to the peripheral growth of the peninsula by stabilizing sediment deposits.

The coastal mangrove swamp covers more than 680,000 acres. Mangroves are also an important geologic indicator. They record changes in sea level. By noting

The coastal mangrove swamp, partially accessible by boat, covers more than 680,000 acres.

Ken DeYonge

is the Ten Thousand Islands began as oyster beds growing on sand bars, which were later overgrown by mangroves.

For the most part, coarse shell particles and carbonate sand called "shell hash" make up Cape Sable, the sedimentary barrier islands, the long shore beaches on either coast, and the small cove beaches fringing bays, sounds, and mangrove islands. Farther north on either coast, quartz sand is more common. Cape Sable is roughly 10 miles long; its southern end, East Cape, is the southernmost point on the mainland United States. The beaches of Cape Sable, along with other secluded beaches, are important nesting areas for sea turtles.

Bordering Florida Bay on the east and south, the Florida Keys are an important part of the larger ecosystem. The archipelago they form extends about 150 miles, from Soldier Key, south of Key Biscayne, to Key West and the Marquesa Keys. Only about 18 feet above sea level at their highest point, the Keys curve

East Cape is the southernmost point on the mainland United States.

Courtesy: Everglades National Park

the amount of peat produced by the decay of previous mangrove stands, it is possible to tell whether a living mangrove forest developed during a period of rising or falling seas.

Mangroves are intertidal species: they inhabit the zone between low and high tides. With no change in sea level other than the ebb and flow of the tides, the most organic detritus that could accumulate would measure no more than the range of the tidal flux—about three feet in this area. Because 10 to 15 feet of peat have been found in some places, the forest that produced the peat could not have formed at the present sea level. The level must have varied, allowing successive generations of mangroves to live and die and contribute their decaying woody matter to the

growing layer of fibrous organic material. For example, if a layer of peat is 15 feet deep, an ancient rise in sea level of 12 feet must have occurred (subtracting the normal 3-foot tidal flux). This change in sea level occurred in the past 4,000 to 5,000 years.

Oyster colonies or bars often cover sand bars and contribute to the growth of calcareous sediment. Some oyster bars, which can be as much as 20 feet wide, are exposed at low tide. Colonies of oysters orient themselves to flowing water—a phenomenon known as "rheotaxis"—and grow at the mouths of rivers and at right angles to tidal currents that carry food to them.

In the intertidal area, mangroves—principally red mangroves—establish themselves on and around oyster bars. The maze that

gently into the Gulf of Mexico. Dense growths of mangroves and shallow tidal flats, almost completely exposed at low tide, border most of the Keys. All the rock of the Keys is limestone.

From the Pleistocene epoch—more than 100,000 years ago—the Key Largo Limestone that forms the Upper Keys was once a living reef about 220 miles long—one of the largest in the world. Drill cores 70 miles west of Key West in the Dry Tortugas, and at least as far north as northern Fort Lauderdale, have found it. Its thickness varies, but in many places it is more than 170 feet thick, suggesting that the reef must have thrived for thousands of years.

The Upper Keys are the remnants of patch reefs that developed in shallow water closer to shore during the third interglacial

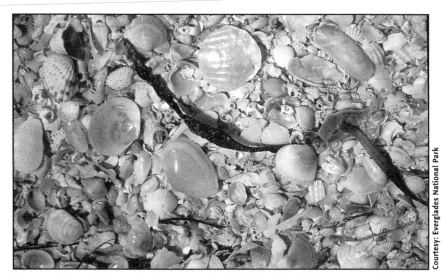

Course shell particles and carbonate sand called "shell hash" form many of the coastal beaches.

Courtesy: Everglades National Park

period. With the next glaciation, water levels dropped, and wave erosion destroyed most of the patch reefs.

Miami Limestone that forms the southern part of the Atlantic Coastal Ridge dips under Florida

Bay and reappears in the Lower Keys. The oolitic part of the Miami Limestone is evident in the rocks of the Lower Keys. The rocks originated from a 15-by-40-mile unconsolidated oolitic sand bar that formed at the same time

Coral

Unfortunately, the fastest growing trend among aquarium enthusiasts is marine reef tanks, an essential element of which is "live rock." Hobbyists demand these chunks of stony coral with their associated algal and other life forms—anemones, sponges, and tube worms—even though they do not survive well in a synthetic aquarium environment.

According to TRAFFIC (USA), an organization of the World Wildlife Fund that monitors the international wildlife trade, about 10 million hobbyists had 2 to 3 billion tropical fish in their aquariums in 1986. The United States is the largest consumer of tropical fish; of the $4 billion spent annually worldwide, more than $1.5 billion is spent in this country.

These figures do not bode well for the Florida reefs or the inshore fish habitats. Demand for live rock and stony coral contributes to the decline

of reefs in some parts of the world. In 1989, the Florida Department of Natural Resources (now part of the Department of Environmental Protection) estimated that three tons of live coral rock were being shipped each day from Miami. Up to 90 percent of the shipments contained state and federally protected species.

Loss of coral is loss of a resource of geological age. Coral rock takes 4,000 to 7,000 years to form; in human terms, it is not a renewable resource. Once lost, it is gone for a very long time—perhaps forever. Many scientists believe that the production of new rock in the coral reefs of southern Florida may be lagging behind the natural loss to erosion. Thus, losses to collectors further jeopardize the long-term integrity of the reef tract.

The harvest of live rock and stony coral at current rates is equal to the

loss of two patch reefs a year. This disturbing trend prompted the Florida Marine Fisheries Commission to accept a recommendation in 1991 that the state phase out the harvest of live rock over a three-year period. It is hoped that this action was not too little, too late.

The harvest of coral, and the consequent damage done to the reefs, stresses critical ecological associations. Food chains on the reefs and the hard bottoms are especially vulnerable because some reef animals feed exclusively on the colonial algae and coral polyps that live together symbiotically. The State Department of Environmental Protection now issues permits to appropriate businesses to seed reefs (deposit old oyster shells back on previously harvested bars to form a substrate) and harvest live rock under carefully controlled conditions.

Cape Sable and other secluded beaches are important nesting areas for sea turtles.

as the Atlantic Coastal Ridge. Younger sediments that once covered the Key Largo reefs but wore away through erosion now compose the Lower Keys.

Corals are coelenterates, a group of invertebrates that includes sea anemone, jellyfish, and Portuguese man-of-war. Corals divide into two general groups: soft corals, such as sea fans and sea whips, and stony corals, the

About 50 species of coral inhabit Florida reefs today.

largest and most important reef building group. About 50 species of coral inhabit Florida reefs today.

Corals live in tropical and subtropical waters, generally between 25 degrees north latitude and 25 degrees south latitude. Like bryozoans, corals may reproduce asexually by budding, so colonies grow quite large. Corals can live only in warm, shallow seawater. If water temperature drops below 60 degrees Fahrenheit, they die. Corals seldom grow more than 150 feet below the surface because the sunlight necessary for growth cannot penetrate any lower. As polyps extract calcium carbonate from seawater and precipitate it at their bases, they produce reefs.

Reef corals and algae have a symbiotic relationship. Algae provide some nourishment, as well as oxygen, for the corals; in turn, algae use carbon dioxide the corals produce. Some corals can survive periodic exposure at low tide, but most cannot live very long out of water.

Water Below

Rock is deceptive. It appears solid, impermeable. Yet, generally, sedimentary rock is porous, and carbonation weathering increases its capacity for water storage. The absorbent layers of rock underlying the greater Everglades divide into three groups of water-bearing strata. The uppermost group opens to the surface, and relatively impermeable layers known as confining units separate the strata.

The layers nearest the surface are collectively called the surficial aquifer (in one area they are also known as the Biscayne Aquifer). In the southeastern part of the watershed, these layers include, from top to bottom: the Miami

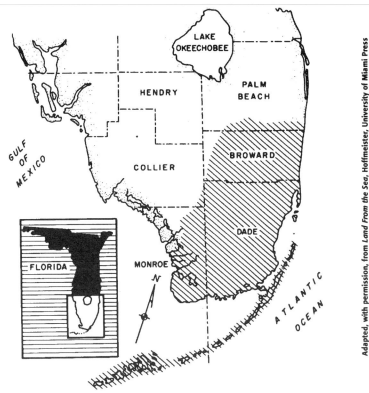

Adapted, with permission, from *Land From the Sea*, Hoffmeister, University of Miami Press

Slanted parallel lines show the geographic extent of the Biscayne aquifer.

Limestone (a good aquifer, very porous and full of solution holes); the Anastasia Formation (a fair to good water bearer); the Key Largo Formation (an excellent aquifer that extends inland as a thin layer); the Fort Thompson Formation (very porous and the best underground watercourse); and the Tamiami Formation (the upper parts of which are permeable).

In the north-central watershed, the surficial aquifer occurs in undifferentiated sediments in the Cypresshead Formation, and in shell beds in the Caloosahatchee and Fort Thompson Formations. To the west, sediments of the Tamiami, Caloosahatchee, and Fort Thompson Formations, along with undifferentiated material, comprise the aquifer. The south-eastern part of the watershed (the

Biscayne Aquifer) consists of the Anastasia, Miami, Key Largo, Fort Thompson, Caloosahatchee, and Tamiami Formations. Throughout the Kissimmee-Okeechobee-Everglades watershed, the surficial aquifer is underlaid by impermeable sediments of the Hawthorne Group.

The surficial aquifer (mainly the Biscayne Aquifer) varies in thickness. Just inches thick in the west, it measures 150 to 200 feet beneath the Atlantic Coastal Ridge between Fort Lauderdale and Miami, and 50 to 60 feet in the Homestead and Florida City area south of Miami. The most important source of water in Dade, Broward, and southern Palm Beach Counties, the aquifer also produces substantial water for domestic and agricultural use in

Lee, Hendry, and Collier Counties.

The intermediate aquifer, composed of interbedded quartz and carbonate sediments of the Hawthorne Group, occurs throughout the watershed. In the east, the Tamiami Formation is believed to form the top of the confining unit. The intermediate aquifer system produces substantial water for southwestern Florida, where it divides into the Sandstone Aquifer, the mid-Hawthorne Aquifer, and the lower-Hawthorne Aquifer.

The Floridan Aquifer, in which water confined by impermeable layers flows under pressure, underlies the intermediate aquifer in older sedimentary formations. In some areas, the Floridan Aquifer lies directly below the surficial. Water in the Floridan Aquifer has traveled considerable distances, having fallen as precipitation or percolated downward from standing water in the northern watershed.

The Floridan Aquifer produces limited potable water, most of it in the northern part of the watershed. In the south, the water quality is substandard, and throughout the greater system the water is generally saline. It may be processed into potable water through an energy-intensive and thus expensive process called reverse osmosis.

In the southwest part of the watershed as much as 1,100 feet of confining beds and other strata overlie the Floridan aquifer, but in Orange County it is near the surface. In most places, the Suwanee Limestone caps the aquifer, followed by the Ocala Limestone and the Avon Park,

· ·

Oldsmar, and upper Cedar Keys Formations. The base of the aquifer lies within or near the top of the Cedar Keys Formation, which rests on 100-million-year-old rock of the Cretaceous Period.

Pages of Stone

Two decades ago, writer-philosopher Alan Tory offered these insights into the nature of Earth and geologic time:

From soft limestone rocks soluble in water . . . from sand carried by wind and tide, from animal waste and mouldering plants over aeons of geological time, earth was formed. Rainstorm beating on rock . . . frost cracking stone, sun drying and splintering particles, flood-swollen rivers bearing freights of silt have played their part in producing this basic gift whose name serves as the title of our globe . . . The gestations of earth are slow and wonderful . . . Whoever wants to work with earth must subscribe to its pace, and submit to the rigors of its time-table.

In the Grand Canyon, we can see a mile down through layers of rock— an entire volume of geology, which Major John Wesley Powell in an 1869 expedition called "the great stony book." In the Everglades, we see the surface of rocks layered with life—just the last few pages of a book. But, just as tree rings and glacial ice record changes in climate and other natural events, these rocks hold the memory of an earlier, different Everglades.

Rummaging through the broken rocks of a quarry or "borrow pit," you find an entry in the Everglades' stony book: a tooth lying among crumbled limestone and fossil shells. Its jagged roots and worn, whorled surface show that it came from the jaw of an ancient mammal—a tiny, three-toed hipparion horse. Geology mixes evidence of past ages, climates, and landscapes: nearby you find ancient shark teeth, the imprint of a primitive plant, and charcoal from an early campfire. Time has placed all these in the fossil record.

Hundreds of thousands of years ago, the small, primitive horse grazed a landscape unlike that of southern Florida today. Saber-toothed tigers, giant tapirs, bear-sized beavers, mastodons, and other now extinct beasts roamed alongside. At different times, predecessors of today's sharks cruised the warm shallows that covered the lower third of the peninsula, and Native Americans cooked at an Everglades campsite.

The most recent geological event in southern Florida was a rise of sea level during the postglacial period, about 10,000 years ago. High water shrank the mainland peninsula and further isolated the Keys. Today, wind and rain, as well as biological and chemical processes, continue to go about the work of geological change. Quietly and subtly, they take from and add to the landscape that, long ago, glaciers left.

In the Everglades we see the surface of rocks layered with life.

Ken DeYonge

Chapter 3

A
Primal Alliance

Sometimes, air touches the Everglades lightly, barely moving a leaf. At other times, it shrieks fiercely, assailing and uprooting centuries-old trees. Air rises and falls, distributing water over the marsh and claiming it again for recycling. It courses above the Glades on hidden currents—the prevailing westerlies, the polar jet stream, and the trade winds—that shape the weather and climate. It influences the Gulf Stream and the North Equatorial Current, great rivers within the oceans, which warm Florida's coastal waters. It holds the compounds of carbon, sulfur, and nitrogen that rain down as weak acid with an appetite for limestone bedrock.

In the most fundamental partnership of all, air carries oxygen from green plants to animals, exchanging it for respired carbon dioxide. In concert with sedge, moonflower, and cypress, air swells and freshens the lungs of the watershed.

Invisible, air reveals itself in many ways. Waves of saw grass

Air reveals itself in a billowed sail.

ripple across an open glade. Summer clouds shift on hidden eddies. Belted kingfishers on a wire all face in the same direction, into the wind. A sail billows on the horizon; the shimmering strands of a golden orb weaver's web shudder; a bird wing cambers perfectly.

Air is inseparably bonded with the life of the watershed. It is essential in the processes of photosynthesis, respiration, transpiration, and the cycling of

elements, including the cycle of fire. Its most obvious role, however, is in the making of climate and weather. Air allied with its elemental counterparts, earth, water, and sun, produces the flux of the seasons. Water is essential to the ecosystem, but air is the vehicle that brings it.

Sun, Rain, and Wind

Weather—the condition in the atmosphere at a given time and place—and climate—weather's long-term trend—are dominant forces in the Everglades watershed. Its proximity to the Caribbean Sea and the Gulf of Mexico strongly influences southern Florida's humid, subtropical climate and generally mild weather. Periodic low-pressure storms from the Atlantic and the Caribbean move over the peninsula in late summer and early fall, bringing heavy and prolonged rainfall. In late fall, winter, and early spring, continental cold fronts advance from the west into the state, mostly in the north. They cause the winter climate there to oscillate between maritime tropical and continental weather.

The climate of southern Florida varies from a mild, dry season (late fall, winter, and early spring) to a warm, wet season (late spring, summer, early fall).

In the most fundamental partnership of all, air carries oxygen from green plants to animals, exchanging it for respired carbon dioxide. In concert with sedge, moonflower, and cypress, air swells and freshens the lungs of the watershed.

Seasonal changes in temperature are subtle, but daily temperature variations may exceed average annual ranges. Seasonal changes in precipitation are much more dramatic. Slight variations in topography and daily weather produce a range of microclimates within the watershed.

Short-term weather extremes punctuate the generally tranquil wet and dry seasons. Tropical storms, hurricanes, tornadoes, and waterspouts come during the summer. Low temperatures and frosts come in the fall, winter, and spring. Sometimes, southern Florida even experiences summer drought and winter flood. These periodic extreme events have a profound impact on the plant and animal communities in the ecosystem. Adapted to gradual changes throughout the year, they cannot always adjust to the stress of random severe weather or unseasonable events like drought.

North and South

Land and water are heated primarily by the sun. The amount of heat depends on the angle of

the sun's rays; the higher the angle, the more intense the heat. Angle is a function of latitude (and of the inclination of Earth's axis). At the equator, the sun is at its highest angle. Except for Hawaii, southern Florida is closer to the equator than anywhere in the United States. While the difference is slight, temperatures tend to be higher in the lower watershed than in northern Florida, which is more than 6 degrees in latitude farther above the equator.

Latitude does not have as much influence on rainfall, but large-scale longitudinal winds—the trade winds from the east and the prevailing westerlies from the west—bring moisture-laden air to the watershed from the ocean and the continent.

Nearly the same amount of rain falls in the upper and lower watershed, but at higher latitudes, rainfall is more evenly distributed throughout the year. The dry season usually lasts seven or eight months (October or November to May) and is characterized by changing temperatures

and low rainfall. In the four- to five-month wet season (June to September or October), temperatures remain about the same, but considerably more rain falls. In southern Florida, the seasons (wet and dry) are more clearly defined than in the north.

The higher the air temperature, the more water vapor air can hold before becoming saturated. In summer at midday in southern Florida, the air is palpably heavy with water. Fifteen cubic yards of air may contain as much as a cup of water. Such humidity is uncomfortable for humans, but other organisms such as mildew and giant palmetto bugs—among the oldest residents in southern Florida—welcome it.

Cool air cannot hold as much water vapor as warm air. If the amount of water vapor remains unchanged, relative humidity rises when temperatures drop at night. Typically, relative humidity at dawn in the heart of the Everglades may be 90 percent or higher.

More than 70 percent of annual precipitation in the watershed falls from May through September. Convection and convergence, processes that force warm, moisture-laden air aloft, most commonly generate precipitation. Clouds form and water vapor condenses into rain, usually from midafternoon through early evening. Much of the rain falls in the evening hours. In the Everglades watershed, nearly a third of daily summer rain falls between 8 P.M. and 6 A.M.

Uneven Heat

Bodies of land and water affect weather differently mainly

Summer storms usually occur from midafternoon through early evening.

Ken DeYonge

because of their dissimilar rates of heat absorption. Land, which is opaque, concentrates absorbed heat near its surface. Water is translucent, allowing sunlight to penetrate and heat it to a greater depth. Evaporation cools bodies of water, preventing their temperatures from rising very high. At night, or in winter, heat radiates more rapidly from land than from water. The fact that southern Florida is a narrow flatland surrounded on three sides by the sea predisposes it to unequal heating, and differential heating is the major cause of the rainstorms so typical of the Everglades region.

The limiting weather factor in the Everglades watershed is rainfall. Rain comes from local storms, larger tropical storms, and hurricanes. All storms result from rising air. In southern Florida, two main types of atmospheric lifting cause rainfall: convective and frontal. Convective lifting results from the unequal heating of a column of air. Heated air rises differentially over land or water. It cools at higher altitude

and falls to be reheated. Convective lifting produces most rain-bearing storms over the Glades. In Florida, frontal lifting most often occurs in winter when cold continental air meets warm oceanic air, and a warm air mass rides up over the cooler air. Cirrus and stratus clouds form with frontal lifting. Various types of cumulus clouds, often towering to great heights, are most often associated with convection and convergence. Convergence occurs frequently, when air moves inland on the breezes from one shore, meets air of the same temperature coming from the other shore, and both are forced upward.

The sea and lake breezes (and associated convection) characteristic of the area result from this differential heating. Normally, the breezes reach inland 15 to 20 miles. Summer sea breezes blowing 8 to 15 miles an hour reach inland 10 to 20 miles with a ceiling, or cloud base, of less than a thousand feet. The Florida peninsula enjoys sea breezes from both the Atlantic Ocean and the

Gulf of Mexico.

During the day, circulation is generally from the direction of the sea. At night, circulation reverses, producing a weaker land breeze. The meeting of eastern and western sea breezes (convergence) at midpeninsula results in thunderstorm activity that reaches maximum intensity in the afternoon.

Because it is so large (730 square miles), Lake Okeechobee generates its own local weather, including a lake breeze. With the sea breezes, the lake breeze affects the development of local convection rainfall. Aerial photographs often show a curtain of clouds around the lake in midsummer.

In a similar fashion, land use can influence local weather. For example, agricultural land like that in the Everglades Agricultural Area around Lake Okeechobee heats at different rates than land in the Everglades marshes to the south.

Rivers in the Sea and Sky

The proximity of the Everglades to the Atlantic Ocean and the Gulf of Mexico affects air temperatures over the Glades. Air tends to assume the temperature of the surface on which it rests or moves. Because Florida is a long peninsula, coastal water warms the watershed on either side, especially at the narrow tip. In the summer, surface temperatures of the Atlantic and the Gulf reach about 84 degrees F. In the winter they drop to 70 degrees F. This heat transfers to the air overhead.

Invisible currents such as the Gulf Stream (ocean), jet stream (atmo-

Lake Okeechobee generates its own local weather.

Storm warnings.

sphere), and others profoundly affect climate and weather in the watershed. The persistent northflowing Gulf Stream snaking around the tip of Florida and, from the Atlantic, the North Equatorial Current bring heated water from the tropics to warm the coastal waters of the peninsula. The wind from either coast brings air heated by contact with coastal water inland to help warm the ecosystem. More shallow than the Atlantic, the Gulf of Mexico tends to be a little warmer in summer and colder in winter. The warming influence comes mostly from the east, with prevailing winds from that direction.

Globally, air rises at the warm equator and sinks at the colder poles, but Earth's rotation causes longitudinal winds (the Coriolis effect). Westerly winds prevail in the area between 30 and 60 degrees latitude, and easterly trade winds blow between the equator and 30 degrees north and south latitude. Because southern Florida is close to 30 degrees north of the equator, both the westerlies and the trade winds influence weather and climate in the region by carrying in large weather systems from the North Atlantic and the continent.

Air considered either "maritime" (from the sea) or "continental"

(from the land), is further described by the terms "tropical" or "polar" depending on the latitude from which it comes. Cool air moving from Alaska or the Pacific Northwest is called continental polar air. However, the maritime influence of the Caribbean Sea, the Gulf of Mexico, and the Bermuda high-pressure cell predominates in effect on Florida's climate.

The Bermuda high, a large, semipermanent high-pressure area in the atmosphere, influences rainfall but has little effect on storms in the fall and winter. In late spring and summer, as the high weakens and expands northward and barometric pressure drops, thunderstorms develop over land in the late afternoon and over the Atlantic and the Gulf at night. Tropical low-pressure systems emerge from the Caribbean, the Atlantic, and the Gulf of Mexico in late summer and early fall, moving inland to drop their heavy burden of water. At that time, lengthy heavy rainfall is not uncommon. The high lies between easterly (to the south) and westerly (to the north) bands of wind at about 30 degrees north latitude. Centered over the Bermuda-Azores area of the Atlantic Ocean, the pressure area swells, shrinks, and wanders.

Air movement in a high-pressure system such as the Bermuda high tends to be downward. Sinking air warms and holds more moisture, so clouds evaporate and bring generally fair skies. Winter storms and fronts still characterize the watershed in March and April, but expansion of the Bermuda high can block penetration of cold air masses

into southern Florida. Conversely, if the high has not extended to the northwest, temperature extremes including frost can occur in the spring.

Rising Air, Falling Water

Frequent convective storms and occasional tropical storms and hurricanes cause most summer precipitation over the watershed. Hurricanes peak in August, September, and October; during a hurricane, 10 or more inches of rain may fall. Thunderstorms in spring and winter, generally produced by the passage of fronts, may occur at any time of day. During one unseasonably productive storm in December 1994, more than 14 inches of rain fell locally in seven hours.

Convection storms are produced by rising warm air. As pressure decreases with height, the air expands and cools, causing atmospheric moisture to condense and form clouds. Clouds may produce precipitation or, if the air is very dry, they may evaporate and disappear. Controlled by prevailing winds and sea breezes, convective storms and rain showers are usually small and slow moving. On average, a typical convection storm forms and dissipates in less than two hours.

It is common on a sunlit summer afternoon drive to see a gray curtain of rain drop down from a cloud hovering over the road ahead. You drive into the shower—often torrential—and emerge into the bright sunlight again a few minutes later. In an hour, three or four brief but powerful showers may wash the car, with enough time in between for the car to dry.

Cumulonimbus clouds (dense, tall cumulus clouds) develop when the air is in violent circulation. Friction between particles such as water droplets and ice crystals causes positive and negative electrical charges to build—much like passing a comb rapidly through dry hair. Air is a poor conductor of electricity, so the difference between the charges grows to enormous proportions—millions of volts—before discharge occurs.

Lightning splits the sky in brilliant traceries, sometimes as a single vivid bolt from cloud to Earth. At other times, it seems like a giant, incandescent web strung among the roiling clouds. Each bolt scent-marks the air with ozone. Its spark hotter than the surface of the sun, lightning electrifies and heats the sky over the watershed. The air resonates with thunderclaps.

Thunder results from the sudden expansion and contraction of air as the lightning bolt passes. It has been calculated that, each year,

Smaller, concentrated storms such as waterspouts develop out of low-pressure areas.

nearly 25 bolts of lightning strike a given square mile of land in southern Florida. In one storm, approximately 2,500 strokes of lightning were recorded in a three-hour period. The brilliant aerial display of lightning signals the birth of a potent rain producer.

Periodic large-scale storms emerge from low-pressure areas. In the northern hemisphere, winds move counterclockwise and inward around areas of low pressure, sometimes growing to enormous proportions. Low-pressure systems that develop within the belts of westerly and easterly winds are generically called cyclones. The largest storms, sometimes hundreds of miles in diameter, often move slowly from west to east across the continent under the influence of the polar jet stream. These big winter storms bring ice and snow to northern climes, while the Everglades basks in tropical warmth. Even so, frosts are not uncommon and in rare years snow has even fallen in the Glades.

As large midlatitude low-pressure storms move across the country, they draw in air from different directions. When they pass over a place, wind direction and temperature change and often there is precipitation. Especially during the winter, passage of these continental lows affects southern Florida's weather and climate. The temperature and moisture content of a low depends on the location of its center at a given time in relation to Florida. Fronts pass through the state from time to time, bringing a continental influence to the Everglades. Sometimes stalling over southern Florida, fronts produce heavy rains, especially along the east coast.

Smaller but more concentrated and violent storms such as tornadoes, waterspouts (rarely violent), and hurricanes also develop out of areas of low pressure. Tornadoes and waterspouts are most common in the spring and summer when, eclipselike, the sky darkens; everything becomes eerily still,

Lightning electrifies and heats the sky over the watershed.

and a funnel of low-pressure air spins down from low clouds. It is not uncommon to see an impressive, tightly spun column of water, a waterspout, dancing across a shallow bay or sound on a summer morning. Tornadoes are associated with the passage of cold fronts; the development of squall lines (lines of advancing storms) as air masses converge; local convection storms; and hurricanes making landfall. Maximum air speed in the eyewall of a tornado may approach 300 miles an hour. Locally, energy concentrated in such violently spiraling air can be very destructive.

Each year, more than a hundred disturbances in the air over the Atlantic, Caribbean, and Gulf have the potential to mature into hurricanes. Hurricanes tend to

form between 20 degrees and 5 degrees north latitude, in an area bound on the north by the Bermuda high and on the equatorial side by the low-pressure intertropical convergence zone. On average, fewer than 10 of these disturbances develop into tropical storms, and about half that number build to hurricane strength. Half of these hurricanes reach the Atlantic or Gulf coasts. The expected return rate varies from 6 to 17 years, depending on the coastal area.

In recent decades, three severe storms—the Labor Day Hurricane of 1935, Hurricane Donna in 1960, and Hurricane Andrew in 1992—completely altered the character of vegetation in parts of the Everglades watershed, especially among the coastal mangroves from Long Sound to the Ten

Thousand Islands. Other hurricanes, such as Betsy in 1964, have visited the area, but have caused less destruction. Is there a 25- to 30-year cycle in which the most powerful storms strike? Perhaps. As with other natural events, big storms periodically revisit the area, the eastern analog of large wildland fires in the West.

These are the hurricane coasts. In the twentieth century, nearly 60 storms have come ashore in Florida. The southern coast has been especially vulnerable. Six years is the longest Florida has gone without suffering a direct hit, from 1979 to 1985. The year 1964 saw three direct hits, the single-year record for the century.

Weather disturbances that sometimes spawn tropical storms and hurricanes are called "tropi-

The most powerful storms form near the Cape Verde Islands off the African coast.

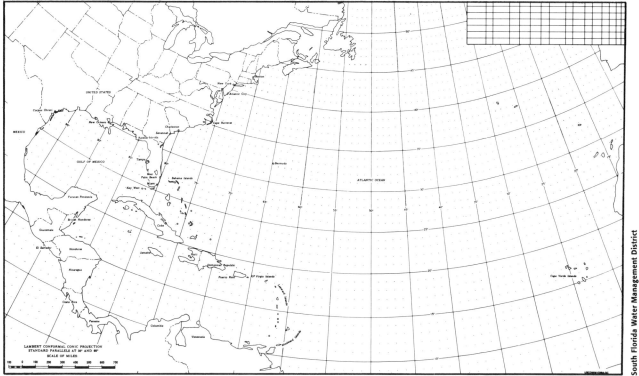

South Florida Water Management District

cal depressions," or "easterly waves." Tropical depressions, large areas of low pressure, often move from east to west over great distances. Sometimes, with well-defined circulation, they evolve into hurricanes. Tropical storms are cyclonic disturbances—storms with sustained circular airflow greater than 39 miles per hour. Hurricanes are also cyclonic disturbances but with winds consistently greater than 74 miles per hour.

Storms forming in the Cape Verde Islands area off Africa are the most powerful. Andrew, Donna, and the 1928 storm that emptied Lake Okeechobee and killed 2,000 people were born in African tropical waters. Cape Verde storms travel farther and have more time to strengthen and mature. In its 14-day lifetime, Andrew traveled over 5,500

miles, varying its latitude by more than 20 degrees to the north and its longitude by more than 70 degrees to the west. Eighty percent of hurricanes that emerge from the Gulf of Mexico originate elsewhere. Fifteen percent do form in the northern Gulf; the rest to the south near the Yucatan peninsula.

In June and from October through November, most storms form in the western Caribbean, follow a track north and west into the Gulf and miss landfall in Florida. Midseason Cape Verde storms form from mid-July to early September and move west-northwest, making landfall in Florida or the northern coast unless they recurve into the North Atlantic. Late-season storms that form in the Caribbean from late September to early November tend to move northeast.

Mechanics of a Heat Engine

All hurricanes require similar conditions. They have the same structure, and behave in a similar way. Air flows into the low-pressure area as if drawn into an expanding lung. There, warm seas heat the air and it rises convectively, carrying water vapor up to merge with clouds massing overhead. If the tropical storm is far enough from the equator to be influenced by the Coriolis effect, the characteristic swirling motion of a hurricane is imparted to it by Earth's spinning on its axis. The warmer the air, the more moisture the air holds, and the more rain that will fall. Condensing water vapor releases latent heat, further contributing to the upward movement of air. The rise of the heated air causes stronger winds, which draw air in

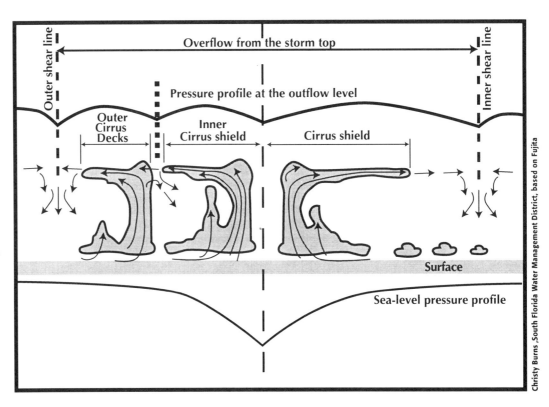

The eye of the hurricane is represented by the dashed line at center. While rotating around the eye, surface air converges toward the storm's center, is lifted in thunderstorms, exits radially in the storm's upper layer, and then sinks along the storm's outer edge. Surface pressure decreases steadily toward the center of the storm before dropping more drastically in the inner core reaching a minimum in the eye.

Christy Burns ,South Florida Water Management District, based on Fujita

Biography of a Maelstrom

One late August, an embryonic disturbance began to grow in the air above the tropical latitudes. A Cape Verde storm, it began in feverish, unsettled air off the coast of West Africa. The storm matured, feeding on its own heat, moisture, and turbulence. It began to turn counterclockwise around a core of low pressure and at the same time slowly accelerated toward the west. As the storm strengthened, it reached further outward and spun more rapidly, drawing more air into the vortex.

The storm's movements seemed capricious and slow; but it followed the sun unerringly across the Atlantic Ocean toward the vulnerable shore of southern Florida. When its circular motion reached sustained speeds of 74 miles an hour, the storm became a hurricane. First of the season, and named according to the alphabetic convention of the hurricane watchers, it was called Andrew. Its landfall in Florida recalled the words of Joseph Conrad in his novel *Typhoon:*

It was something formidable and swift, like the sudden smashing of a Vial of Wrath . . . This is the disintegrating power of a great wind. It isolates one from one's kind. An earthquake, a landslip, an avalanche, overtake a man incidentally, as it were—without passion. A furious gale attacks him like a personal enemy, tries to grasp his limbs, fastens upon his mind, seeks to rout the very spirit out of him.

Hundreds of thousands of people remember 1992 as the year that Andrew came, and their memories are vivid, sad, and indelible. It is the year that a great wind roared out of the Atlantic to visit the power of wind and water on southern Florida, a humbling reminder of humanity's subservience to nature. To people who suffered through those late August days and nights, huddled together in vulnerable dwellings, Hurricane Andrew has been added to the benchmarks of a human lifetime.

To the Everglades, Andrew was just another natural event, no more, no less. Hurricanes and their cyclonic kin frequent all the oceans except the South Atlantic. In all the seasons during which hurricanes have swirled about the seas, there has always been one somewhere approaching a rendezvous with the land. The visitation of Andrew (like the 1988 fires in Yellowstone and other large-scale manifestations of natural power) exacted a human toll. But from nature's vantage point, sadness and despair would be inappropriate. Rather, the event was a reminder of the inevitability of change.

Andrew was born when a line of thunderstorms moved offshore from the coast of West Africa on or about August 13. The storms were carried west-northwest by a trough of low pressure, an "easterly wave." As the wave moved farther from equatorial waters, winds, twisted by the Coriolis effect, began to circle about the low pressure center, forming a tropical depression.

By August 17, the mass of circling air had tightened and increased in speed, transforming the depression into a tropical storm that was christened Andrew. Andrew's adolescence was short lived. In the next five days, the storm intensified and became better organized. On August 22, with winds sustained at 74 miles an hour, Andrew matured into a hurricane. By the next day, August 23, winds exceeded 145 miles an hour. Overnight, Andrew had grown to deadly proportions and had struck the Bahamas.

At 4:52 A.M. on August 24, just 11 days old, Andrew moved inland toward the Everglades with winds gusting to 175—possibly as high as 200—miles an hour; their speed was more than any instrument could measure. The peak storm surge, when the ocean surface was drawn up by the low pressure and pushed inland, measured nearly 17 feet.

Passing quickly over the peninsula but marking it for decades, Andrew moved offshore into the Gulf of Mexico on August 25, weakened, and continued toward Louisiana, where it made landfall on August 26. By August 27, Andrew began to die, dissipating into torrential rain and tornadoes over Mississippi, Alabama, Georgia, and Tennessee, where "he" passed into the weather history books.

What was Andrew's legacy to the Everglades? The most obvious effect of the storm was major structural damage to trees. Most hammock trees were affected; as many as 30 percent of them were felled or broken. Twenty to 25 percent of the royal palms fell down, and perhaps 40 percent of the pines blew over or broke. Seventy thousand acres of mangroves were blown down, and 90 percent of the known nesting trees of the endangered red-cockaded woodpecker were destroyed.

Very little evidence of direct animal mortality was observed. Although adult alligators were little affected, many nests were destroyed and many young gators may have suffered. Coastal wading bird rookeries were severely damaged, but relatively few birds were found dead, and hundreds were seen alive. Resident white ibis and egrets were apparently unaffected. Freshwater fish and larger invertebrates were also relatively untouched, although more than 7 million dead fish were found in oxygen-depleted waters around the southeast coast of the peninsula. Fish in Everglades National Park may suffer longer-term loss due to the disruption and loss of periphyton.

Marine environments fared better than terrestrial ones. There was some scouring of the shallow bottoms, but most submerged areas were intact. Cape Sable and the west coast beaches experienced overwashes of 10 to 40 feet, which probably improved them as sea turtle nesting sites. The mangrove fishery was unchanged. Plankton blooms were observed and low oxygen levels recorded, but the major effect on inshore habitats was increased turbidity. Ironically, more manatees were counted following Andrew than at any other time since monitoring began. Watchers counted 209 of the giant sirens in less than 10 hours. Known crocodile nesting sites were not affected.

One hoped-for consequence of the storm did not occur. Had Andrew tracked across the park farther south, it might have helped break up the malignant algae bloom that is spreading in parts of Florida Bay. While water levels and water quality were affected to some extent, Andrew was, by hurricane standards, a dry storm. It produced a maximum of only about 8 inches of rain, and most areas only received about 4.5 inches.

One of the more insidious effects of the storm may be the spread of invasive nonnative species. Disturbed terrestrial habitats may be overtaken in larger numbers by competitive, hardy, and prolific nonnative species, confounding existing efforts to exclude them. Also, the storm released many alien pets and laboratory and zoo animals that may find their way into the fastness of the park. After the hurricane, a monkey was seen at Cape Sable.

What was the measurable human cost of Andrew? In southern Florida, 43 lives were lost. In terms of devastation and economic loss, Andrew was the most destructive hurricane to date. Eighty thousand homes were destroyed and another 55,000 severely damaged, leaving 160,000 people homeless—nearly half of the population of southern Dade County. Eighty-five thousand people lost jobs. Perhaps 25,000 people chose to leave Florida altogether. Fifteen thousand boats were smashed, and Andrew generated 20 to 40 million cubic yards of debris, much of it the outfall of shattered human homes and businesses. The total loss was estimated at about $30 billion.

To date, Andrew is the costliest natural disaster in U.S. history, exceeding the others by tens of billions of dollars. Below Andrew on the list of the 10 worst natural disasters in the country are historic events like the 1889 Johnstown Flood, the 1906 San Francisco Earthquake, and the 1993 Great Mississippi Flood.

The World Meteorological Organization "retires" the names of particularly severe or destructive hurricanes, like the numbers of great athletes. Andrew has joined 33 other great storms, including Donna and Betsy, in what has been called a "hurricane hall of infamy." Other storms will come to southern Florida, but Andrew will never again visit the Everglades.

at the base of the growing storm like a vacuum cleaner sucking up dust. Sometimes, in an intensifying depression, more air exits from the top of the storm than enters at the bottom, increasing the exchange of heat and moisture.

Someone once aptly called a hurricane a "giant, self-sustaining heat engine." The main energy source for tropical storms is latent heat released when water vapor condenses. Only very moist air can supply the enormous energy necessary to spawn and maintain a tropical storm, and the warmer the air, the greater its moisture-holding capacity. Thus, tropical storms and hurricanes tend to form over oceans with water temperatures of at least 80 degrees F. After they form, tropical storms grow more powerful when they pass over warm water, and weaker when they pass over cold water or land. Peak hurricane activity is from mid-August to mid-October, when ocean temperatures are warmest and atmospheric patterns most favorable.

The rate of heating from the condensation associated with heavy rainfall in a hurricane can produce energy equivalent to 2,400 billion kilowatt-hours in one day. High altitude infrared photographs clearly show this intense heat in the storm's center; from space, Andrew was an angry red vortex tracking straight toward southern Florida.

Hurricanes may expand to diameters of more than 400 miles. Maximum wind velocity may exceed 200 miles an hour, with sustained winds averaging closer to 100 miles an hour depending

on category, or strength. Hurricane-force winds typically extend 50 miles from the storm center. A storm moves at an average speed of 10 to 15 miles per hour. As a storm's energy dissipates, its forward speed may actually increase. A hurricane is always most powerful in its right-front quadrant, a result of sustained counterclockwise winds and the storm's forward speed over water. Storm surge, too, is most pronounced to the right of center.

A well-developed hurricane has a circular eye, around which violent winds move. Strangely calm and cloud-free, the eye may extend above 50,000 feet and measure from 6 to 60 miles across. It is the area of lowest pressure and highest temperature in the storm. Sometimes, pelagic birds imprisoned in the eye circle and rise endlessly, unwilling riders carried along on the storm.

Winds in the eyewall rotate counterclockwise at a maximum velocity of more than 180 miles per hour. Winds of 200 miles an

hour or more wreaked havoc in the Florida Keys and along the southwest coast during the 1935 Labor Day storm. The pressure differential between the eye and the outer margin of the storm causes the eyewall winds. Three hundred miles from the center, winds usually blow at less than 20 miles per hour. Deceptively mild, these marginal winds foretell the banshee wail of the wildly swirling eyewall.

The strong convection in the eyewall produces the heaviest precipitation. The hurricane generates thunderstorms that may produce rainfall of up to 10, possibly even 20 inches per day. Released latent heat associated with rainfall helps maintain low pressure and strong winds. A typical hurricane lasts about 3 to 12 days, so total rainfall can be enormous.

Like an ice skater spinning faster as she brings her arms down, air spins faster closer to the axis of rotation as it is pulled in toward the center of the storm. A wind of

A well-developed hurricane has a circular eye, around which violent winds circulate.

Courtesy: Everglades National Park

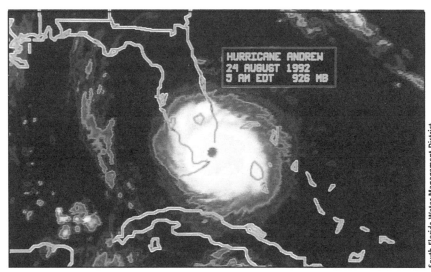

HURRICANE ANDREW
24 AUGUST 1992
5 AM EDT   926 MB

South Florida Water Management District

The eye of Hurricane Andrew passed over Homestead and Florida City.

only 3 miles per hour at a distance of 300 miles from the storm center increases to 160 miles per hour in the eyewall. Ten miles up in the convective eyewall, rising air cools and moves outward, and its counterclockwise rotation slows. About 190 miles from the center of a 300-mile-wide storm, the air changes direction.

We know much about hurricanes and other weather phenomena, but forecasting is still an imprecise art. We understand the general mechanisms of the storm's origin and growth; we can measure temperature, wind speeds, barometric pressure, and rainfall, and make predictions. But hurricanes move erratically, governed by larger phenomena such as the general movement of winds. Hurricanes are fickle.

The large-scale prevailing wind currents in which the storms are imbedded control storm movement across the ocean. Typically a storm moves at 10 to 15 miles per hour, but it may stall and remain stationary for several days. Often,

hurricanes move north along the coast and diminish when they reach the horse latitudes, an area in which the air and water are cooler. When this happens, they may turn back to the northeast to dissipate at sea.

Sometimes a storm intensifies when a continental high-pressure area moves east to meet the Bermuda high. A trough of low pressure forms between them, funneling hurricanes north up the coast. If the Bermuda high is shrinking eastward and the continental high moves out to sea, storms are likely to move back out over the Atlantic. If a continental high remains positioned midcontinent, storms are much more likely to move inland.

As hurricanes move inland over extensive land, they lose the latent heat source of open water and begin to deteriorate. Because peninsular Florida is narrow, a powerful storm can diminish then regain intensity when it is back over water. But, like a renegade, Andrew may have even gained

strength when it passed over-land—namely, over hapless Dade County.

Hurricanes also diminish in power when they meet a current of cold, dry air from the mainland, as did Emily in 1993. A cold front forced her back out to sea, sparing much of the northeast coast. Cold air, which holds little moisture, weakens a storm; a hurricane must have heat and moisture to survive.

Typically, a storm tracks east to west over open water in the lower latitudes. As a storm approaches 25 to 30 degrees latitude it tends to recurve and, moving into higher latitudes, comes under the influence of westerly winds. These tend to shift the storm path northeast. Thus, many storms blow back out into the North Atlantic and never make landfall.

Costs and Benefits

Hurricanes touch the lives of every organism in southern Florida. Consider the mangrove. The tree is clearly hurricane dependent. In all three species (red, black, and white mangroves), maturation of seeds coincides with the peak of hurricane season. Storm winds and tides carry seeds, their passage to maturity shaped by a coincidence of the primal elements; their

Sign in visitor center of Everglades National Park.

PARDON OUR DUST
WATCH US REBUILD
FROM
HURRICANE ANDREW

Ken DeYonge

Wind damage and flooding are major effects of hurricanes.

South Florida Water Management District

death, and the beginning of yet another cycle, are foreshadowed in swirling currents of hot, moist air rising from distant waters. In 1960, Hurricane Donna destroyed nearly 75 percent of the Everglades' coastal mangrove forest. Thirty-two years later, 70,000 acres were snapped and broken by Hurricane Andrew. The effects of these storms will be visible for decades. Hurricane Donna killed mangroves that survived the Labor Day storm of 1935, and plants that survived Donna were killed by Andrew.

Wind damage and flooding are the major effects of hurricanes. Wind damages trees by stripping leaves and branches, shearing trunks, girdling, and uprooting. The collective effect of wind-generated waves, tides, and storm surge causes flooding. If heavy, precipitation aggravates flood conditions—and a storm can generate 10 to 20 inches of rain in a single day.

Waves and storm surges generated by wind also cause damage along the coast. Impervious mud suffocates roots, and storm surges carry excessive salinity inland. Heavy precipitation lessens these effects. Storm surges are caused by winds piling water up into a dome 10 to 20 feet high (capillary action accounts for about 10 percent of the surge). Surges are more pronounced in coastal shoals; thus, Gulf coastal areas experience greater storm surges. Storm surges are also greater if a storm coincides with high tide, as happened during Hurricane Camille.

The surge that accompanied Hurricane Donna's landfall was nearly 11 feet. The dome of water Andrew pushed up measured nearly 17 feet. The 1935 Labor Day storm produced a surge of more than 18 (possibly 20) feet. The highest surge on record in the U.S., caused by Hurricane Camille, was 22.4 feet. If you've ever been knocked down by surf at the beach, you can imagine the power of a storm-driven dome of water four or five times as high. Through storm surge, hurricanes cause geomorphic changes—they alter the landscape as beaches and impoundments are created, extended, and washed away.

Hurricanes affect marine creatures not only by pummeling them in the turbulent upper waters, but also by fogging shallow waters with accumulations of silt, and clogging the delicate breathing membranes of fish and invertebrates.

Temporary damage aside, however, hurricanes are important agents of diversity. Like large wildland fires, they help create vegetative mosaics, replacing old vegetation with biologically rich edges (ecotones). Storms also break up unnatural algal blooms that threaten inland waters and embayments. Hurricanes and tropical storms are instruments of biogeographic dispersal. They carry life forms from distant shores to new environments. On hurricane-driven winds and currents, new life forms have colonized watershed communities over the years. Plant seeds are less frail than animals and more likely to survive the tumultuous passage to a new land. But tropical storms have introduced some animals to southern Florida too. One example is tree snails, those spiral rainbows from the Caribbean that decorate the trees of hardwood hammocks.

A Hurricane Richter Scale

Hurricanes fall into five categories according to maximum wind velocity, central barometric pressure, height of storm surge, and expected damage. A "major" storm is of category three or higher. Through 1989, only one of the 56 twentieth-century hurricanes that hit Florida ranked in

Hurricane Andrew – The Human Cost

All photos: South Florida Water Management District

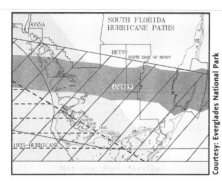

Andrew cut a wide swath through southern Florida.

category five: the Labor Day Hurricane of 1935. Hurricane Donna in 1960 ranked as a category four storm, and Betsy in 1965 was a category three. The severe hurricanes of 1926 and 1928 were category four storms, and those of 1945 and 1949, category three.

These major storms substantially affected the Everglades watershed, both its life and landscape. But until Hurricane Andrew, only 25 percent or fewer of the people living near the Everglades had experienced a hurricane's direct hit. Often, major storms threaten to come ashore, but veer away at the last moment, so most people have only experienced a hurricane's weaker margins. Perhaps this explains the disturbing complacency in populations untested by a storm's full force.

The Labor Day storm (in 1935 a system for naming hurricanes had not been devised) is still considered one of the most violent storms to have hit North America in the twentieth century. Small but powerful, it is the only category five storm to have struck Florida in recent memory. When it passed over Long Key at the southern edge of Florida Bay,

barometric pressure measured 26.35 inches—the lowest ever recorded at sea level in the United States. Instruments that measured wind velocity were destroyed, but damage assessment led to an estimate of gusts between 200 and 250 miles an hour. The storm surged up to 20 feet above sea level, virtually scraping Islamorada clear of human structures.

J. E. Duane, a weather observer on Long Key, experienced and wrote about the eye of that violent storm beginning on September 2, 1935.

> *9:20 P.M.— Barometer now reads 27.22 inches, wind has abated . . . a very light breeze continues throughout the lull; no flat calm . . . the sea began to lift up it seemed, and rise very fast . . . I could see walls of water which seemed many feet high. I had to race fast to regain entrance to cottage, but water caught me waist deep . . . Water lifted cottage from its foundations and it floated.*

> *10:10 P.M.—Barometer now 27.02 inches; wind beginning to blow.*

> *10:15 P.M.—The first blast from SSW, full force. House now breaking up—wind seemed stronger than any time during storm. I glanced at barometer which read 26.98 inches . . . I was then struck by some object and knocked unconscious.*

> *September 3, 2:25 A.M. — I became conscious in tree and found I was lodged about 20 feet above ground.*

Mr. Duane survived the storm, but more than 400 other people did not, including several at Cape Sable. Only the storm of September 16, 1928, was more deadly.

That storm blew all the water out of Lake Okeechobee, burying more than 2,000 people in an avalanche of mud and debris. In the late 1940s, consecutive hurricanes precipitated a hue and cry for flood control.

An Enduring Presence

While hurricanes have probably been active since the primal elements first joined to create them, only a few accounts in the logs of early Spanish and English mariners make reference to them in Florida waters. The earliest recorded hurricane in Florida occurred in 1559, in the north. A powerful storm is also known to have touched southern Florida in 1759. With the exception of these occasional references, the record of intense storms is incomplete until about 1871. From about 1887 to the present, we can construct a complete time line though most hurricane tracks prior to radar (1940s) and satellites (1960s) are estimated.

Several facts emerge from a look at the historical record. Very few storms developed in November. Eleven percent of the tropical cyclones that have affected Florida have arrived early in June; 7 percent came in July. Most of the storms—mainly the powerful Cape Verde hurricanes—came in late summer: 16 percent in August and 31 percent in September. Another 31 percent of the storms, mainly from the south, the western Caribbean, the Gulf of Mexico, and the Straits of Florida, arrived in October.

The southeast coast of Florida is one of the most hurricane-prone, vulnerable areas in the country. The frequency rate for hurricanes there is one every seven years and the probability of a hurricane striking the area in a given year is as high as 16 percent.

There always were and always will be hurricanes. Hurricanes are an enduring presence, and in spite of the persistent human imperative to manipulate and control Nature, we can do nothing when she chooses to show her power. We can only prepare, observe, and hope to survive, all the while marveling at her unmatched strength.

Too Little, Too Much

A drought is a period of more than six months with little or no rain. Drought may seem a doubtful occurrence in a place where water plays such a dominant role. Although it is one of the wettest places in the country, southern Florida's rainfall varies greatly from year to year. In some ways the watershed is similar to the eastern Great Plains—it has been visited by severe droughts as well as periodic floods, though these events are less severe in southern Florida. Unusual conditions in the

air masses reaching southern Florida seem to trigger drought. Ordinarily, warm air is unstable. Because it is lighter, it rises, and its temperature progressively drops. The more rapid the temperature loss, the more unstable the air becomes as it continues to rise.

Sometimes the temperature gradient becomes reversed and air temperature begins to increase, instead of decrease, as air moves upward. This is called an inversion. Because warmer, lighter air is above colder air, it is no longer compelled to rise. This phenomenon is familiar to city dwellers who must, from time to time, cope with low-lying smog on otherwise clear days.

In winter and spring, inversions form over Florida at lower altitudes, preventing air from rising to form cumulus clouds and produce rain. By late spring or early summer, hot air converging over the area causes the inversion layer to either form higher in the atmosphere or to dissipate completely. During the

summer, tropical low-pressure areas frequently move into southern Florida. They too lift air and dissipate the inversion, enabling warm moist air to rise and form rain clouds. Sometimes, though, the inversion remains well into the summer, and little or no rain falls. In summer, the angle of the sun is high and its heating and drying power is at its greatest. When these conditions occur simultaneously, a dry spell or even drought is imminent.

In May and June, and again in September and October, moderate to severe dry spells are likely to develop. In several of the years since 1950, severe and extended dry conditions have occurred, necessitating restrictions on water use.

The drought of 1980-82 was especially severe. It came after a decade in which only four years had seen normal or above normal rainfall. In July 1982, Lake Okeechobee—critical to the survival of the Glades—dropped to levels never before recorded (9.75 feet above mean sea level). One major concern during drought in Florida is that, with insufficient rainfall to recharge it, the Biscayne Aquifer (the major source of water in its area for human use and consumption) will be drawn down so far that salt water will invade it. If this happened, it could take many years to eliminate salt water contamination in coastal wells.

Drought also alters fire's relationship to the vegetation of the watershed. Lightning-caused fires are normal in the Glades during the dry season, but drought accelerates drying and increases the likelihood of abnormally

Even in an area that receives more than 60 inches of rain a year, seasonal drought can occur.

Courtesy: Everglades National Park

large, intense fires that may burn in and destroy organic muck soils.

One of many connections between climate, weather, and sun has correlated sunspot activity and drought, but specific cause and effect relationships are not known. It may also be that large volcanic eruptions contribute to drought. Great volumes of ash in the atmosphere may decrease solar radiation and evapotranspiration, and strengthen high atmospheric pressure that is already suppressing rain. This relationship was first postulated during the 1980-82 drought, which coincided with a major eruption in Mexico.

Historically, wetlands composed 75 percent of the area south of Lake Okeechobee. Drainage for flood protection, agriculture, and urban development has reduced that amount by half. One theory suggests that diminished wetland area results in less evaporation and a consequent decrease in the normal buildup of cumulus and cumulonimbus clouds, the principal sources of southern Florida precipitation. But records do not support this theory. The greatest sources of evaporation in the area are the Gulf of Mexico and the Atlantic, not the Everglades marshes. Evapotranspiration returns 80 to 90 percent of average rainfall (48 to 54 inches) to the hydrologic cycle.

During winter, periodic heavy rains fall on the watershed. Moisture-laden low-pressure systems emerging from the Gulf of Mexico usually cause this unseasonable precipitation. In January and February of 1983, following the three-year drought, unexpectedly heavy rain fell—

Heavy rain may prompt water managers to release billions of gallons of water through flood control structures.

more than three times the average for the period. It was almost as if nature was hurrying to balance the books. Old "crackers" in southern Florida often say you're either in a drought on the way to a flood, or vice versa. That's life in the subtropics.

Winter and spring of 1983 were among the wettest in history. Probably, the interaction of low-pressure systems from the Gulf of Mexico and strong cold fronts produced unstable air and storms. Meteorologists believe that these unseasonable events may have been caused by unusually warm offshore currents that winter—in particular a recurring phenomenon called El Niño.

The heavy rain prompted the South Florida Water Management District to release billions of gallons from swollen Lake Okeechobee into shallow basins or conservation areas south of the lake, and subsequently into the Everglades and estuaries, to minimize the threat of flooding and the breaching of Okeechobee's Hoover Dike. The

releases came at a time when water levels are typically low, and adversely affected nesting birds and other reproducing wildlife. In addition, large amounts of fresh water discharging into coastal estuaries resulted in high mortality of sea grasses, fish, and shellfish. The situation is just one of many that illustrate the challenges of managing water to meet the needs of both people and nature.

Heavy rain fell again in late 1994—so much that, in places, water levels were two feet higher than normal. A naturalist in Everglades National Park saw cormorants diving for bass in a parking lot. Another wet year

Water levels affect wildlife.

was 1995. For weeks, water levels in Lake Okeechobee exceeded 18.5 feet above mean sea level, forcing major discharges. And so the cycle continues.

The Water Calendar

Sporadic severe weather plays an important part in the Florida climate; it contrasts with the still, measured seasons that come and go predictably, with little fanfare. The cycle of the seasons is not as showy and dramatic as it is in more northern latitudes, yet seasons are distinct here, with some blending that is true to the watershed. Observers of natural phenomena will note the falling or the emergence of cypress needles, fresh fiddleheads on ferns, and the exchange of old oak leaves for new ones. A year in southern Florida is counted in the coming and going of water. Air, the medium that brings water to the Glades in clouds, exchanges it with the earth as rain; the sky is the canvas on which the sun paints colorful arcs of light and water called rainbows.

For nearly five decades, water has been managed for people first. However, through lessons learned, people have begun to connect the health of natural systems with the health of human society. In many ancient cultures, the rainbow symbolized a bridge. Perhaps our culture could also use it to symbolize, and remind us of, the connections among saw grass, alligators, wood storks, and people.

Emergence of cypress needles indicates a change in seasons.

Courtesy: Everglades National Park

Chapter 4

A Green Patchwork

My advice is to urge every discon-tented man to take a trip through the Everglades—if it doesn't kill [him] it will certainly cure him. All who are suffering from "ennui," who have no taste for the good things of the world and can feed on nothing but the dainties of the table—after a few days of such experiences as we went through, fat white bacon warmed through will be as delicate to the taste as turkey's breast, and "sinkers" will sit as lightly on the stomach as the finest white bread. One may have been raised to think iced champagne the only drink fit for a gentleman, but one will grow to think cold coffee, without milk or sugar, equal to nectar. If a man is a dude, a trip through the 'Glades is the thing to cure him. A day's journey in slimy, decaying vegetable matter which coats and permeates everything it touches, and no water with which to wash it off, will be good for him, but his chief medicine will be his morning toilet. He must rise with the sun when the grass and leaves are wet with dew and put on his shrinking body his clothes heavy and wet with slime and scrape out of each shoe a cup full of black and odorous mud—it is enough to make a man swear to be contented ever afterwards with a board for a bed and a clean shirt once a week.

—Alonzo Church, in his
A Dash Through the Everglades, a
personal record of the Everglades
Exploring Expedition of 1892.

Florida is flat. Its soils are often sandy and surface water is limited due to the porous lime-stone substrate and sandy soils. Given these conditions, one might imagine that Florida's vegetation would be sparse and uniform. Nothing could be further from the truth. The plants of the watershed are lush and diverse. How diverse? Some 3,500 plants thrive there, many found no-where else.

What offsets the potentially limiting features of soil and water? One factor is the latitude of Florida; positioned between temperate and tropical zones, it contains habitats for species from both. In addition, Florida's peninsular shape, with shores washed by warm seas, provides a very humid environment that nurtures plant growth. Finally, Florida has a large range of landscape ages. Plants and animals have inhabited parts of the state for millions of years; other parts for only a few thou-sand.

Sometimes, boundaries between plant communities are blurred and indistinct, but in this water-shed boundaries are often clearly

Tree islands dot the saw grass landscape.

defined. Differences in moisture, soil fertility, fire frequency, and patterns of human use create this definition. Unlike in other parts of the country, a few inches' difference in elevation can create associations of plants and animals that are totally different from those a few feet away. For ex-ample, hammock communities support diverse, lush vegetation with a low fire frequency. Yet they dot saw grass landscapes that thrive in the extremes of flood, fire, and drought.

Plant associations of the water-shed include pine flatwoods and dry prairies; scrub and high pine; pine rockland; hardwood ham-mocks; freshwater swamps; freshwater marshes; mangrove swamps; coastal marshes; and inshore marine systems.

Pine Flatwoods and Dry Prairies

As is implied by their name, pine flatwoods thrive in areas of low

The plants of the watershed are lush and diverse. How diverse?

Some 3,500 plants thrive there, many found nowhere else.

Southern Florida slash pine grows throughout the central and southern regions of Florida.

relief. The soil is generally sandy, acidic, and not very well drained. In the past, when humans did not control them, fires frequently burned through these areas.

Pine flatwoods make up the most extensive plant community in Florida, but are probably the most altered by human use. With the construction of roads, developments, and other "fire breaks," flatwoods have not burned as frequently as in the past. Large areas have been lumbered, and nonnative species have taken over in some forests. Therefore, current stands differ from those of the past. Records of early pine flatwoods describe an understory "open enough to drive wagons through easily." Since current forests experience fire less frequently, trees are more likely to be the same approximate age, and the understory has greater shrub cover.

Four types of trees dominate the flatwoods: longleaf pine, typical slash pine, southern Florida slash pine, and pond pine. Live oak is a

minor species in central Florida. In the understory, saw palmetto, dwarf huckleberry, wax myrtle, dwarf live oak, gallberry, and fetterbush live.

Flatwoods exist throughout the watershed in the following areas: the southeastern coastal plain, the southwestern lowlands, the east coast lowlands, and the central portion of the peninsula. The dominant pine in the flatwoods varies from central to southern Florida. To the north, depending on soil and drainage, are longleaf pine (well-drained areas); slash pine (swamps and areas adjacent to ponds); and pond pine (wet areas). Further south, only southern Florida slash pine grows.

The longleaf pine has the longest needles and largest cones of the eastern pines. The crown of the tree is open and one new row of spreading branches grows each year. The needles, three in a bundle, are evergreen. Longleaf pine produces "naval stores." The term comes from the seventeenth

century when pine tar and pitch sealed the planking of wooden ships and preserved ropes. The trees are wounded to obtain turpentine and resin and after a few years are logged. These practices have impacted the flatwoods. Tapping trees for sap collection weakens them, lowering their resistance to fire, wind, and insect infestation. Heavy equipment used to collect sap disrupts the understory. Unfortunately, when fields are replanted after logging, slash pine often replaces longleaf pine, and the habitat the new species provides is not identical.

Slash pine is also logged and tapped for naval stores. A large, beautiful pine, it is popular as a shade and ornamental tree. One variety of slash pine, the southern Florida slash pine, grows throughout the central and southern regions of Florida.

Pond pine prefers wet habitats such as swamps, shallow bays, and ponds. Its Latin species

Southern Florida slash pine.

Dry prairie interspersed with hardwood hammocks.

name, *serotina*, means "late." This refers to the cones, which may remain closed for years, often opening after a fire or other disturbance.

Florida dry prairies are open, grassy expanses. Some botanists maintain the only difference between dry prairies and pine flatwoods is trees. Dry prairies occur on very flat terrain interrupted by cypress strands, cypress domes, isolated freshwater marshes, and hardwood hammocks. Dry prairies host many native species of grasses, sedges, herbs, and shrubs, including saw palmetto, fetterbush, staggerbush, gallberry, wiregrass, blueberry, carpet grasses, and bluestems.

Historically, a large area of this type of plant community lay just north of Lake Okeechobee, and was frequently swept by fire. Now, much of the dry prairie has been converted to pasture. In southern and central Florida, dry prairie includes palmetto prairies—former pine flatwoods where the overstory has been reduced or removed.

Current practices are heavily impacting flatwoods and dry prairie ecosystems. Stands are being removed or altered to accommodate agriculture, urban development, and the timber and cattle industries. In *Ecosystems of Florida*, edited by Ronald L. Meyers and John J. Ewel, contributing authors Warren C. Abrahamson and David C. Hartnett predict, "If present trends continue, the most extensive future alterations and declines in natural Florida ecosystems will occur in the flatwoods and dry prairies."

Scrub and High Pine

Scrub and high pine communities occur within the watershed, but are less frequent—particularly south of Lake Okeechobee. Scrub and high pine appear to be very different communities, but they have several common characteristics. They occur in upland areas that are dry and infertile. Soil characteristics often overlap. Both communities depend on fire to maintain their integrity. In the absence of fire, hardwood forests may replace them. The scrub community depends on fires ignited in more volatile areas, such as among the nearby high pine. And finally, both communities likely serve as aquifer recharge areas.

Scrub is a unique Florida habitat. Early settlers did not care for it since it was difficult to traverse and was conducive neither to agriculture nor to the grazing of cattle. A vanishing shrub community, scrub is characterized by dry, infertile, sandy soils with a variety of small oaks or Florida rosemary—sometimes both—with or without a pine canopy. Sand pine (also scrub pine) generally forms the canopy, but sometimes it is slash pine. Considered endangered, scrub pine communities can be seen at Jonathan Dickinson State Park and along the coast, particularly on the Florida Atlantic University

Courtesy: Everglades National Park

campus and at Boca Raton (the Yamato parcel).

In contrast, the high pine community is open. It consists of longleaf pine with a ground cover of wiregrass and other grass species. Most often, turkey oak grows in this system, occurring individually and in clusters. The high pine community is not unique to Florida; once it occupied lands from Virginia to east Texas, providing habitat for the endangered red-cockaded woodpecker and numerous other species.

Elevation, not tree height, distinguishes pine flatwood from high pine areas. High pine inhabits upland areas and sand ridges, whereas flatwoods occupy places of low relief. High pine often blends into longleaf pine flatwoods. Some species frequent both communities, but deciduous oaks are found only in high pines, while gallberry and fetterbush live only in flatwoods.

Clearing for agricultural and urban development threatens

scrub communities. However, some state parks offer protection, such as Lake Louisa, Lake Kissimmee, Blue Springs, Gold Head Branch, and Jonathan Dickinson. Other protected areas include Little Manatee River State Recreation Area, sections of the Avon Park Bombing Range and Lake Cain-Marsha Park in Orlando, Lake Wales Ridge National Wildlife Refuge, and the Nature Conservancy Disney Wilderness Preserve. However, even this degree of protection does not ensure the survival of scrub communities. Scrub must burn, and burn intensely, to maintain its species composition. Now, because scrub communities have become so fragmented, the only fires that burn are prescribed, and these are tightly controlled for air quality and safety. A possible mechanical alternative to burning is cutting.

Like scrub, high pine also depends on fire for its integrity. Unlike scrub, however, high pine requires frequent, low-intensity fires. More easily controlled, these fires make prescribed burning for high pine less difficult than for scrub.

South Florida Rockland

In extreme southern Florida, limestone characterizes upland areas. On these limestone outcroppings grow tropical hardwood hammocks and pinelands. The rocky pinelands of Everglades National Park are good places to get a feel for these plant communities, as well as for the exposed limestone topography. Tropical hardwood hammocks contain trees of primarily West Indian origin and are rich in tropical epiphytes such as orchids, bromeliads, and ferns. A more detailed discussion of the species that grow in these hammocks follows.

In *Ecosystems of Florida*, researchers write: "Rockland pine forests in southern Florida occur in locally elevated areas of the limestone bedrock bordered primarily by wet prairies and, to a small extent, by mangroves." Indeed, exposed rock makes up 70 percent or more of the surface in these pine forests. Plants take root in pockets of soil collected in the bedrock, and solution holes are common.

Some southern Florida plant communities related to elevation.

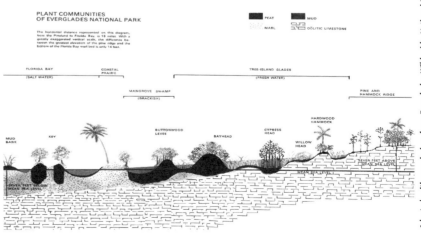

Adapted, with permission, from *Everglades Wildguide*, National Park Service

In its natural state the rootstock of the coontie is poisonous, but properly prepared it was an important food for Native Americans and early settlers.

The single canopy species in these pinelands is the southern Florida slash pine, sometimes called Dade County pine. Saw palmettos, coontie, and many endangered plant species also characterize these southern rocky pine forests. The saw palmetto's thick, branched stem creeps along the ground.

Because of its thick underground rootstock, the fernlike coontie can survive fire. Fire kills only the top of the plant; the hearty rootstock survives. Coontie was an important food plant for Native Americans and early Florida settlers. In its natural state, the underground rootstock is poisonous, but properly prepared, coontie yields starch. Julia Morton writes, "The rootstocks were scraped or peeled, then pounded, grated or ground, or boiled until soft and mashed; washed with plenty of water, drained, and the resultant starch dried in the sun." Early settlers ran coontie mills; however, the red water produced by the process proved fatal to cattle that drank it. Native Americans

made a food called "sofkee" with the starch.

Temperate and tropical species blend in the shrubs, palms, and herbs of the rockland pine system, but the animals are primarily temperate. Species include the black racer snake, the rough green snake, the Carolina anole, the red-bellied woodpecker, the northern cardinal, the opossum, the raccoon, and the white-tailed deer.

Because they are elevated, the pinelands are a pleasant place to walk at any time of the year. In summer, however, if a mosquito hatch has occurred, a breezy day might prove more comfortable.

Hardwood Hammocks

In technical terms, a hammock is a forest of broad-leaved trees on a slightly elevated area. Without these mounds of green, saw grass marsh would stretch unbroken to the horizon. From the air, hammocks look like a legion of turtles, large and small, ponderously making their way across the flat terrain. Hammocks also characterize pine rocklands.

The sites on which hammocks develop generally rise only a few feet above the surrounding area. By thriving where floods and burns are rare, they increase their chances of establishing themselves before fire destroys them and fire-tolerant tree species replace them. In this way, fire maintains balance among plant communities. When species from mature hammocks spread into neighboring pinelands or marsh-

Tropical hardwood hammocks develop on slightly elevated sites.

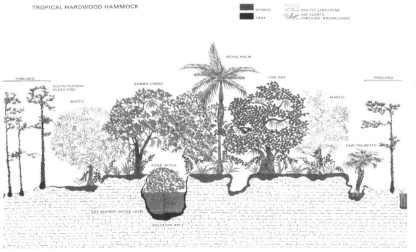

Interior of a hardwood hammock.

lands, fire controls their advance. However, when hammocks burn, their location determines whether pine trees will replace them. For example, in the East Everglades, species such as wax myrtle colonize hammocks. Exotics may also invade burned hammocks.

Hammocks can include both temperate and tropical species. Tree islands of the southern Everglades, influenced by the warming effects of the sea, are composed largely of tropical trees. Hammocks farther north contain tropical as well as temperate species (live oak, red bay, mulberry) growing near the southern limit of their range. While hammocks fit a general description, they are individualistic, varying in species composition, size, shape, and density. Areas of abundant rainfall support lush forests with large trees; less moisture provides for a more open hammock with smaller trees and fewer air plants.

Hammocks accessible to the public include Royal Palm and

Mahogany Hammock in Everglades National Park, and Chekika Hammock northeast of the park. Experiencing a hammock is a little like eating the fruit of the prickly pear cactus: once you peel back the spiny covering you're in for a delicious experience. On the edge of a hammock, your first instinct may be to turn back. The perimeter is generally dense—the result of the "edge effect." Pineland or grassland usually surrounds a hammock, and at the edges where the two communities meet, vegetation overlaps.

Royal Palm Hammock, ENP.

As you attempt to enter a hammock, a 50-foot thick tangle of low shrubby bushes, saw palmettos, and vines impedes you. Devil's claw, a vine with nasty curved spines, grabs at your hair and clothing. The erect leaves of saw palmettos may measure as much as four feet wide. Each leaf's segments radiate from a central point, in the manner of a Chinese fan. Saw palmettos should always be approached cautiously as they may harbor rattlesnakes.

The inside of a hammock, however, is not junglelike. Mature hammocks are "closed." The dense foliage of the "roof" or canopy allows little sunlight to filter through to the forest floor below. Because most herbs, vines, and shrubs will not grow in the shade of the canopy, the forest floor is generally open.

The interior of a hammock has a magical quality. With its bark deeply furrowed, and its massive branches cradling air plants and rare, fragile orchids, a venerable live oak reminds one of cultures that believed trees housed the spirits of ancestors. This belief is still common today among some rain forest peoples.

If we personify the live oak as good and noble, then the strangler fig is a scoundrel. One researcher maintained that the various species of figs, like most "criminals," are difficult to identify. Why such harsh judgments of a species whose only offense is that it manages to

Strangler fig.

establish itself where sunlight is at a premium?

Unable to work from the ground floor up, the fig begins at the top. Birds, cleaning their beaks and defecating, deposit seeds in the upper branches of the tree canopy. Bathed in sunshine, the seeds sprout, and roots begin their descent of the host trees. When the roots reach the soil and begin to absorb nutrients, they thicken, entwining their "victim." The fig thrives, depriving its host of sunlight and constraining its vascular system. In the end, the host tree dies and decays. Only the fig remains.

With a far less sinister public image, the gumbo limbo is an interesting and easily identified species of the tropical hammock. Commonly called the tourist tree because it is always red and peeling, the tree's reddish brown bark has the texture of onionskin paper.

Gumbo limbo is sometimes confused with poisonwood, a hammock tree that grows close to

Gumbo limbo.

Poisonwood leaves exhibit "drip tips" characteristic of tropical trees.

oak. Like the gumbo limbo, poisonwood sports a thin, flaky, reddish brown bark. What distinguishes it from the harmless gumbo limbo tree is its caustic sap, which turns black upon exposure to the air. Any tree with tarlike streaks or patches should be avoided; contact with any part of the tree can cause a rash or blisters and can even result in hospitalization.

Two groups of trees with different needs grow in the shadow of live oaks, gumbo limbos, and strangler figs: other mature trees that require less sunlight, and young trees that will eventually push up into the canopy. The pungent odor of one of these trees, white stopper, earned it the name "skunk tree." White stopper inhabits the understory of almost every tropical hardwood hammock.

Unlike in the pine forests, identifying species in a tropical hammock is not easy. Some hammocks contain more than 44 species of trees and shrubs. Because of the height of some canopy species and the way in which branches overlap in the

constant struggle for sunlight, it can be difficult to determine which leaves belong to which trees. To further complicate things, leaves of tropical trees often look similar. Leathery leaves with smooth edges and long, pointed "drip tips" dominate. In an area that receives considerable rainfall—in some parts of the watershed, in excess of 60 inches per year—"drip tips" allow leaves to shed water more efficiently.

Distribution of temperate and tropical species in hammocks throughout the watershed follows a pattern. Temperate species extend farther south in the center of the state than along the coasts. However, because of maritime temperature buffering, tropical species range farther north along the coasts than in the interior. Plant species are not alone in varying from northern to southern hammocks; forest structures vary as well. As hammocks range southward, overstories become lower and less layered. Understories and shrub layers increase. Epiphytes, or air plants, also increase in diversity.

Bromeliads anchor to rough-barked trees.

Epiphytes grow on other plants, though they do not take any nutrition from their hosts. Southern Florida hosts three major groups of epiphytes: bromeliads, ferns, and orchids.

Bromeliads usually prefer rough-barked trees to smooth-barked trees because they need a firm anchor. A tree branch may support many bromeliads, but sometimes snaps under their weight when the plants retain great amounts of water. The most commonly seen bromeliad is the stiff-leafed wild-pine, with its tight cluster of overlapping leaves at the base. Succumbing to gravity's pull, the slender leaves arch gracefully from the base and taper to a point. A shaft of

brilliant red bracts, the blooms of the wild-pine, harbors the plant's true flowers, which are tubular and lavender in color.

Another common bromeliad, Spanish moss, festoons the branches of live oak and other trees with a tangle of gray, filamentous stems. It is not a true moss, but a relative of the pineapple, although it has no roots. Among epiphytes, Spanish moss dominates hammocks along the Atlantic and Gulf coasts.

The bromeliads' water-holding capacity greatly enriches the diversity of life in the hammock. The bases of the stiff-leafed wild-pine and other bromeliads form reservoirs for rainwater. In and above these microponds, mosqui-

toes and tree frogs breed and spiders build their webs. These small reservoirs also provide moisture for a variety of snakes, snails, lizards, insects, and spiders. Around no more than a cup of water, entire food webs may grow.

Depending on light and moisture, bromeliads and orchids occupy different levels of a hammock. Some species that prefer low light live in the subcanopy; sun lovers grow in the tops of trees, in gaps in the canopy, or in hammock margins.

Vibrant green ferns, often with intricately fashioned fronds, contribute color and beautiful texture to a hammock. The strap fern grows on living or dead trees and humus. Its long, leathery leaves look like a barber's strop. Young, coiled fern leaves, called fiddleheads, uncurl as they grow. Brown cases sometimes cover the undersides of ferns. These erupt when mature, releasing millions of spores. Should these spores land in moist, shady areas, they will develop into young plants.

One of the most interesting ferns in southern Florida hammocks is the resurrection fern. Viewed in winter, the brown, withered ferns seem to have succumbed to drought. Yet summer rains cause the small fronds, now vivid

Resurrection fern.

Strap fern.

Butterfly orchid.

green, to unfurl, creating miniature gardens on logs and limbs.

In bloom, orchids add splashes of bright color to the greens and browns of hammocks. Though a few orchids stand out—such as the cowhorn, which can weigh up to 75 pounds—the blooms of most hammock orchids are diminutive. Common names express these species' beauty or unusual form. A sun lover, the butterfly orchid's central lobed petal looks like tiny butterfly wings. The night-blooming epidendrum with its white, spiderlike flowers is especially sweet smelling.

Florida Freshwater Wetlands: Swamps and Marshes

Originally, wetlands covered more than 50 percent of Florida. Wetlands are defined as landforms characterized by the presence of shallow water on a regular or periodic basis, hydric or saturated soils, and hydrophytic (water tolerant) plants. More than just areas where surface water occurs, wetlands are also regions where ground water can occasionally rise to the surface to saturate the soil. Saturated soil promotes the growth of wetland plants.

Diverse systems fit into the category of wetlands, but there are two primary types: swamps and marshes. The dominant vegetation of swamps is trees; marshes are more prairielike, with nonwoody plant cover, though trees may grow individually or in clumps throughout a marsh.

Cypress is the most prevalent wetland tree in Florida.

Courtesy: Everglades National Park, Glen Van Nimwegen

Freshwater Swamps

Heads, domes, bogs, bays, and strands are swamps. Examples of major swamps in the Everglades watershed include Okaloooacoochee Slough, Corkscrew Swamp, Big Cypress Swamp, and the Fakahatchee Strand.

The most prevalent wetland tree in the state is the cypress. A deciduous member of the redwood family, cypress drops its needles in November and flushes in March. Cypress trees are divided into bald cypress and pond cypress, although botanists argue whether they are separate species or varieties. In general, bald cypress prefer moving water and pond cypress prefer still water.

Cypress trees cover about one-third of Big Cypress Swamp. Most are dwarf pond cypress. The great bald cypress trees are rarer; some are 600 or 700 years old. Cypress trees may develop "knees" as an outgrowth of their root systems. Scientists believe the knees provide support for the

tree and help the tree cope when oxygen is low in the root area.

Heavy logging of the great bald cypress began in the 1930s. The giant trees' heartwood is so resistant to decay that it earned the nickname "wood eternal." After years of logging, oil exploration, and drainage in Big Cypress Swamp, and more recently, the threat of a major jetport, Congress set aside about 40 percent of the swamp as a national preserve in 1974 in order to protect the watershed. Corkscrew Swamp Sanctuary, a National Audubon Society refuge, is located northwest of the preserve, and Fakahatchee Strand State Preserve lies to the west of it.

Dwarf cypress is a smaller form of the pond cypress; it grows in nutrient-poor areas. The dwarf cypress's size does not correlate with its age. Only a few feet tall, these trees may be hundreds of years old. Dwarf cypress may be seen in Everglades National Park along the main park road near Rock Reef Pass.

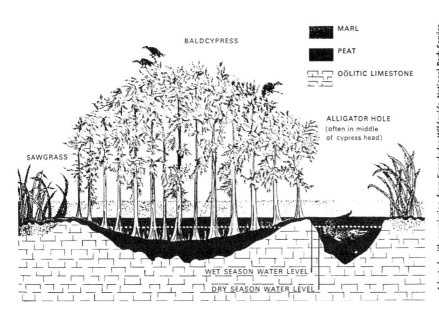

BALDCYPRESS

SAWGRASS

MARL

PEAT

OÖLITIC LIMESTONE

ALLIGATOR HOLE
(often in middle
of cypress head)

WET SEASON WATER LEVEL

DRY SEASON WATER LEVEL

Adapted, with permission, from *Everglades Wildguide*, National Park Service

Cypress heads stand out conspicuously on the Glades landscape. They are tall, dome-like tree islands of bald cypress. Unlike hammocks, which occupy elevated sites, cypress heads, or domes, occupy depressions in the limestone bedrock.

In Big Cypress Swamp—named for its expanse, rather than the size of its trees—dwarf pond cypress edge the wet prairies. Cypress strands outline the sloughs, and there are cypress domes. Cypress heads or domes occupy depressions in the limestone bedrock. These depressions hold water, usually even in the dry season. Water-loving cypress take root in the accumulated peat and soil. Taller trees grow in the center of the water-filled depression, where the collection of peat is greatest, and smaller trees occupy the edge. Interiors of cypress domes have often been described as cathedral-like. This may be because of the high canopy, which resembles a vaulted ceiling, and because of the special quality of the light filtering through the leaves.

The swamp hosts more than cypress trees. Islands of slash pine, mixed hardwood hammocks, wet and dry prairies,

marshes, and estuarine mangrove forests also characterize the swamp.

Freshwater Marshes

Topography, rainfall, evaporation, and geology all influence the development of marsh ecosystems. Marshes in the state divide into five major groups: highland marshes, flatwoods marshes, the

Kissimmee marsh complex, the Saint Johns marshes, and the Everglades.

Similar plant populations throughout Florida marsh systems respond to a range of conditions. These conditions include hydroperiod (the amount of time a marsh is flooded), fire frequency, soils, and drying time. Six categories of marshes have been identified in Florida: water lily marsh, submersed marsh, cattail marsh, flag marsh, saw grass marsh, and wet prairie.

The Everglades is the largest Florida marsh system. One hundred years ago, this marsh covered all of central southern Florida, flowing gently from Lake Okeechobee southwest to Florida Bay. Predominantly a saw grass marsh, the Everglades is also a mosaic of wet prairie, slough, and pond.

In the late 1800s, travelers contemplating a trip through the Everglades had second thoughts if they listened to rumors. Alonzo Church, who served as compassman on an Everglades expedition, recorded the warnings.

The Everglades is predominantly a saw grass marsh.

Courtesy: Everglades National Park

Of the Everglades they gave conflicting accounts, one man assuring us that there was nothing to be met with but terrible sawgrass. . . . The sawgrass, he said, is from five to ten feet tall, very thick and so stiff and sharp that it cuts like the edge of a razor; no gloves or clothes can withstand it.

This saw grass, Church claimed, "extended all the way across the Glades and would be an impenetrable barrier to our advance."

Mr. Town assured us that as we advanced through the sawgrass the snakes in front of us crawling out of our way would make such a crackling in the dry leaves that we would not be able to hear each other speak; and as for alligators, he said when you get to water they will just be so thick you can walk across on their heads.

The vastness of the saw grass prairie inspires awe. In the past, in the northern Everglades, saw grass grew up to nine feet tall in the thick peat soils. It was the dominant plant. Although some saw grass remains protected in

conservation areas, sugar cane fields have replaced much of it. Saw grass has low nutrient requirements. In areas where many nutrients have been introduced into the system, other species such as cattails generally replace the saw grass.

Saw grass marshes are generally categorized as dense or sparse. Travel is difficult in tall, dense saw grass. On foot, a person must almost throw himself against it and walk the length of it. Early people would "fire" the saw grass to burn a path through it. Tall saw grass provides little cover for wildlife, though alligators take advantage of it in the nesting season. Generally, saw grass does not reach great heights in the central and southern Everglades, where it intermixes with other marsh vegetation.

On their margins and on the back of their midribs, saw grass leaves have small teeth that slant upwards. As long as you move your finger along the leaf in line with the teeth, there is no problem. But if you slide your finger in the

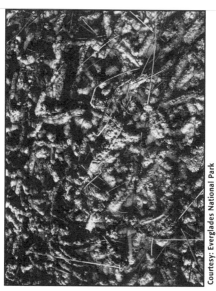

Periphyton is essential to Everglades food chains.

opposite direction, you will receive a painful cut. Surprisingly, about one to three inches of the saw grass "heart" (the base of the plant, where the central leaves overlap) is edible and quite tender. It tastes bland, like celery, not bitter or unpleasant.

Periphyton forms the base of the Everglades food pyramid. An association of different types of algae, periphyton grows on the soil surface and on plant stems throughout the saw grass marsh wherever sunlight is adequate. During wet periods, this spongy mass covers the marl or peat substrate in a mat. The mat consists mainly of cyanobacteria but also contains many other organisms, both plant and animal. The larvae of mosquitoes, tadpoles, and other tiny creatures feed on periphyton. Small fish and other animals eat the periphyton-feeders. Finally, larger fish, birds, and mammals feast on these creatures in this most fundamental Everglades food web.

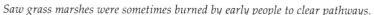

Saw grass marshes were sometimes burned by early people to clear pathways.

Wet Prairie

Of all Florida marsh types, wet prairies spend the shortest amount of time under water. Their hydroperiod, or period of submersion, ranges from 50 to 150 days per year. A saw grass marsh is flooded for an average of 300 days, but may be wet all year.

In southern Florida, marl forms the base of most wet prairie. The bedrock of marl wet prairie is limestone. Although walking may appear to be easier in these areas because of the sparse vegetation, the bedrock is actually deeply pitted with solution holes and rough and jagged with rocky projections called pinnacle rock. Saw grass grows here with a mix of other species, including beak rush, spike rush, white-top sedge, and muhly grass.

Although solution holes can be hazardous for the hiker (especially in the wet season, when they are disguised by floating algae), they provide important feeding areas for wading birds early in the dry season.

A second type of wet prairie developed on peat soil, generally in the northern and central Everglades. Its hydroperiod is longer and it hosts fewer plant species. As the end of the dry season approaches, peat wet prairie is important for wading birds.

In places, Shark River Slough is 20 miles across.

Bladderwort grows on the edges of ponds and gator holes.

Sloughs

Sloughs are channels of slow moving water. Shark River Slough and Taylor Slough are the main waterways through which water flows into Everglades National Park. Sloughs measure as much as three or four feet deep and may remain flooded for years. In Everglades National Park, Shark River Slough is about six miles wide; in the south-central Everglades, it stretches to 20 miles across. Occurring over peat soils, sloughs harbor fish, turtles, alligators, otters, and aquatic invertebrates. They provide important refuges during the dry season.

Alligator hole in the Glades.

The vegetation of a slough may include bladderwort, white water lily, and spatterdock. Saw grass is sparse, but maidencane, a common aquatic grass, may be found. Some bladderwort float freely. With ovoid, bladderlike traps on their leaves, they engulf small aquatic organisms. Spatterdock, a rooted aquatic plant, is easily identified by its large, oval, floating leaf, deeply notched at one end, and its bright yellow flower. Spatterdock's leaves extend from the rootstock on long petioles.

Ponds

Small areas of open water appear throughout the Everglades marsh. Many of these ponds become alligator holes. In an alligator hole, vegetation such as spatterdock and bladderwort grows only on the fringe of the hole; the alligator keeps the center open. Alligator flag, its green, arrow-shaped leaves often measuring over two feet long, also marks these ponds. Ferns and tree seedlings may take root

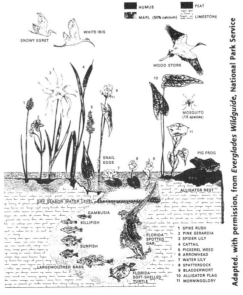

in decaying plants and debris the alligator piles by the hole. Eventually, the alligator pond may give way to a tree island.

Particularly in times of drought, these holes provide important oases for aquatic organisms. In exchange for its efforts, the alligator only requires an occasional meal. Dr. Peter Rosendahl believes significantly fewer alligator holes exist in 1995 than did in the early 1800s. He suggests that alligators now congregate in canals. This hypothetical loss of refuges would also negatively affect numerous other organisms.

Mangrove Community

The stress of life on the water's edge requires special structural and physiological adaptations. Mangroves provide many examples of these. Mangroves appear to grow out of the water. Living at the edge between land and sea, between salt water and fresh, they are one of the most highly modified organisms of the watershed. Mangroves have evolved special root structures, physiological mechanisms, and reproductive strategies that enable them to survive the rigors of coastal life. A brief exploration of some of those modifications underscores both the engineering skill and the frugality of nature.

Early fishermen navigate mangrove channels.

Courtesy: Everglades National Park

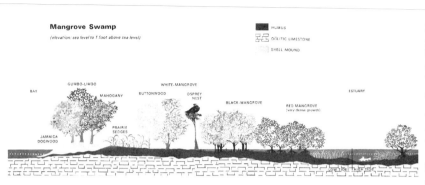

Adapted, with permission, from Everglades Wildguide, National Park Service

Mangrove swamp (elevation: sea level to 1 foot above sea level)

Mangroves are what is known as "facultative halophytes." This means that they can use either salt water or fresh water, depending on availability. They grow well in fresh water, but competition from freshwater vascular plants inhibits their growth in exclusively freshwater environments. Salt water limits potentially competitive species.

The cyclic wash of tidal water and runoff from the terrestrial environment helps transport nutrients and clear water to the mangroves, and carries away accumulations of salt and the hydrogen sulfide that develops in submerged, anaerobic soil. Tidal flux and wave energy also play important roles in the reproduction and spread of mangroves. Mangrove forests develop most extensively in low-lying areas where tidal exchange is extreme. In the Glades, substantial terrestrial runoff of fresh water from the marsh subsidizes the exchange of tidal water.

Mangroves flourish in depositional environments with little wave activity. High wave energy retards establishment of propagules, the modified reproductive parts of the tree. It also limits accumulation of the fine, anaerobic sediment in

which mangroves are adapted to grow, and destroys the shallow root system.

Mangroves develop root systems without a deep tap root. Their shallow roots manage to hold the trees above the salty water, to stabilize both tree and shoreline, and to obtain necessary nutrients and oxygen all at the same time.

It is generally accepted that different species of mangrove grow in distinct zones. The red mangrove grows closest to the water, followed by black, white, and then buttonwood, moving inland. However, climate, wave energy, rising sea level, and other factors can alter this pattern of distribution.

The red mangrove has developed prop roots from the lower stem and drop roots from branches and the upper stem. The roots are very shallow and extend only a

Red mangroves appear to "walk on water."

Courtesy: Everglades National Park

Black mangrove.

few inches into the soil. The above-ground portion of the roots contains small pores, or lenticels, which allow oxygen to enter the plant. Oxygen moves downward to the roots through air space tissue, called aerenchyma. Lenticels are further adapted to prevent water penetration into the aerenchyma during high tide. They are called hydrophobic because they repel water.

The black mangrove's cable roots penetrate only a few inches into the ground and radiate outward many feet from the stem. Aerial roots called pneumatophores extend upward from the cable roots. Pneumatophores contain lenticels and aerenchyma which aid in gas exchange. These odd "breathing tubes" often extend several feet into the air. The pneumatophores are believed to help the black mangrove to oxidize the reduced organic material around its roots more efficiently than the red mangrove.

The white mangrove usually doesn't have prop or cable roots; lenticels on the lower trunk aid in

respiration. Sometimes white mangroves develop "peg roots" which filter salt from sea water, an ability these trees share with the red and black mangroves. Black and white mangroves also maintain balance by excreting excess salt through salt glands on the underside of leaf surfaces.

Ironically, the highly modified root system that enables mangroves to thrive in anaerobic soils and to stand tall and secure above the constant motion of the sea is also one of its most vulnerable structures. The exposed lenticels are subject to clogging by fine material suspended in the water, and also to attack by insects.

Water conservation modifications, called xerophytic adaptations, characterize all mangroves. Modifications include thick, succulent leaves, a thick leaf cuticle, and sunken stomata—or pores—on the lower leaf surface for air and water exchange.

Two adaptations have allowed mangroves to reproduce successfully in a marine environment:

The white mangrove has rounded leaves.

vivipary—the plant equivalent of live birth—and propagule dispersal by water.

The embryonic mangrove begins germination and development in a thick, protective sheath on the parent tree. The young mangrove and its sheath are more appropriately called a propagule than a seed because its development includes no intermediate resting stage. White and black mangroves, generally located in higher parts of the intertidal zone, have smaller propagules, while red mangroves, located in lower intertidal areas, have large ones.

The propagules float and remain viable for long periods of time, but germination must be completed within an obligatory dispersal time. For white mangrove propagules, time is up in eight days. Black mangrove propagules can drift for up to 110 days. The red mangrove embryo is the true long-distance traveler; it can drift aimlessly on ocean currents for up to a year, giving it enough time to reach the fertile coasts of other countries and even

other continents.

Red, black, and white mangroves belong to different plant families, but their adaptations to coastal habitats link them. Buttonwood belongs to the white mangrove family but generally lives on the fringe of mangrove swamps on higher ground.

Though mangrove forests have provided protection against hurricanes (early Florida settlers frequently secured their boats in mangrove channels when storms approached), hurricanes have devastated these same forests. Like the 1935 hurricane, Hurricane Andrew destroyed mature forest growth along the coast of Florida Bay and Cape Sable. Hurricane Donna in 1960 was even more devastating, with 36 hours of wind that reached a sustained velocity of 140 miles per hour and gusts up to 180. This hurricane followed the coastline on the west side of the peninsula and heavily impacted the area from Madeira Bay and Flamingo

around Cape Sable north to Chokoloskee and Everglades City. Some mangrove islands simply disappeared.

People have found some interesting uses for parts of the mangrove tree. Reportedly, dried mangrove leaves make a fairly decent cup of tea. However, according to a botanist who drank it for two weeks, "subsequent research" indicated the tea should not be consumed in excess.

In some countries people collect salt from the leaves and roots of the black mangrove, while the pale yellow flowers provide "mangrove honey." Black mangrove was particularly important to early settlers of Flamingo, in what is now Everglades National Park. Smoldered in smudge pots, decomposed black mangrove produced a pungent smoke that discouraged mosquitoes. Each home had a room called a "loser" where the smudge pot burned. There, residents beat mosquitoes out of their clothes lest they carried

them into the rest of the house.

According to early accounts, wood from the buttonwood tree was so hard buttons could be made from it—hence the name. The flowers and fruits also resemble clusters of buttons. When storm-killed, this twisted, gnarled, rough-barked tree turns into beautiful driftwood, artfully sculpted by wind and water and sun bleached a silvery gray. In the 1900s, buttonwood was an important source of firewood; it fed an early southern Florida industry: charcoal production.

Mangrove communities can be observed on the coastlines of the Florida Keys and Everglades National Park, in the Ding Darling National Wildlife Refuge on Sanibel, and along the Loxahatchee River in Jonathan Dickinson State Park. The occurrence of mangroves in the state park indicates salt water intrusion, and correlates with the death of many cypress trees.

Mangrove swamps play a vital role in southern Florida fisheries. Leaves, bark, and twigs that the trees shed decompose in the water; the shrimp, larval crabs, and tiny fish that consume the mangrove detritus form the base of an extensive food web. The mangrove swamp provides not only food but also shelter for the young of many fishes (mullet, tarpon, snook, and mangrove snapper) and invertebrates (spiny lobster and pink shrimp). It has been documented that when mangrove ecosystems are destroyed, sport and commercial fisheries decline.

Coastal Marshes

Salt marshes exist along the coasts

Buttonwood is related to the white mangrove but usually lives on higher ground.

Courtesy: Everglades National Park

in areas sometimes covered by salt water. These intertidal zones support nonwoody salt-tolerant plants. Mangrove trees, more sparse in these areas, do not shade out the salt marsh vegetation.

Many plants known as succulents grow in the high marsh area (above mean high water). The thick, waxy-surfaced tissues of succulents store water. It is often as difficult for these plants to extract water from the coastal soil as it is for plants living in the desert.

Saltwort is a common succulent in this habitat. The stems creep along the ground and form masses. They are covered by slim, fleshy leaves that resemble pickles, about an inch in length. Edible and crunchy like a pickle, the leaves are very salty.

Another common coastal plant is sea purslane. This herb also has sprawling stems covered with fleshy, oblong leaves. The leaves and stems may also be eaten as a vegetable, raw, pickled, or boiled. If you boil the plant, you can change the water often to lessen the salty flavor.

When trodden upon, the succulent, segmented stems of woody glasswort sound like glass snapping under foot. Sea oxeye has light green leaves and a lovely yellow flower that resembles a daisy. These species frequent coastal prairies.

Plants that range in habitat from high to low marsh include black needlerush and smooth cordgrass. Smooth cordgrass is the most seaward of the nonwoody marsh plants in the state.

The salt marsh is a rigorous environment; residents must adapt to rapid changes in water level and salinity, with accompanying alterations in dissolved oxygen and temperature. Highly productive areas, salt marshes provide both food and shelter for insects, mammals, fish, shellfish, and birds. *Ecosystems of Florida* identifies four major habitats within salt marshes: "an aerial habitat amongst the leaves and stems of salt marsh plants; the intertidal sediment-water interface beneath the stems and leaves; salt marsh creeks and associated marsh edges; and salt marsh tidepools."

In the aerial habitat, a variety of organisms such as grasshoppers and planthoppers feed on the juices and tissues of plants. In turn, spiders, wasps, and beetles feed on the grasshoppers and planthoppers. Snails and marsh crabs also eat the stems and leaves of salt marsh plants. Many kinds of birds—great egrets, swallows, marsh wrens—feed on members of the aerial habitat. Further, salt marsh plants provide nesting places for salt marsh birds.

Organisms that live beneath the stems and leaves of salt marsh plants—including gastropod mollusks, bivalve mollusks, and crustaceans—filter feed, and also forage on the sediment layer. These creatures become food for others including mud crabs, killifish, blue crabs, raccoons, and herons. Stems and leaves of salt marsh plants also contribute detritus to the food chain.

Finally, many species of fish and shellfish of commercial or recreational significance inhabit tidal creeks and pools. These include mullet, oysters, blue crabs, and shrimp. This food supply attracts predatory fish such as snook and red drum, as well as wading birds and dolphin.

Inshore Marine Habitats

Florida's inshore marine habitats are unique and invaluable. The entire system is an estuary. Estuarine systems nurture many marine and freshwater species at some time in their life cycles. Florida's coastal systems support spiny lobster, penaeid shrimp,

Florida Bay is an important inshore marine habitat.

Courtesy: Everglades National Park

blue crab, oyster, spotted sea trout, stone crab, and many other species of commercial and recreational interest.

A variety of features characterize primary inshore habitats. Sea grass beds—highly productive systems—are also extremely vulnerable to human activity. Oyster bars, found on both coasts of Florida, provide food and habitat for a number of species such as larval sponges, gastropods, mollusks, and crustaceans. Soft-bottom, or unvegetated, areas occur on both coasts. The microorganisms they support form the base of a food web that determines the makeup of the community in the overlying water column.

Inshore marine habitats associated with the watershed include the southern reaches of the Indian River Lagoon, Biscayne Bay, the Lake Worth Lagoon, Florida Bay, Cape Sable, the Ten Thousand Islands, Cape Romano, Estero Bay, San Carlos Bay, and Charlotte Harbor. Currently, flood control discharges, industrial and agricultural activities, urban expansion, and changes in freshwater drainage patterns are adversely affecting the Indian River Lagoon, Biscayne Bay, Lake Worth Lagoon, San Carlos Bay and other inshore marine habitats. Many of the effects are reflected in the loss of submerged aquatic vegetation, an indicator of water quality in these shallow marine systems.

The relationship between aquatic vegetation loss and anthropogenic stresses has been documented in other systems—in the Chesapeake Bay, for example. With the population explosion

Florida has experienced in the past 30 to 40 years, declines in aquatic vegetation have occurred in several systems around Florida. Sea grass beds have diminished in Biscayne Bay, and in Florida Bay, extensive sea grass habitat is undergoing serious deterioration.

Florida Bay is a large, shallow marine system (its average depth is less than three feet). Extensive mud flats, irregularly shaped islands called keys, and deeper channels characterize the bay, which is located almost entirely within Everglades National Park.

Exposed at low tide, the mud flats of the bay provide a valuable feeding area for a number of birds. Flowering plants, such as turtle grass, horned pondweed, sea grass, and manatee grass, stabilize the mud flats. A number of different species of algae also live there. Sea grass beds serve as nursery areas, feeding grounds, and refuges for many species.

Man-of-War, Bottle, Derelict, Porjoe—these are names of some

of the 100 keys of Florida Bay. The keys generally fall into one of two categories. Mangroves cover islands mainly in the northeastern part of the bay. On the majority of keys, however, a mangrove fringe encloses a depressed central area. Tropical hardwoods occupy this inland bowl. Extensive hammocks, often covered with moonflowers, exist on some of the keys. Moonflower vines have delicate, fragrant white flowers that open at night.

The Florida Bay keys are important rookeries and nesting places for many bird species. Isolated from the mainland, the keys protect nestlings from some predators. Because of their value as refuges for birds, it is illegal to land on most of these islands. If people landed boats during nesting, stressed parent birds might abandon their young, leaving them as "easy pickings" for crows or at the mercy of the sun. Frantic parents might also jostle young birds out of the nest; on the ground they would become food for ghost crabs and

Activity of producers, consumers, and decomposers beneath prop roots forms a complex estuarine food web.

. . . .

other scavenging predators. Birds one might expect to see on these keys include roseate spoonbills, brown pelicans, double-crested cormorants, ospreys, egrets, great blue herons, and others.

Though hidden from view, the activity going on beneath the mangroves' prop roots is important both to the birds in the tree's branches and to the humans watching them. A mangrove leaf falls into the water. Bacteria and fungi coat it, then break it down, adding nourishment to the detritus. Shrimp and worms feed on it; larger animals feed on the shrimp and worms. A food web eventually evolves that includes important recreational and commercial species such as snapper, snook, mullet, tarpon,

pink shrimp, and spiny lobster.

Deeper areas of the bay are called "holes," or if they are extensive, "lakes." Submarine meadows, these areas are often covered with seaweed and other vegetation that tolerate the deeper, darker water.

In a Foreign Country

The vegetative communities of the Everglades watershed are not only diverse in plant and animal species but also in the experiences they offer those who venture into them. Alonzo Church wrote, "The grass was high and thick, the ground so boggy that at every step we sank into it up to our thighs."

However, the reward of sinking into muck up to your thighs and

navigating pinnacle rock may be the excitement of exploring a tropical hammock that you have discovered; or finding a sense of peace as you stand in the cool waters of a cypress head, bright splashes of color from the blooms of orchids and airplants punctuating the still greens and browns of the trees.

Church ended the account of his Everglades trek, "I felt that I had been in a foreign country and had come back to the comforts and blessings of home." Saw grass, gumbo limbo, strangler fig . . . there is much that is unusual or "foreign" about the Everglades. Indeed, it is the unique character of this place that makes a visit, an adventure.

Ken DeYonge

Chapter 5

Blood and Bones

Few places are as biologically rich as the Everglades ecosystem. Nearly 45 species of mammals, including about 10 marine forms, frequent the Everglades and related bays, sounds, coastal estuaries, and offshore waters. Hundreds of species of fish and thousands of species of marine, estuarine, and freshwater invertebrates ply the waters of the ecosystem. More than 50 kinds of reptiles, including the legendary alligator, lend truth to the perception that the Everglades is infested with crawly things. And nearly 20 types of salamanders, frogs, and toads live in or near alligator holes, sloughs, and marshes in the watershed.

Aside from insects—which number in the thousands— perhaps no other animals represent the area's biological diversity and wealth better than birds. Almost 350 species of birds, both temperate and tropical, have been recorded.

As the following sections show, the Everglades ecosystem is teeming with wildlife.

Animals without Backbones

Invertebrate fauna—animals without backbones—include such diverse life forms as sponges, jellyfish, snails, corals, crabs, lobsters, oysters, insects, and arachnids. With few exceptions— among them the blue crab and the pink shrimp—most marine invertebrates are of tropical origin, having found their way to southern Florida on ocean currents or the wind. Freshwater invertebrates such as dragonflies, water striders, and grass shrimp are mostly from the temperate zone.

Perhaps no other invertebrates are as colorful as the golden orb weaver spider, the Florida tree snail, the zebra butterfly, and the endangered Schaus' swallowtail butterfly. Golden orb weavers are yellow gold with black velvety patches on each of eight legs. These spiders are lovely and huge; a mature female is about the size of an adult's palm. The spider's web can be three feet across and anchored at face level between two subcanopy trees. Though it can be unnerving for a person to walk into a spider's web, the sticky threads adhering to hair and lips, it is equally disturbing for the spider. A human is too big to truss and eat, and now the web must be repaired.

If the trees that support the anchor lines of the weaver's web are closely examined, an equally fascinating hammock resident may be discovered. On smooth-barked trees, such as lysiloma or Jamaica dogwood, slime trails through growths of algae, fungi, lichens, and molds are evidence of tree snails.

The tree snail moves slowly on its muscular gray foot, carrying with it a shell that shimmers as if it has just been freshly painted. There are some 58 differently colored forms of Florida trees snails of the single species *Liguus fasciatus.* Outside of southern Florida, *Liguus* snails are only found on

The tree snail moves slowly on its muscular foot.

Courtesy: Everglades National Park

Few places are as biologically rich as the Everglades ecosystem.

. . . the Everglades ecosystem is teeming with wildlife.

Zebra longwing.

two Caribbean islands: Cuba and Hispaniola. The snails most likely came from the West Indies on logs or other floating materials, aided by their ability to seal themselves up during periods of stress.

Populations of snails are generally isolated from each other by barriers of water, saw grass, and forests of cypress, buttonwood, and pines. Transplantation and crossing experiments have shown that the diverse color patterns of the shells are genetically determined. Most hammocks contain only one particular color form; this is because individuals remain within their isolated groups and do not breed with members outside of them.

During winter, tree snails affix themselves further up the trees. If it is a time of drought, the snails will be motionless; they are sealed, waiting out the dry period. The snails are more active during the summer rainy season.

Striped with wide or thin bands, colored with every hue of the rainbow, and often tipped a dusty rose, the snails are singular treasures. Unfortunately, even before the establishment of Everglades National Park, they had attracted the attention of collectors, and some forms are extinct today.

The zebra longwing moves among hammock blooms in its slow, measured flight. The long, narrow black wings with yellow horizontal bands have a rapid but shallow beat. Active during the daylight hours, zebra butterflies roost at night in groups of 25 to 30 individuals in hammocks and thickets. They may change their roost location periodically, but their usual return to the same site night after night indicates that zebras learn and remember features of their environment.

The zebras are poisonous and distasteful to predators but exhibit an interesting feeding behavior of their own. In foraging local flower sources, they follow a set route each day; this behavior is commonly known as traplining. Zebras do not feed on nectar; they collect pollen, which their systems are specially adapted to utilize as a food source.

The dwindling population of Schaus' swallowtails is limited to the extreme southern part of the Everglades watershed. These beautiful brown and yellow butterflies are listed as threatened, but may be found on Elliott Key in Biscayne National Park and on Key Largo.

Animals with Backbones, Gills, and Fins

The Everglades' fish fauna is large and diverse. The region's fish are divided into freshwater, marine, and estuarine groups, based on species' tolerance of salt water. The freshwater fishes are further divided into "primary," "secondary," and "peripheral" categories. Primary freshwater

Florida gar are frequently seen near the surface.

fishes cannot tolerate salinity; their ability to colonize new areas is limited by the availability of freshwater routes. The group includes largemouth bass, bluespotted sunfish, yellow bullheads, bowfins, and bluegills.

Secondary freshwater fish can tolerate brief exposure to saline water. They can colonize new areas by moving from the mouth of one river system to another through brackish estuarine waters, so they are more likely to be widely distributed in the watershed. Among them are Florida gar, golden topminnows, eastern mosquitofish, flagfish, and least killifish. Florida gar are long and slender and have sharp teeth and thick scales. They are frequently seen near the surface gulping air; gar suffocate if they cannot surface. Mosquitofish are the most common freshwater fish in the Everglades. This two-inch insect eater is an important food for birds and larger fish.

Peripheral freshwater fish live part or most of their lives in salt water, but occasionally move into freshwater habitats. Among this group are important game fish such as tarpon, snook, and mullet.

Fish are essential parts of virtually every food chain in the

Walking catfish, an alien species.

Everglades watershed, and represent a substantial part of its biomass. The greatest diversity of fish can be found in marine and estuarine habitats, where species may number several hundred, especially in the rich waters near reefs. Diversity of marine species is due to two facts: that they can travel the open sea, and that they sometimes have planktonic larvae that are easily carried to the shore.

Freshwater, marine, and estuarine habitats all produce game fish, or commercial fish, which are important to southern Florida's economy. Among these are largemouth bass, speckled perch (black crappie), bluegill, tarpon, common snook, spotted sea trout, red snapper, and amberjack.

Alien fish species have also been introduced into the ecosystem. By the mid-1970s, the nonnative walking catfish had spread throughout the southern Florida canal system, and had even invaded the Kissimmee marshes. Introduced species compete aggressively and can significantly alter an ecosystem's natural composition. Such is the case in certain parts of Everglades National Park, where tilapia and oscars are occurring in greater and greater numbers.

Sirens, Newts, and Other "Slimy Things"

Frogs are the dominant amphibians in the watershed, but they are more often heard than seen. Fewer than 20 native amphibians live in the area, none of them tropical (with the exception of introduced species such as the Cuban tree frog and the giant toad from Mexico; the latter has displaced the American toad in southern Florida). One of the reasons that no tropical species have been established here is that all amphibians must have fresh water, at least during the early stages of their life cycles.

Among the amphibians are the two-toed amphiuma and the greater siren, both large, secretive, mostly nocturnal eel-like creatures that can grow up to three and a half feet long. The amphiuma is usually found in acidic swamps and drainage ditches. Young sirens are often seen among water hyacinth roots in canals. To survive periods of drought, the greater siren estivates, going dormant in a mois-ture-conserving "cocoon" of mucus.

Other watershed amphibians are the Florida chorus frog (heard at night near ponds and sloughs), the pig frog (in the southern watershed), the bullfrog, the southern toad, the lesser siren (in the watershed's extreme northern area), the squirrel tree frog, the secretive eastern newt, and the dwarf salamander (found under damp pine needles in pinelands south of Lake Okeechobee). Next to the bullfrog, the pig frog is Florida's largest. Both of these frog species are hunted; if you order frog legs in southern Florida restaurants, they are likely to be those of pig frogs.

The pig frog's gruntlike call echoes day and night all year long. "Frog calls" in urban environments may not be from frogs at all, but from the marine toad, *Bufo marinus*. From May through October you will likely be treated to choruses of green tree frogs. These small, bright green creatures with their identifying light stripe along the upper

The green tree frog is identified by a light stripe along the upper jaw and side.

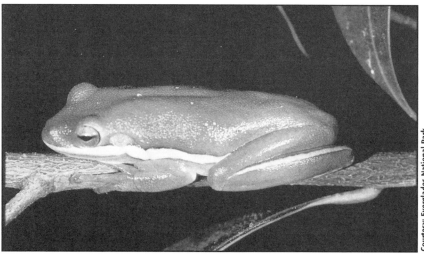

jaw and side are common in freshwater marshes, but also cling to trees in hardwood hammocks or pinelands. The toe pads of tree frogs expand into large discs that secrete mucus, allowing the frogs to stick to vertical surfaces. With their protruding eyes, gawky limbs, and long toes, green tree frogs resemble the character Gollum from J. R. R. Tolkien's book, *The Hobbit.*

Along with mosquitofish, frog larvae and tadpoles are among the first organisms to repopulate droughty wetlands following rains. Tadpoles are small and mobile, and can spread rapidly into areas of shallow water. Larval and adult frogs are an important food source for many other watershed animals—among them, water birds, otters, raccoons, and certain fish. Wet-weather or seasonal ponds are extremely important to the successful reproduction of amphibians, which in turn contribute much of the biomass to the base of the vertebrate food chain.

Dinosaur Memories

Reptiles are often associated with southern Florida and among them, the crocodilians—the American alligator from the temperate zone and the American crocodile from the tropics. Human interest in alligators and crocodiles parallels our fascination with dinosaurs. Indeed, crocodilians, with their armor of rough scales and sharp claws, have more in common with dinosaurs than appearance alone. Though alligators and crocodiles are not "living dinosaurs," their ancestors who searched for prey in humid swamps of great tree

ferns and mosses provide a window to an era millions of years past.

The thecodont was a primeval, crocodile-like ancestor. As thecodonts evolved, they moved their legs in different ways and became smaller and quicker. Finally, over great spans of time, they evolved into the earliest dinosaurs. Therefore, crocodile ancestors lived before the dinosaurs and during their reign; their descendants still exist today. Fossil evidence suggests that these first crocodiles may have scavenged dinosaur remains.

Alligator lineage also reaches back into time. The significant discovery of *Albertochampsa langstoni* provided us with alligator fossils. *Albertochampsa* lived around 70 million years ago and may have inhabited some of the same swamps as the dinosaurs in their final days.

In the 1980s researchers learned that alligator and crocodile gender was not decided by sex chromosomes, as it is in humans.

Instead, incubation temperatures determined the ratio of males and females in a nest. Alligator eggs incubated at temperatures between 90 and 93 degrees F produced males, and those incubated between 82 and 86 degrees F produced females. Temperatures from 87 to 89 degrees F produced about the same number of males and females. In crocodiles, the relationship between gender and temperature is reversed: females tend to come from warmer eggs.

Scientists studying today's alligators and crocodiles may be able to uncover clues that will help solve the mystery of dinosaur extinction. How do alligator and crocodile nesting conditions relate to the study of dinosaurs? One theory is that the cooling of the earth produced temperature changes among incubating dinosaur eggs so that the sex ratio was altered—resulting in either all males or all females. This generation of all one sex could not reproduce.

The American alligator is symbolic of the Everglades.

Ken DeYonge

Today there are 24 species of crocodiles worldwide, but only two species of alligators—*Alligator mississippiensis* and its cousin in China, *Alligator sinensis*. The Chinese alligator, or tulong (earth dragon), is thicker-bodied and smaller with a shorter tail. Both alligators have primitive North American ancestors.

Round Snouts: Alligator Tales

Characteristics that separated ancient alligators from crocodiles are similar to those of their modern-day counterparts. Distinctive features of the alligator include a rounded nose (the crocodile's snout is elongated), blunt teeth, and sockets in the upper jaw into which opposing teeth from the lower jaw fit.

Alligators have often been attributed with exaggerated longevity and size. Under natural conditions, scientists estimate that a male alligator may live for 30 to 35 years; in captivity he may see 50. Females have reached the age of 30 or so in captivity. But even naturalist John

James Audubon was fooled by the perception of a relationship between large size and great age in alligators. Audubon estimated that a 17-foot specimen was hundreds of years old!

An old Florida "cracker" might estimate the size of a gator by the distance from its bulging eyes to the tip of its knobby snout. By this rule of thumb, 1 inch equals approximately 1 foot. Although alligators have been described in guide books as measuring 6 to 19 1/2 feet long, an alligator greater than 14 feet long is rare. When alligators are born they measure between 9 and 10 inches.

In keeping with its unusual, primitive appearance, the largest reptile in North America is the subject of a repertoire of equally unusual tall tales. Often, folklore that originated with the African Nile crocodile was applied to the alligator. Interestingly, many of these fables contain a modicum of truth.

Alligator gastroliths, or "stomach stones," were purported to have medicinal value. According to an

ancient Nile crocodile legend, the animal was believed to swallow a stone for each person that it ate in order to keep a tally of its quarry. Truth is stranger than fiction. Alligators do not chew their food, but swallow it in large chunks along with nonfood items such as stones, wood, and sand. An alligator has a two-lobed stomach. The first section is gizzardlike and crushes large pieces of food. The sand or stones aid in this process. Strong digestive juices in the second lobe finish breaking down food items. It generally takes two days for food to pass through both lobes of an alligator's stomach. The alligator does swallow stones, but not for bookkeeping purposes.

Native Americans also developed myths about alligators. They wore the reptiles' teeth around their necks, believing the charm would prevent snakebite. If the teeth failed, the blood of an alligator was supposed to ease the effects of a painful strike by a poisonous snake. This belief may have developed from early people's observation of alligators eating such snakes without incurring harm.

Early colonists in North Carolina are reported to have eaten powdered alligator teeth to cure sterility and impotence. Alligator fat was believed to reduce fever and to cure arthritis and sprains. In the mid-1800s jewelers touted alligator teeth as "baby pacifiers." The teeth were polished to an ivory white, set in silver, and intended to be worn around a baby's neck. The painful process of "cutting teeth" was eased by the baby working his or her

Alligators soak up the sun's warmth on banks of sloughs or creeks.

Courtesy: Everglades National Park

"Gator Gape."

throbbing gums against the hard alligator tooth.

Alligators may be observed lying on banks of sloughs or canals with their mouths open. Observers once believed that alligators filled their mouths with "bait" such as shrimp to entice birds between those powerful, poised jaws. One researcher maintains that the purpose of this "gator gape" is to allow the sun to dry leeches or lice that sometimes attach themselves to the animal's tongue. Another possible explanation of the open mouth is that it helps with temperature regulation, since alligators are cold-blooded. Recovering from a cool night, alligators will lie in the sun to warm up. Their massive heads generally heat before the rest of the body, so they may open their mouths to cool off.

Until the 1960s, it was considered appropriate (and legal) to return from a Florida vacation with a live baby alligator. Black with yellow bands and needle-sharp teeth, baby alligators are appealing. However, an animal that

grows a foot every year for the first seven or eight years in captivity will quickly outgrow the bathtub. With a flush, many baby alligators went the way of unwanted goldfish. These baby alligators often became the subject of legend, which said massive gators lurked in the underground network of New York's sewer system, preying on traumatized sewer rats. The tale made great material for writers. One children's author wrote *The Great Escape or The Sewer Story*, in which homesick sewer alligators disguise themselves as humans and return to the Everglades.

No matter how fascinating, the tales are not true. The reptilian nature of alligators dictates their range of adaptability, and New York is too cold. If periods of cold are not too long or too intense, alligators can survive in areas with an average January temperature of 45 degrees F. However, the lowest average winter temperatures cannot drop below 15 degrees F. New York and other northern municipalities are too far out of the alligator's comfort zone.

Although the alligator mating season fluctuates with water levels and temperatures, alligators breed from mid-April through May, a period audibly marked by the impressive bellowing of both sexes—the alligator equivalent of elk bugling in the Rockies. After a courtship ritual that can extend for days, copulation takes place underwater. A male may mate with several females in a single season and assumes no responsibility for nest building or rearing of young. In fact, a bull alligator will cannibalize its young if more suitable prey is scarce.

Female alligators in the Everglades generally begin nest construction in mid-June. Each female builds her nest with earth, saw grass, cattails, and other marsh materials. The mound is usually 2 to 3 feet high and is about 15 feet from water or in the open marsh. The female digs an opening in the top of the nest, lays a single egg about every 30 seconds, and pushes her eggs into the cavity with her hind foot. When she is finished, she covers the eggs with more vegetation. The heat generated by the decaying vegetable matter will incubate the eggs—the mother does not lie on the nest, as one might expect.

Nest construction begins in mid-June.

Young alligators hatch from eggs in 65 to 70 days.

Although alligator mothers vary the amount of time and the degree of protection they afford their nests, a female guarding a nest can be dangerous to humans, raccoons, foxes, bobcats, and other species that may raid the nest to feed on the eggs. In general alligators are not aggressive, but they will react when threatened. Hissing, a vigilant female will lunge off of a nest at intruders.

The young alligators hatch from the eggs in 65 to 70 days. They make a grunting sound that attracts their mother. She digs the newly hatched young out of the nest and carefully carries them in her mouth to the water. If the mother is not in the area when the babies hatch, they will head for the water on their own. These tiny baby gators are food for many creatures. Wading birds such as great egrets as well as otters, raccoons, and even bass pick them off fairly easily. John James Audubon recorded this phenomenon in the illustration "Whooping Crane" in his book *Birds of America*.

The first two years of life are tenuous for the young gator, especially during drought. By constructing and maintaining alligator wallows at these times, older alligators play a vital role in the survival of not only their own offspring but also a myriad of other species.

The alligator population today is a shining example of resource management success. Due to intense hunting pressure, the alligator was listed as an endangered species in 1967, even though the State of Florida had legally eliminated hunting after 1961.

The process of tanning alligator hides had been perfected and fashion-conscious people adored the "look of gator." In the late 1960s alligator shoes sold for $70 to $350 per pair. Recognizing the profits to be made, many alligator hunters accepted the risks of poaching. For rangers and game wardens protecting Everglades alligators, this was a dangerous and frustrating period of high-speed chases, generally at night, through mangrove labyrinths or

across saw grass prairies. Few offenders were caught, and those that went before judges received mild sentences. Loren G. "Totch" Brown, a native of Chokoloskee, described the poacher's lifestyle in his autobiography, *Totch: A Life in the Everglades*; he learned the life from his "daddy" and found it difficult to change as the culture of Everglades City did.

Progress against poaching came at last when legal action was taken to stop tanners and marketers. The 1969 Mason-Smith Act prevented the sale of endangered species parts within New York State. Later, other states followed suit. A number of legal actions transpired until protection was granted the alligator and other endangered species through CITES (the Convention on International Trade in Endangered Species) in 1973. Congress passed the Endangered Species Act the same year.

Considerable human time, energy, and money—and most important, the endangerment of a species—could have been minimized if consumers had accepted responsibility for their role in the alligator's plight. The loss of this species would have impacted an entire ecosystem—a horribly inflated price for a pair of shoes, a handbag, or a piece of designer luggage.

Baby alligators are black with yellow bands.

Thanks to the protection afforded the alligator, the animal is no longer listed as threatened in Florida. In fact, a tightly regulated alligator hunting season was opened there in 1988. In Everglades National Park, all animals are fully protected. No hunting, specimen collecting, or commercial fishing is allowed. The greatest threats to the alligator today are motorists, weekend gun enthusiasts who shoot alligators for sport, and the destruction of alligator habitat. The preservation of wetlands is critical for this species.

The American alligator currently ranges from the coastal areas of the Carolinas and Georgia to the southern tip of Florida. It is found in southern Alabama and Missis-

Alligator strolls Anhinga Trail in Everglades National Park.

sippi, throughout Louisiana, and north to southeastern Oklahoma, southern Arkansas, and southeast Texas. Symbolic of the Everglades watershed, it serves as the mascot of the South Florida Water Management District. Each district-managed flood control canal is identified by a prominent sign featuring Freddy the Alligator, protector of the Everglades. The alligator also graces a postage stamp commemorating Florida's sesquicentennial (1845–1995).

Pointed Snouts

If you see an armored reptile on the Florida mainland and wonder what it is, your best guess would be an alligator. Crocodiles prefer coastal mangrove swamps and bays, creeks, and canals with salt water or brackish water (a mixture of fresh and salt water). Crocodiles are scarce: with fewer than 500 animals, the Florida crocodile population was placed on the federal list of endangered species in 1975.

Crocodiles do not tolerate cold temperatures as well as alligators. Southern Florida is the northern-

most limit of their range. Colonies of the animals are found in Cuba, Jamaica, Hispaniola (Haiti and the Dominican Republic), coastal Venezuela, Colombia, coastal Ecuador and Peru, and parts of Central America and Mexico. In several areas, persecution and hunting pressure are seriously reducing populations.

The crocodile is distinguished from the alligator by its tapering snout and by the fourth tooth in its lower jaw, which is visible when the animal's mouth is closed. There is also a difference in color; the alligator is generally gray or black with yellow highlighting, whereas the crocodile is dark and has a green cast to its hide.

Although female crocodiles also assume complete responsibility for constructing nests, they either dig holes in the substrate or build up mounds, often made of sand. A female crocodile may build her nest in the same site year after year. The nests are generally located so that the adult can approach the nest from water. In late April or early May, the female deposits some 20 to 80 eggs in the nest in one night. After the eggs are laid the female returns less often to the nest. The frequency of visits goes up as the end of the incubation period approaches. Hearing the "peeps"

Pointed snout and visible lower fourth tooth identify the American crocodile.

Crocodile nest in Florida Bay.

of her hatchlings, the mother digs up the nest and assists the young, which immediately go to the water. They generally hide among mangrove roots, but mortality is high; raccoons, birds, sharks, fish, and even other crocodiles feed on them.

Crocodiles, too, are the subjects of myth and misinformation. Many people assume that crocodiles are vicious and fierce; this is probably the result of association with the much larger and more aggressive Nile crocodile. However, American crocodiles are reported to be more timid than even alligators. For example, crocodile mothers may not defend their nests, as alligators are known to do. In fact, human disturbance may cause the female to desert her nest. Still, the crocodile is a large and powerful animal and should never be threatened.

Writing in the late 1700s, naturalist William Bartram described what was supposedly an American alligator involved in a territorial dispute. "Clouds of smoke issue from his dilated nostrils. The earth trembles with his thunder . . . the floods of water and blood rushing out of their mouths, and the clouds of vapor rising from their wide nostrils, were truly frightful." One suspects that Bartram was using

poetic license in his description of this confrontation, but perhaps he was recalling male crocodiles who have been observed involved in "narial geysering," a discharge of water or mist from the nostrils.

Fortunately for the crocodile, Florida Bay was made part of Everglades National Park in 1950 (the park was originally established in 1947). If this protection had not been afforded, providing safe habitat and nest sites, the American crocodile would be extinct today in the United States. The crocodile population within the park is fairly secure, but adult mortality, attributed to automobiles, is high. Researchers have suggested management actions to promote a viable American crocodile population in southern Florida: public education, adaptation of roadways to decrease the number of animals killed by automobiles, protection of nesting sites, and captive breeding. To protect crocodiles, the National Crocodile Refuge has been established in northern Key Largo.

A third crocodilian that may be sighted on occasion in Florida

drainage canals or sloughs is the South American caiman. Caimans were introduced into Florida when the trade in native alligators was outlawed. Imported for the pet market, baby caimans quickly outgrew their appeal and were often released in the wild. Some survived and fed on fish, birds, mammals, and insects. They are native to Central and South America, and generally do not grow as large as alligators and crocodiles.

Slithery Serpents

Snakes are probably the most reviled and the most intriguing of animals. Of the nearly 30 kinds of snakes found in the Everglades watershed, only four are poisonous. Because of the difficulty in discriminating among species, snakes should be observed but not handled. Snake bite injuries are rare but occur most often when people poke at snakes, grab them by the tail, or attempt to kill them.

The eastern coral snake is the most deadly of the area's poisonous species. Bright bands of red, yellow, and black encircle its body. Not generally aggressive,

The poisonous coral snake lives under leaves or in rotten logs.

the coral snake lives under leaves or in rotten logs. This snake is the most venomous snake endemic to the United States. Its small, fixed fangs inject a neurotoxin that causes paralysis, suffocation, or loss of sight within an hour or two. Antivenin is readily available at snakebite treatment centers in the coral snake's known range, so fatalities are rare. One has a greater chance of being killed by lightning (or on the interstate highways of southern Florida) than by a snake.

The order of its bands distinguishes the coral snake from others that mimic it. Numerous jingles have been developed to help identify the coral snake—for example, "Red on yellow, kill a fellow." The black nose of the eastern coral snake also differentiates it from the harmless scarlet snake and the scarlet kingsnake ("Red on black, friend of Jack") whose snouts are red. The scarlet kingsnake is known to eat other smaller snakes, including rattlesnakes.

Except for the coral snake, the region's poisonous snakes have flattened, triangular heads. The eastern diamondback rattlesnake's thick body often has a yellow and deep brown diamond pattern on its back, but color varies with age, sex, habitat, and season. When threatened, the snake normally strikes, but if given an opportunity to escape it usually chooses that option; it may also coil, hiss, and vibrate its rattles. A common myth is that you can tell the age of a rattlesnake by counting the tail segments. This is not true. Each time the snake sheds, it adds a section to its rattle. A healthy snake may shed four times a year. Also,

Eastern diamondback rattlesnake courtship behavior.

segments may get broken off as the snake crawls through underbrush. Although the diamondback is endemic to pinelands, hardwood hammocks, and coastal prairies, it can be found in just about any habitat, including mangrove keys. Visitors should be particularly alert when walking through saw palmettos, which fringe hammocks and are abundant in other habitats throughout the watershed. These dense, low plants can obscure vision.

The Florida cottonmouth moccasin is common in freshwater marshes, ponds, and mangroves, but is sometimes seen coiled on dry rockland. Its habitat overlaps that of other snakes. Its rough, brown scales make the cottonmouth confusingly similar to harmless water snakes. However, when disturbed, water snakes often slip away; a cottonmouth typically holds its ground. Cottonmouth water moccasins do not have rattles. When agitated,

Florida cottonmouth moccasin.

they will commonly shake their tails and provide an open-mouth warning display. This exposes the cottonlike mucous membrane in its mouth, which gives this snake its common name.

A fourth poisonous snake, the dusky pygmy rattlesnake, is a resident of pine rockland and flatwoods. This small snake, rarely exceeding 20 inches in length, is gray with black splotches. Ounce for ounce, it is as venomous as a large diamondback rattlesnake—and much harder to see. On a trek in the pinelands of the Everglades watershed, a visitor might step over a pygmy rattlesnake and

Dusky pigmy rattlesnake.

never know it was there. Down the center of its back, rust-colored splotches alternate with black ones. The sound of this small snake's rattles is faint and simulates the buzz of insects. The pygmy rattler delivers a small but potent dose of venom. The animal may also strike repeatedly at its target. Although its bite is unlikely to cause death, it can be painful.

One nonpoisonous snake is the eastern indigo snake. The indigo is bluish black and marked with red or orange on the chin, throat, and lips. Thick-bodied and muscular, indigos are impressive in size and gentle in temperament—thus their popularity with collectors. In the 1940s, one researcher heard reports of indigos 11 feet long, like thick black ropes, and maintained that

Eastern indigo snake.

the Seminoles avoided them because they believed the snakes endangered their babies. The average length of an indigo is about five feet. The indigo may be found throughout the watershed in all areas, from saw grass and hammocks to the coastal prairie. The snake was listed in 1978 as threatened due to the destruction of its habitat and commercial collecting. Within Everglades National Park and other sanctuaries its population seems secure, although elsewhere this magnificent snake is vulnerable.

Some other common nonpoisonous snakes in the Everglades watershed are the southern black racer and a subspecies limited to southern Florida, the Everglades

Everglades rat snake.

racer; the rough green snake, often seen looking like a bright green vine coiled around low branches; the Everglades rat snake, an accomplished tree climber that seems to defy gravity by clinging to rough bark as it searches for unwary prey in bird nests; the yellow rat snake, similar to its southern neighbor but found in the northern watershed; and the mangrove salt marsh snake, a mainly nocturnal resident of coastal mangrove forests.

The eastern hognose snake is nonpoisonous but mimicks venomous snakes; it illustrates how we can be fooled by appearances. When approached, the hognose snake will often assume an aggressive posture. The snake must suffer from an identify crisis: it coils like a rattlesnake and inflates its neck like a cobra. It may hiss and even strike with a closed mouth. However, if approached, it will flop over on its back, open its mouth with its tongue lolling out, and play dead. Even when picked up, the snake will remain limp. If left undisturbed, it will compose itself and crawl away.

Unfortunately, snakes—along with bats and spiders—are animals few people love. Most people will never relate to snakes as they do to baby birds or white-tailed fawns. Yet, as members of the watershed community, snakes play a critical role in food chains. By feeding on mice, rats, and other prolific breeders, snakes help to maintain balance in the system.

Hard Shells, Soft Shells, and Snorkel Noses

A visit to the wilder parts of the watershed can be particularly rewarding. The Everglades, less famous for its scenery than for its ecological players, is alive with possibilities and serendipitous discoveries. A wealth of birds live in the Everglades in winter, but with the change of seasons there are other things to see, more subtle perhaps, but no less interesting. The watershed is a busy place year-round

Common near ponds, lakes, and sloughs in early summer is the Florida softshell turtle, digging nests and laying eggs. This animal may be seen swimming with its snorkel-like nose breaking the surface of the water, or crawling up on the bank to dig its nest. The

Florida softshell turtle.

snorkel snout and the long neck allow the turtle to remain submerged while taking a breath. The leathery shell of the turtle grows darker as the turtle ages.

Morning is the best time to observe nesting activity. The female turtle may try several spots before she finds a suitable nesting location. Each season, she lays one to three clutches of eggs. Quite often, raccoons dig up turtle nests and eat the eggs. Evidence of their nightly marauding are excavated nests and the scattered remains of leathery shells. Although its soft shell makes the turtle vulnerable to predation, adaptation and natural selection have endowed it with a vicious temper and a powerful bite; these show when it is molested. Humans and other predators beware!

The striped mud turtle is also common in wet places and hardwood hammocks. This turtle may have three stripes on its shell, but the marks that allow for consistent identification are the two light stripes on its head. Not a picky eater, the striped mud turtle feeds on insects, snails, plant material, and dead fish. A classic omnivore, in some parts of Florida it is called the "cow-dung cooter," since it has been observed foraging in cow manure.

An interesting but rarely seen turtle species, due to its nocturnal habits, is the snapping turtle. This animal has three saw-toothed ridges running down the top of its long, tapering tail. In a closeup frontal view, the turtle looks like an old man who failed to put in his false teeth when he got up in the morning. The snapping turtle has no teeth, but that does not diminish its ability to defend itself. These turtles have long

Snapping turtle.

necks and can strike with lightning speed. They can snap a sizable twig with ease, or snip off a foolishly proffered finger.

The diamondback terrapin is a saltwater creature. Terrapins may be seen soaking up sun on mud flats, in bays, or among the prop roots of mangroves. They were collected by early settlers, since their meat made an excellent soup. Coastal development and collecting resulted in the destruction of their habitat and greatly reduced their numbers. Where protected, they are fairly common in estuarine areas.

The Florida box turtle is commonly seen along roads and in pinelands and hammocks. Lovely and dark with yellow, radiating lines on their highly domed shells, box turtles are sometimes

Florida box turtle.

fire scarred from the frequent fires in their pineland habitats. Some have been recorded to live 100 years. Collection for the pet trade has jeopardized the population of this docile species.

Five marine turtle species are occasionally sighted in Florida Bay or offshore on either coast. Four are listed as endangered, and the fifth, the loggerhead, is threatened. The loggerhead gets its name from its oversized head—large compared to that of

Loggerhead turtle.

other sea turtles. Loggerheads may be found in Florida Bay or on Cape Sable and other protected beaches from May through August. Only female loggerheads are seen on the beaches as they nest during this four-month interval. Everglades National Park researchers have been studying loggerhead nesting since 1964 and estimate that there are between 400 and 900 nests each season on Cape Sable.

Identifying loggerhead turtle nests can be challenging. The female crawls from the water and may move from place to place on the beach. Sometimes she initiates digging in one place, then moves to another spot and starts digging again. The female digs a body pit and egg chamber. While laying her eggs, she sheds "tears." Legend suggests that these are due to pain or to the mother's concern about the fate of her hatchlings, but marine turtles shed this liquid even at sea in order to exude excess salt. On land the fluid washes grit from their eyes. After she finishes laying, the mother turtle covers the 100 to 120 eggs with sand.

The loggerhead mother would be justified in lamenting the fate of her young. Predation is heavy on eggs and hatchlings. Raccoons either snatch the eggs as they are

Loggerhead turtle hatchlings.

laid or dig up the nests. Although turtle mothers are picky about nest sites, once they start laying eggs they are not easily distracted from their task—even by raccoons lurking nearby. Although baby turtles usually hatch under cover of darkness, many are picked off on their way to the sea by raccoons, ghost crabs, and other predators.

Around the world, humans also prey heavily on the eggs, though turtles and most nesting sites in Florida, the other U.S. states, and most countries are safeguarded. Beyond protected waters, turtles are affected by commercial shrimping operations. When shrimpers trawl in areas that turtles frequent, the animals often get caught in the nets. An "escape hatch" called a TED—turtle excluder device—cuts down on turtle mortality.

Development of beaches also reduces turtle populations by eliminating nesting sites. When baby turtles emerge from their nests, they can become disoriented by lights from condominiums and beach residences. The hatchlings tend to move toward the brightest horizon—a phenomenon known as positive phototropism. If they do not move in the direction of the sea, they will not survive. By protecting places such

as Blowing Rocks Preserve, McArthur State Park, Everglades National Park, and others, we protect not only turtle habitat and species but also timeless biological processes. Although we may never see a mother turtle crawling ponderously from the sea, searching, digging, and finally depositing her clutch of eggs, this event is part of a process that was set in motion thousands—perhaps millions—of years ago. Like the alligator and crocodile, sea turtles are living fossils.

Changing Colors and Throwaway Tails

At the other end of the size spectrum from alligators, crocodiles, and marine turtles, but still within the realm of reptiles, are the lizards. Anoles, skinks, and geckos thrive in the Everglades. You may not see a loggerhead turtle on a visit to the ecosystem, but you will almost certainly see a green anole.

The green anole is a slender, bright green lizard with a long, tapering tail and long toes. Both males and females have throat fans, or "dewlaps." The dewlap is generally larger in males than females and is bright pink or red in color. The green anole can change color, and is often identified as a chameleon. It is not a true Old World chameleon, and

Green anole.

whether it turns green or brown depends upon temperature, background environment, or "mood." At temperatures above 70 degrees F, it tends to remain green. If perched on a brown background, it may turn brown to match. Interestingly, color changes can be attributed to behavior. After a dispute between two male anoles, the victor turns green and the loser brown. These external color changes are controlled by hormones.

However, a brown anole is not always a green anole that has changed color. The brown anole (*Anolis sagrei*) was introduced into southern Florida from Cuba. It has been successful and in some

Brown anole displays dewlap.

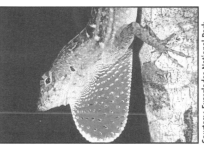

areas of southern Florida appears to have replaced the native green species. The brown anole can only turn darker brown—not green.

The southeastern five-lined skink is usually brown or black with five narrow light stripes along its back. The skink has a shiny, metallic appearance. The tail is a beautiful iridescent blue, particularly in the juvenile; the stripes and tail color fade with age. There are conflicting theories explaining the reason for the startling blue tail. One is that the tail attracts predators to a part of the lizard's body that, if lost, would not

Southeastern five-lined skink.

prove fatal for the reptile. Others have proposed that the blue tail warns predators that the lizard makes a poisonous meal. Cats and small dogs that have dined on skinks experience paralysis. Common in the Everglades watershed, the skink is found on boardwalk trails, in wooded areas, and in wetlands. Although it can climb, it is usually found on the ground where it hunts insects.

Mammals, Wet and Dry

Mammals (not including humans, black rats, and house mice) form the smallest group of organisms in the Everglades watershed. No native, land-based Florida mammals migrated from the tropics;

Raccoon, commonly observed southern Florida mammal.

the nine-banded armadillo, which is fairly common, was probably introduced, or it ventured here on its own from Mexico. Fewer than 20 terrestrial and aquatic species of mammals, and only two marine and estuarine species (the Atlantic bottle-nosed dolphin and the West Indian manatee) exist in the Everglades region. The most commonly observed mammals are raccoons, marsh rabbits, white-tailed deer, and, occasionally, gray and fox squirrels. Three terrestrial species endemic to the watershed are the Florida panther, the diminutive Key deer, and the semiaquatic Everglades mink, all of which are endangered.

The plants and animals of the southern part of the watershed are a mix of temperate and tropical species. Several geographic and meteorological pathways led them to southern Florida. Most land mammals moved into the area from the north, since there is no geographical barrier; if a northern species could tolerate the climate, it could live in the Everglades ecosystem. Tropical species that inhabit the ecosystem today were carried to it by wind or water. Air masses generally move from the West Indies toward Florida, and hurricanes often move up from the Caribbean in the direction of the peninsula. The Gulf Stream flows north from the Gulf of Mexico through the Straits of Florida, carrying the seeds or eggs of species—or the animals themselves. A diverse group of plants, insects, snails, frogs, lizards, and a few land birds— species that were light, tolerant of salt water, or located in areas from which they could be carried—made the voyage.

White-tailed deer.

Most visitors travel to the southern Everglades expecting to see an alligator, a snake or maybe a lizard or two. But in this shallow saw grass river few anticipate sighting a deer, bear, or bobcat; these animals are normally seen in drier areas. However, deer have been observed wading belly deep while foraging here, and bobcats have been spotted negotiating tangled mangrove roots just above the water.

A local subspecies of the white-tailed deer is the Key deer, found in the Lower Florida Keys. This diminutive deer, weighing 50 pounds or less, is an endangered species. It is particularly vulnerable to habitat loss and fast moving automobiles: deer are often attracted to roadsides by people who feed them illegally.

One mammal visitors probably will not encounter in the Everglades is the black bear. Although bears live in the Glades, they are few in number and are seen

Black bear.

infrequently. Do bears hibernate in southern Florida? They do not den for the winter as in colder climates, but on chilly days they may become lethargic and sleep in nests of leaves and twigs.

Another rare Everglades animal is the Florida panther, one of the most endangered mammals in the world. Only between 30 and 50

Rare Florida panther.

live in the state of Florida. A sighting would be a rare and fortuitous event. Only one male panther is known to range regularly through Everglades National Park, primarily in the Long Pine Key area. The Florida panther has a tan or tawny back and head and a white underside. Its head is small compared to its long, lean body. Although the cat is solid and muscular, its movements are fluid and graceful.

The decline of the Florida panther began with the arrival of the first European settlers, who killed the animals to protect their livestock and because they feared the big cat. The panther is characteristi-

cally elusive and solitary. Its mysterious nature worked against it as myth and legend made up for the lack of information. Early settlers' fears were unfounded; the Florida panther is not inclined to kill livestock, and attacks on humans are unknown.

Today, these secretive animals are protected not only in Everglades National Park but also in Big Cypress National Preserve, in Fakahatchee Strand State Preserve, on the Big Cypress Seminole Indian Reservation, and in the Florida Panther National Wildlife Refuge. Panthers mainly eat white-tailed deer, although they also feed on feral pigs, raccoons, opossums, and marsh rabbits.

The bobcat comes by its name because of its short or bobbed tail. About twice the size of a house cat, the bobcat has characteristic tufts of hair on the tips of its ears. The bobcat's coat is yellowish or reddish brown with black or brown spots or streaks. Its underside is white with black spots, and the underside of its tail is white. Found only in North America, the bobcat is the most common of the wildcats. In the Everglades watershed, bobcats frequent pinelands, hardwood hammocks, and the coastal prairie. They feed on smaller animals such as rabbits, birds, and rodents. This felid appears to

Bobcat.

cope fairly well with human disturbance. Hikers who have sighted bobcats in the Everglades report that the animals did not flee, but watched them with apparent curiosity.

Everglades water mammals include both freshwater and saltwater species. River otters may be observed in sloughs and canals; the Anhinga Trail and the Shark River Slough in Everglades National Park are especially good spots for sighting these sleek, streamlined creatures. Otters feed on turtles, fish, an occasional baby gator, and even apple snails and ram's horn snails.

Some folks believe that the area's convoluted mangrove channels are monotonous in their green

River otter.

uniformity. The charms of the coastal fringe are the sense of possibility and the unanticipated discovery: craning to see, around the next turn, a dolphin or a manatee.

Sometimes—in the Ten Thousand Islands and other inshore marine or estuarine areas—Atlantic bottle-nosed dolphins surf in the waves produced by boats. They try to beat the surge, to dive ahead of it, then they ride the current. Sometimes, as they leap from the water, they roll on their sides and seem, briefly, to ap-

Atlantic bottle-nosed dolphin.

Mother manatee with calf.

praise the passengers on board with one bright eye.

Depending on the season, West Indian manatees seek the warm waters of inland waterways and the coasts of Florida, the Caribbean islands, Mexico, Central America, and northern South America. The entire U.S. manatee population winters in Florida waters.

A marine mammal, the manatee is related to an unlikely cousin—the elephant. At maturity, each manatee is about 15 feet long and can weigh up to 2,000 pounds; while growing, it can gain as much as 300 pounds in 14 months. Its bulbous body is equipped with flipperlike appendages in front. It has no back

legs, but has a tail shaped like a broad, flat paddle. Nearly hairless, the animal has no neck, and its wrinkled face looks like that of a Chinese Shar-Pei dog.

Manatees graze on aquatic vegetation, consuming 60 to 100 pounds a day, and have earned the nickname "sea cow." They have been observed feeding at the water's edge on mangrove leaves. Early mariners—perhaps too long at sea—identified these corpulent creatures as mermaids.

One of the manatee's greatest natural assets, its steel gray to blackish color, has become its greatest liability. Although the color serves to camouflage and protect manatees in the wild, many have been seriously injured or killed by speeding boaters who were unable to see them close to the surface of the water. Boat speed zones have been established in areas where manatees are known to congregate, but the growing number of boats has imperiled the manatees. According to the Florida Department of Environmental Protection, more

than 400 manatees died in boating accidents between 1982 and 1992. Manatees can also be crushed in navigational locks and flood control structures. The U.S. Army Corps of Engineers and the South Florida Water Management District have designed and installed manatee sensors to reduce or eliminate this problem.

Despite its size, the manatee is a gentle giant that avoids confrontation. Manatees respond to danger by fleeing. To escape human intruders, some animals have been known to move into cold water where they suffer from hypothermia, become sick, and die. Mothers protect their young and will shield them from harm with their own bodies. However, an orphaned calf is doomed unless human rescuers intervene.

Today, the manatee is an endangered species and has state and federal protection. The population is estimated at approximately 2,500. Some people believe that the animals are attempting to adapt. More manatees move about at night and stick close to the water's edge, perhaps to avoid boat traffic. Can the manatee alter millions of years of evolution and modify its habits quickly enough to save itself? Or are we expecting the wrong species to adapt—perhaps

Early sailors misidentified manatees as "mermaids."

humans should be adapting to the needs of manatees.

Living Airfoils

Four hundred species of birds have spent time in southern Florida, and about 350 are commonly observed throughout the Everglades watershed. About 60 percent of these birds are winter residents, enjoying the long, mild season. Approximately 116 species (about 70 percent land birds, 30 percent songbirds and perching birds) are native to the watershed, living and breeding in southern Florida. Unfortunately, those species limited to shrinking natural habitats are endangered. Such is the case with the Cape Sable seaside sparrow and the Florida snail kite.

The following scene is replayed for thousands of bird watchers in southern Florida. A large white bird skims across the water, its dangling feet just breaking the surface of the pond. Although its long neck and legs should give it an awkward, ungainly appearance, the effect is just the oppo-

site—the bird moves with the poise of royalty. In a confederacy of stately birds at a watershed pond, the great egret becomes the center of attention. Only the egret stands and feeds in deeper portions of the pond. Other wading birds, with shorter legs, feed in the shallows along the edge or roost in branches of nearby trees.

The egret can be compared to an elegant performer who knows she holds her audience captivated. Hunting from a standing position or moving slowly and deliberately, the egret spears a fish that comes within its range. The bird holds its wiggling prey in its yellow beak, then with the unhurried discipline of the gourmet, swallows the hapless fish.

Finally the bird retreats from center stage, its lovely wings outstretched as it flies to a snag on the edge of the pond. As the bird shakes and fluffs out its feathers, its delicate breeding plumage drapes down its back, the white lacy tips nearly touching the water.

Ken DeYonge

Elegant plumage.

For Florida bird watchers, the great egret might be the star, but there are numerous bit players here as well. With a slender black bill and legs and bright yellow feet, the snowy egret is smaller than the great egret. Its colorful feet have earned it the name "golden slippers." The great white heron, the largest heron, has a yellow bill and legs. The great egret is often misidentified as the heron, but the egret has a yellow bill and black legs, and is smaller. The great white heron was once considered a distinct species, but is currently seen as being the white phase of the great blue heron, which is blue gray in color.

The cattle egret is common in all seasons. Old World birds, the cattle egrets probably flew from Africa to South America then came up through the West Indies to southern Florida. By the early 1960s, the birds had moved as far north as southern Canada. Cattle egrets are small and white with a brush of orange color on their

A great egret skims across the water.

Ken DeYonge

heads and orange bills. They frequent fields where they ride on the backs of cattle, picking insects from them, or eating bugs stirred up by their movements. Cattle egrets are probably the most commonly observed egrets in the watershed. Bird watchers and scientists debate whether or not the cattle egret has displaced an endemic species from its niche.

Because of its coloration, the roseate spoonbill is never confused with an egret, but people seeing this bird at a distance have, with great excitement, misidentified it as a flamingo. Adult roseate spoonbills are vivid pink with a white neck and back and an orange tail. Their bills look like flattened spoons. These birds spend a great deal of time in shallow coastal bays, swishing their bills back and forth to scoop up whatever happens by—generally fish and shrimp.

Are there flamingos in Flamingo, a historic village on the edge of Florida Bay in Everglades National Park? Although the town was named for the bird, it is rarely seen there. Observers maintain that those flamingos occasionally seen on the mud flats of Florida Bay are escapees from captive groups, such as the one at Hialeah Race Track. However, in *The Cruise of the Bonton,* an account of an 1885 plume-hunting trip through the Everglades, William Pierce writes, "There were two large flocks of flamingos on the bank, but they took wing when we were at least a half mile from them, and did not give us any chance for a shot at them." Some researchers contend that until the early 1900s, large

numbers of flamingos migrated from the Bahamas to Florida Bay to molt. When flamingos molt, they remain flightless for a short time. The extensive mud flats of the bay would have afforded them protection from predators during this vulnerable period.

Whether or not they view flamingos on Florida Bay's mud flats at low tide, bird watchers can expect to add a number of species to their life lists in southern Florida—particularly during dry, winter seasons. In addition to wading birds such as egrets, herons, roseate spoonbills, ibis, and others, they may site migratory birds like warblers, or year-round residents: cardinals, blue jays, meadowlarks, bobwhites, and red-bellied woodpeckers.

Flamingos are rarely seen in Florida Bay.

Local birds of prey include ospreys, bald eagles, owls, snail kites, and the most common hawk, the red-shouldered hawk.

Noted naturalist and writer Aldo Leopold once said, "The life of every river sings its own song . . ." In the "river of grass" the musicians are a diverse lot. Colorful birds riding above the Glades on wings with perfect camber or wading gracefully in a shallow pond are among the area's most prominent players. But all animals contribute their sounds, colors, and movements to a harmonious whole orchestrated by natural processes.

A Gathering

Courtesy: Everglades National Park

Snowy egret.

Courtesy: Everglades National Park

Great white heron.

Courtesy: Everglades National Park

Roseate spoonbill.

South Florida Water Management District

Barred owl.

South Florida Water Management District

White ibis.

Courtesy: Everglades National Park

Bald eagle.

Courtesy: Everglades National Park

Red-bellied woodpecker.

Courtesy: Everglades National Park, Cawley

Red-shouldered hawk.

Chapter 6

Connections

In southern Florida, temperate and subtropical zones merge to form one of the largest and most complex wetland ecosystems in North America. The Kissimmee-Okeechobee-Everglades ecosystem is composed of more than a dozen plant communities, hundreds of distinctive habitats, and thousands of ecological niches, all of which fit together like pieces of a jigsaw puzzle. Florida has never been physically connected to the West Indies, but its peninsula has always joined the mainland, providing pathways for colonizing animals from the north. Most of the Everglades continental plants and animals came south from portions of the northern and central peninsula over the past million years; these areas remained above water, even when much of the southern peninsula was submerged by the rising sea. The dispersion pattern of these continental organisms, especially of the vertebrate animals, is called the "peninsular effect."

In the history of the Everglades watershed, "vagile" life forms—

The Kissimmee-Okeechobee-Everglades ecosystem is composed of more than a dozen plant communities, hundreds of distinctive habitats, and thousands of ecological niches, all of which fit together like pieces of a jigsaw puzzle.

those capable of dispersing— were most successful. They were able to cross the intervening expanse of salt water from the West Indies, or to traverse the sometimes wet, sometimes dry Glades and northern prairies to reach the youthful, dry ground of southern Florida. Many of these successful immigrants were birds, other creatures gifted with flight, or those structurally adapted to travel by sea. Relatively few land animals successfully negotiated the saltwater passage from the tropics. Over the past 10,000 years, since the most recent retreat of glacial ice, the small number of terrestrial West Indian species that have passed overseas includes mostly insects, plants, reptiles, and amphibians.

Most tropical components of the Everglades watershed are botanical. The light seeds of plants are adapted for easy dispersal. Some have made the passage to the Florida peninsula on ocean currents and winds. Others have been carried in the intestinal tracts of birds. Among these are

pigeon plum, saffron plum, coco plum, satin leaf, mastic, Jamaica dogwood, and silver palm. Proximity to the Gulf of Mexico and the Atlantic Ocean contributes to the region's luxuriant vegetative cover, which includes profuse epiphytic plants, especially orchids, bromeliads, and ferns. Temperate and subtropical zones merge here, and the warm, moist climate is suitable for West Indian life forms. For example, it is not unusual to see a cardinal perched in a gumbo limbo tree. Together, the native and immigrant inhabitants of the Everglades watershed make it one of the most biologically diverse ecosystems on the continent.

A complicated interaction occurs at the margins of living communities. Regardless of the size of their organizational unit—a biome, an ecosystem, a community, etc.— species and individuals from each area mix when two or more biological assemblages come together. This phenomenon is known as the edge effect, and the place where it occurs is called an ecotone. The edge effect causes a greater abundance and diversity of plants and animals in the ecotone. In addition, with a superficial resemblance to the Venn diagrams that math teachers use to explain set theory, some life forms that do not occur in the adjacent areas are found in the

© The Watercourse, 1996

88

From Where Do You Hail?

Florida panther, temperate zone.

Courtesy: Everglades National Park

Red-shouldered hawk, temperate zone.

South Florida Water Management District

Royal palm, the tropics.

Courtesy: Everglades National Park

Tree snails, the tropics.

Courtesy: Everglades National Park

overlapping sections. For example, the Cape Sable seaside sparrow is endemic to the southern Florida ecotone, but it is neither temperate nor subtropical in origin.

As in the study of all living things, the organisms and environments in southern Florida are assigned an organizational hierarchy. Populations of plants and animals living and interacting together in particular places (e.g., a freshwater marsh, hardwood hammock, or cypress swamp) are organized into communities. The combination of a community (or group of communities) and its nonliving environment is called an ecosystem. An ecosystem can be as small as a cup of water, or as large as the entire Kissimmee-Okeechobee-Everglades watershed.

Groups of animals or plants with similar characteristics are also organized so that we may study them. Those that interbreed under natural conditions are called species. For example, the American alligator is a species. The place in the ecosystem where a species lives—for instance, the alligator's hole—is called its habitat. The ecological niche of a species describes the food requirements, nesting sites, feeding behavior, and other physical, chemical, or biological conditions that the species needs to survive in an ecosystem. In other words, a species' ecological niche is its position in the community, in relation to other species. For example, a bird that feeds on fish in deep water might have a long spearlike bill and no oil gland for "waterproofing" its feathers, and it might hold its wings out from its body after diving as a means

Anhinga feeding.

of drying its feathers and maintaining body temperature. In this example, the species is the anhinga. The anhinga's habitat is an alligator hole or slough. Its ecological niche includes the type of food it eats (fish), the feeding methods it uses (swimming underwater and spearing the fish), its physical characteristics (e.g., the lack of a uropygeal, or oil, gland), and its behavior (e.g., thermoregulation). The bird has developed its place in the community in order to fit its habitat and survival needs.

The concept of an ecological niche can also be illustrated by the feeding behavior of various water birds. Special structural adaptations or methods of feeding allow different species to occupy the same habitats. Within the Everglades watershed, this means they can survive without the threat of competitive exclusion. For example, the wood stork, which feeds on small fish and invertebrates, is a "touch feeder."

Thermoregulation behavior.

It slowly probes shallow water with its partially open bill, which it snaps shut when it detects food. Its neighbor, the great blue heron is a "sight feeder": it impales its larger prey on its long, spearlike bill. As their common names imply, night herons (black-crowned and yellow-crowned) seldom feed in daylight when other water birds are more active; they fill the same niche as other species, but feed at a different time.

A species is further classified as specialist or generalist, depending on the extent of its habitat, its diet, its tolerance of environmental conditions, etc. For example, the bird called the snail kite is a specialist, feeding exclusively on apple snails and limited to habitats in which this prey is available. The alligator, on the other hand, is a generalist; it eats a wide variety of food and ranges throughout most of the watershed.

Certain animals have special importance to the overall health and integrity of an ecosystem. These are called keystone species, because they affect other organisms in critical ways. For example, the alligator excavates holes that become dry-season refuges for many other animals. The apple snail, because it is the exclusive food source for the snail kite, is a keystone species for that endangered raptor. Human beings are also a keystone species. But unlike other animals, people have the capability of altering or adapting the environment to accommodate their needs.

We may think of the organization of the natural world as similar to that of a giant corporation. A biome is the largest unit in nature: a wetland, a forest, a

Gator holes provide refuge for many species.

desert, etc. It corresponds to the larger corporation—a group of businesses or factories. Within this biome, an ecosystem is equivalent to a single business or factory. Communities are like the factory's different departments or divisions. Habitats represent offices or workspaces in the departments. Species are the workers, and the ecological niches are their different jobs or occupations. Some of the workers are specialists, others are generalists.

Despite their diversity, organisms and their places in the Everglades ecosystem share fundamental relationships that bind the region's elements together into an ecological whole. The connections of living things with the watershed and with one another are myriad. Some are simple; others are complex. Most involve exchanges of air, nutrients, and energy. Many are dependent on periodic fire. All are influenced by the ebb and flow of water.

Dry Land, Wet Refuge

The alligator—the signature species of the Everglades—lives throughout the watershed. Like the beaver, the gator is a hydrological engineer. As water becomes scarce with the onset of the dry season, alligators excavate reservoirs in the peat and marl, and deepen sinkholes already filled with water. Often these "gator holes"—some quite large and deep—are in the center of a cypress or bay head. (A head is a high or low spot on which tree islands develop. A head is frequently named according to the dominant plant species.) Gator holes become retreats, called refugia, for all kinds of life, and may be used year after year. Gator holes are vital to the system's ecological balance. Some scientists believe that the development of southern Florida's extensive canal system has altered this balance by attracting alligators to ready-made refuges that cannot replicate the many functions of the original gator holes.

The most important effect of a gator hole is its concentration and, thus, conservation of water. Each hole becomes a water sanctuary, and harbors a micro-

cosm of Everglades life. As the larger world of water grows smaller during the dry season, living things are drawn to gator holes. Snakes, turtles, raccoons, marsh rabbits, fish, and wading birds abound. Like scarecrows, anhingas dry their wings above these small ponds. Chorus frogs fill the night air around them with sound, and moonlight reflects red in the eyes of alligators waiting in them. Small plants and animals, some only visible with a hand lens, flourish, thickening the water.

Gator holes also "weed out" weaker individuals—demonstrating natural selection in action. Wintering and nesting birds rely heavily on the concentrations of fish in gator holes and other water-filled depressions. When water levels drop, dissolved oxygen decreases in the pond, but predation keeps fish population levels low enough that the demand for oxygen doesn't exceed the supply. With the advent of the wet season in May, gambusia (the common mosquitofish) and other small fish recolonize the marsh. They are omnivorous, so find food easily, and they produce live, fully developed young through internal fertilization. The stimulant for these fish to disperse rapidly from their dry-season

Common mosquitofish.

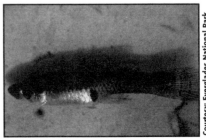

Each organism is tied to the next in an endless cycle of birth, life, and death.

home is the slight current generated by the onset of rains. Congregations of fish at the downstream end of perceptible currents are appropriately called "jubilees." As if in celebration of the return of rain, the fish and other aquatic organisms gather just before they begin to move out into the rewatered marshlands.

When the rains come, life begins to bloom again in the prairies. Tiny life forms—algae, bacteria, protozoa, crustaceans—emerge from the shelter of eggs and cysts. They reproduce and disperse widely. The algal microflora begin the production of simple sugars through photosynthesis. As they work with the sun, they become a nutritious food source and produce oxygen for a rapidly swelling population of consumers. A host of flying aquatic insects appears, as do glass shrimp, crayfish, snails, turtles, garfish, catfish, and frogs. The rains bring noisy hordes of mosquitoes; they are always present, but in summer they often fill the sky like a living mist. Mosquitoes, in turn, nourish the new generation of frogs and fish, dragonflies and birds. Rainfall signals an accelerated pace in the watershed, a period of renewal, of continuation, of new life. When the rains come, the ecosystem prospers, and the timeless cycle of regeneration continues as it has for thousands of years.

The change from wet summer to droughty winter is gradual, but by early January in an average year, drought is imminent. As winter proceeds, higher land drains and lower muddy areas dry and crack. In dry areas, grasses and weeds lose moisture and become tinder for fires; these fires burn large areas, paving the way for new growth. Drying is so widespread that from November to April the Shark River Slough at the lower end of the watershed, normally miles wide, withers to a few narrow streams. Throughout the watershed, wood storks and other species flock to evaporating pools. The annual transition from wet to dry season has perpetuated the living components of the watershed for thousands of years. Each organism is tied to the next

in an endless cycle of birth, life, death, and interdependence. Water is the connecting thread.

Normally, the periodic stress of annual drought is accommodated by the system. It has always been a part of the cyclic natural mechanisms in the watershed. Plants and animals have adapted to drought over time. It serves as a natural regulator, and under most conditions, the ecosystem remains stable. The system has the capability of adjusting to change, of resisting and bouncing back from disturbance. Only when people have intervened, by channeling and diverting water flow and encroaching on native habitats, has its resilience been tested.

Ironheads and Mosquitofish

The wood stork—locally known as the "ironhead" because of its characteristic black head and neck—is another indicator of the importance of water in the Everglades ecosystem, and of the profound effect that human manipulation of water can have on the life of a single species.

Emblematic of the Everglades, the wood stork usually nests at the beginning of the dry season. It is an opportune time of year, because the wet season has just increased the population of fish to

Wood stork or "ironhead."

peak levels. The onset of drying concentrates these fish into ponds where they are more easily caught to feed the stork's ravenous nestlings. The concentration of fish is critical because large numbers are needed, and because wood storks feed by touch, their long bills feeling then snapping shut on their prey. Drying and the subsequent concentration of food apparently trigger the wood storks instinct to nest and breed.

It has been estimated that a single stork family, including both adults and two hatchlings, requires nearly 450 pounds of fish, primarily gambusia, during the four-month breeding season. A colony of 6,000 nesting pairs plus offspring—a memory of bygone days because there are no longer colonies that large—would consume more than 2.5 million pounds of mosquitofish in a four-month period.

Occasionally, when breeding has already begun, unseasonable rains cause storks to abort the reproductive process and abandon nests. When water must be released from Conservation Area 3A (a storage area just north of the Tamiami Trail) out of sync with the bird's biological clock, or if late-season tropical storms or hurricanes bring rains, storks will terminate nesting as rising water levels in the southern watershed reduce the normal concentration of forage fish. In better times— just a few decades ago—wood storks would nest in drying wetlands throughout the southern Everglades in winter. Recently, unseasonable high water levels have made it difficult for the birds to begin nesting before March. This altered cycle does not

The status of the wood stork population indicates the health of the ecosystem.

give the young wood storks enough time to fledge before the onset of the next rainy season.

Regrettably, in this time of fragmentation and loss of habitat, species extinction sometimes reflects human influence. In the late 1980s, we came very close to another loss—the death of the last wood stork. Historically, the Everglades may have been home to as many as 250,000 nesting pairs of wood storks. Nearly 50 years ago—about the time that Everglades National Park was established—an estimated 6,500 wood storks inhabited the region. In the 1970s, as many as 2,600 still lived, but by the 1980s, there were fewer than 1,000, and these failed to produce offspring. The stork's reproductive cycle was interrupted because water levels for those years were too high too late in the season. Fish were too widely dispersed at a time when a concentrated food source was critical for wood stork offspring. In 1990, only 115 wood stork nests were found. For breeding wood storks, survival depends on

having the right amount of water at the right time.

Curved Beaks and Snails
Water touches the life of an endangered bird called the snail kite, too, but in a different way. While the last few years have been relatively good ones for the kite, there were fewer than 200 of these birds during the 1970s, and no more than 800 altogether in recent decades.

Snail kite.

The snail kite is the most highly specialized North American bird of prey. Named for its diet, it feeds exclusively on apple snails. The snail kite's bill is specially adapted to force open a snail's operculum (the thin disk that seals the snail inside its rather large shell) and to sever the muscle that holds the fleshy meat to the shell. Unlike most operculate snails, the apple snail has a type of "lung" that it uses to breathe air at the water's surface. As it crawls up onto broad blades of saw grass or other emergent aquatic vegetation to deposit masses of eggs, it is snatched with one outstretched talon by the swooping kite.

The apple snail is an aquatic organism. To live and reproduce, it must have standing or slowly moving water and emergent vegetation. The availability of such water is critical to the survival of the kite, and is important to the limpkin and the boat-tailed grackle too. The apple snail is the only food of the kite, a

The apple snail, only food of the snail kite, lays eggs on plant stems.

major part of the diet of the limpkin, and a fare of opportunity for the omnivorous grackle. Many reptiles, amphibians, and mammals, such as river otters, also eat snails and mussels. So do bullfrogs, turtles, alligators, and even certain fish. Studies have shown that there is very little conflict among the kite, the limpkin, and the grackle even though they eat the same food. This noncompetitive coexistence is largely due to the differing manners and locales in which the birds eat. The kite flies overhead and dives to catch snails in open water; the limpkin feeds on the ground in dense aquatic vegetation. Conflicts between the grackle and the other two seem only to arise when the grackle tries to steal food from them. The snail population has declined in

Photos courtesy: Everglades National Park

recent years because of natural drought and variations in the managed flow of water, and perhaps other factors such as loss of habitat. The kite may not compete for food openly, but it is losing its food source.

It's the Little Things that Count

Water is the world of snails, mussels, pea clams, limpets, and mosquito larvae. These small creatures number in the millions. They go quietly about their business, largely unnoticed, near the bottom of Everglades food chains, filtering plankton, eating algae, and awaiting their passage into the alimentary canals of larger consumers.

Enough water to produce an abundance of these tiny life forms is essential to the overall economy of the watershed and the larger ecosystem, especially during drought periods, when death often takes the largest organisms first. In a drying pond, the first fish to die are bass. Next, medium-sized fish such as sunfish succumb. Gar and other "rough fish" such as the bowfin (or blackfish) survive longer, but mosquitofish outlive them all. The annual cycle of the watershed begins and ends with small things making the transitions, maintaining continuity from one generation to the next. In the bioeconomics of the Everglades watershed, size is not the only measure of importance.

In powers of ten, the small things nourish the world of water. In a few hours, one small fish may eat 50,000 copepods, the small marine and freshwater crustaceans of the order Copepoda that are part of plankton. Each cope-pod may have eaten 120,000 diatoms, unicellular or colonial algae of both freshwater and saltwater varieties, in a day. During an algal bloom, as many as 70 million diatoms may exist in a cubic foot of brackish water. In an estuary or marsh, billions of diatoms and other microscopic plants thrive. They are consumed by millions of copepods and other single-celled animals which are, in turn, eaten by thousands of tiny crustaceans. The crustaceans are eaten by hundreds of small fish. The fish are eaten by tens of larger fish, which are eventually consumed by a large predator like an alligator, a dolphin, or a human. From bottom to top of the food pyramid, the numbers decrease as the size of the organisms increases. It may require billions of diatoms to support one panther, or one person. In the Everglades ecosystem, the medium in which the energy exchanges occur is water.

Life on the Edge

As the water pendulum swings from drought to flood, two critical adaptive behaviors are essential to the survival of Everglades watershed creatures: the capacity to live through near suffocation and total dehydration, and the ability to spread rapidly and recolonize when the rains return.

Gambusia and other killifish, such as golden topminnows, flagfish, least mosquitofish, and lucanias, are adapted to "breathe" the oxygen-rich surface layers of shrinking ponds of water long after other fish like bass and bream have succumbed. Their heads are flat on top, and their mouths are angled upward so

that they can gulp air at the water's surface. Bass and other fish have rounded heads and horizontal mouths, and must swim at unnatural angles to breath at the surface.

The structural adaptation of the gambusia has considerable significance to the wood stork. It enables large numbers of the fish to survive in basins of shrinking water during the time that adult birds are searching for food for their young. The modified mouth structure of the mosquitofish enables it to breathe in marginal conditions.

Other organisms have interesting structural and behavioral adaptations that help them cope with the lack of water. Tree snails become dormant behind a seal of mucous in winter. Apple snails, crayfish, frogs, and turtles dig down to moist soil and enter a state of torpor, a resting state similar to estivation. Birds migrate to moister places. Land mammals range farther abroad in search of water, and carnivores and omnivores subsist on other animals that have succumbed. Garfish and bowfins have primitive "lungs" that enable them to survive at least short periods completely out of water; the bowfin even burrows into moist ground on the bottoms of drying ponds and manages to survive. During the dry season, alligators depend on stored fat, largely ignoring the other tenants of the gator hole.

Bromeliads and other air plants trap and hold water in their upturned leaves. Other plants have thick, succulent leaves, or body parts that conserve water. The algal mat of periphyton—the "ark" of the Everglades—holds

Mosquitoes

The mosquito is one member of the saw grass community that never goes unnoticed. Florida has 67 species of mosquitoes. Their life cycles, habits, and behaviors vary. Some bite only at night, others only during the day; a few don't bite at all. If a mosquito bites you, it is most likely a female, who requires one or more meals of blood before she can lay her eggs.

Glades mosquitoes lay their eggs in mud and detritus, from May through August. The eggs "keep" until the rains begin. As soon as the eggs are flooded they hatch into the larval stage, and after four to ten days they become pupae. The adult mosquito develops from the pupa in two to four days. Adults generally live two to four weeks. The mosquitoes of Cape Sable and Flamingo are the persistent black salt marsh mosquitoes.

As irritating as the mosquitoes of the Glades can be, they are critical to the food webs in the watershed. Many kinds of insects and other creatures are dependent on the large food mass of mosquito larvae. Mosquitofish or gambusia prey on the larvae and, in turn, are food for other animals, such as frogs, snakes, and birds. These animals are fed upon by otters, raccoons, alligators, and other large predators.

Urban areas frequently experience migratory swarms of mosquitoes from wetlands. In these areas, mosquitoes are controlled by aerial spraying of insecticides designed to kill the adult form. A perennial issue arises when we try to balance our desire for comfort with the fact that mosquitoes, in all life stages, represent a critical food source for many watershed animals.

eggs, cysts, larvae of insects, and other creatures in its moist interior, enabling them to survive the dry season.

The Paradox of Fire

The bond between fire and the Everglades ecosystem is as important as the region's connection with water. Telltale deposits of charcoal imbedded in marsh peat, as well as soil profiles from mangrove areas, suggest that fire has occurred repeatedly throughout the history of the watershed. Fires are second only to hurricanes as periodic events that shape the plant communities of the ecosystem.

Forty species of plants, mostly herbaceous plants or shrubs, have evolved in southern Florida, including some temperate and tropical forms. Seventy percent of these species are fire-dependent—they require fire at some time during their life cycles. Since the fossil record indicates little change in plant species from the last lowering of the sea level, it appears that the frequency of lightning-caused fires today is similar to pre-aboriginal times. Lightning fire has been a factor in the maintenance of these fire-dependent species throughout the area's geologic history.

Fire helps shape the ecosystem.

Fire recycles nutrients into the soil and atmosphere.

Fire is essential to the maintenance of certain communities and to the general stability and health of the ecosystem. Periodic burning reduces fuel accumulations, strengthening the ecosystem by making it less susceptible to more catastrophic fires. The harvest of fire is measured in increased biological diversity and complexity—both indicators of good ecosystem health. Fire creates edges, or ecotones, which are biologically rich. Because natural fires tend to burn in random patterns, creating mosaics of vegetation where different communities of plants merge, they contribute to the edge effect. Fire enhances habitat rather than destroying it.

The principal effect of fire on wildlife is habitat alteration. Fires and hurricanes make some areas inhospitable, but they also create new habitat for some species.

Fire also modifies succession, composition, and stability in the plant community, helping to maintain the region's wetlands and pinelands. It stimulates vegetative reproduction in certain woody plants, and causes flowering and seed production in other species. Some species—such as southern Florida slash pine, sand pine, and others—are called serotinous. For these plants, the heat of fire triggers release of seeds, and promotes seed germination. Fire reduces or removes older, weaker, or diseased individuals from the plant community, and helps to control undesirable species, harmful insects, and disease. Fire contributes to the recycling of nutrients by releasing them from leaf litter on the forest floor back into the soil and the atmosphere. It improves seedbed conditions and increases overall productivity, thus helping to increase the biomass—the total weight of living matter in a given area. Periodic fire opens the canopy and reduces shading of the forest floor, altering the microclimate. It prunes lower branches and reduces understory, decreasing hazardous fuel loads and improving forage and

Intense fire can affect air quality.

South Florida Water Management District

grazing for consumers. Indeed, pinelands are maintained by fire. Without fire, the pinelands can be invaded by a thick understory of hammock species. Conversely, a hammock community can be devastated by fire.

Intense fire can affect air quality, but it contributes only small, temporary amounts of pollution to the already low annual atmospheric pollutant level above southern Florida. Persistent sea breezes help to clear the region's air. Fire can affect the quality of nearby surface waters and watersheds, but there are no indications of major problems. Big fires, burning uncontrolled during the dry season or drought, can penetrate deep into organic soils, destroying them or causing the soils to be less permeable and water retentive, increasing their susceptibility to erosion. Loss of rich peat soils can significantly alter normal plant succession (the sequence of plant types that appear in an area over time) following a disturbance.

Fortunately, most fires are not large and burn under the watchful eye of resource managers. Natural fires that are allowed to burn under certain sets of conditions (defining favorable levels of wind, relative humidity, temperature, and fuel moisture) are said to be burning in prescription. Fires burning out of prescription, especially those occurring during the dry season, can cause serious damage. The potential for damage is increased because human adjustments to natural drainage patterns have extended the dry season in the region, affecting normal water levels.

How do animals fare in a fire? Large mammals are generally unaffected by fire's passage, since their speed and mobility allow them to escape the flames. Birds are able to fly away, although nests and nestlings may succumb. Insects may suffer substantial short-term losses, but flies, roaches, and mosquitoes have survived in southern Florida for hundreds of thousands of years. Smoke has little consequence for wildlife, and fires have positive effects on fisheries since they enrich aquatic systems by transporting ash into watersheds.

Fires are essential in maintaining an equilibrium between forests and grasslands, hammocks and prairies. Except in localized areas where conditions are more favorable for islands of palm or hardwoods, periodic fires in the Everglades prevent broad-leafed trees from invading grasslands. Many plant reproductive parts are underground, and are thus unaffected by fire. Since nutrients are rapidly released from plant materials by fire, many plants on

the forest floor produce luxuriant growth following destruction of the overstory. Among the more common of these are fire grass, which signals the passage of fire with flower stalks 6 to 8 feet high; coontie, which has a root that Native Americans used to make flour; and partridge pea, which has bright yellow flowers and leaves that are sensitive and curl up when touched. Herbivores such as white-tailed deer and grasshoppers thrive on new growth of these herbaceous plants.

A Parade of Plants

Over time, an area's plant cover naturally changes through a process called plant succession. One community gradually gives way to another in a predictable series (called seral stages), until a final dominant vegetation (called climax vegetation) emerges. Sometimes, because of the influence of a periodic event like a fire or hurricane, the normal sequence of plant succession is arrested at an earlier stage called subclimax.

The climax plant community for southern Florida is the hardwood hammock, an island of mixed hardwood trees on elevated ground. Why isn't all of southern Florida covered by hammocks? The normal succession to climax forest is based on a stable, unchanging climate, but southern Florida's climate has shifted since its most recent emergence from the sea. Also, fires, hurricanes, frosts, other cyclic events, and human intervention alter succession by changing its direction or forcing a return to an earlier stage.

Plant succession begins on sites that have been disturbed by

The climax plant community for southern Florida is the hardwood hammock. (Mahogany Hammock, ENP)

people or nature. Primary succession begins on sites often unfavorable for the development of living systems, like landscapes that have been devastated by volcanic eruptions, or substrate that has never supported a plant community. The opportunity to observe this phenomenon is rare. Secondary succession begins on sites previously occupied by plant communities, like those in the ecosystem that have been disrupted by fire or hurricane. Secondary succession occurs after any kind of disturbance; it can happen on abandoned farmland or in bulldozed areas. Plant succession is analogous to a play. Seeing the climax vegetation is like witnessing the final act. Fires and other phenomena that reset the stage allow us to see the curtain rise, to observe the play from the first scene.

Fire is also an artifact of human culture. Early people of southern Florida included the Calusa Indians along the west coast and the Tequesta Indians on the east coast. These people lived here some 10,000 years ago. They knew about fire, but neither group used it as a tool for habitat management. Later, the Seminoles probably used fire to open travel routes, clear land, drive game, improve game habitat, and control insects. They may have burned pinelands to increase production of coontie, a valued food plant that responds to fire with rapid regrowth. Fires set by Native Americans probably contributed to the vegetative mosaics of scattered hammocks among pinelands and tree islands in saw grass prairies. These fires were probably started when soils and hammock vegetation were still too damp to burn, so the fires were less destructive than ones later in the dry season.

Little is known about the use of fire by the Spanish and British people who came to Florida. Early American explorers used fire to clear routes for foot and boat travel. Later settlers burned more extensively for the same reasons as the Seminoles.

Permanent settlement changed the landscape of southern Florida.

Settlers drained and lowered water levels, which led to more frequent and severe fires that resulted in destruction of organic soils and hardwoods in some places. Later extensive drainage and flood control structures altered natural hydrologic conditions. As humans caused natural surface water levels to drop, the dry season was extended, and fires had greater potential for changing large areas. In the 1930s and early 1940s, when people began to harvest timber heavily in Florida's pinelands, they also began burning slash pine. The fires were frequent, extensive, and sometimes severe. Rapidly spreading, wind-driven fires during the dry season were difficult to control. The historic wet-season fire regime was altered by firefighting activities, and by the proliferation of canals, roads, and farmlands as more and more of southern Florida was developed. This interrupted the natural succession in fire-dependent communities, so plant associations skipped stages in the vegetation sequence, progressing toward a different climax community.

Ecologist Ronald H. Hofstetter says, "Modification of natural cycles of water level and patterns of water flow, unseasonable burning, the uncontrolled dispersal of tenacious exotic species . . . and reckless land clearing have left southern Florida without truly natural ecosystems."

Prescribed burning—the use of fire as a resource management tool that takes advantage of the favorable attributes of surface fires—is done to perpetuate fire subclimax communities where wildfires cannot penetrate; to reduce fuel loads and prevent fires from entering developed areas; and to reclaim abandoned farmland and other developed areas. Of prescribed burning, Hofstetter says,

. . . [it] can be used to supplement inadequacy of natural fires. It can also be used to prevent, or at least reduce, the destruction of wildfires. When conditions are favorable for prescribed burning, areas with a high frequency of incendiary fires can be burned to reduce fuel and, therefore, intensity of a possible wildfire under drier conditions later. Fuel can also be burned out around ecologically important areas. . . . Prescribed burning can also be used to break up the continuity of fuels in large areas . . . to lessen the area traversed by a potential wildfire.

Prescribed burning is ecologically and economically sound. Effective prescribed burning creates vegetative mosaics, or patchworks, of burned and unburned areas at different stages of succession. It also contributes to species and community diversity and stability. Essential to certain plant and animal communities, it maintains the general stability and health of the ecosystem. Prescription fires were initiated in saw grass prairies in 1969. Until the 1980s, managers set prescribed burns mainly during the cooler dry months, but since then they have started fires during the wet season as well. The first prescribed burn was a resource management benchmark. Since that time, hundreds of fires have been set by resource managers in pinelands, scrub, and marshes alike to limit invasion by hardwoods, to maintain natural

community associations, and to retain a semblance of primitive conditions. Guided by science, this human intervention in the affairs of nature was necessary in order to regain some equilibrium in a system thrown out of balance by other human activities.

Like wind and water, fire has been a constant companion of the Glades since the end of the Ice Age. Smoke still rises above the watershed, signaling continuity and change. It marks beginnings, not ends; diversity, not uniformity. As long as fire periodically sweeps across pinnacle rock, pineland, and grassy waters, a part of the ancient Everglades will abide.

Webs, Chains, Pyramids, and Cycles

The sun energizes the entire Everglades ecosystem, from the tiny diatoms and copepods to the tropical hurricanes. Primary producers convert and concentrate solar energy into food. Animals and certain plants, like the bladderworts, are primary consumers, utilizing, rearranging,

and decomposing the material made by the producers. Decomposers are the link between death and new life. In a way, each organism in this flow of energy eats a little bit of the sun, since the primary energy source for producers is light, required for photosynthesis.

Gross primary production is the total amount of organic matter converted from solar energy in a given area and time. This includes maintenance energy, the portion used by the plants to keep themselves alive. Net primary productivity is the amount of organic matter stored in the plant in excess of its own needs, and therefore available to consumers. Net community production is a measure of the amount of food remaining after the producers and consumers have used what they need. Secondary production is the energy stored as food in consumers that may themselves be consumed at some point—for example, energy stored in the tissues of a prey animal such as a garfish that may be consumed by a predator like an alligator.

Bladderworts are primary consumers that feed on insects.

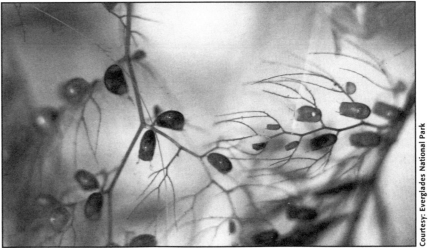

Courtesy: Everglades National Park

Marsh rabbit.

Primary production is high in natural ecosystems where water, nutrients, climate, and other physical factors are favorable. This is especially true if energy from outside the system helps to reduce maintenance energy requirements. For example, organisms in vital coastal estuaries (such as the Saint Lucie and Caloosahatchee systems) have an energy subsidy; they can devote more energy to production because tidal energy brings in nutrients and carries away waste products. In a similar fashion, energy levels in watershed marshes are subsidized by the cyclic rise of fresh water as the "pendulum" swings from the dry to the wet season.

Primary consumers—like marsh rabbits—eat plants. Secondary consumers ingesting primary consumers eat meat—for example, a bobcat that eats marsh rabbits. The term "food web" conveys the complex energy interactions in a natural system. A food web is a composite of several food chains, or sequences of production and consumption, of life and death. Each level or link in a food web is called a trophic level.

Grazing food chains involve consumption of living matter. A typical grazing food chain in the

Everglades could include periphyton fed on by mosquito larvae, in turn eaten by sunfish. The sunfish becomes food for the largemouth bass, which is then eaten by a river otter—or an angler.

Detrital food chains are those in which consumers eat dead matter. Some microbes are part of food chains in which dissolved organic matter is consumed. Detrital food chains are most common in natural systems like the Everglades, where less than ten percent of the primary production is grazed. In such a rich system, substantial and complex buildups of biomass can occur, increasing energy storage in the system. A typical detrital food chain in the watershed could begin with dead plant material eaten by bacteria and fungi, which are consumed by single-celled animals. The protozoans are then eaten by worms and

insects which are consumed by birds. Mangrove systems, such as those in Rookery Bay near Naples, are classic examples of detrital food chains.

Nutrients, elements, and inorganic compounds that are essential to life are circulated through the watershed in what are called material cycles. Among the elements that are repeatedly moved through the ecosystem in large quantities are nitrogen, phosphorus, sulfur, and carbon.

Nitrogen is critical to life. It is a basic component of amino acids, nucleic acids, and proteins that carry the genetic templates of a species. Available in large quantities in the atmosphere, nitrogen is unusable in its atmospheric form. It must be fixed, or converted from gas into ammonia, nitrite, or nitrate before plants can use it to produce food. Nitrogen is fixed in

MARL

PEAT

LIMESTONE

PERIPHYTON (ALGAE AND ONE-CELLED ANIMALS)

DEAD LEAVES AND STEMS

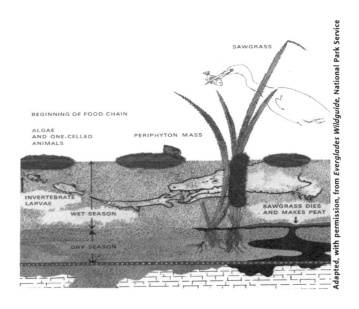

the soil of the Everglades by bacteria living on the roots of legumes and other higher plants. Lightning strikes also fix atmospheric nitrogen, and southern Florida is the lightning capital of the world.

Phosphorus moves from phosphate-bearing rocks to the sea through weathering, erosion, and sedimentation. It returns to the land when sedimentary rocks are uplifted and exposed to the abrasive effects of wind and water. Ocean currents bring dissolved phosphates to the water's surface, making them available to photosynthetic aquatic plants, which are consumed by fish, which are in turn eaten by birds. Phosphorus is also returned to the land and sea through the waste products of birds and the deposition of skeletal material. While the Everglades ecosystem is oxygen rich, it is naturally low in phosphorus and other nutrients—a condition known as oligotrophy. Human activities over the past hundred years have altered this condition, causing changes in natural plant communities.

The sulfur in the Everglades ecosystem is found in both gaseous and sedimentary cycles. Large quantities of sulfur are held in sediments, especially in the dark, anaerobic sediments in wetlands. Smaller amounts can be found in gaseous form in the atmosphere.

Carbon is one of the most important materials for living organisms. The cycle of carbon in plants is known as photosynthesis. The chemistry is complex, but photosynthesis can be simply defined as the combination in green plants of carbon dioxide and water, with radiant energy from the sun to produce carbohydrates, water, and oxygen.

The carbon dioxide used in the process is a byproduct of respiration of the animals in the ecosystem; the oxygen produced keeps these animals breathing. Air breathers change glucose (and other complex compounds they synthesize, eat, or decompose) back into carbon dioxide and water through respiration. Respiration is a carefully controlled slow burning of organic compounds that takes place inside the cell. The chemical energy released in the process is stored in other molecules until it is needed by the organism. As the energy is used, most of it is changed into low-temperature heat that flows back into the environment, where it helps to fuel weather and climate.

During photosynthesis, oxygen and water are released to the air through the pores, or stomata, on the surface of leaves. Carbon dioxide and water are released for reuse with each compression of an animal's lungs. The carbon cycle includes respiration, transpiration, burning of fossil fuels, storage in the earth, and the exchange of sediments between land and sea.

Air is subject to increasing human pollution, especially near large urban areas such as those along Florida's east and west coasts. Due to the burning of fossil fuels, toxic oxides of nitrogen and sulfur are occurring in greater concentrations in the air over these regions. Sulfur dioxide harms the photosynthetic process, and it combines with water vapor to form sulfuric acid that falls to earth as acid rain. Nitrous oxide and nitrogen dioxide also mix with water vapor, producing nitric acid, another component of acid rain. Another negative property of nitrogen dioxide is that it combines with the hydrocarbons in auto exhaust to produce photochemical smog. Fortunately, due largely to the persistent sea breezes that sweep away the polluted air above the narrow peninsula, there is relatively little smog in the air over the Everglades.

Other pollutants affect the watershed. Carbon monoxide is a form of carbon and part of the carbon cycle. It is a byproduct of incomplete burning of fossil fuels in internal combustion engines. Carbon monoxide is a major air pollutant in urban areas where there are millions of cars, and thousands of boats, lawn mowers, and airplanes.

One of the best ways to visualize interrelationships in the watershed is to think of the ecosystem as a living organism. Air and water are its metaphoric breath and blood; carbon, nitrogen, phosphorus, and other compounds are its foods, which, if not properly balanced, can cause illness. Green plants and air-breathing animals—including people—are the lungs of the ecosystem. Fire is part of both the reproductive and the waste removal systems. Just as arteries and veins carry blood in a complex circulatory system, air, water, and nutrients are carried to the watershed and its life forms through various cycles that connect everything.

Chapter 7

Looking Back at Eden

Southern Florida is a land rich in stories, a writer's paradise. Authors, painters, and songwriters have often retreated to its sun-bleached beaches and blue seas for inspiration, or just to rest. Ernest Hemingway was a popular figure in Key West. Frederic Remington, famous cowboy artist, went west—west of Lake Okeechobee that is—to paint a different kind of man in the saddle. Florida cowboys were called "cowhunters," and with their skinny, ragged frames and floppy hats, they did not match the image of their Western counterparts. The cracking of their whips over the heads of wild (feral) cattle gave rise to the nickname "cracker." Popular Western writer Zane Grey liked what he saw in southern Florida. In 1924, he said, "A certain kind of lure began to dawn on me. This was a country that must be understood."

Songwriter and performer Jimmy Buffett has lived in the Florida Keys and portrays the area's easy lifestyle through his music. Country-western entertainer John Anderson sings about the Seminoles. In his novel *Killing Mister Watson*, noted writer Peter Mathiessen has examined the characters, landscapes, and legends of the Everglades' Ten Thousand Islands of 100 years ago. And, although she is known widely for her works of nonfiction—in particular *The Everglades: River of Grass*—author, lecturer, and Everglades activist Marjory Stoneman Douglas wrote wonderful stories that drew upon the rare and untamed character of the people here and the place in which they lived.

But this nearly tropical land has known other storytellers, early ones who drew close to the fire, using its sooty smoke as a thin veil of protection against the mosquitoes and no-see-ums. Women told stories as they hugged their children to their bare breasts and arranged their

Early Calusa women.

Courtesy: Everglades National Park

skirts of Spanish moss. Men shifted the fancy raccoon tails that hung from their breechcloths to sit more comfortably as they talked. The southern Florida night air was heavy with the sounds of frogs humming ageless tunes, with the mysterious, haunting call of an owl seeking a mate. In this atmosphere, the early people—the Ais, Jeaga, Calusas, and Tequestas—told stories of hunts, battles, and the foolish, sometimes deadly, passions of men and women.

Conch Shells and Wooden Masks

Almost 11,000 years ago, native

The southern Florida night air was heavy with the sounds of frogs humming ageless tunes, with the mysterious, haunting call of an owl seeking a mate. In this atmosphere, the early people—the Ais, Jeaga, Calusas, and Tequestas—told stories of hunts, battles, and the foolish, sometimes deadly, passions of men and women.

Early Native Americans of Florida.

From Florida from Indian Trail to Space Age, Vol. I, Chapt. XXIV, Adelaide K. Bullen, © 1965.

people migrated to Florida; most likely, they came from the region that is now the southern United States. Four thousand years later the first settlements appeared.

By the time the first European explorers reached Florida in the late 1500s, six main groups of Native Americans lived in the region: the Apalachee and Timucua of northern Florida and the Ais, Jeaga, Calusa, and Tequesta of southern Florida.

Although they ranged some 20 to 30 miles inland, the Ais lived along the coastal and Indian River regions from south of Cape

Calusa hunters.

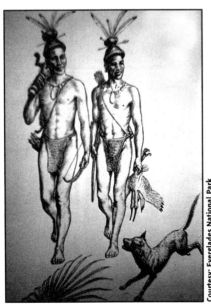

Courtesy: Everglades National Park

Canaveral to the Saint Lucie River. Jonathan Dickinson, who was shipwrecked with his family south of the Ais territory in the late 1600s, wrote about these early people in his journal. From Dickinson we learn that the Ais did not farm the land, but fished and gathered wild fruits such as coco plums, sea grapes, and palm berries. Apparently the Ais had great respect for their chief, but not for the elder members of their society. Theirs was a "youth" culture where the old people served as slaves for the young. By 1760, the Ais had died out as a result of introduced diseases, slave raids, and the effects of rum provided by the Europeans.

The Jeaga people lived along the Florida coast between the Ais and the Tequestas. Dickinson also contacted these people and described them as less powerful than the Ais. But their lifestyle was similar: they were nonagriculturalists, and they supplemented their fish diet with berries and roots. The Jeagas disappeared about 10 years before the Ais did.

The Tequestas lived on Florida's east coast and probably ranged as far north as present-day Pompano Beach. To the west and south, their territory merged with that of the Calusa, who claimed the area from Tampa Bay south to Cape Sable. The Calusas were the more dominant group of the two, and Charlton W. Tebeau, noted Everglades historian, maintained in *Man in the Everglades* that "the Calusa appear to have exercised some degree of cultural if not political leadership over most of the Indians south of Lake Okeechobee." The Calusas and

the Tequestas mainly lived along the coasts, occupying the fringe of the Everglades. They too were primarily hunters and non-agriculturalists. The land and sea were rich with food. The people made flour from the coontie root, and ate fruit: palmettos, coco plums, sea grapes, and pigeon plums. Freshwater and saltwater fish were abundant, and oysters, conch, and turtles were also common fare. The large turtles that crawled from the sea to dig nests in the warm sand provided the people with meat and eggs.

The Tequesta were regarded as great fishermen who sometimes varied their diets with sea cows or manatees. Accounts maintain that in winter they hunted the animals from their canoes with ropes and stakes. They also caught sharks, porpoises, and stingrays. The Tequesta had fishing gear but also bows and arrows for hunting and warfare. They crafted simple pottery. The women wore skirts of Spanish moss; the men wore breechcloths.

Much of what we know about the Calusa people comes from Escalante de Fontaneda, a Spaniard who was shipwrecked in Florida when he was 13 years old. He lived with the Calusa and other groups for about 17 years. Although Fontaneda's *Memoir* provides some insight into Calusa culture, the Calusa themselves left behind artifacts in mounds of shell, bone, and earth that preserve stories of these now extinct people. Some of the mounds were built for ceremonial purposes, others for burial. Sometimes the Calusas used them for habitation, and they often served as refuse heaps.

Artifacts of the Calusa

Horse conch—source of tools, weapons, and utensils.

Carved bone pendant.

Decorated potsherds.

Sticks thrust through holes drilled in conchs converted the shells into weapons or tools.

Artifacts discovered in mounds reveal much about early people in the watershed.

Courtesy: Everglades National Park

The conch shell served as a Calusa tool, weapon, and drinking cup. The Calusa people removed the delicious meat of the conch from a large hole knocked in one side of the shell. They drilled a smaller hole on the opposite side, then thrust a stick through both holes and tightly secured it. This heavy curved instrument could subdue an enemy or shape a dugout canoe. With its columella or spiral end removed, the conch shell served as a drinking cup.

The Calusas made pots by rolling long snakes of clay and coiling them on a base. At first the pots were simple and heavy with no adornment. But as time passed, their function was enhanced by art. Native artisans began to decorate pieces with lines, crosshatching, and patterns. With the invention of the shark tooth knife, personal adornment was also refined. Using the cutting edge of the knife, artists crafted bone hairpins and created pendants from bone and shell to hang

around their necks or from belts. But some of the craftspeople's finest work was in wood. They carved animal masks for ceremonial purposes. A deer mask with cords attached to its ears allowed the wearer to twitch the ears back and forth, as if listening for the footfall of the hunter.

As their culture progressed and trade with other people introduced new ideas, the Calusas developed intricate ceremonies. They buried their dead with greater care, establishing mounds for internment at a distance from their villages. In the mounds, the Calusa positioned the bodies of their dead in a particular manner; in some cases they boiled the bodies to remove the flesh so that only bundles of bones were consigned to the mound.

But even their mounds, sacrificial rites, and shamans could not protect the Calusas and Tequestas from the forces that brought these once healthy and thriving people to an end. By the early 1800s both the Tequestas and the Calusas

were gone from the lower peninsula of Florida. Disease, slave raids, and wars took their toll. Some believe that these people migrated to Cuba; others say they took refuge in the Everglades and later joined the Seminoles.

The Calusas constructed many of their mounds within the Everglades watershed. Unfortunately, many Indian mounds have been damaged or in some cases completely paved over by modern development. Today, anthropologists examine surviving mounds to "hear" the stories of an extinct people: the Calusas speak to us through the clay their hands once worked and the bones of the ancestors they honored.

Chickees, Patchwork, and Frybread

In a beautiful John Anderson song called "Seminole Wind," the singer laments the draining of the Everglades, home of the Seminole people, and calls upon the ghost of Osceola, their leader during the Seminole Wars.

The Miccosukee people also made their home in the Everglades. To see a Miccosukee village along the Tamiami Trail is to visit a place from another time. Old men carve small dugout canoes to be sold as children's toys. Women in skirts of complex patterns and

Miccosukee craftwork.

Ken DeYonge

bold colors weave baskets, sew dolls from palmetto fiber, stitch beadwork, or make frybread. Sitting on their open-air platforms or "chickees," the breeze rustling the dry palm fronds on the roof, their hands forever busy, the people are quiet and calm. They reply pleasantly to visitors' questions. Here, an earlier culture struggles to hold on to its rich traditions and yet belong to a world whose stated values are often inconsistent with its actions.

After it was drained and channelized, the Everglades could no longer support the Miccosukee people in the old ways. Stephen Tiger, public relations manager for the Miccosukee tribe, often uses the term "space-age Indian." He believes that the young people of the tribe must have a non-Indian education. Tiger contends that if the region had been left alone, the Miccosukees would still be living as they did 100 years ago. Today, the Miccosukees who cling to the old ways must also adopt new ones—they must be like a chameleon, changing, yet remaining the same.

Although the stories, beliefs, customs, and history of the Miccosukees and the Seminoles overlap, the Miccosukees are not Seminoles. For a long time the U.S. government withheld its consideration of the Miccosukee as an official tribe. A Miccosukee delegation met with Cuba's leader Fidel Castro, who acknowledged them as a new Indian nation and offered them a place to live. Finally, in 1962, the tribe was recognized by the United States, and its constitution was at last approved.

Stephen Tiger frequently refers to the Everglades as the geographic "savior of the Miccosukees." History supports his statement. In the early 1700s, Native Americans living in what are now the states of Georgia, Alabama, North and South Carolina, Tennessee, and Mississippi were pressured to move to western reservations so that their traditional lands could become available for non-Indian settlement. Some of these people, collectively called the Five Civilized Tribes, fled to Florida, which at that time was controlled by the Spanish. Many of the people were Creek Indians. Later, joined by others—including some escaped slaves—they came to be known as the Seminoles. Diverse languages were spoken by the Seminole people, but eventually two favorites emerged—Muskogee and Mikasuki.

In 1763, Spain was forced to give up Florida to Britain in exchange for Cuba. When Florida came under British ownership, a period of prosperity began for the Seminoles. They had no strife with other Indian groups because the Timucua, who had inhabited their area about the same time that the Calusa were on the peninsula, had become extinct.

William Bartram, a British naturalist, visited the Seminoles during this agricultural-pastoral period and left a written record of his observations. Bartram was graciously received by Chief Cowkeeper, and conducted "to an apartment prepared for the reception of their guests . . ." He was treated to a feast ". . . consisting of venison, stewed with bear's oil, fresh corn cakes, milk, and hominy; and our drink, honey

and water, very cool and agreeable . . ." Bartram continued his description of the Seminoles and their lands:

> . . . fragrant orange groves, droves of cattle, herds of sprightly deer, squadrons of the beautiful fleet Siminole [sic] horse, flocks of turkeys . . . their towns are clean, the inhabitants being particular in laying their filth at a proper distance from their dwellings, which undoubtedly contributes to the healthiness of their habitations . . .

This peaceful Seminole life preceded a time of conflict, the Seminole Wars.

After the Revolutionary War that freed the American colonies, Britain was forced to return Florida to Spain. At this time, the fertile lands of the Seminole did not go unnoticed. Soon, settlers from the former northern colonies began moving onto the Indians' lands. The Seminoles protested and threatened to attack. When settlers ignored the warnings, Seminoles raided their homesteads. Hostilities between the Seminoles and the settlers heightened until the United States declared war on the Seminoles in 1817. General Andrew Jackson drove these people south, killing many Seminoles on the way. Those that survived escaped to the marshes. Some historians maintain that Jackson's deadly raid against the Seminoles was meant to eliminate former slaves that lived among the Indians, suggesting that southern plantation owners resented the sanctuary that Florida had become for runaways. They also feared an alliance between the Seminoles and the former slaves.

In the treaty of 1823, the Seminoles agreed to move to a reservation in the center of Florida, which by that time belonged to the United States. Under Spanish rule, the Seminoles had been granted citizenship. However, under the rule of the U.S. government, they were not enfranchised. Neither were they left alone. In the Indian Removal Act of 1830, the U.S. government dictated that all eastern Indians must move west of the Mississippi River. Settlers who continued to push into the Seminoles' fertile land supported this action. But the Seminoles resisted, and the Second Seminole War began. It was a long, bloody conflict with great loss of lives on both sides, and the most expensive war ever waged against Native Americans. The Seminoles were led in battle by their chief, Osceola. As leader of the Seminoles and thus an ally of slaves, he became a hero to Northern abolitionists.

The Second Seminole War was brutal. Federal troops did battle not only in the field but also on the hearth, burning Seminole villages and stealing or destroying food stores. The troops took women and children as hostages. Captured by government soldiers under a flag of truce, Osceola died in prison in South Carolina. (The late Will McClean, Florida poet and troubadour, wrote a haunting song about Osceola's final days.) No treaty terminated the Second Seminole War; it merely faded away. Many Seminoles had been killed, captured, or sent west of the Mississippi on the "Trail of

The dugout canoe was perfectly crafted for navigating shallow Everglades waters.

Tears." The survivors fled farther south into the Everglades.

About 500 Seminoles took refuge in the Everglades, a place where soldiers hesitated to follow. The swamp differed from land the Seminoles had known. They lived on the high, dry hammocks, where they planted their crops. They hunted deer, bears, rabbits, raccoons, otters, and many species of birds. They fed heavily on turtles and alligators. They gathered roots, berries, and herbs. They adapted their clothing, their houses, and their lifestyle to this

domain of mosquitoes, snakes, and wet and dry seasons.

Before the Civil War, the U.S. government tried to remove the Seminoles from the swamp. This struggle, called the Third Seminole War, lasted from 1855 and 1858. Some Seminoles agreed to move to the West, but others stayed. By the end of the 1800s, the Florida Seminoles numbered fewer than 500. The survivors lasted into the twentieth century by hunting egrets for plumes, alligators for hides, and otters for furs; these items were much in

An early Miccosukee village.

Miccosukee women sew colorful patchwork clothing.

religion. This placed them at odds with the predominately Christian and progressive leadership of the Seminole Tribe.

The Miccosukees continue to change and adapt, but also strive to maintain cultural continuity with their rich and ancient traditions. An example of this cultural constancy is the Green Corn Dance. Conducted annually, the Green Corn Dance lasts four days. It is a time of renewal and new beginnings for the people, intended to restore balance to their society. Few non-Indians have witnessed the rituals of the Green Corn Dance, a ceremony that the Creek Indians of Georgia and Alabama also celebrated. Many other tribes who did not till the ground observed First Fruit ceremonies. The celebration combines fun and solemnity. Men and boys play a ball game, competing against girls and women. There is dancing and storytelling. Tribal justice is meted out: the elders hear cases involving violations of tribal laws and customs. In a curious custom called "scratching," medicine men scratch themselves with needles until they bleed. This bloodletting is intended to purify the body.

demand for the fashion market. As Florida developed and added canals and roads, reservations were again set aside for the Seminoles, this time in Florida.

Through the First and Second World Wars and the Great Depression, the Seminole people struggled to adapt to new ways of earning a living, educating their children, maintaining their traditions, and organizing themselves. Under the Indian Reorganization Act (IRA) of 1957, the Seminoles drafted a constitution and established themselves as the

"Seminole Tribe of Florida." Not all of Florida's native people aligned themselves with the official Seminole Tribe. People along the Tamiami Trail chose to follow a path more appropriate for them, establishing themselves as the Miccosukee Tribe of Indians of Florida. Of the Miccosukee tribe historian Charleton Tebeau writes:

These so-called Trail Indians were themselves highly factionalized, but they had a number of things in common: they were cultural traditionalists who observed the old ways of housing, dress and

Another Green Corn Dance purification rite is fasting, combined with the consumption of "asi" or the "black drink." Made from the leaves of a Glades plant, this concoction is a powerful emetic. In the past, gourds were filled with the drink. Young boys ran them to the elders and chiefs and gave the "black-drink cry"—Asi-ya-ho-lo—while the men emptied the gourds. Whoever does not drink this liquor cannot

Chickees keep occupants cool, dry, and relatively safe from snakes.

eat the new green corn. With the medicine men joining in, dancing begins as the drink is consumed. The participants eat green corn the following day and fast the day after that, in order to keep the sacred food away from common food. Then, on the third day, they hold a great feast. Scholars maintain that this ceremony is not so much "thanksgiving" as worship, ensuring that the spirits of the corn are revered. Spirits who are offended might deprive the people of their crops or wild fruit.

The Everglades provided refuge for the Seminole and Miccosukee of the past, and offer a spiritual connection for their people today. Today, the "Seminole Wind" that singer John Anderson describes is blowing stronger; in its breath it holds the memory of a people who struggled to live free among the grassy waters. During the time of the Seminole Wars, on a ship bound for New Orleans, a deported Seminole chief watched as the coast of Florida faded in the distance. "It was my home,"

he said. Today, it would be his home again.

Explorers and Wanderers

Many explorers touched Florida's shores in their search for gold and slaves. Much of what we know about the early native people of southern Florida was reported by these early adventurers.

One of the explorers was the now legendary Juan Ponce de Leon. On his second trip to Florida, he had hopes of establishing a settlement. But when he landed on the peninsula's west coast and strode in full shimmering armor across the white sands, the arrow of a Calusa warrior mortally wounded him.

The Indians of the coast and the Florida Keys became salvage artists as well as soldiers. They watched for wrecked ships, particularly during the hurricane months, from June through November. Escalante de Fontaneda was taken captive by the Calusas when the ship that

was to carry him to school in Spain foundered in the violent seas. Fontaneda was only 13 years old at the time, but on his journey to the main village he picked up a few words—enough so that he was able to understand and respond to a command given by Carlos, a Calusa leader. His life was spared because of it, and for the next 17 years he lived among these people. Eventually he was rescued, and in the latter part of the 1600s he wrote his *Memoirs*, the first written record of the early Everglades. In his book, he observed, "These Indians occupy a very rocky and a very marshy country. They have no product of mines, or things that we have in this part of the world [Spain]."

While the Calusa, the Tequesta, and later the Seminole and Miccosukee adapted to the seasons and moods of their environment, the explorers, soldiers, and adventurers of other cultures strode rigidly against it. In *The Everglades: River of Grass*, Marjory Stoneman Douglas describes what the experience of the Spanish or American soldier in his full wool uniform and soggy leather boots must have been:

> But the men suffered always the discomforts of the thundering rains, wet clothing, clouds of salt-water mosquitoes in the mangrove country, wet food, sleeping in wet boats or on wet ground haunted by moccasin snakes also seeking dry land, and the roaring and thrash-ing of alligators that invaded the muddy flats. Nights in the drowned glades with a norther blowing on chilled skins and sodden garments were a singularly penetrating agony.

Maps of explorers provide us a glimpse of early Florida.

Courtesy: Everglades National Park

Moving with the grain of the saw grass and oiling their bodies against the mosquito's sting, the native people molded themselves to the land. European soldiers and adventurers thrashed against the sharp-edged saw grass and cursed the sun and insects, suffering greatly. They did not know the country. When asked by explorers how long it would take them to cross the Everglades and reach Miami, an old Seminole woman replied, "Indian two days, whiteman ten, fifteen."

Accounts of Everglades travelers describe the maddening whine of mosquitoes, the bite of the saw grass, the muck that sapped the strength of the fittest, and the sound that made the bravest man sweat—the buzz of a big rattler by his bedroll. Alonzo Church made an expedition through the Everglades in the late 1800s. Describing his passage, he wrote:

The grass was high and thick, the ground so boggy that at every step we sank into it up to our thighs, and the sun was scorching hot; it soon became evident that at the rate we were going we could not reach the island by night fall. [Travelers generally set as their goal a hammock for their night camp; if they were unable to make it by dark, they were forced to sleep in their boats. They often fired the saw grass in order to create a pathway.] . . . *We now pushed our way towards the island, lighting fires every hundred yards or so, knowing that if the wind held and the saw grass burnt with its usual fury, there would soon be behind us a clear path for the boats. . . . On all sides the grass was burning with a fury that I have never seen equaled; to my rear the smoke and flames completely hid the boats and the men struggling to bring them forward, while very soon the fires, kindled ahead, swept down towards me and but for the bayou in which I stood would have burned me up. I thought little of the fire, but rather of the dreadful fatigue.*

In addition to detailing hardships, early accounts also describe the wildlife of the area. In the 1885 cruise of the sloop *Bonton*, Charles William Pierce and his companions, including Guy Bradley (who would later become an Audubon warden) killed birds for a naturalist named Mr. Chevelier. In his account of the trip, *The Cruise of the Bonton* , Pierce wrote, "Mr. Chevelier has a market for all of them in Paris. He gets fifty cents for the pelican skins, twenty-five cents for sea swallows or least tern, $10 for great white heron, and $25 for flamingo skins." He maintained that if the great white herons and flamingos had not been scarce, "we would [have] soon [made] the old man rich." Dr. Bill Robertson, senior Everglades National Park biologist, did an analysis of *The Cruise of the Bonton* and found that 1,397 birds of 36 species had been shot.

Pierce also described a shallow pond in which he estimated were 50 alligators. He immediately

The sloop, Bonton.

Courtesy: Everglades National Park

opened fire on them, since "gators eat wounded plume birds." As soon as he used up his 15 shells, he left, noting, "There were too many gators there still alive when my gun was empty."

The cruise was undertaken in the spring and summer, and the mosquitoes were often quite thick, prompting Pierce to observe:

Dead calm all night, and this morning. When we got out from under our mosquito bars there was not a spot as large as a pin head on that boat from the water line to the tip of the mast that did not have a mosquito on it. We fought them for about two hours before we could stop to make coffee.

In the 1830s, John James Audubon collected bird specimens from the rookeries of Florida Bay and the Florida Keys. From these models he painted accurate and beautiful portraits of the bird species. Books including reproductions of Audubon's paintings are collector's items. His original works are priceless treasures.

Settlers and Orange Blossoms

Some people who came to southern Florida were ready to quit wandering and make this place their home. They faced challenges and discomforts, but they were an adaptable and hearty lot. Some didn't admit to a past; the mangrove wilderness camouflaged these individuals so well that the law forgot all about them. Some of them settled, if only for a short time, in out-of-the-way places such as the Ten Thousand Islands or the village of Flamingo. Others chose a place called Fort Dallas,

Historic Florida collage.

now known as Miami.

In 1896, the year of its incorporation, the city of Miami had a population of 1,500. In the past 100 years its population has exploded; it is now home to nearly half a million people, with 12 million visitors annually. The impact of so many people on the land and water resources of an area that was virtually untouched for millions of years is difficult to imagine.

Many settlers who arrived in the Miami area between 1840 and 1880 made their living making starch from the coontie plant and trading it. These people depended on a boat that ran between Key West and the Miami River. They ordered supplies a month in advance; the boat was supposed to make a round trip every two weeks, but quite often it was late. The settlers raised a few fruits and vegetables, such as sweet potatoes and pumpkins, but they also bought produce from the Seminoles.

The first vegetables raised for a commercial market were tomatoes. The crop was a risky venture, since tomatoes were picked and packed green. The trick was to get the tomatoes to market before they rotted. On a Monday, the tomatoes left Miami on a sailboat to Key West. The boat had to arrive in Key West by Friday, when a steamer for New York would depart. If the sailboat captain did not feel compelled to push his craft, the tomatoes might arrive late in Key West and sit on the dock for a week before shipment to New York.

Another Florida industry was ship wrecking. According to J. K. Dorn, an early settler who wrote *Recollections of Early Miami*, a wrecking operation took precedence over any other activity taking place—even a court trial with a jury.

There's a wreck on the Beach! There's a wreck on the Beach! He went all around Miami yelling this. In less than ten minutes there was not a juryman in the box.

They jumped out the window, ran down the stairs, and made for their fishing smacks, for in those days the first man to arrive at a wreck was made captain of the wrecking operations, and others received shares according to the time of their arrival.

Settlers who came to Miami hoped for something to start, and they were always sure it was coming. Some of these people looked for the railroad that would connect Miami to the rest of the East Coast. Although it was Henry Flagler who finally brought the railroad to Miami, Mrs. Julia Tuttle, who settled in the area permanently in 1891, may have sold him on the idea. In 1894-95, northern Florida experienced a terrible freeze that killed most of its orange trees and vegetables. Millionaires became paupers overnight. According to the many stories surrounding this event, Mrs. Tuttle sent an orange blossom (or a box of fresh fruits and vegetables) to prove to Mr. Flagler that the southern part of the state was not affected by the frost and therefore represented a good investment for a railroad. Flagler went immediately to Miami, met with Mrs. Tuttle, and agreed within the day to build the railroad. Once it leaked out that trains were coming to Miami, people began moving there by the hundreds—a trend that has only occasionally been interrupted in the past 100 years. Some historians maintain that this account is a myth, and that Henry Flagler had every intention of extending the railroad south of West Palm Beach, regardless of Mrs. Tuttle's negotiations.

Flagler Railroad, Knight's Key Bridge ca. 1908.

Guns and Mangroves

At about the same time the railroad went south to Miami, people settled Fort Myers and various spots in the Ten Thousand Islands area: on Chokoloskee Island, on Barron River, on Halfway Creek, on Turner River, and on Sandfly Island. Only two of these settlements are occupied today: Everglades City on Barron River and Chokoloskee. Mounds in some of these areas indicate that Native Americans also found them good places to live.

What attracted settlers to such isolated spots? With the mild weather, living was easy. A person could hunt crocodiles or alligators for their hides; birds for their feathers; bears, deer, bob-cats, and raccoons for food, hides, or sport. Soil for farming was adequate and fish were ample. Mullet predominated but mack-erel, kingfish, trout, snapper, and redfish were taken in season. Settlers harvested sea turtles and produced charcoal from the buttonwood tree. But life in the

Ten Thousand Islands was not all good: no modern weather technology and no means of communication with the outside world meant that hurricanes hit without warning. And the number of mosquitoes in the rainy season could take on the proportions of a Biblical plague. In his book *Totch: A Life in the Everglades*, Loren G. "Totch" Brown recalls such events and tells readers what it was like to grow up in Chokoloskee.

Chokoloskee eventually had a post office and a school, but island living—and island teach-ing—certainly wasn't for every-one. After the local teacher decided to depart, one resident wrote, "Our schoolteacher, we understand, is going to give up her school today; it is too much for her nerves . . . Maybe we don't need any school—we all know enough anyway."

Some interesting characters lived in the Ten Thousand Islands. Old Man Gomez, who lived on Panther Key, was said to be 124

years old when he died. He maintained that he had met Napoleon Bonaparte, had been a member of Gasparilla's pirate gang, could speak seven lan-guages, and had married a 78-year-old woman when he was 106! Perhaps there is something to that Fountain of Youth story after all.

The story of Ed Watson is part of almost any account of the Ten Thousand Islands. Watson raised crops on the Chatham River and was a good farmer. He also produced syrup from sugar cane. Although the stories that sur-round him often conflict, there is no doubt that Watson had a bent for trouble. He was a contradic-tion of sorts. He worked hard and was successful, making a good living where others had failed. But he often had to give up what he had when he was forced to flee from a bad situation—frequently of his own making. People said he was kind, generous, and helpful, but that his temper was something fearful to behold.

Watson employed many people on his farm at Chatham Bend, including friends, neighbors, drifters, and fugitives. But people who crossed him turned up dead. Stories about Ed Watson began to grow and, true or not, they scared people. In 1910 Watson hired an unsavory lot. At least three of his crew were murdered, including one woman, Hannah Smith. When the sheriff was turned back by the 1910 hurricane, Watson pursued the man who suppos-edly did all the killing. Watson reportedly showed up at Chokoloskee and told his neigh-bors that he had killed the mur-derer. They didn't believe him and wanted to see the body.

Someone questioned whether Watson should be allowed to keep his gun. This enraged Watson, who, true to character, attempted to fire on the crowd. Edgy and frightened, his armed neighbors gunned him down.

Fact or fiction, the story of Ed Watson has become part of the literature of Florida. In his novel *Killing Mister Watson*, Peter Matthiessen explores Ed Watson's story. Set in the mangrove wilderness, the tale is based on legends passed down from early pioneering families. Travelers on the Wilderness Waterway in Everglades National Park can visit Watson's farm site and other historical points of interest from this era.

The End of the Road

In the late 1800s, six families who lived in the village of Flamingo— the southernmost spot in the continental United States— applied for a post office. To have a post office, a town had to have a name. As they stood around pondering options, the residents' gaze must have wandered to Florida Bay. At that time, large flocks of flamingos migrated from Cuba and the Bahama Islands. Flamingo seemed a good name, representing something of the area.

The natives would have done better to name their town Pelican or Mullet. The flamingo is not native to Florida, and after 1902 it was sighted infrequently. Perhaps Mosquito would have been the

best choice. Although residents claimed that after a bit "you just got used to them," mosquitoes were relentless, particularly during the rainy season.

Interesting stories and folklore grew up around mosquitoes. Mothers were reported to bundle their children in layers of newspaper so that they could play outside amid the bugs. One Flamingo resident bought a milk cow and built a screened stall for it. In the morning, once the sun and the breeze were up, the cow went out to graze; in the evening, before dark—and the mosquitoes—descended, it headed on its own for the barn. Cows left out at night suffocated when their noses swelled shut from mosquito bites.

Early fishing shack in the village of Flamingo.

Courtesy: Everglades National Park

Hat decorated with "aigrettes."

Courtesy: Everglades National Park

In his historical novel, *A Land Remembered*, Patrick Smith chronicled the death of cattle being driven to Punta Rassa from the inhalation of mosquitoes.

Most folks kept a sense of humor about the insects. According to one tale, a health official was surprised at the lack of enthusiasm when he told residents that the U.S. government had the means to wipe out 95 percent of the mosquitoes in Flamingo. One native was reported to have replied, "You wouldn't miss 'em."

Flamingoites made their living in several ways. Buttonwood trees were common to the area, so many residents burned them for charcoal. Others hunted, fished, grew sugar cane, smuggled whiskey or refugees, or shot plume birds.

In the late 1800s and early 1900s, fashionable ladies everywhere wore hats decorated with plumes, also called aigrettes. "Egret" comes from the French word *aigrette*, which really means heron. Aigrettes, however, came from both egrets and herons, which grow long, lacy feathers during the breeding season. Hat ornamentation was not limited to gracefully arching plumes but included avian breasts and even whole birds. The millinery industry claimed that the feathers were gently plucked from the birds, or that they dropped off when the birds molted. This was a terrible deception. Birds were actually shot in rookeries while nesting or caring for young. When the parent birds were killed, their eggs rotted, or their fledglings were left to starve or die of exposure under the merciless sun.

Many bird rookeries, or breeding places, are still located on mangrove islands in Florida Bay and the Ten Thousand Islands. Leaves and branches are whitewashed with the guano castings of fish eaters such as herons and egrets. Rookeries are smelly, noisy, frantic places, characterized by the insistent squawking of hungry nestlings and the comings and goings of harried parents. Plume hunters nearly wiped out whole rookeries in pursuit of the aigrettes, which were worth their weight in gold.

Although early hunters were often careful to shoot the birds late in the season after the young had fledged, as the birds became scarce, all conservation measures were sacrificed to avarice. Eventually, even hunters began to complain of the scarcity of birds. In 1901 the National Association of Audubon Societies got behind a law that prohibited the killing of any birds, except game birds. Guy Bradley, who lived in Flamingo with his family, was hired as an Audubon warden to protect the birds of Cape Sable and the Cuthbert rookery.

Guy Bradley had grown up on the Florida peninsula; he was among the first group of pupils who sat at the rough, splintery table in the first red schoolhouse in southern Florida. He even played in the Hypoluxo String Band for dances on Palm Beach. As boys, Guy and his brother

Plumes removed from birds shot in rookeries.

Courtesy: Everglades National Park

Guy Bradley.

Louie had sailed with Charles William Pierce on the *Bonton*. While pursuing poachers—men who were his neighbors—Guy Bradley was shot dead. The accused killers were acquitted. The decision so angered the people of Flamingo that they burned the house of the accused murderers and told them never to come back to the community. The death of the young warden was not in vain. A bitter battle with the millinery trade ensued, and the U.S. government made it illegal after 1910 to even own an egret plume.

Park People

Even after Bradley's death and the murder of a warden near Charlotte Harbor three years later, and after protective legislation had been passed, the battle over plume birds persisted. Poachers continued to kill birds. In some cases whole rookeries were "shot out" by men who passed themselves off as Audubon wardens.

Other resources also declined. Pine, cypress, and mahogany trees were logged in large numbers. Commercial fishers impacted certain species of fish, and hunters bagged great quantities of wildlife. Collectors emerged from hammocks with tree snails, orchids, and other plants and animals. The Florida real estate boom was in full swing. Dredges had been active in the state for several years, since the early 1900s view of wetlands was that they were wastelands. People believed the right thing to do was to get the water off the land so that the land could be used. They dug canals and channel systems to drain the fresh water and divert it to the ocean.

Dredge at work.

Fortunately, there were other people, people of vision, who appreciated the special qualities of this wide, silent land. Biologists recognized that the mix of temperate and tropical species in southern Florida was unique in the United States. Anthropologists surveyed the mounds of early Native Americans and advocated their preservation; stories that rightfully belonged to all generations must not be converted to dust under developers' bulldozers. The life lists of birders swelled with the native and migratory species; ornithologists identified the area as a critical wintering ground and stopover for migratory birds on the eastern flyway, and they acknowledged its extensive rookeries.

The struggle to establish a representative part of the Everglades watershed as a national park involved the efforts and energy of many people. A name that emerges in the park literature but is not widely recognized is that of Ernest F. Coe. At the dedication of Everglades National Park, Ernest Coe was recognized as its

Early dredge on the old Homestead Canal.

"Daddy." A former landscape architect, Coe was the first chairman of the Tropical Everglades National Park Commission, established in 1929. The intent of the commission was to acquire land. At one point, the recommended park boundaries enclosed two million acres, including part of the Florida coral reef. Unfortunately, obtaining this much Florida real estate was not practical. After boundary negotiations, the area established in 1958 comprised 1,406,000 acres.

Recently, Congress extended the eastern boundary of the park. Although not all lands within the extension have been acquired, the park acreage today is 1,506,539 acres. In February 1995, the South Florida Water Management District purchased over 5,000 acres of the Frog Pond, east of Everglades National Park's main entrance, to restore more natural water regimes to Taylor Slough.

Once the U.S. Congress authorized its original boundaries, the proposed park was surveyed by a group that traveled by car, houseboat, plane, and blimp, and, of course, on foot. In his book, *The Birth of the National Park Service: The Founding Years 1913-1933*, Horace M. Albright, former director of the National Park Service, described the presentation of the group's findings to a congressional committee. According to Albright's account, it was a memorable day.

At the hearing, the committee seemed quite impressed by the testimony. Then Representative Owen called on a physician from Johns Hopkins University who had been going to Florida for years and had a famous collection of shells

and pictures of plants and birds. He laid it out on a table and put on an impressive presentation. Just as he was gathering up his collection to leave, he said, "Oh, I forgot something," and reached down under the table. He pulled out a live king snake five feet long and tossed it on the table.

There was instant pandemonium. Members of the Congress drew back. The court reporter looked up, saw the snake coming toward him and toppled over backwards, his stenotype machine crashing down beside him. A woman in the audience fainted and another screamed. Then Representative Ruth Owen, bless her, reached over, picked up the snake and calmly wrapped it around her neck. The sight of the congresswoman with the big snake harmlessly draped over her shoulders restored calm to the session . . .

Although the presentation generated interest, Congress moved slowly. World events also delayed the establishment of an Everglades park as the Second World War consumed the finances and attention of the

nation. Finally, on December 6, 1947, Everglades National Park was dedicated. President Harry S. Truman attended and delivered an address in Everglades (now Everglades City). From the podium, he said:

We have to remain constantly vigilant to prevent raids by those who would selfishly exploit our common heritage for their private gain. Such raids on our natural resources are not examples of enterprise and initiative. They are attempts to take from all the people for the benefit of a few.

A three-cent commemorative stamp was issued the day before the dedication of the park; on it was a map of the state of Florida with Everglades National Park highlighted. The stamp also pictured the simple but elegant long-legged heron—emblematic bird of the entire watershed, saved by stewardship.

Ken DeYonge

· ·

Calusa Memories

The old man was awakened by a sudden breeze as it rustled the leaves of the palm fronds above him. He sat up very slowly and brushed away the black, whining insects that settled on his arm. He shook his head; even the heavy, black smoke from the fire did not discourage them. Some of the people had left the village to escape their whining and bloodletting. But the old man knew he would never leave the village on such a journey again.

He thought of his canoe, hollowed from a great tree; it had carried him on many trips through the narrow, winding channels among the trees that waded into the water on arching, spindly legs. He had followed the canals built by slaves captured in wars waged by his people.

He had been a fine hunter. Many times he had returned to his village with deer, tufts of their soft, brown fur snagged on the rough wood of his canoe.

His mouth watered as he remembered the great feasts of his people. His wife had cooked the deer meat, the juices popping and sizzling as they fell into the fire. The old man had once savored the tangy juice from clams and oysters as he dug the gray meat from the shells and swallowed without chewing. His people had returned time and time again to the same places to feast, sing and tell stories. Eventually, great mounds grew from the shells, bones, and pieces of broken pots that they left behind.

In his mind, the old man saw his people drawing close to the fire and its sooty smoke. As they sat, the women arranged their skirts of tangled, gray moss and held their children close. The men shifted the raccoon tails that hung from their belts to sit more comfortably. The gold ornaments that hung around their necks sparked in the firelight.

The old man was not a chief or even a priest in his village, but his skill was greatly respected. He was a woodcarver. He had created masks of deer, turtles, wolves, bears, and others for the clans who took their power from these creatures. His masks were special; the ears of the deer moved back and forth and the jaw of the wolf opened and closed. The masks were worn by dancers who turned and twisted in the firelight, their figures silhouetted on the great mounds built for such special rites.

He had also learned to work the smooth metal that looked as if it burned with the brightness of the

Ken DeYonge

sun, but was cold to the touch. This metal came from a strange people. Their great canoes struggled in waves and wind that threw them upon the shore and scattered their riches. The villagers had pulled the people from the sea and gathered their bright things.

Some of the villagers feared these strange people. But the old man did not; his people were strong. These strangers who came from the sea would have no power over them. The spears and bows and arrows of the Calusa would turn them away.

The old man felt a tightness and burning in his chest. His head ached and his skin felt hot. He thought, This is what it must feel like to grow old. How could a person know? A person only grew old once. But then the old man thought he remembered hearing children cough and cry that they too were hot. Perhaps he only dreamed it.

He was tired. He had worn himself out with remembering. He lay down on the wooden platform; soon he was asleep. And in his dream his canoe carried him on his final journey.

As to the extinction of the Calusa, a gifted and powerful people, experts differ in their theories. Unrecorded epidemics [diseases introduced by the Spaniards and others] may have been an important factor in their disappearance . .

—Adelaide K. Bullen
Florida Indians of Past and Present

Southern Florida's resources have been affected by events occurring not only within the watershed, but also outside of it: world wars, major weather events such as hurricanes, human migrations due to political unrest in other countries, the establishment of parks. The following Florida time line of the past 100 years or so provides insight into these events and some of their effects on the watershed.

100 Years in the Watershed

1881

Hamilton Disston begins drainage of southern Florida wetlands with a promise from the state of one million acres for 25 cents per acre if he is successful.

1880-1900

Steamboats ferry passengers and cargo from Fort Myers through Lake Okeechobee to Kissimmee and on the Indian River from Jupiter to the Cape Canaveral area. Key West serves as a hub of steamship routes to the Gulf of Mexico, Cuba and the Northeast.

1912

Henry Flagler's railroad to Key West is opened: southern Florida is connected economically to the East Coast and the rest of the nation.

1924-25

The real estate boom reaches its height in southern Florida.

1926

A major hurricane hits Miami, killing about 390 people; the real estate crash begins.

1928

A major hurricane strikes Lake Okeechobee and pulls down 22 miles of muck dike. Between 1,800 and 3,000 people drown. The goals of water management in southern Florida change to include flood protection as well as transportation and drainage of the land for development.

1930s

The economy of Florida, which is heavily based on land speculation, crumbles with the Great Depression that is sweeping the rest of the country.

1935

The Labor Day Hurricane kills 409 people and destroys the railroad through the Florida Keys.

1942-45

Many military personnel are trained in southern Florida for World War II. After the war many of these people return; this is believed to be one of the reasons for Florida's postwar population boom.

1947

Everglades National Park is established.

1949

The Central and Southern Florida Flood Control District is created as the local sponsor of the U.S. Army Corps of Engineers' Central and Southern Florida Flood Control Project.

1965

The freedom flights from Cuba begin; within a period of seven years, more than 261,000 Cuban people flee to Florida.

1971

Disney World opens in Orlando and brings to the watershed not only millions of visitors but also many new permanent residents.

1972

The state legislature passes the Water Resources Act.

1976

The Central and Southern Florida Flood Control District is renamed the South Florida Water Management District in accordance with new responsibilities.

1980

More than 120,000 Cuban people come to southern Florida through the Mariel boatlift.

1992

Hurricane Andrew strikes southern Dade County; damages approach $16 billion.

1994

The Florida Legislature passes the Everglades Forever Act.

Part II

The Altered Watershed: Rearranged Pieces

* *

Rapid population growth in southern Florida and increasing

demands on limited resources, have greatly accelerated natural

change. Parts of the ecological puzzle have been rearranged.

Some may have been lost. The ability to balance human needs

while maintaining the integrity of our environment is being tested.

Chapter 8

Troubled Waters

Recent headlines from Florida newspapers read: "Florida's Water Torture Not Helping Everglades," "The Dead Zone," and "Murder in the Everglades." The advocacy group American Rivers listed the Everglades as the third most endangered American river system. Everglades National Park is frequently cited as the most threatened park in the National Park system. The Everglades watershed is indeed experiencing troubled waters.

Whether we like to admit it or not, people are part of the problem. If the Kissimmee-Okeechobee-Everglades ecosystem is to survive, people must also be part of the solution. What is happening in the Everglades watershed may be a test case for the human ability to achieve balance between needs and desires, and to maintain the ecological integrity of other living things on the planet.

In *Everglades in the Twenty-First Century, The Water Management*

Future, the Everglades Coalition, a consortium of national and Florida conservation organizations, wrote:

The Everglades has been so altered by previous human decisions that survival of the Everglades biological system now depends on the choices that people in Florida and the United States will make in the next few years. The regional water management system and the land use changes made possible by the system have altered the volume, distribution, timing and even the chemical composition of water supplies in the Everglades. Half the historic area of the Everglades has been drained and developed.

Lake Okeechobee is often referred to as the "fluid heart" of the Kissimmee-Okeechobee-Everglades ecosystem. Before the era of Everglades reclamation, water moved from the Upper Chain of Lakes, south of Orlando, into the Kissimmee River and then into Lake Okeechobee. During times of high water, water flowed over

More than 5 million people live in southern Florida.

the southern rim of the lake and spread across the Everglades in a wide, gently moving sheet that finally emptied into Florida Bay and the Gulf of Mexico.

In the late 1800s, drawn by the warm climate and a spirit of exploration, people who migrated south looked for ways to drain the land and make it useful to them. Today, computer modeling demonstrates that settlement in southern Florida could only have occurred naturally on the coastal ridges. Historically, the ridges were dry, and surrounded by coastal and freshwater marshes. Florida's west coast, from the Ten Thousand Islands to Fort Myers, was lined predominantly with a mangrove fringe that blended as a subtle ecotone toward the interior marshes and other plant communities.

Today, most people are aware of the value of wetlands as habitat for wildlife. Wetlands act as filters, clarifying waters; as their plants inhibit the flow of sedi-

What is happening in the Everglades watershed may be a test case for the human ability to achieve balance between needs and desires, and to maintain the ecological integrity of other living things on the planet.

ments, particles settle out of the water column. Wetland plants even metabolize certain pollutants. If not saturated, wetlands can retain water—like a sponge—and serve as catchment areas. These environments, which exhibit a great diversity of plant and animal life, are also valuable for aesthetic and recreational purposes.

But in the late 1800s, people did not understand and appreciate the many functions of wetlands. Wetlands were perceived to be wastelands. As early as 1881, Hamilton Disston began to drain the land around Lake Okeechobee by constructing canals. The state of Florida encouraged this and other drainage programs in order to entice farmers to work the rich, dark soil of the Everglades. Disston was offered one million acres for 25 cents per acre if he could drain it. The fertile soil and the ability to harvest a crop year-round drew settlers to southern Florida. By 1927, the Everglades Drainage District had dug 440 miles of canals and had constructed levees, locks, and dams.

Towboat on the old Homestead Canal.

The state stepped up its flood control programs after the hurricanes of the late 1920s. More than two thousand people died and two thousand were injured in the Lake Okeechobee Hurricane of 1928. Fierce winds blew water out of the lake, causing much of the death and destruction. Will Mclean's song, "Hold Back the Waters," tells of this haunting event. Congresswoman Ruth Bryan Owen described what she saw in Belle Glade on the southeastern shore of Lake Okeechobee 10 days after the storm:

Houses were folded together like a pack of cards. Some places you would see a foundation protrude without walls, here and there were houses upside down. . . . The people were still hunting for bodies. As many had been recovered in the early days, many hundred of them were sent to the coast. . . . It soon became evident that they would have to burn the bodies as they were found, and they were piled in piles and covered with oil and burned.

Herbert Hoover Dike, Lake Okeechobee.

In 1930, the Herbert Hoover Dike was constructed around the lake, and flood protection became not only a state but also a federal responsibility. After seesawing between too much and too little water from 1931 to 1945, southern Florida experienced drought in the late 1940s. As coastal water supplies dwindled, salt water intruded into the aquifer. Fires raged out of control in the Everglades; they were so intense that even the rich muck burned. Then, in 1947, the rains returned, followed by devastating back-to-back hurricanes late in the year. Many lives were lost, much property was demolished, and the region was flooded for a prolonged period. At the unanimous request of state and federal elected officials, the U.S. Army Corps of Engineers was authorized to create a $208 million flood control project that would include 1,400 miles of canals throughout central and southern Florida. In 1949, the Central and Southern Florida Flood Control District was formed to serve as local sponsor and manager of the federal project.

In 1950, the population of the state of Florida was less than 3 million people. By 1990, it had grown to nearly 13 million. With so many people moving to southern Florida, and with the accompanying urban and agricul-

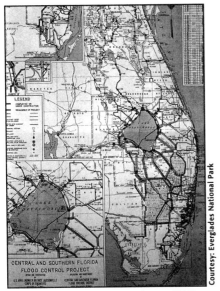

Flood Control District canals, ca. 1970.

tural development, demand on the water system was double the original projections. Initially, the emphasis of water management was on flood control and water supply. As people have developed greater environmental awareness, the district has accepted the broader challenge of "protecting water quality and preserving environmental values."

Who makes decisions about water for southern Florida? The Water Resources Act of 1972 set watershed boundaries for five water management districts in the state. Most of the former Central and Southern Florida Flood Control District remained within the new boundary of the South Florida Water Management District. The district is run by a nine-member board appointed by the governor and confirmed by the state senate. With a budget of more than $300 million, about half of which is derived from property taxes, the district employs nearly 1,600 people and is responsible for a 17,000 square mile area in 16

counties extending from Orlando to Key West, and from Fort Pierce to Fort Myers. The budget is devoted to the seemingly impossible task of balancing the needs of 5.5 million people with the needs of a unique and priceless biologic treasure.

The South Florida Water Management District is responsible for moving water through its system of canals. The network of canals moves water away from farms and urban areas during hurricanes and severe storms. It provides water supplies for populated areas and for agriculture. It maintains a flow of fresh water to the lower east coast to prevent saltwater intrusion. It also provides water to the historic Everglades.

Water is the life-blood of the Everglades. Not only are the quantity and quality of water reaching the marsh critical, but so is the time of year that it comes and the way that it spreads out across the land. Engineers and managers have tinkered with this system for a little more than 100 years; but the plants and animals of the Everglades have matched their life rhythms to natural cycles for thousands of years. In the past, managers seem to have made no attempt to imitate these natural systems. During dry times, only a trickle of water was allowed into the Everglades. For a short time, Everglades National Park was deprived of sheet flow altogether and forced to rely solely on rainfall. Alligators scratched futilely in the parched, cracked marl in search of water. Desperate rangers blasted holes in the bedrock to create refuges for dwindling wildlife—a mea-

sure that rangers today would not likely resort to, although some have advocated it to make up for the natural holes lost when alligators are lured to artificial canals.

Alternately, when water was abundant, managers released great slugs of fresh water into the Everglades. Alligators had built their nests in response to some internal stimulus perceived by their small but ancient reptilian brains—these nests were flooded by the sudden addition of water. Deer, unable to find high ground, swam until they were exhausted then drowned, or slowly starved on tree islands with insufficient vegetation to support them. Nesting birds, dependent on lower water levels to concentrate fish, deserted nestlings when food was too difficult to obtain. Wood storks survived the plume-hunting era only to suffer years of failed nesting due to the radical changes in water levels.

The 1960s was a decade of controversy as concern grew for Everglades National Park. The water management district was criticized for allowing muck fires to burn out of control during dry times and for drowning deer in human-made floods in wet seasons.

Tom Huser, formerly of the water management district, recalls that

Parched, cracked marl.

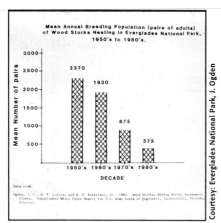

Mean Annual Breeding Population (pairs of adults) of Wood Storks Nesting in Everglades National Park, 1950's to 1980's

Wood stork nesting trends, decades of change.

in 1965 a Mr. R. T. Fisher of the Boston Whaler boat company bought full-page national advertisements in outdoor magazines, headlined "Take a Long Last Look at a Famous National Park or Wake Up the Army Engineers." Fisher called the Corps the "guys in black hats" for cutting off the park's water. According to Huser, a new district board member, Bob Padrick, met with Fisher and pledged to help the park. Fisher must have been convinced: he bought new full page ads that read "Florida Dons the Biggest White Hat."

In an article published on May 6, 1967, noted author Wallace Stegner did not seem convinced of the district's white-hat status. He maintained that as the park dried out, the Corps continued to dump water into the ocean.

Stegner put a new twist on the issue: he maintained that if the park were located in the American West, there would be a law to take care of this situation, "since western water law very early developed the right of prior appropriation." Water law was developed in the West because of

quantity issues. The East, however, is a water-rich area. Further, the state of Florida owns all of its waters and sovereign lands. In southern Florida there was an abundance of water, but getting it to the park was not a political priority. Colonel Tabb of the Army Corps of Engineers, Stegner pointed out, admitted that "agricultural interests did not suffer for water during the years when the park was dying of thirst."

There is a common expression associated with Western water rights: "Whiskey's for drinkin' and water's for fightin'." Many people and organizations in southern Florida fought for the Everglades to have water. Like the Lorax, in the book of the same name by Dr. Seuss, individuals and groups spoke not only "for the trees" but also for alligators, wood storks, deer, tree snails, and orchids. In 1970, Congress put the Water Resource Development Act in place, requiring a minimum water delivery per year to Everglades National Park.

Supporters voicing the needs of wildlife as water users have never been able to rest upon their laurels. One issue that came up in the 1960s and continued into the 1970s and beyond was the building of a jetport just north of the park. Former Interior Secre-

People spoke out for alligators to have water, too.

tary Walter J. Hickel said, "Our best information is that the impact of constructing and operating a commercial jetport at the proposed site, plus the related development that would build up around it, would probably destroy the Everglades." The jetport issue died in 1974; it was resurrected again in the late 1980s and thwarted, but it still deserves watching. The runways constructed before the project was terminated are still there, a discernible scar seen from very high altitudes.

The first executive director of the Florida Conservation District wrote:

Central and southern Florida are not naturally suited for intensive human habitation and use . . . So formidable was the area that, although it was one of the first known to western man, it was one of the last to be settled. In spite of various inducements, it was almost 400 years after discovery of the peninsula before appreciable settlement got underway.

Taking advantage of a marvelous climate and a year-round growing season, people in large numbers finally settled in the Florida wetlands. How much did they know about the ecology of the area before they began tampering with it? Much was lost before we even knew we had anything to lose.

No Shortage of Issues

Most visitors seeing the Everglades for the first time are unaware of the issues associated with the ecosystem. Scientists who commented on the ability of the system to recover after Hurricane Andrew qualified their statements. South Florida Water

Management District biologist Dr. Nick Aumen said, "Though it will take decades for the mangroves and tree canopies to fully return, ecosystems recover—as long as they are healthy."

The health of the Everglades system is impacted by the cumulative effects of myriad stresses that act upon this region. Tom MacVicar, former deputy executive director of the South Florida Water Management District, believes the word "fragile" is misapplied to the Everglades. He has said:

> We had a great biologist named J. Walter Dineen. He wrote a paper in the mid-1970s called "Life in the Tenacious Everglades." His favorite word to describe the Everglades was "tenacious." It was a system designed by nature to burn, flood, go through droughts and extremes of all kinds of weather and it always comes back.

But the tenacity of the Everglades is being tested. Many of the stresses introduced into the

Growing closely together, melaleuca trees squeeze out competitors. The bark peels like scrolls of paper.

system—unlike hurricanes, fires, floods, and drought—have not evolved with it. Many of these stresses are fairly new, originating within the past 50 years or so, and it remains to be seen how the system will accommodate them.

What are these stresses? Pete Rhoads, former director of the Everglades Restoration Program for the water management district, lists three major problems: melaleuca and other nonnative plants; water quantity, or the right amount of water at the right time; and water quality.

Melaleuca is an invasive, nonnative plant species brought from Australia to southern Florida in the early 1900s. It may have been introduced as an ornamental

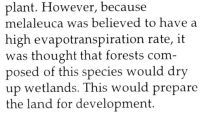

plant. However, because melaleuca was believed to have a high evapotranspiration rate, it was thought that forests composed of this species would dry up wetlands. This would prepare the land for development.

Within its own native system, melaleuca is kept in check by natural enemies; in southern Florida, where it has no natural controls, it is wildly out of balance. The prolific trees grow so closely together that most native vegetation is squeezed out in the competition for water, sunlight, and nutrients. A typical melaleuca produces thousands of seed pods, which burst open after periods of stress such as fire, flood, or virtually any other disturbance. After Hurricane Andrew, scientists worried that melaleuca seeds might have been distributed throughout the southern Everglades. In the 40-mile swath cut through the Glades by Andrew, melaleuca would have outcompeted native vegetation.

Pete Rhoads agrees that the potential spread of the exotic plant was of great concern; but there may be a few factors working in the watershed's favor. Melaleuca trees do not generally disperse seeds until *after* a trauma, so hurricane winds would not have carried the seeds across the Everglades. Water levels were up during and after Hurricane Andrew (although maximum rainfall was only about 8 inches), and the seeds would not have been able to germinate in the saturated or flooded soil. No one is breathing a sigh of relief—the final verdict will not be in for a few years.

Photos: South Florida Water Management District

Melaleuca can grow up to 50 feet tall. In dense stands, the trees adapt and are quite narrow in diameter. Older, isolated trees may be several feet across. On large trees, the bark can be 5 to 6 inches thick. Also called the paperbark tree or cajeput, the melaleuca's bark is white and soft, and it peels off like paper. The seeds are dustlike and easily dispersed by wind. Melaleuca forests can be so dense that people and animals have a tough time traveling through them. Unfortunately, the wet Everglades with its periodic fires is ideal for melaleuca growth. Recent surveys suggest that over 480,000 acres of the Everglades have been infested with the exotic trees.

Stopgap measures to control the spread of this species include aerial application of herbicides, bulldozing, and the hack-and-squirt method (complete girdling of the cambium layer below the bark and application of herbicides). On the ecosystem level,

Casuarina *forest.*

these methods are expensive and temporary.

Considerable effort is going into developing biological controls. More than 400 species of Australian insects have been screened. Melaleuca weevil, which feeds on the growing green tips of the invasive plant, is going through the United States Department of Agriculture's stringent quarantine and testing to ensure that, if released, it would not affect other southern Florida vegetation. To date, according to Rhoads, the USDA has been successful with other biological control programs. Some 60 species of organisms have been released with no known deleterious effects.

A fungus may also be used to infect and kill the melaleuca. Roger Webb, a University of Florida biologist, believes he may have found a natural enemy of the tree, the black fungus *Botryispheria ribis.* The only problem is getting the fungus inside the trees. One idea is to sprinkle the fungus on the backs of the weevils, in a sort of double dose.

When asked if he thinks biocontrol will work, Rhoads replies, "There is a need for continued funding—we must maintain a high level of effort and research. If this doesn't work, I think we may lose the Everglades."

Although melaleuca appears to be the most serious invasive plant at this time, other species affect the Everglades ecosystem. *Casuarina,* also an Australian native and often called the Australian pine represents a threat to coastal areas. Red Reef Park of Boca Raton is one affected area. Australian pines are controlled by

Casuarina *needles.*

mechanical means (cutting down trees and pulling up seedlings) and chemicals. The trees are tall and ungainly and have a shallow root system. They border many of the highways and canals in southern Florida; Hurricane Andrew toppled scores of them into flood control canals. The trees, along with other debris, were a serious and dangerous impediment to flood control. Had 20 inches of rain fallen—not unheard of in tropical storms—even greater property damage and loss of life would have occurred.

Schinus, or Brazilian pepper, a member of the poison ivy family, has established itself all over the watershed. In former agricultural areas in and near the park, where the process of rockplowing was used, Brazilian pepper quickly colonizes the disturbed site. Rockplowing is the technique of augmenting shallow soils overlying the rock ridge by scraping and crushing the top layer of

Brazilian pepper, a nonnative species, has invaded the entire watershed.

limestone. The process makes the substrate more oxygen- and nutrient-rich. Areas that were improved for crops and later abandoned (and virtually any disturbed habitat) are vulnerable to invasion by this introduced species.

Enough Water?

Because Everglades plants and animals adapt their lifestyles to the cycles of wet and dry, it is critical that water managers hold and release the resource in accordance with these seasons. Too much water at the wrong time can be as damaging as too little. Deer starve because their food is under water; submerged alligator eggs rot in the nest.

Why does this happen? One intent of the original canal system was to provide flood control. Flood waters are discharged into Everglades wetlands on a schedule that does not always coincide with natural rhythms. So, in the short term, more water is being introduced into the Everglades than would have been sent there historically. But in the long term,

there is less water moving into the area.

Why less? From Fort Pierce to Key West are some 4 million people with water needs. To protect these people from floods, an East Coast levee system keeps virtually all rain falling east of the levee going to tidewater (the estuary). Some percolates through soils to recharge the aquifer or run off into canals, but this runoff is no longer part of the Ever-

glades system. In fact, it cannot be by law, since it contains urban pollutants that would violate federal and state clean water standards if they were introduced into the Everglades Protection Area.

Southern Florida is water-rich, receiving an average of 60 inches of rainfall annually. In 1994, nearly 90 inches fell. But the physical system of canals now in place was intended to drain the land, and so has affected the amount of water available to natural areas. Serious plans to "replumb" the system are being made by the U.S. Army Corps of Engineers with cooperation from the South Florida Water Management District. The cost will soar into the billions of dollars.

Cities along the Florida coast get their water mainly from well fields. During dry periods, enough fresh water must be pumped into these well fields to keep salt water from moving inland into the drinking water supply. With an average per capita consumption of 185 gallons per day, 50 percent of which goes

Water is metered into the Glades through flood control structures.

to irrigate lush landscapes, there is competition for the resource. The South Florida Water Management District must balance these demands. Today, the agency is giving the Everglades environment first priority.

What's being done to create a more equitable or more natural distribution of water? Pete Rhoads focuses this issue more sharply by asking, "What do the remnants of the Everglades system need in the way of water supply?" Rhoads does not feel anyone really knows what the optimal freshwater inflows to the Everglades should be right now.

Some scientists (including Rhoads) feel that a "vision" should be established of what we want the remaining wild Everglades to look like in 2010. Recognizing the stresses that the environment is currently experiencing, where along the spectrum of possibilities do we set our sights? At one extreme, we would return the natural system to the pristine conditions of 150 years ago, at the other, we would allow it to be swallowed up by development. The first is impossible to obtain, the second undesirable.

In *Flatland*, author Edwin Abbott said, "We cannot return to days gone by, nor avoid the coming of tomorrow. We can neither hasten nor retard our journey into the future." The question is, how can we balance what we want with what we can reasonably expect to have in light of the present stresses on the system? Manipulating the water regimen in order to plan for the Everglades of tomorrow is a complex task.

One example of the complexity is the problem of accommodating sea level rise. Documentation confirms that the sea level is rising in southern Florida and that this trend will continue. The real issue is, will it accelerate?

Much of the watershed is at a low elevation—south of Lake Okeechobee, the land is typically less than 25 feet above mean sea level. Many sections are less than 3 feet above sea level. If the sea level rises some 12 inches over the next 50 years, a significant portion of the Everglades will be affected. How will this change the management of the ecosystem? According to Rhoads, "What we had . . . and what we have now [are] not going to be the same as what we will have for the future, if for nothing else than the sea level rise issue." There is considerable scientific debate about how soon and how high the sea level will rise, as well as about potential effects.

What are the potential effects? If nothing is done about changing freshwater flows, the rise will have a vegetative effect. It may change the range of mangroves and the inward extent of salt marsh vegetation, thereby reducing freshwater marshes. Sea level rise is one more variable in a whole set of tough questions on southern Florida water management. Water Management District Environmental Education Coordinator Roy King describes the situation simply and directly: "Nature bats last."

Other problems in the watershed are more imminent than sea level rise. Florida Bay, located between the Florida mainland and the Florida Keys, is the watershed's largest marine system. It sits at the downstream end of the watershed, and suffers the cumulative effects of everything that happens upstream. The bay supports a multimillion dollar commercial fishing industry, involving about 3,200 jobs. Recently, fishing guides, commercial fishers, motel owners, dive boat operators, real estate agents, and Keys residents joined environmentalists and others to stop the degradation of the bay, which is affecting the economic and social structure of the Florida

Florida Bay, the watershed's largest marine system, supports an abundance of life.

Courtesy: Everglades National Park

Keys. But, in the words of cartoon character Pogo, "We have met the enemy and it is us." There are 87,000 permanent residents and some 2 million visitors to the Keys each year, and the area has no comprehensive sewage treatment system. Most homes and businesses have septic tanks. This is just one root of the crisis.

Florida Bay has a large bird population. About 25 percent of the U.S. population of roseate spoonbills nests on its mangrove islands. Great white herons, brown pelicans, cormorants, ospreys, bald eagles, white pelicans, numerous shorebirds, and many other species either nest or winter in the bay. The mangroves and sea grass beds support lobsters, shrimp, and many finfish such as mangrove snapper, snook, and mullet. The endangered American crocodile nests on the bay's sandy beaches.

But in some areas the bay's clear waters are clouded by massive algal blooms. Large die-offs of sea grass have been occurring since the late 1980s. In 1991, mangroves began dying in certain areas. Hurricane Andrew contributed significantly to mangrove destruction in its devastating trek across the southern Everglades. The decomposition of the dead materials introduced nutrients

Algal bloom, Florida Bay.

South Florida Water Management District

into the waters that fostered large algal blooms. The blooms have seriously affected sea grasses and sponge beds, which act as protective nurseries for juvenile spiny lobsters.

Another dilemma stems from the fact that the degraded waters of Florida Bay are not contained. Many believe that the deteriorating conditions of the bay are affecting the coral reefs on the ocean side of the middle Keys. Since Florida Bay is very shallow, considerable evaporation takes place during the summer months. When sea water evaporates, it leaves salts behind; the remaining water becomes hot and even more salty. These conditions are exaggerated in years of drought; then, rainfall and upstream flow from Taylor Slough (through Everglades National Park) do not replenish and freshen the system. The bay's hot, saline water is denser than normal sea water. It flows through channels between the Keys to the reef system. Coral cannot tolerate high temperatures, high salinity, or low oxygen.

Via the media, a concerned public talks about the catastrophe as the meltdown of Florida Bay. "The Dead Zone," an article appearing in *The Miami Herald*, reported: "It may be the Keys' worst crisis since missiles were pointed at it from Cuba three decades ago." "This is like an atomic bomb hitting the Keys," said former state representative Ron Saunders, noting that nearly every job in the Keys is linked to tourism or fishing. "If the ecology goes down, the economy goes down."

Many scientists agree that a factor in the degradation of Florida Bay

Courtesy: Everglades National Park

Conditions in Florida Bay may affect coral reefs.

is reduced freshwater flow. In this intricately connected system, freshwater input is as critical for spiny lobsters and mangrove snappers as it is for alligators and nesting birds. The South Florida Water Management District and the U. S. Army Corps of Engineers have taken emergency measures to address this problem. A total "replumbing" may be necessary for a lasting solution.

The Bay is the terminus of the Kissimmee-Okeechobee-Everglades watershed. Fresh surface water moves into Florida Bay from sheet flow across the prairies of the southern Everglades. Fresh water also enters from 20 creek systems that receive water from Taylor Slough and the C-111 canal. Shark River Slough drains into Whitewater Bay. This water moves around Cape Sable and enters western Florida Bay. In this estuarine environment, these waters bathe the eggs and young of many species—at least 22 of particular commercial and recreational interest. Water temperature, salinity, and chemistry, which must remain within tolerance levels for these developing organisms, depend on amount of rainfall, freshwater flow, evaporation, circulation, and flushing.

In the past, fresh water moved into Florida Bay directly from Taylor Slough. Dr. G. Thomas Bancroft, a scientist with the National Audubon Society, maintains:

Everglades National Park personnel have examined in detail the management of water in the Taylor Slough Basin. They have shown that the construction of the Central and Southern Florida Flood Control Project decreased flows through Taylor Slough and contributed in a major way to the degradation of Florida Bay.

Through predictions derived from computer modeling and physical research, scientists have determined that water flowing into Florida Bay from Taylor Slough should be three to five times greater annually. Water managers have the capability to move more water into the bay. East Everglades tomato farmers in an area called the Frog Pond, fearing their fields would be flooded, did not support this action. The Florida legislature gave the South Florida Water Management District authority to condemn approximately 1,700 acres as part of the 1994 Everglades Forever Act. Farmers opted to sell out completely. In early March 1995, the water management district took title to 5,200 acres of the Frog Pond.

Researchers estimate that Florida

Bay receives less than one tenth of the fresh water that flowed into it before channelization of the southern Florida ecosystem. In addition, areas filled for the construction of the Flagler railroad reduced circulation within the Bay itself. Some believe that the Bay has become stagnant because a major hurricane has not flushed the system in 33 years. Further freshwater flow does not just moderate salinity in estuaries, it also carries nutrients for primary producers.

Since the summer of 1987, large areas in western Florida Bay have been stripped of turtle grass. This event is historically unprecedented in the Bay, nor has tropical seagrass mortality of this extent been reported in the scientific literature. Reduced freshwater flow into Florida Bay is believed to contribute to this die-off. While several factors may be at fault such as seagrass density, storm frequency, and flushing rate, some researchers maintain that long-term saline stress may have contributed to making turtle grass more suscep-

tible to other negative conditions.

Two types of blooms have also occurred in the Bay. The release of nutrients in sediments probably caused blue-green bacteria (cyanobacteria) blooms in the central and eastern bay. Such releases are directly related to seagrass dieback. The bloom in western Florida Bay is caused by other nutrient sources, possibly from the Shark River Slough or the Gulf of Mexico.

In resolving resource issues, people frequently become polarized as the argument focuses on "jobs vs. the environment." In the book *Entering the Watershed*, authors Doppelt, Scurlock, Frissell, and Karr contend that it is not a matter of jobs against the environment, but of jobs against jobs.

Maintaining or increasing the nation's primary production—in agriculture, fisheries, or forestry, for example—is the foundation of a sustainable economy. Maintaining the natural ecological and biological systems that produce those products is the fundamental step

Florida Bay is the terminus of the Kissimmee-Okeechobee-Everglades watershed.

required to achieve sustainability. Protection and restoration of healthy riverine systems and biodiversity is essential, not just for the potential value of genetic resources, recreation and tourism, but also because these systems provide important ecological functions that support all economic activity and human welfare.

Most agree that in the Bay, it is not just a matter of water quantity, but also of water quality. Many reports indicate that improper sewage disposal in the Keys is causing a far greater problem for Florida Bay than was previously thought. Since some pollutants originate farther north—in the area of Lake Okeechobee and in the headwaters of the Kissimmee-Okeechobee-Everglades system near Turkey Lake—some prefer to place responsibility there.

The Florida Bay ecosystem is analogous to a fine watch. If its gears become worn and slightly out of sync, the watch continues to run but will begin to lose time. The change is imperceptible at first—just a second lost here or there. But the watch falls behind, and when it is no longer functioning as a unit it stops. Although the situation may not be as radical as the watch metaphor suggests, many contend that Florida Bay is running out of time.

Undoubtedly, many complex factors have contributed to the decline. Fortunately, citizens, scientists, students, water managers, and government leaders have joined forces to begin healing the Bay.

Good Enough?

The Everglades functions as a low-nutrient, oligotrophic system, with particularly low levels of phosphorus. Although the addition of nutrients enriches the system, overenrichment in the Everglades causes changes in water quality, in levels of oxygen and sediments, and in the growth of algae and other plants; it even alters food chains. The transition from saw grass to cattails is indicative of nutrient loading. When nutrient levels are high, cattails outcompete saw grass, initiating a domino effect that has ramifications throughout the natural system. Steven M. Davis, in *Everglades: The Ecosystem and its Restoration*, notes that:

Accompanying the shift from sawgrass to cattail at eutrophic sites are changes in organic sediment texture, periphyton communities, dissolved oxygen, microbial communities, macroinvertebrate communities and plant transpiration rates.

Front of cattails advances on a saw grass community.

How is phosphorus entering the Everglades system? Some researchers maintain that agriculture makes a sizable contribution. Runoff from sugar cane and vegetable fields south and west of Lake Okeechobee in the Everglades Agricultural Area contains large concentrations of phosphorus and nitrogen. Although phosphorus in fertilizers makes crops grow, it also helps cattails prevail over saw grass. Water flows from the Everglades Agricultural Area into the Water Conservation Areas, then into Everglades National Park. Some scientists identified this nutrient problem in the Everglades 20 years ago, but at that time it was not of major public concern. Others maintain that phosphorus is removed by wetlands that separate the Everglades Agricultural Area from the park.

South Florida Water Management District

Everglades National Park

Stormwater Pollutants

Some Stormwater Pollutants, Their Sources, and Their Effects

Pollutant	Sources	Effects
sediment	cropland; urban surfaces; construction sites	decreased clarity; sedimentation; damage to coral reefs; loss of recreational potential
nutrients	agricultural land; sewage; lawns	increased plant growth; algal blooms; concentration of organic debris; reduced oxygen levels; change in species; reduced sport/ commercial fishery
pesticides	cropland; mosquito control; lawns	loss of aquatic microflora/ fauna; sea grass mortality; altered aquatic populations; loss of recreational potential; reduced sport/ commercial fishery
toxic waste	industry; acid rain; highways	death of organisms; human health hazards; loss of recreational potential; loss of sport/com- mercial fishery; nonpotable water

In 1988, the federal government sued the state of Florida (the former Florida Department of Environmental Regulation) and the South Florida Water Management District for not maintaining the quality of water flowing into Everglades National Park and Loxahatchee National Wildlife Refuge. The suit threatened to drag on for years at great expense to taxpayers, until Florida Governor Lawton Chiles vowed to end the legal struggle and get on with saving the Everglades. He conceded in 1991 that the state was polluting the region. The settlement agreement reads:

In recognition of the serious and potentially devastating degradation threatening the Park and the Refuge as a result of nutrient-laden waters, and to further a process that resolves ongoing litigation, the Parties commit themselves to guarantee water quality and water quantity needed to preserve and restore the unique flora and fauna of the Park and the Refuge (the Arthur R. Marshall Loxahatchee National Wildlife Refuge, also known as Water Conservation Area 1).

The agreement commits the state to achieve water quality standards by July 1, 2002. In reference to water quantity it states, "Quantity, distribution and timing of water flow to the Park and Refuge must be sufficient for maintaining and restoring the full abundance and diversity of the native floral and faunal communities throughout the Park and the Refuge." The settlement was challenged by the Miccosukees (a Florida Native American tribe) and by agricultural interests, and, once again, restoration of the

Everglades was put on hold.

In 1994, the Florida legislature passed the Everglades Forever Act. The law calls for the construction of 40,000 acres of Stormwater Treatment Areas (STAs). Ironically, the problem has become the solution. Scientists have proposed setting up large "filters" using cattails, which thrive on phosphorus, to create natural treatment systems that are, in fact, cattail wetlands. Water from the Everglades Agricultural Area will move into the STAs for filtration, then into the Water Conservation Areas, and finally into the park and Florida Bay. By the end of the summer of 1993, the district had completed construction of the prototype STA known as the Everglades Nutrient Removal Project (ENR). Some 3,700 acres of constructed wetland, the project is an engineering test case for STAs. Water leaving the ENR has had phosphorus loads reduced from 150 parts per billion to 50 parts per billion or less.

Farmers are also assuming responsibility for the Everglades cleanup. They will pay an "agriculture privilege tax" and are now employing Best Management Practices (BMPs), which could include more conservative use of fertilizers. They have financial incentives to clean up the water before it leaves their land.

Still, farming activities in the 700,000-acre Everglades Agricultural Area are hotly disputed. Some environmentalists acknowledge that they will not be satisfied until farming is eliminated from the area. Some say that farmers do not pay a fair price for

Lagoon traps wastes and nutrients from dairy farm.

the water they use. Others maintain that sugar cane and vegetables are the lesser of evils—the Everglades would suffer greater degradation if condominiums, golf courses, and shopping malls replaced sugar cane fields.

Although most people agree that water quality and quantity should be restored to Everglades National Park, the question is who pays. In response to a proposed tax increase, some southern Florida taxpayers argue that they should not bear the financial burden. They claim that because "big sugar" has profited while degrading the system, "big sugar" should pay. The issue of "fair share" was negotiated with leading environmental agencies (representing the people), and the contribution of industry mandated by the Everglades Forever Act was considered its fair share.

Farming interests maintain that they are not entirely responsible for the degradation of the Everglades because they did not construct the canal system. The Everglades Forever Act recog-

nizes that urban encroachment on the Everglades also contributes to its malaise. The law authorized the South Florida Water Management District to levy a homeowners tax for the STAs. The average homeowner pays about $10 a year toward the restoration.

The diking of Lake Okeechobee affected the natural flow of water to the Everglades. But the lake itself has also experienced serious

degradation. In the 1980s algal blooms blanketed large areas of the lake. Scientists maintained that these blooms were the result of phosphorus and nitrogen introduced from dairy farms north of the lake and from backpumping to drain the Everglades Agricultural Area. Many dairy farms were bought out by the state. Some relocated or installed Best Management Practices and systems that removed the nutrients. These measures, of course, had a negative impact on the economy of the area. Backpumping has been curtailed but not eliminated. Flood protection is necessary in southern Florida, and when water levels reach a certain height above mean sea level, the pumps are turned on. In 1994, with a total rainfall of over 90 inches, backpumping took place on several occasions for extended periods of time. Heavy rains in late 1995 forced the district to backpump again. However, the agricultural industry maintains that only about 5 percent of the

Sugar cane production is a major industry.

lake's water budget is contributed by backpumping. Further, the Everglades Forever Act calls for reducing this amount to less than 1 percent through local drainage district diversion to future STAs.

Long Water Returns

Situations affecting the Everglades and Florida Bay originate even farther north. The largest tributary of Lake Okeechobee, the Kissimmee River (Kissimmee is a Calusa Indian word meaning "long water"), once meandered nearly 103 miles before it was channeled. Now it is a 56-mile, 30-foot-deep canal that could best be described as a straight shot from the outlet of Lake Kissimmee to Lake Okeechobee.

Work began on the channeling project in 1961 and was completed about 10 years later. Even before the project was finished, there was a movement under way (led in part by Art Marshall, for whom the National Wildlife Refuge in Water Conservation Area 1 is named) to have the river restored. Since 1984, the South Florida Water Management District has been involved in research to design an approach to Kissimmee River restoration.

Lou Toth has been a principal biologist on the project since that time. He explains that the Kissimmee River restoration will be restoration in its purest sense. That is, there will be a total reversal of human-induced environmental degradation. "Once you reestablish the determinants of ecological integrity," Toth says, "the system will reorganize or evolve into a system you had historically."

How will the river be restored? In simple terms, the engineers will

Water managers are now restoring the Kissimmee River to its historic channel.

be "putting the dirt back in the ditch." In reality, the restoration is much more complicated. Part of the process involves reestablishing historic flow patterns from the headwaters area to the river. In addition, a center section of the canal will be filled in, and former isolated river channels will be recarved by natural water flow. The remnant sections of the river channel will be connected. This will result in about 40 linear miles of continuous, connected river channel fed by natural inflows from the Upper Basin. Within this section will be a completely restored ecosystem. The canal, levees, and local drainage structures will be gone. The feasibility of this process has been demonstrated through construction of a scale model and a 1,000-foot engineering test fill.

Because of flood control restraints, including those for the Kissimmee-Saint Cloud area and nearby Disney World, only a middle section of the river will be restored. However, this represents 40 square miles of river floodplain ecosystem that will be reclaimed, and within that area some 320 fish and wildlife species will benefit. According to Lou Toth, there is no other restoration project that represents the range of benefits that this project has. In terms of area, it is the largest restoration project in the world.

How does the restoration of the Kissimmee River benefit the lower watershed and Florida Bay? The restored area will provide additional habitat for waterfowl and wading birds. It will add additional feeding and breeding grounds for many species. From the Kissimmee

Photos: South Florida Water Management District

A River Comes Home,
The Kissimmee

Twisting and turning, the little river flowed patiently, unhurried on its way from Lake Kissimmee to Lake Okeechobee or "big water." The river was named by the Seminole Indians of southern Florida. These same people said the river was made by a big snake that crawled down the center part of the peninsula to the large lake.

The Calusa Indians, who lived hundreds of years before the Seminoles, named the river Kissimmee or "long water." Imagine a Calusa following the small winding river as he poles a cypress canoe. He is bronze colored with long, black hair. In his canoe are pottery, shell, and bone ornaments that he will trade for flint and some copper.

He follows the river north. He sees black bears feeding on palmetto berries and deer grazing in the marshes on each side of the river. The green tree tops turn white as thousands of ibis and egrets roost on the branches. Ducks settle in great flocks on the wetlands created by the river. Many fish come to the water's surface to feed on insects. As the evening air grows cooler, alligators slide silently into the warmer water from their "sunning" places on the river's banks. A red wolf howls in the distance. The bear, the fish, the bird, the man–the river provides for all of them.

Many years pass. The Calusa Indians no longer exist. Seeking a new home far to the south in the Everglades, the Seminoles follow the little river to escape the soldiers who pursue them. Settlers build their houses on the banks of the river. Steamboats travel up and down the watercourse to bring flour, salt, guns, and bullets to the homesteaders in exchange for deer meat, alligator hides, and other animal skins. The river provides for the people, but not enough. It is too narrow and too shallow. The river is widened and deepened.

More and more people move to the river and to Lake Kissimmee from which it flows. But in some seasons, the sky boils with black clouds that block out the sun. Wind blows with a terrible power, and the rain falls in sheets. The little river overflows its banks. Water from the lake gets deeper and deeper. Homes and businesses are flooded; lives are lost. The people say the river must be controlled.

Huge dredges move across the land and change the shape of the river. Now it is deep and wide and very straight. The water in its bends and folds becomes still and stagnant. Its name is changed. It is now called C-38. A once 103-mile winding river is a straight canal 56 miles long.

Water that overflowed the river's banks during the rainy season wet the marshes where ducks and other water birds rested and fed. When the wetlands dried up, most of the birds did not return. The deep waters of the canal could not provide for the fish in ways the river had. Soon there were fewer and smaller fish for birds, otters, and people to catch. The bends and folds of the river that had traveled some 100 miles from Lake Kissimmee to Lake Okeechobee cleaned and refreshed the water that flowed thróugh them. "Big Water" into which C-38 flowed became more and more polluted.

Many people were concerned; they wanted to be protected from flood waters, but they missed the abundant wildlife and the river. They asked, was it possible to return a river to its home? In southern Florida, there has been a call to restore the Kissimmee River, to allow it to flow through its old river channel, the curves and folds that had once been its home. Engineers and biologists from government agencies which included the South Florida Water Management District, the Army Corps of Engineers, and

the Florida Game and Fresh Water Fish Commission have developed restoration plans. A huge model–100 feet by 100 feet (half the size of a football field)–was designed in an indoor laboratory to test their ideas.

When the canal was originally dug from 1960 to 1971, the dirt or spoil was left on the river bank. About 23 miles of the middle section of C-38 will be "backfilled." This will force the water into the abandoned bends of the Kissimmee River and bring back 43 miles of river channel and 26,500 acres of floodplain wetlands. More than 300 fish and wildlife species, including several endangered species, are expected to benefit.

Will it work? When engineers did a test fill in one small part of C-38, the water moved to the old bends. Wetlands plants and animals returned to the reflooded land that had been dry pasture.

Restoring the Kissimmee River is the largest project of its kind in the world; it will require about $300 million, over 50 million tons of dirt, and 15 years to complete.

As we learn more about the environment and the effects of our actions on it, there will be more restoration projects around the world. The area of restoration offers many interesting career opportunities. Maybe someday your efforts will allow a river to return home.

Because of its limited range in southern Florida, the Cape Sable seaside sparrow is threatened by habitat alterations.

longer periods, as they were historically, but finds this may affect the threatened sparrow. Dr. John Ogden, former restoration biologist for the park, maintains that we are forcing these species to go back to where they started. Ogden feels that restoration projects must work together "with some element of faith in this transition period" while species sort themselves out.

In the document *Everglades in the Twenty-First Century*, the Everglades Coalition makes the following statement:

> More than any other of our great national parks, Everglades National Park lives in its waters. More than any other, it is dependent on human choices—water management choices—to sustain its life. More than any other, its whole fabric is threatened by the choices we have made. . . . We will repeat our fundamental view about the proper human relation to it: No cause can be permitted to degrade Everglades National Park or reduce its value to the ecosystem and to future generations of Americans . . .

When asked if they are hopeful or pessimistic about the survival of the Everglades, park administrators, naturalists, researchers, South Florida Water Management

River through Lake Okeechobee and into Everglades National Park, benefits will spread throughout the landscape.

Because the restored area will represent a mosaic of habitat types and will provide prime breeding grounds, it is expected that the population of birds throughout the Okeechobee and Everglades area will increase. Because the Kissimmee Basin will provide habitat for migratory waterfowl in winter, the benefit to these species will extend throughout their range. The Kissimmee area attracts white ibis, snowy egrets, glossy ibis, great blue herons, great egrets, and wood storks.

"I Belong"

The managers of the Kissimmee-Okeechobee-Everglades ecosystem struggle daily with water quantity and quality considerations and the effects of invasive, nonnative species, and with many other issues as well. In their attempts to restore the Everglades, federal, state, and local agencies often find themselves in

a kind of Catch-22. The area is home to several endangered plants and animals. As scientists work to restore the Everglades through a "greater ecosystem" management approach, they find their goals conflict with those of other agencies whose mandates require them to focus on endangered species. Resource managers might attempt to drain impoundments and move water to areas that were traditionally wet and are now too dry, but they may run into opposition from species-specific managers. For example, water management district officials were stymied in an effort to move more water into the area east of Everglades National Park because the seaside sparrow— listed as threatened— nested in the area.

Many species have rearranged themselves in response to the hydrology imposed by canals and levees, among them the Cape Sable sparrow, which has moved into overdrained marshes. Everglades National Park wants to keep those marshes wet for

Everglades naturalist with school group.

· ·

District scientists, educators and governing board members, and leaders in the environmental movement consistently reply that they are "cautiously optimistic."

In the face of these diverse issues, how is optimism warranted? John Ogden and long-respected park biologist Bill Robertson both feel that there is now a real spirit of cooperation among state and federal agencies. A hopeful sign was the formulation (in 1993-94) of a "collective vision" for the Kissimmee-Okeechobee-Everglades ecosystem by the South Florida Water Management District (see sidebar). Among the strategic goals of the district stated in *Vision 2050* are the following: determine the feasibility of changes to the Central and Southern Florida Project to restore the southern Florida ecosystem; restore the Kissimmee River; protect and enhance Lake Okeechobee; restore the Everglades and Florida Bay; develop water supply plans for all "reasonable-beneficial" uses; and protect and enhance estuarine systems.

Alan Milledge, a third-generation Floridian and former chairman and member of the South Florida Water Management District Governing Board, maintains that "the mandate of the South Florida Water Management District is that the health of natural systems comes first." "The mother system comes first!" he adds. Milledge's comments reflect his personal commitment to southern Florida, and further, a positive political atmosphere in which the Everglades may get the attention, the financial resources, and the time the area needs to heal. Secretary

Vision 2050

Vision 2050, which presents the South Florida Water Management District's view of what southern Florida will look like in the year 2050, is based on assumptions articulated in the District Water Management Plan, Volume I (October, 1994), and is repeated here verbatim:

• The South Florida ecosystem will more closely resemble its natural, predevelopment state and will function more naturally, in terms of hydrology, water quality, and environmental values. The Kissimmee River Restoration and the Upper Chain of Lakes project (higher lake levels) will be completed. The Lake Okeechobee water quality improvement work will be completed. The various projects to improve water flow and quality to the Everglades will be completed. More natural hydroperiods and flow distribution in the Water Conservation Areas will be established. Everglades National Park will receive water of appropriate quality and quantity, delivered at appropriate locations and times to insure restored environmental values. The distribution and timing of fresh water flows will be improved from Everglades National Park to Florida Bay.

• Population will approximately triple in the district. To accommodate this growth, urban development will expand beyond current urban areas. Publicly owned buffer areas will be established between urban and natural areas to protect sensitive natural features from potential pollutants generated in urban areas.

• The urban Lower East Coast will need to rely less on the regional water management system for future water supplies. This can be accomplished via a variety of actions: multifunctional regional and local water storage areas; aquifer storage and recovery; reverse osmosis treatment of ground or ocean water; wastewater reuse and other new ultraefficient water technologies that may be developed within the next 50 years.

• Agriculture will continue to be a major industry in southern Florida, focusing in the Everglades Agricultural

Area (EAA), the areas around Lake Okeechobee, and the Kissimmee River Basin. Soil subsidence will reduce the land area available for agriculture in the EAA. In addition, some portion of the EAA will be devoted to Stormwater Treatment Areas associated with Everglades restoration.

• Acquisition of environmentally sensitive land will continue to be a major tool for environmental restoration and preservation and will be a high priority of the public and the district.

• Estuarine and coastal water quality will more closely resemble predevelopment conditions than at the present. The development of areas to store urban stormwater runoff will reduce the flow of runoff and its accompanying pollutants into estuaries and coastal waters. In addition, releases from Lake Okeechobee into the Indian River Lagoon, Biscayne Bay, and Charlotte Harbor will be reduced to lessen the impacts of large freshwater flows into these important estuaries.

• In the Florida Keys, centralized wastewater systems and/or other new treatment technologies will eliminate the use of septic tanks, major contributors to nearshore water quality problems. Actions in other issue areas, such as dock and marina siting and regulation and surface water management, will contribute to improved water quality.

The magnitude of the changes necessary to move from current conditions to the realization of *Vision 2050* will require the ongoing commitment and participation of all levels of government—local, regional, state, and federal. The water resource management responsibilities of the district, the State of Florida, and the federal government must be clearly delineated, communicated, and accepted by all involved agencies. In particular, the significance of local governments' land use decisions in determining the water supply and flood protection needs of southern Florida must be recognized. These decisions also directly impact water quality, and the level of effort and cost of restoring various elements of the ecosystem.

of the Interior Bruce Babbitt has said, "The Everglades is a test case for all ecosystems in the entire country. This is the one that needs attention now."

Recently, Bill Laitner, formerly of Everglades National Park, said, "The Everglades can change people's lives forever." In the 1970s, the park began an environmental education program that has connected nearly half a million young Floridians with their wild Everglades heritage. In the early years, naturalists conducted an activity called "Web of Life." Students were given brightly colored buttons, each one bearing a picture of a plant, an animal, a person, or one of the primal elements (soil, air, water, sun). There were pictures of garfish, alligators, egrets, mosquitoes, and people. Under each picture were the simple words, "I Belong." Students pinned on the buttons and stood in a big circle. A ranger introduced a large ball of yarn and handed it to the student who was

Young people discover the Everglades.

the sun; this student connected to a plant, who in turn connected to a deer, and so forth. The circle was quickly transformed into a marvelous web. The activity pointed out that humans, like saw grass and alligators, "belong" to and are part of—not apart from—the web.

"You know," Bill Laitner said, "we hired a seasonal ranger this year who brought with her an "I Belong" button that she received from an Everglades ranger when she was 12 years old. Talk about the web of life!"

The South Florida Water Management District also invests in the

future by promoting public education today, especially that of teachers and schoolchildren. Each year, nearly 450 teachers participate in a two-day workshop. Approximately 200,000 instructional booklets are delivered annually to the schools in the 16-county area of the watershed. Over the past five years, the South Florida Water Management District has entered into nearly 30 environmental education partnerships with schools, organizations, and agencies, including Everglades National Park. This book is the result of such a collaboration between the water management district and The Watercourse.

The district's vision of 2050 is also concerned with educating adults—providing them with opportunities to recognize their connection with the web of life in this unique watershed. The Everglades cannot wait 10 years until children grow up, graduate, and become responsible voters. For all of our "guarded optimism," the Everglades needs our attention, now. If we want to provide a legacy of saw grass and cypress, alligators and tree snails, and still, quiet places where tomorrow's children can belong, the preservation of the watershed must be the responsibility of citizens today. Margaret Mead said, "Never doubt that a small group of thoughtful, committed citizens can change the world; indeed, it's the only thing that ever has!"

A Question of Values

What is the significance of seeing an alligator basking in the sun at the edge of a pond? Of discovering a rainbow-colored tree snail grazing a field of lichens on a tree trunk? Of hearing a chorus of tree frogs; of marveling at the acrobatic ability of a corn snake climbing a tree in search of eggs; of observing an egret, a spoonbill, or a rare bird madly dashing about the mud flat—as it has done for far longer than we have been in this place? What is the value of a swarm of mosquitoes; of a golden orb weaver spider; of a family of river otters; of a snail kite delicately eviscerating an apple snail? Partly value lies in the idea of constancy. Wordsworth wrote about rainbows, but he might have been treating all things natural when he wrote:

So was it when my life began;

So is it now I am a man;

So be it when I shall grow old . . .

Perhaps seeing an uncommon white bird or a relative of a long extinct giant reptile reminds us of the ultimate meaning of preservation, stewardship, and wise management. We preserve a legacy for the children of the future in the hope that they will care about alligators, snakes, panthers, tree snails, and rare white birds. It is in places like the relatively pristine portions of the Everglades watershed where Wordsworth's young boy and old man may share a common experience with another sovereign nation. It is a place where we can make this connection, where we can better appreciate our bond with other living beings, and accept the responsibility of saving them for future generations.

In southern Florida, the ability to satisfy human needs while maintaining the integrity of the environment is being tested. Other countries with fewer resources are monitoring our success or failure in restoring this system. But more importantly, the Everglades ecosystem represents an opportunity for people and a river to come home again—to belong.

South Florida Water Management District

Chapter 9

A Portfolio of Problems

Perhaps more than with any other large natural system, the natural mechanisms of the Kissimmee-Okeechobee-Everglades ecosystem have been altered by human intervention.

People generally agree that water quality and quantity problems in the Everglades and southern Florida estuaries have resulted from human manipulations of the natural systems of the watershed. The watershed and its ecological processes have been significantly changed, though the changes are not necessarily irrevocable. Since the first canal was dug by Native Americans, people have been unsuccessful in restoring the complex natural balance among atmospheric, surface, and ground water. Perhaps of greatest concern to the integrity of the Everglades is the timing, distribution, quantity, and quality of waterflow.

To aid in planning and management of the watershed's water resources, the South Florida Water Management District is developing modeling tools that simulate water quantity and quality, as well as environmental responses to various conditions within the watershed. These

Forty percent of the state's population lives in southern Florida.

planning tools offer resource managers a means of predicting and evaluating the effects of changes to the natural system. The South Florida Regional Simulation Model, the Natural System Model, the Wetlands Water Quality Model, the Everglades Landscape Model, and others now being developed for the Kissimmee-Okeechobee-Everglades-Florida Bay ecosystem are helping resource managers and citizens put the pieces of the watershed puzzle back together.

It is in the nature of human affairs for conflicts to develop. They arise from differing human traditions, perceptions, needs, and values relative to the watershed and its resources. Change is an inevitable consequence of natural process, but the demands

of an increasing population on limited resources have greatly accelerated change in southern Florida. New issues emerge each day, so a one-time listing cannot depict the constantly shifting mosaic of water-related issues in southern Florida. What follows is a brief sampler of conditions that affect all or part of the southern Florida ecosystem—conditions or circumstances that have, in effect, rearranged the pieces of the ecological puzzle that is the watershed.

Population Growth

Southern Florida has a rapidly expanding population that now approaches 5.5 million people; most live in upland areas such as the Coastal Ridge in the southeast, but some live in the wetlands. The population of southern Florida represents 40 percent of Florida's total population. This large human presence, with its needs and demands, has changed the region's ecosystem. In addition to hydrologic alterations through the development of flood control structures, there is increasing water demand by all users. The ground water supply has been diminished by the conversion of land to agricultural and urban uses essential to the support of a growing population. Water supplies have also been reduced when fresh water, previously stored in wetlands,

Perhaps of greatest concern to the integrity of the Everglades is the timing, distribution, quantity, and quality of waterflow.

South Florida Population

Population (millions)

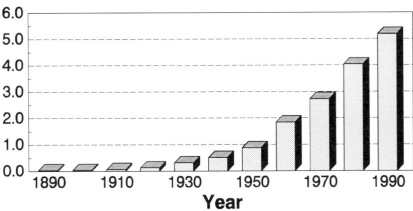

Source: U.S. Census

soils, and aquifers, has been shunted to the coast.

Soil Loss and Water Quality

One of the first observed harmful effects of large-scale drainage was the compacting and oxidation of organic soils in the agricultural lands south of Lake Okeechobee. The original maximum depth of soil there was probably only 12 to 14 feet, but in some areas 5 or more feet of organic soil had been lost by 1984. More recently, the rate of soil loss was calculated at 1.2 inches per year. Through oxidation, loss of soil continues today, although the process may be slowed in most locations if managers can reflood fallow fields and maintain a high water table.

Because of southern Florida's low relief, soil loss of such magnitude affects Everglades hydrology and ecology. In the upper and central Everglades, elevation has changed due to soil loss. The land has subsided, and this has meant a loss of the hydraulic head that once drove water south. Moving

water from north to south now requires pumping; the effort necessary to move water increases with time as the soils continue to erode. The soil loss has also reduced the area's ability to absorb water and thus to carry it through short- and long-term variations in rainfall. The problems caused by soil loss are magnified by the enormous area over which the loss has occurred. The loss is not confined to the Everglades Agricultural Area but actually extends into the northern parts of Water Conservation Areas 1 and 3A, where water diversion has caused additional soil loss.

The loss of soil may have resulted in a concentration of compounds and minerals in the remaining soil. It seems likely that soil loss has nearly overstretched the binding capacity of remaining soil. When this happens, the soil's highly concentrated compounds and minerals are released into waters that flow downstream. In conjunction with the long-term use of pesticides, this release poses a potential ecological threat.

Well fields of East Coast cities are supplied with water from Lake Okeechobee and the Everglades through major canals. Discoloration of the water is evidence of the presence of dissolved organic carbon compounds, precursors to hazardous chemicals formed in the process of chlorinating drinking water. Dade County water treatment plants have switched to a different purifying process, but by-products of this process may cause public health concerns, too. Historically, Everglades waters were naturally clear. Organic soils that are oxidizing due to drainage are believed to be a source of the dissolved organic compounds causing problems in water treatment.

Nutrient Enrichment and Contamination

The drainage and development of much of the southern Florida wetland system have introduced contaminants into remnant wetlands. Phosphorus and other

Contaminants have been introduced into wetlands.

Mercury has concentrated in large-mouth bass.

nutrients entering Lake Okeechobee, principally through tributaries to the north, have added to the deterioration of the lake's water quality. High concentrations of pesticides or their derivatives have been found in the tissues of great egrets and other wading birds from Water Conservation Area 1, and Lake Okeechobee has experienced proliferation of blue-green bacteria.

Particularly alarming are the elevated levels of mercury in fish and wildlife throughout much of the southern Florida wetlands. The source is uncertain, but approximately one million acres of the Everglades are under health advisories recommending that anglers completely avoid consumption of largemouth bass and several other fish species. Alligators harvested from the Water Conservation Areas cannot be sold for human consumption because of elevated mercury levels in their tissue. In 1989, a Florida panther died from mercury poisoning, and mercury is suspected as the cause in the deaths of two other panthers. Analysis of raccoons (a major prey of panthers) from certain areas of southern Florida revealed very high concentrations of mercury in liver and muscle tissue.

Fragmentation of Landscapes and Habitats

The southern Florida ecosystem is now highly fragmented, with diminished habitat diversity. Four major wetland landscapes are reduced to remnants: the cypress strands fringing the western side of the Atlantic Coastal Ridge, the pond apple forest/swamp on the southern shore of Lake Okeechobee, the tall saw grass plain of the Everglades Agricultural Area, and the biologically important peripheral wet prairies in southeastern Dade County. On the East Coast ridge, most of the natural areas have been replaced by urban development. Only 10 percent of the former rocky pinelands and 10 percent of the tropical hardwood hammocks persist. Both are seriously stressed by the combination of a lowered water table and introduced species—conditions which make them much more vulnerable to natural disasters such as hurricanes.

Subdivision of much of the remaining Everglades for various human uses has fragmented the system by creating a series of poorly connected wetlands. Similarly, urbanization has fragmented upland systems. The former role of these systems in

Southern Florida has been subdivided by human activity.

regulating both the hydrology and the ecology of the southern Florida ecosystem was no doubt enormous. The urban area now exerts a stress on both the ecosystem's water supplies and its water storage capacity.

This compartmentalization, along with the channelization of the Kissimmee River and construction of a canal network from Lake Okeechobee to the coast, has almost eliminated the natural sheet flow that sustained the wetlands and estuaries. Water conveyance networks capture much of the rainfall that the system receives during the wet season; they deliver the fresh water to the estuaries, but they do it in large pulses that can drastically lower salinities, stress estuarine life, and lower estuarine productivity. Wetland productivity is lost as well, because the elimination of large volumes of fresh water from the system results in shorter hydroperiods. This lowers wetland carrying capacity—the maximum population of a species that can be supported by a given area. The dry season loses the important delayed flows originating from wet season rainfall. Lost also are the base flows that, in the natural system, sustained the estuary during dry times.

Loss of Wetlands and Their Functions

Roughly 50 percent of the historic wetland area has been lost to human use and development. In particular, humans have diminished the critical peripheral, or short hydroperiod, wetlands on the eastern side of the Everglades. Loss of this wetland area significantly reduces landscape diversity, habitat options, and long-term population survival ratios for vertebrate species that require large areas. Wading birds, snail kites, and panthers have become increasingly stressed by the fragmentation and loss of their habitat. The decrease in southern Florida wetlands has reduced the area over which sunlight can be transformed into food and oxygen by aquatic plants. The reduction in topography variation has narrowed survival options for plants and animals. By any measure of species richness, there has been a drastic erosion of biodiversity in southern Florida.

The decrease in wetland area has meant a loss of wetland function, including the loss of gator holes and other refuges, as well as the loss of sheet flow and base flow mentioned before. The Everglades and other wetland systems of southern Florida were naturally flowing, or lotic, systems that not only covered greater area but also had longer periods of inundation (hydroperiods) and more sustained outflows to estuaries than exist today under managed conditions.

Southern Florida wetlands have been reduced by half. Wading bird populations have dropped to under 10 percent of their former sizes. The correlation suggests that the lost wetlands may have been especially critical to the wading birds' feeding and nesting success; or, that the remaining wetlands are so diminished in quality that their carrying capacity for birds is only a fraction of former levels. The estuarine system serves as a foraging ground for many

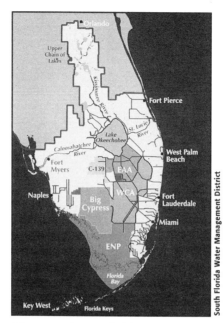

Most water impounded in Water Conservation Areas (WCAs) is diverted to the Atlantic coast during the dry season for water supply.

South Florida Water Management District

waders, and loss of estuarine feeding opportunities also may have decreased the carrying capacity of the southern Florida ecosystem for wading birds.

Disconnecting Wetlands and Estuaries from Rainfall

Water supply and regulatory releases involved in the management of water levels in Lake Okeechobee, the Water Conservation Areas, and the East Everglades have altered the historic rainfall-driven sheet flow through the system. Flows to the Everglades from Lake Okeechobee have shifted from primarily wet season flows (those that occur in response to rainfall) to dry season flows (occurring in response to human water demands). Water is impounded in the Water Conservation Areas and diverted in surface water flows to the Atlan-

tic Coast. Combined with ground water and levee seepage losses eastward, this diversion significantly reduces flows to the southern Everglades. It also shortens hydroperiods in this area. These changes have resulted in larger flow variations within the year.

Because of the smaller wetland area and the reduction in water storage capacity in remaining wetlands, large volumes of rainwater now drain to the sea. This did not occur historically. The diversion of water eastward results in a loss of several million acre feet of water per year from southern Florida.

In the Everglades, reduction in flow from upstream has reduced the maximum area covered by water each year, and the hydroperiod, or duration of flooding. Peak flows are higher after major rainfall and flow rates decline more abruptly following the end of the wet season than

Canals and impoundments have affected water depths.

Ken DeYonge

they did in the natural system. Channelization and impoundment have disrupted the annual pattern of rising and falling water depths in the remaining wetlands of southern Florida. In particular, the effects of dry season rainfall have been aggravated by increases in the depth and duration of reversals in the natural drydown process—causing rainfall to have a greater disruptive effect on the concentration of secondary production upon which the whole system depends.

In most southern Florida landscapes, human development accelerates the rate of runoff, resulting in sporadic waterflow and more frequent and longer drying of wetlands. Reduced hydroperiods in wetlands appear to adversely affect aquatic production at all levels of the food chain. Surface water refuges—such as alligator holes—that support aquatic animals during drought have shrunk. Fewer of them exist, and many of those that do are relocated in the managed system.

In a few areas, such as the southern parts of the Water Conservation Areas, channelization and impoundment have increased water depth and hydroperiod. This has not been good news either, though. Unseasonable water releases from the Water Conservation Areas flooded alligator nesting sites in Everglades National Park, resulting in nest failure. In addition, these releases have disrupted the nesting of wading birds, which depend upon concentrated food supplies.

Nonnative Species

Prolific nonnative plant and

The walking catfish is a nonnative species.

animal species are changing the southern Florida landscape and affecting its hydrologic conditions and ecological relationships. Water management has encouraged the spread of invasive species such as hydrilla and water hyacinth, which often choke waterways with their dense growth.

Twenty-one species of nonnative fish breed in Florida. The walking catfish startled some Florida residents when they first saw the fish struggling across meadows and roads. Within the past few years, a new alien fish has been found in some waters, including some in Everglades National Park. Mozambique *tilapia* was discovered nesting in Taylor Slough at Anhinga Trail. In Everglades National Park, the addition of this *tilapia* brings the number of introduced fish species to eight.

Bill Laitner, former chief of interpretation for Everglades National Park says:

Tilapia, a nonnative fish, has been found in Everglades National Park.

Exotic fish are an issue we haven't been paying enough attention to. If you walk the Anhinga Trail, for example, and look down, virtually all the fish you see were not there ten years ago . . . there are a few gar, a few bass, but there are mainly tilapia, oscars, and cichlids . . . Some of these may not matter. But these fish often differ in size from the native species. If you're a bird that eats predominantly small fish, and suddenly the fish are all larger, it may make a difference. I wonder if exotic fish is an issue that will blow up and we're going to say we didn't know.

Canal networks provide a type of deep-water refuge that may create a completely different living community—particularly of predatory fish—than in the natural system. Some researchers have suggested that canals may have supplanted natural alligator holes as refugia. Canals may also be the conduit for dispersing invasive species.

Probably the most important way these and other water control structures encourage the spread of alien species is by creating spaces where conditions are more favorable to introduced species than to natives. For instance, altered hydrologic conditions within remnant wetlands have increased their vulnerability to invasion by melaleuca.

Loss of Hydraulic Head and Recharge Value

Draining southern Florida's wetlands drastically lowered the water table and increased its rate of recession on Florida's east coast ridge. This affected water flow to both interior wetlands and estuaries. It also affected the plant communities of the ridge, the interface between salt water and fresh water, and the potable water supply.

Changes in the Role of Fire

The role of fire in the region has also changed. Because of changes in seasonal burning patterns and overdrying of wetlands, the ecological role of fire in the watershed may have shifted from one of increasing habitat diversity (in the natural system) to reducing diversity (in the managed system). Fragmented vegetative communities interfere with the ability of fire to maintain natural mosaics. Fire patterns have also been altered by prescribed burning, a practice that retards the annual variation in the number and severity of fires. Because species have adapted to natural variations, managing and controlling natural disturbances such as fire can lead to loss of biological diversity. Any modification of physical factors in an ecosystem may favor some species over others and thus affect species composition.

A change in the fire regime results in hardwood species invading pinelands.

Effects on Estuaries

Water management in southern Florida has resulted in short-term, high-volume water flow to estuaries and reduced life-sustaining base flows. Regulatory releases send abnormal pulses of fresh water to estuaries, causing rapid, drastic decreases in salinity that stress estuarine organisms. In addition, water flows have been diverted from one receiving basin to another, changing long-term salinity levels in both systems.

As a result of both diversion and increased runoff, Florida Bay receives less water now than it did historically. Salinities greatly exceeding concentrations in the ocean are common in Florida Bay. Biscayne Bay sometimes exhibits abnormal negative, or reverse, salinity levels; salinities in Manatee Bay have dropped substantially in a matter of hours due to abrupt regulatory releases from the South Dade Conveyance System. This is particularly disruptive, because loss of natural freshwater inflow ordinarily causes Manatee Bay to experience extremely high salinities. The

Fisheries productivity may be affected by changes in water flow.

same is true in northeastern Florida Bay.

Long-term changes in freshwater flow to many southern Florida estuaries have shifted salinity zones upstream or downstream from where they originally occurred each season. As a result, some areas have salinities within the optimum ranges for various species; but, these salinities may no longer coincide with physical features of the estuary that are conducive to the growth and survival of these same species. And, shifts in salinity may have reduced or eliminated the habitat available to other species.

The fisheries productivity of southern Florida marine waters and estuaries, so critical to the economy of the watershed, largely depends on the quality and quantity of habitat. Decreased fisheries productivity may be reflected by declines in catches and catch rates. The effect on lobster productivity of the recent and continuing sponge die-off has not yet been determined, but it may soon be observed in declining catches and catch rates. Harvests of Tortugas pink shrimp (dependent on Florida Bay nursery grounds) have declined sharply since the mid-1980s; this comes after long-term catch rates declined from the 1960s through the 1970s.

Fish displaying abnormal dorsal fins and misaligned scales are found in northern Biscayne Bay, and are also present in the Saint Lucie Inlet and the lower Indian River. The same abnormalities have been seen in at least 10 species. Occurrence of the abnormalities in multiple species suggests that something common to the environment of all the species is causing the problem.

Going to the Solution Hole

He may never have attended a public meeting or been a member of a prestigious commission, but the alligator has always had his priorities straight. Natural or instinctual wisdom acquired from surviving as a species for thousands of years has taught the alligator that the key to its survival is water. As this primeval reptile thrashes about in a gator hole, ripping out vegetation and widening and deepening his refuge, he is demonstrating the need to conserve water resources;

this practice will ensure that his species—along with the wood storks, killifish, apple snails, mosquito larvae, and periphyton that share his refuge—will survive.

But the gator's actions are not linked to conscious decisions on his part. Instead, a genetic code that lives deep in the strands of his double helix is programming the need to match natural rhythms of wet and dry with actions that conserve this most precious resource, water.

Consciously or not, humans have learned from the alligator. Within the last 20 years we have learned that the Everglades and its critters are dependent upon the quality, quantity, distribution, and timing of water.

We cannot deny that our actions have disrupted this system. As one study concludes: "Rapid population growth, land development, water management activities, and land conversion have negatively impacted the Everglades ecosystem; its water quality has been degraded and the associated natural systems no

longer adequately perform the function they once performed." As a species, we can now begin to thrash and struggle to clear our own solution hole of the vegetation that chokes it. We have taken one of many first steps: honestly identifying problems and their real and potential impacts.

The next step is defining what we can hope to accomplish. In their article "Toward Ecosystem Restoration," Steven M. Davis and John C. Ogden write:

Going back in time to that lost world [the Everglades of over 100 years ago] is not an achievable goal of Everglades restoration, although many of its attributes and functions are achievable. Perhaps a more realistic vision is going forward, into the 21st century, toward the creation of the next generation of the Everglades. The new Everglades will be different from that of the past, but it must (if restoration is successful) be one that rekindles to the extent possible the wildness and richness of the former system.

We have several reasons to be hopeful in spite of the many problems that face the southern Florida ecosystem. A massive restoration effort is under way. The South Florida Water Management District and the U.S. Army Corps of Engineers are committed to this project. The water management district has drafted a South Florida Ecosystem Restoration Master Plan (1995) that outlines an ambitious program. The program coordinates local, state, and federal government partners, and integrates the efforts of planning, research, monitoring, regulation, land acquisition, design, and construction. The

For people, and alligators, the key to survival is water.

Courtesy: Everglades National Park

master plan summarizes the restoration goals for each part of the ecosystem, and describes strategies, schedules, and resource requirements for accomplishing them.

Numerous public opinion polls conducted across the country have tabulated similar results: people want a clean and healthy environment, and they are willing to pay for it. Both homeowners and agribusiness are paying for Everglades restoration and will need to continue to do so, perhaps for decades.

The concept of sustainability, "meeting the needs of the present

without compromising the ability of future generations to meet their own needs," is also more prevalent in our dialogues and our literature today. On March 3, 1994, Governor Lawton Chiles signed an executive order that created the Governor's Commission for a Sustainable South Florida. "This Commission was created to assure a healthy Everglades ecosystem can coexist and be mutually supportive of a sustainable south Florida economy." Its Mission Statement reads:

"There are no other Everglades in the world." (Douglas, 1947) All life in southern Florida is influenced by this vast ecosystem. It is the mission of the Governor's Commission for a Sustainable South Florida, representing diverse interests, to develop recommendations and public support for regaining a healthy Everglades ecosystem with a sustainable economy and quality communities. The Commission will recommend a five-year action plan containing strategies, actions, and measures of success to the Governor and the South Florida community for achieving positive change that enhances the ecological, economic,

Restoration Objectives

System-wide objectives for the Everglades restoration effort are to:

* Increase the area and landscape diversity of the system in order to recover its ecological structure and function, preventing further wetland loss, recovering undeveloped degraded wetlands, and restoring landscape elements that have been lost to development.

* Restore the natural hydrologic structure and function of the system by restoring sheet flow, reestablishing strong hydrologic linkages between areas, restoring the fundamental relationships of ground and surface water levels and water flow with rainfall, and reestablishing the natural quality, timing, and distribution of freshwater flow throughout the system and into estuaries.

* Gradually decompartmentalize the Water Conservation Areas to reinstate sheet flow through them to the south.

* Recover populations of threatened and endangered species.

* Restore natural biological diversity.

* Reestablish natural vegetation and periphyton communities, particularly where they have been lost or altered as a result of human impacts.

* Reduce the dependence of urban and agricultural areas on water supplies in Lake Okeechobee, the Everglades, and Big Cypress Swamp.

* Restore natural rates of productivity throughout the ecosystem.

* Reestablish sustainable wading bird breeding populations and colonies.

* Stop the invasion of southern Florida by exotic plants and animals.

* Prevent point and nonpoint air and water pollution, including contaminants, excessive nutrients, sediments, and thermal pollutants.

* Reestablish the corridors for movement, dispersion, and interactions of vegetation and animals.

* Increase the hard coral cover on Florida Keys reefs.

* Restore natural estuarine and coastal productivity and fisheries.

* Link agricultural and urban growth management with ecosystem management.

* Restore a system that is self-maintaining with minimum human intervention.

* Restore the sustainability of systems of people and nature in southern Florida that support cities, farms, and industries in an environment of clean air, clean water, and abundant and diverse natural resources.

and social systems upon which South Florida and its communities depend. Once implemented, these strategies will bolster the regional economy, promote quality communities, secure healthy South Florida ecosystems, and assure today's progress is not achieved at tomorrow's expense.

There are many positive signs of change in southern Florida. Scientists, governmental decision makers, conservationists, farmers, industrialists, educators, and other citizens are cooperating and working together toward solutions. Looking to technology, farmers, industrialists and others are adapting their operations in order to conserve and protect natural resources. People are aware that continued research is vital; they make the distinction between short-term "fixes" and long-term solutions. Instead of clinging to the memory of an Everglades Lost, they have developed a vision of a twenty-first century Everglades. Organizations such as the Governor's Commission for a Sustainable South Florida and others have recognized that the region's economic and social health is intrinsically linked to the health of its ecosystem—people are connected to the ecosystem and are responsible for it. The State Department of Environmental Protection has a lead role in coordinating an "ecosystem management" approach to resource management among all appropriate resource agencies. The Everglades ecosystem is one of several demonstration sites.

And, like the alligator, we have begun by focusing on water. The report of the Governor's commission states, "Water is central to all of south Florida. Recognition of this fact is essential if a sustainable ecosystem, which meets the needs of the environment (the natural system), and the demands of the built human system (urban/rural, tribal, and agricultural uses) is to be achieved and maintained."

As we go to the solution hole—like the alligator—we recognize our dependence upon this priceless natural resource. Unlike the alligator, we must consciously assume responsibility for the restoration of this unique and troubled ecosystem. In fact, we are the only species that can.

Courtesy: Everglades National Park

Epilogue

Escape from Flatland

· ·

Of the experience of sailors Edwin Abbott said, "The far-off land may have bays, forelands, angles in and out to any number and extent; yet at a distance you see none of these . . . nothing but a gray unbroken line upon the water . . . Whenever you open your eyes, you see a Plane." We hope that as you have drawn closer to the flatland called the Everglades, you have gone past the lines of two dimensions. We hope that you have seen beyond the shadows to the real world of earth, air, fire, water, and life, and that you have come to better understand their inseparable connections. If you have, perhaps you can say with the person just escaped from Flatland, "I looked, and, behold, a new world! There stood before me, visibly incorporate, all that I had before inferred, conjectured, dreamed, of perfect Circular beauty . . . a beautiful harmonious Something."

For many people, especially young folks, a trip to the wilder parts of the Everglades watershed may be their first time away from a city. In the Glades they may find their first opportunity to see

Courtesy: Everglades National Park

an alligator or deer in a setting other than a zoo; to touch a snake; to feel the cutting edge of a blade of saw grass and taste its tender shoots; to listen intently and not hear the sound of cars, airplanes and thousands of other people. For all of us, the greater Everglades ecosystem is a place where we can renew our contracts with nature. Here, we can keep in mind humanity's inseparable ties to the natural world and remember that in our pursuit of higher levels of sophistication and technological achievement, we may endanger wild places. The redundancy of human manipulations in the Everglades ecosystem make its restoration and preservation even more urgent. In managing large ecosystems, our concerns must reach beyond the

boundaries that conventionally define those systems. A Mexican proverb says, "Quien quiera el arbol tiene que querer sus ramos." It means, "He who cares for the tree must also care for the branches."

Everglades is not a featureless two-dimensional land. It is a very different kind of country, enciphered in the code of the primal elements. It is a place of diversity and depth, a complex, multidimensional world. In his poem "Seeing Things," novelist John Updike wrote: "Strike through the mask? You find another mask, Mirroring mirrors . . ." In this great watershed, one part of the story is a reflection of another, and another, and another. Marjory Stoneman Douglas, who has devoted much of her life to the preservation of this place, reminds us: "There are no other Everglades in the world."

Courtesy: Everglades National Park

We hope that you have seen beyond the shadows to the real world of earth, air, fire, water, and life, and that you have come to better understand their inseparable connections.

Part III

Investigations: Putting the Pieces Together

. . . .

Interdisciplinary explorations of parts of the watershed puzzle

help to put some of the pieces into proper context.

Water on the Move

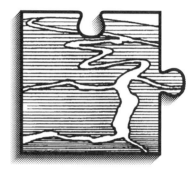

Have you ever tickled the nose of an alligator? Bounced along the bottom of a swamp? Leaped thousands of miles above the ground? You can when you're on the move with water.

Summary
With the roll of a die, students simulate water cycling through the K-O-E watershed.

Objectives
Students will:

• describe the water cycle in the K-O-E watershed.

• identify processes that move water through the water cycle.

Materials
• *Water on the Move Map*

• *9 large pieces of paper*

• *Copies of Water Cycle Table (optional)*

• *Marking pens*

• *9 boxes, about 6 inches (15 cm) on a side.* (Boxes are used to make dice for the game. Gift boxes used for coffee mugs are a good size; inquire at your local mailing outlet. There will be one die [box] per station of the water cycle. [More boxes at each station increase the game's pace, especially at the cloud station.] Labels for the sides of dice are in the *Water Cycle Table*. These labels represent the options for pathways that water can follow. Explanations

for the labels are provided.)

• *Bell, whistle, buzzer, or some sound maker*

NOTE: An alternative board game teaching method—drawing numbers out of a bag—is also presented.

Making Connections
One can imagine a drop of water traveling from the Kissimmee River to Florida Bay. In reality, this rarely happens. The forces of nature and the sun's energy cause water to move in a variety of pathways called the water cycle. When students think of the water cycle, they may imagine water traveling in a circular route from a stream to an ocean, evaporating into the clouds, raining down on a mountaintop, and flowing back into a stream. Role-playing a water molecule helps students conceptualize the water cycle as more than a predictable two-dimensional path.

Background
While water does circulate from one point or physical state to another in the water cycle, the paths it takes may vary.

Heat energy increases molecular movement, causing water to change from solid to liquid to gas. With each change in state, physical movement from one location to another, caused primarily by gravity and air currents (wind), usually occurs.

One of the most visible states in which water moves is the liquid state. In this form we see it in lakes, rivers, runoff, and canals. Liquid water also travels slowly underground, seeping, flowing, and filtering through particles of soil and pores in rocks and aquifers.

Although unseen, water's most dramatic movements take place during its gaseous phase. Water is constantly evaporating, changing from liquid into gas. As a vapor, it can travel through the atmosphere over Earth's surface. In fact, water vapor surrounds us all the time. Where it will condense and return to Earth depends on loss of heat energy, gravity, and the structure of Earth's surface.

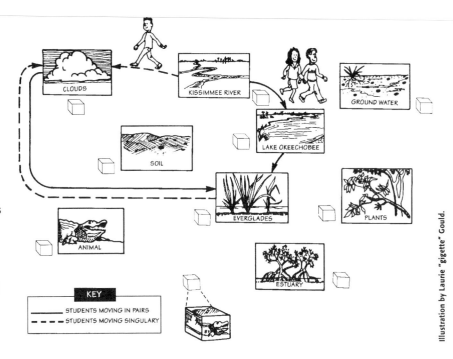

Illustration by Laurie "gigette" Gould.

Water condensation from a gas to a liquid is visible as dew on plants or water droplets on the outside of a glass of cold water. In clouds, water molecules collect or condense on tiny dust particles. Eventually, the water droplets become too heavy and gravity pulls the water to Earth as rain.

Living organisms also help move water. Humans and other animals carry water in their bodies, transporting it from one location to another. Animals consume water directly, remove it from foods during digestion, and excrete it as a liquid or a gas (for example, through respiration). When water is present on the skin of an animal (for example, as perspiration), evaporation may occur.

The greatest movers of water among living organisms are plants. Plant roots absorb water. Some of this water is used in the body of the plant, but most of it

travels up through the plant to the leaf surface. When water reaches the leaves, it is exposed to the air and the sun's energy and evaporates easily through pores called stomata. This process is called transpiration.

The processes of the water cycle move water around, through, and over the planet. Water travels great distances. A water molecule in a snowpack in western Montana might end up in the Gulf of Mexico or in a cloud over China.

On a smaller scale, water cycles through watersheds, like those in southern Florida. A drop of rainwater landing at the headwaters of the Kissimmee River might flow into Lake Okeechobee, on to the Everglades, and out to sea via an estuary. This, however, is not water's only pathway in the K-O-E watershed. Rainwater may land on a house, an orange grove, or wetlands. Water seeps into the

ground, filling pores and spaces in limestone and other rock and recharging aquifers. Chances are good that water flowing through the Everglades will never make it to an estuary. Evapotranspiration (the transpiration of water from plants and the evaporation of water from land areas) accounts for as much as 80 percent of rainfall in the Everglades. Evaporated water is often transported back over the upper portions of the watershed, where it condenses and falls as rain onto Lake Okeechobee or other portions of southern Florida. Ultimately, global winds and ocean currents carry water to and from southern Florida, making the K-O-E watershed's water cycle really just a small detour in the larger water cycle of Earth.

Additional information about water's movement through the K-O-E watershed can be found in chapters 1 and 3.

Procedure

Warm Up

Have students identify the basic layout of the watershed and sketch their description on the board (Kissimmee River, Lake Okeechobee, the Everglades, Florida Bay). Ask the question, "Is it possible that a drop of water could flow from the source of the Kissimmee River to Florida Bay? What else might happen to water as it flows through the watershed?" Have students identify different places water can go as it moves through and around the K-O-E watershed. Encourage students to be specific, naming wetlands plants (cabbage palm, saw grass, cypress tree) and animals (wood stork, human, alligator, water strider). Write responses on the board.

The Activity

1. **Divide places through which water can move in the K-O-E watershed into nine stations: Clouds, Plants, Animals, Kissimmee River, Estuary (Florida Bay), Lake Okeechobee, Ground Water, Soil, and Everglades. Write these names on large pieces of paper. Arrange the pieces of paper representing the river, lake, Everglades, and estuary in a row on the ground in the order in which they appear in the watershed. Place the other stations around the room or yard.** (Students may illustrate station labels.)

2. **Have students identify the different places water can go from each station in the water cycle. Discuss the conditions that cause the water to move.** Explain that water movement depends on energy from the sun, electromag-

netic energy, and gravity. Sometimes water will not go anywhere. Have students make the dice, checking to see if they have shown all the places water can go. The *Water Cycle Table* explains water movements from each station.

3. **Students should discuss the form in which water moves from one location to another.** Most movement from one station to another takes place when water is liquid. However, any time water moves to the clouds, it is in the form of water vapor, with molecules moving rapidly apart from each other.

4. **Tell students they are going to become water moving through the K-O-E watershed. Instruct students to line up in groups of two or three at the river station.** As liquid water, students will move in groups, representing the many water molecules together in a water drop. When they move to the clouds (evaporate), they will separate from their partners and move alone as individual water molecules. When they reach the clouds, they condense into tiny water droplets, so they should grab a partner again.

5. **How many students think they will go straight from the river to the lake, through the Everglades, and into the bay? In this game, a roll of the die determines where water will go.** Students roll the die and go to the location indicated. When students arrive at the next station, they get in line and roll again. If they roll *Stay*, they roll again. If they roll *Stay* three times in a row at any station other than the estuary and cloud stations they go to the end

of the line. In the clouds and in the estuary, if they roll *Stay* three times in a row, it means they have left the watershed (the cloud has drifted into another watershed or the water drop has drifted into the ocean). These students should leave the playing area and watch.

6. **Students should keep track of their movements.** Have students record each move on the map, including *Stays*. Students may record their journeys by leaving personalized stickers at each station. In another approach half the class plays the game while the other half watches. Onlookers can track the movements of their classmates. In the next round, onlookers play the game, and the others record their movements.

7. **Tell students the game will begin and end with the sound of a bell (or buzzer or whistle). Begin the game!**

NOTE: Alternatively, you can make the activity into a board game. Arrange the stations on a desk or table in the layout described in step 1. By each station place the applicable portion of the *Water Cycle Table*. Give each group a die or a small sack containing six numbered pieces of paper. Students place their playing pieces (pebbles, buttons, or seeds) at the river station. The first player draws a piece of paper or rolls a number, refers to the "Kissimmee River" section of the *Water Cycle Table,* and moves to the designated location. For example, if "2" is rolled or drawn, move to "Ground Water." If using the bag of numbers, instruct students to replace the drawn number after each turn. Make sure students understand that when they move to the clouds they move as individual water molecules; between other stations, they move as water drops. Instruct students to track their movements on the map. Challenge them to move through the watershed from the river to the bay. The first student to visit each station and make it to the bay wins!

Wrap Up and Action

Have students refer to their maps and write stories about where the water has been. They should include descriptions of conditions necessary for water to move to each location and the physical state water was in when it moved. Did any student "flow" from river to lake to Everglades to estuary? Do they think this would be possible in nature? Discuss any *cycling* that took place. That is, did any students return to the same stations?

Provide students with a location (e.g., parking lot, stream, glacier, or a place in the human body—the bladder!). Have students identify ways water can move to and from that site. Have them identify what physical states the water would be in.

Have older students teach "Water on the Move" to younger students.

Assessment

Have students:

• role-play water as it moves through the water cycle (step 7).

• identify water's different physical states as it moves through the water cycle (step 3 and *Wrap Up*).

• write a story describing the movement of water through the K-O-E watershed (*Wrap Up*).

Extensions

Ask students to compare the movement of water during different seasons and at different locations around the globe. They can adapt the "Water on the Move" game (change the faces of the die, add alternative stations, etc.) to represent these different conditions or locations.

Have students investigate how water becomes polluted and cleaned as it moves through the K-O-E watershed. For instance, water might pick up contaminants as it travels through the soil, then leave them behind as it evaporates at the surface or is cleansed in the Kissimmee River floodplain. Challenge students to adapt "Water on the Move" to include these processes. For example, rolled-up pieces of masking tape could represent pollutants and be stuck to students as they travel to the soil station. Some materials would filter out as water moves to the lake; students could rub their arms to slough off tape. If they roll *Clouds*, they remove all the tape, since evaporating water leaves pollutants behind.

Resources

Alexander, Gretchen. 1989. *Water Cycle Teacher's Guide*. Hudson, N.H.: Delta Education, Inc.

Marsh, William M. 1987. *Earthscape: A Physical Geography*. New York, N.Y.: John Wiley & Sons.

Miller, G. Tyler, Jr. 1990. *Resource Conservation and Management*. Belmont, Calif.: Wadsworth Publishing Co.

Water on the Move

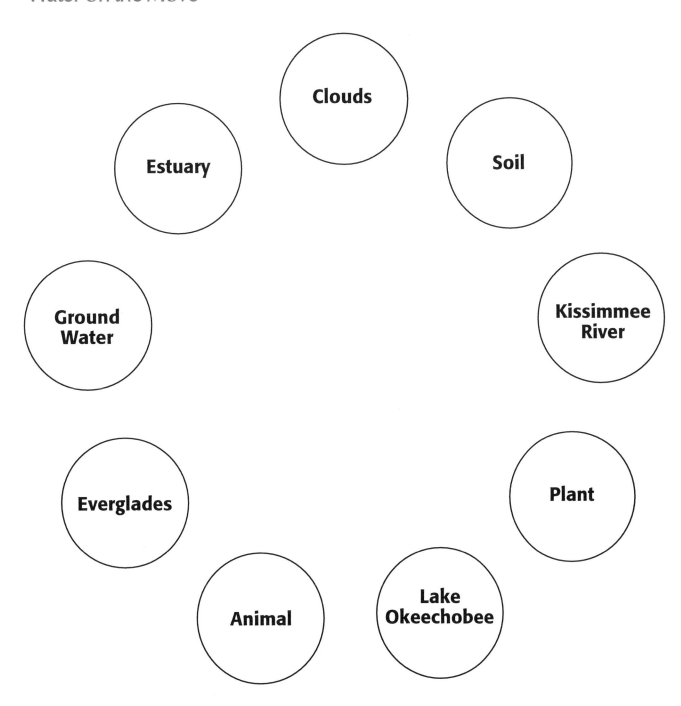

Water Journey Table

NOTE: **Die labels do not represent actual probability of water's movement from one station to another, nor do they comprise all possible movements.**

STATION	DIE LABELS (for running game)	STATION DESTINATION (for board game)	EXPLANATION
Soil	one side *Plant*	1	Water is absorbed by plant roots.
	one side *River*	2	The soil is saturated, so water runs off into a river.
	one side *Ground Water*	3	Gravity pulls water; it filters into the soil.
	two sides *Clouds*	4 or 5	Heat energy is added to the water, which evaporates and goes to the clouds.
	one side *Stay*	6	Water remains on the surface (perhaps in a puddle, or adhered to a soil particle).
Plant	four sides *Clouds*	1, 2, 3, or 4	Water leaves the plant through the process of transpiration.
	two sides *Stay*	5 or 6	Water is used by the plant and stays in the cells.
Kissimmee River	one side *Lake*	1	Water flows into Lake Okeechobee.
	one side *Ground Water*	2	Water is pulled by gravity; it filters into the soil.
	one side *Animal*	3	An otter drinks water.
	one side *Clouds*	4	Heat energy is added to the water, which evaporates and goes to the clouds.
	two sides *Stay*	5 or 6	Water remains in the current of the river.
Clouds	one side *Soil*	1	Water condenses and falls on soil.
	one side *River*	2	Water condenses and falls into the Kissimmee River.
	one side *Everglades*	3	Water condenses and falls onto the Everglades.
	one side *Lake*	4	Water condenses and falls into Lake Okeechobee.
	one side *Estuary*	5	Water condenses and falls into the estuary.
	one side *Stay*	6	Water remains part of a droplet in a cloud.

Water Journey Table (Cont.)

Estuary	two sides *Clouds*	1 or 2	Heat energy is added to the water, which evaporates and goes to the clouds.
	two sides *Stay*	3 or 4	Water remains in the estuary.
	two sides *Plant*	5 or 6	A mangrove plant absorbs water.
Lake Okeechobee	two sides *Everglades*	1 or 2	Water flows from the lake through canals to the Everglades
	one side *Animal*	3	A wood stork drinks the water.
	one side *Clouds*	4	Heat energy is added to the water, which evaporates and goes to the clouds.
	two sides *Stay*	5 or 6	Water remains in the lake.
Animal	two sides *Soil*	1 or 2	Water is excreted through feces and urine.
	two sides *Clouds*	3 or 4	Water is exhaled or evaporated from the body.
	two sides *Stay*	5 or 6	Body tissues incorporate water.
Ground Water	two sides *River*	1 or 2	Water filters into the Kissimmee River.
	two sides *Lake*	3 or 4	Water filters into Lake Okeechobee.
	two sides *Stay*	5 or 6	Water stays underground.
Everglades	two sides *Plant*	1 or 2	Water is absorbed by saw grass plant.
	two sides *Clouds*	3 or 4	Water evaporates and goes to the clouds.
	one side *Estuary*	5	Water flows into the estuary.
	one side *Stay*	6	Water remains in the Everglades.

Heart of a Watershed

Grade Level:
Middle School

Subject Areas:
Ecology, Earth Science,
Geography

Duration:
Preparation time: Part I, 50
minutes; Part II, 50 minutes

Activity time: Part I, 50
minutes; Part II, two 50-
minute periods

Setting:
Classroom

Skills:
Organizing (mapping);
Analyzing (contrasting and
comparing); Evaluating
(testing, critiquing)

Vocabulary:
drainage basin, watershed,
divide, tributary, runoff,
eutrophication

Why is Lake Okeechobee often called the "heart" of the K-O-E watershed?

Summary
Students build a model landscape to illustrate the uniqueness of the Kissimmee-Lake Okeechobee-Everglades (K-O-E) watershed and use the model to demonstrate how alterations have affected the watershed.

Objectives
Students will:

• design a model depicting the main components of the K-O-E watershed.

• compare the K-O-E watershed to other watersheds.

• illustrate how alterations to the K-O-E watershed have affected it.

Materials
Students are encouraged to develop their own ideas for creating a model of the K-O-E. Following is a list of materials used in suggested strategies described in the activity (students can supply some of the materials).

• *Large quantities of moist soil*

• *Shallow tray*

• *Shallow pan, pie plate, or bowl* (preferably made from sturdy aluminum)

• *Cardboard strips*

• *Plastic or dampened newspaper*

• *Water*

• *Silt, pepper, torn paper, and other small insoluble objects to represent sediments*

• *Pond or lake water*

• *Liquid fertilizer (NOTE: Make sure use of fertilizer is permissible.)*

• *Water test kit that includes test for chlorophyll*

• *2 plastic glasses*

• *Blue-colored salt water (add salt to water until saturated)*

• *Hydrometer (optional)*

• *Index card*

• *A nail to punch holes in aluminum tray*

• *Straws*

• *Duct tape or wood glue*

Making Connections
The K-O-E watershed is unique among watersheds. Failure to understand its complexity contributed to unforeseen complications during engineering projects. A greater awareness of this unique watershed will support prudent and effective restoration and protection of the Everglades and other resources of southern Florida.

Background
When the ground is saturated or impermeable to water, excess water during heavy rains flows over the surface of land as runoff.

Eventually, this water collects in channels such as streams. The land area that drains water into the channels is called the watershed or drainage basin.

Watersheds are separated from each other by areas of higher elevation called ridge lines or divides. (The Central Florida Ridge is a divide.) Near the divide of a watershed, water channels are narrow and water moves fast. At lower elevations, the slope of the land decreases, causing water to flow more slowly. As smaller streams merge together, the width of the channel increases. Eventually, water collects in a wide river that empties into a body of water, such as a lake or ocean.

Areas of the K-O-E watershed deviate from this pattern. While there are smaller streams draining into Lake Okeechobee (e.g., Fisheating Creek), the principal conduit for water from the north is the Kissimmee River. However, there is not a single recognizable watercourse on the southern border of the lake. Instead, historically, water spilled over the southern portion of the lake and moved in a wide sheet through the saw grass. This sheet flow created the Everglades, "the river of grass." Since the lake was diked in 1948, all water movement into and out of the lake except local rainfall is controlled by water managers.

Unlike many national parks, Everglades National Park is located at the base, rather than the origin of its watershed. This aspect of the K-O-E watershed has led to many engineering problems. Water quality and

quantity for the Everglades depends primarily on what happens to upper portions of the watershed. Channelizations, diversion projects, dikes, and levees have all made their mark on the Everglades.

For additional information about the K-O-E watershed, refer to chapters 1, 2, 8, and 9.

Procedure
Warm Up
Ask students to describe the functions of the human heart. Tell them Lake Okeechobee has been called the "heart" of the K-O-E watershed. Challenge them to cite reasons for the analogy. Have them sketch what they believe are the parts of the K-O-E watershed, including the Kissimmee River, Lake Okeechobee, and the Everglades.

The Activity
NOTE: This activity is divided into two parts. In the first part students create a model of the historical everglades. In the second part, students add representations of human made alterations to the model.

Part I

1. **Provide students with a diagram of the historic K-O-E watershed (prior to human alterations—see activity "In the Year 2020"). Their task is to make a model of the watershed. The model must include the Kissimmee River, Lake Okeechobee, Caloosahatchee and Saint Lucie Canals, and the Everglades.** Caution students that even with detail, their model will be a simplified representation and cannot identify all aspects of this complex watershed.

A suggested strategy is to arrange moist soil in a long tray or on the ground. Label one end North and the other South. Make sure the northern end is higher than the southern. Bury a pie plate, shallow pan, or bowl in the middle of the strip of soil so that its lip is even with the surface (the southern lip should be tilted slightly lower than the northern). The bowl represents Lake Okeechobee. Fill the lake with water. Create a meandering stream (the Kissimmee River) in the Northern portion of the soil that leads to the lake. Line the river bottom and banks with cardboard strips. Pour water into the river and check to see if it flows into the lake. The lake should overflow at its southern end. Check the soil south of the lake; is it becoming more saturated? To mimic a wide river similar to the Everglades, create a shallow J-shaped channel that begins at the lake and heads toward the tip of Florida. Line the channel with plastic or dampened newspaper.

2. **Discuss aspects of the watershed and how each component affects the others. Now that they have created this model, do students agree that Lake Okeechobee is the heart of the K-O-E watershed?**

3. **Briefly describe branching patterns found in other watersheds around Florida and the country (e.g., Mississippi, Colorado, Columbia). How are they similar to and different from the K-O-E watershed?**

Part II

Inform students they will use this model to demonstrate how

changes to the K-O-E watershed have affected the health of the watershed. Encourage students to locate newspaper and journal articles that describe these changes. If necessary, remind students again that these are incomplete representations that do not portray all conditions and outcomes of change.

Suggested alterations include the following:

• **Channelization of the Kissimmee River.** Pour water that contains sediments into the meandering Kissimmee River. These sediments, materials carried into the river by runoff from surrounding land areas, can be represented by silt, pepper, torn paper, and other small insoluble objects. As water flows through the channel, note how much of the material actually makes it to the lake. Now change the river to a straight channel and pour in water containing sediment. Does more or less material make it to the lake? What happens to the depth of the lake as more materials are added?

• **Eutrophication of Lake Okeechobee.** *NOTE:* This demonstration can be done separately from the model. Fill a shallow bowl with pond water or if possible, with water from Lake Okeechobee. What does the water look and smell like? Does it contain any living organisms? To represent additional nutrients being added to the lake, such as those back-pumped from agricultural lands, add three drops of liquid fertilizer once a week. Cover the bowl with plastic wrap to prevent evaporation. Observe the quality of the water, or

measure the amount of chlorophyll using a chlorophyll test kit. For comparisons, repeat the procedure with different bowls adding different amounts of fertilizer (e.g., one drop per week, two drops per week, and a control with no added fertilizer). What are the problems associated with increasing the nutrients in a lake?

• **Diverting water from the Everglades.** Demonstrate density differences between salt water and fresh water. Fill a plastic glass to the brim with blue-colored salt water; fill another to the brim with fresh water. If an aquarium hydrometer is available, have students use it to measure the specific gravity of the liquids. Students can convert specific gravity to density and salinity using tables from aquarium or physics books.

Place an index card over the top of the fresh water glass and invert it. Place the inverted glass on top of the salt water glass, and line up the edges of the glasses. Ask students to predict what will happen when you pull out the card.

Carefully pull out the card allowing the two types of water to come into contact (the clear water should remain as a layer above the blue salt water). Have students provide explanations for why this happens. Discuss how salt water is denser than fresh water and can support fresh water. Slowly turn the glasses upside down. The blue salt water should slide under the clear fresh water. With continued turning, the two types of water will eventually mix; agitation from wind and tides also mixes water

in estuaries.

Explain that proper proportions of ocean (salt) water and fresh water are vital to life forms in Florida Bay. To show how alterations to the K-O-E watershed have contributed to alterations in these proportions, place a clear container at the base of the model to collect water from the sheet flow. Time how long it takes a cup of water to flow into the container. After that time, add an equal amount of colored water to the collection container. For example, if it takes about 3 minutes for a cup of water to collect in the container, add a cup of colored water every three minutes. The colored water represents ocean salt water. Note the color of the collected water that is a mixture of water from the Everglades and the ocean.

Demonstrate water diversion projects by punching holes in the side of the aluminum bowl representing Lake Okeechobee. Place straws into the holes and seal the spaces around the straws with duct tape, modeling clay, or wood glue. The arrangement of straws can match the placement of canals. Pour water through the model. Add a cup of colored water to the collection container at the intervals of time increments measured in the previous step. Less water should be coming to the collection basin from the Everglades, but the same quantity is being contributed by the oceans. Compare the color of the water to that in the previous exercise. The water should be darker. If the color represents salinity, what does this say about the proportion of salt in the estuary?

. . . .

Wrap Up

Have students summarize the components of the K-O-E watershed and compare the watershed before and after alterations. Ask students to locate where they live in the watershed. Do any of their actions impact the watershed? Could water from their yard flow into the river, the lake, the estuary, or the Everglades? Students can trace actual pathways through storm drains and rivers or they can generalize. If students live outside the watershed, does this mean they don't have impact on the watershed? Do they eat sugar? Tomatoes? Do they vacation in Florida?

Encourage students to identify practical ways they can help sustain the health of the K-O-E watershed. Tell students one of the most powerful ways to help the watershed is to remain informed and to behave as responsible citizens. Students can keep a record of newspaper articles about the K-O-E watershed and arrange them to match the layout of the watershed. Arrows drawn between articles might designate connections and how changes to one part of the watershed affect other sections. Have students organize class discussions on diverse issues. Compile a list of citizen behaviors (actions). Discuss the pros and cons of each behavior. Moderate the discussion to ensure fairness regarding time and points of view.

Assessment

Have students:

• design a model and describe the main components of the K-O-E watershed (*Part I*, step 1 and *Wrap Up*).

• cite similarities and differences between the K-O-E watershed and other watersheds (*Part I*, step 3).

• demonstrate how channelization contributed to the amount of sediment load delivered into Lake Okeechobee (*Part II*).

• test how increased fertilization affects algae growth in pond water (*Part II*).

• illustrate possible relationships between water diversion projects and salinity in Florida Bay (*Part II*).

• keep a record or log of K-O-E watershed issues in the news and relate the stories to components of and alterations to the watershed (*Wrap Up*).

Extensions

Students may want to finish their models by painting landscapes and constructing scale models of trees, wetlands, and riparian areas. They may introduce human influences such as towns and roads. Natural and human-made environmental problems such as sink holes and erosion could be incorporated into the design.

Involve students in making a contour model of the K-O-E watershed. Locate a topographic map with contour lines. Divide the map into sections and give one or more sections to each group of students. Each group is to construct a 3-D model of the section. The first sheet of cardboard serves as a base and represents 0' elevation. Determine the increments of elevation the contour lines represent. Each group should trace the next highest level of elevation (the contour line should either connect in a circle or its ends should

intersect with the boundaries of the section). Build up layers to represent elevations according to the contour lines on the map. Then piece together completed sections to form the whole watershed. Students can cover the model with papier-mâché or gesso, paint it with acrylics, and illustrate it with major landforms, agricultural areas, and cities. Students should compare their map with a contour map. They can predict where water will flow on the model, then sprinkle water on it to confirm predictions.

Resources

Coble, Charles, et al. 1988. *Prentice Hall Earth Science.* Englewood Cliffs, N.J.: Prentice Hall, Inc.

Duplaix, Nicole. 1990. "South Florida Water: Paying the Price." *National Geographic* 178(1): 89-114.

Marsh, William M. 1987. *Earthscape, A Physical Geography.* New York, N.Y.: John Wiley & Sons.

South Florida Water Management District. *How Much . . . How Good? The Story of South Florida's Water.*

"Water—The Power, Promise, and Turmoil of North America's Fresh Water." 1993. *National Geographic* (special edition).

KOE Watershed

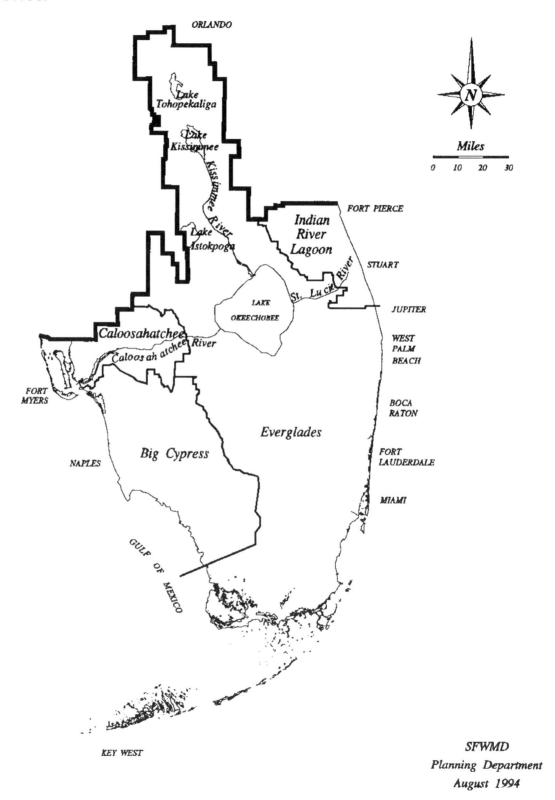

*SFWMD
Planning Department
August 1994*

Ground Water Window

Have you ever wished you had a window into the earth so you could see what's beneath your feet?

Summary

Students will observe and learn about basic ground water phenomena and principles as they create their own geologic cross section or "ground water window."

Objectives

Students will:

- identify the parts of a ground water system.

- compare movement of water through diverse substrates.

- relate different types of land uses to potential ground water contamination.

- design a model of a ground water system.

Materials

Part I

- *25 strips of white paper, 1" x 12" (number the back of the strips 1 through 25)*

- *Blue crayon or colored pencil*

- *Copies of **Well Log Data Chart***

- *Copies of **Ground Water Student Page***

Part II

Students are to develop their own ground water model. Here are some materials they may use, but students should be encouraged to use other items in the classroom or to bring materials from home.

- *Water*

- *Assorted food colors* (to simulate various pollutants)

- *Aquarium or large jars*

- *Gravel* (washed)

- *Sand* (washed)

- *Clay* (If unable to obtain clay locally, place unscented, nonclumping kitty litter in a blender and grind until fine. Mix with enough water to make moist.)

- *Objects to form underground storage tanks, sewage lagoons, etc.* (e.g., assorted paper towel or toilet paper rolls, plastic bottles)

- *Large syringe, hand-held pump, or pump from a bottle of dish detergent to extract water*

- *Assortment of clear plastic tubes or straws* (2 to 3 dozen of various lengths and diameters for injection and pumping wells. If pumps from detergent bottles are used, they may be inserted directly into the model.)

- *Fine wire screen or cheese cloth* (to cover ends of simulated pumping wells)

- *Scissors, pliers, wire cutters*

- *Waterproof glue, wire, string*

Grade Level:
Middle School, High School

Subject Areas:
Ecology, Environmental Science, Earth Science, Government

Duration:
Preparation time: Part I, 30 minutes; Part II, 50 minutes

Activity time: Part I, 50 minutes; Part II, two 50-minute periods

Setting:
Classroom

Skills:
Organizing (matching, charting); Analyzing (identifying patterns); Interpreting (inferring, translating)

Vocabulary:
ground water, hydrogeologist, zone of saturation, zone of aeration, well log, confined aquifer, unconfined aquifer, water table, permeable layer, impermeable layer

Making Connections

Out of sight is out of mind. Because ground water is hidden below Earth's surface, students do not have a visible reference point as they do when they look at water in lakes or rivers. The aquifers of southern Florida supply nearly 90 percent of the water used by people. Most students drink ground water every day. Creating a geologic cross section helps students become aware of this hidden source of water.

Background

Water stored in the pores, cracks, and openings of subsurface rock material is called ground water. Wells dug by hand or machine have been used throughout history to retrieve water from the ground. Scientists use the word "aquifer" to describe an underground formation capable of storing and transmitting water.

Aquifers come in all shapes and sizes. (See *Well Log Ground Water Chart [Cross Section]* for identification and definition of parts of a ground water system.) Some aquifers may cover hundreds of square miles and be hundreds of feet thick, while others, only a few feet thick, may cover only a few square miles. Water quality and quantity vary between aquifers and sometimes within the same system. Some aquifers yield millions of gallons of water per day and maintain water levels, while others may produce only small amounts of water each day. In some areas, wells might have to be drilled thousands of feet to reach usable water, while in other areas water is located only a few feet down. One site might contain several aquifers at different depths, while another site yields little or no ground water.

The age of ground water, the length of time it has been underground, varies from aquifer to aquifer. For example, an unconfined surface aquifer might hold water that is only a few days, weeks, or months old. On the other hand, a deep aquifer covered by one or more impervious layers may contain water that is hundreds, even thousands of years old.

The rate of movement of ground water depends on the rock material in the formation through which the water is moving. After water percolates down to the water table, it becomes ground water and starts to move slowly down the gradient. Water movement responds to differences in energy levels. The energies that cause ground water to flow are expressed as gravitational energy and pressure energy (both are forms of mechanical energy). Gravitational energy comes from the difference in elevation between the recharge area (where water enters the ground water system) and the discharge area (where water leaves the system). Pressure energy (hydraulic head) comes from the weight of overlying water and earth materials. Ground water moves toward areas of least resistance. (Ground water encountering semi-impervious material such as clay will slow down significantly; when it moves toward an open area, such as a lake, water's rate of movement will increase.)

Hydrogeologists—scientists who study ground water—are familiar with these variables and know that to really look into the ground they must build "ground water windows" by drilling wells. Wells provide the best opportunity to learn the physical, hydrologic, and chemical characteristics of an aquifer. As a well is drilled deeper and deeper into the ground, it passes through the different rock layers that form the aquifer. The driller records the exact location of the well, records the depth of each formation, and collects samples of the rock material penetrated (limestone, clay, unconsolidated sediment, etc.) for testing and further examination. This data becomes part of the well's record or *well log*. The driller's record provides valuable information for determining ground water availability, movement, quantity, and quality. The well driller then caps and seals the well to protect the aquifer from contamination.

If hazardous waste, chemicals, heavy metals, oil, etc., collect on the surface of the ground, rain or runoff percolating into the soil can carry these substances into ground water. When hydrogeologists or water quality specialists analyze the quality of ground water, they consider land use practices in the watershed and in the vicinity of the well.

Ground water is one of southern Florida's most valuable natural resources. The geologic foundation of the watershed is very porous and permeable. The rock is mostly limestone, and in some places there are intermediate impermeable layers of silt or clay. Throughout most of the watershed, layers of rock or sediment called the surficial aquifer intercept water—mostly rainfall—as it percolates down through shallow organic soil. Several layers of marine and freshwater sediments make up the surficial aquifer. The surficial layers underlying most of the watershed south of Boynton Beach—including the Keys and Florida Bay—are called the Biscayne Aquifer. Older rock layers beneath the surficial aquifer form what is called the intermediate aquifer. The intermediate aquifer is only found in some parts of the watershed, its deepest layer forming an impermeable barrier above the Floridan Aquifer. The Floridan Aquifer is under artesian pressure: it is confined by impermeable layers, top and bottom. It carries much older water to southern Florida from its recharge areas in central Florida. This water is fresh when it enters the aquifer, but becomes brackish—thus less potable—as it dissolves aquifer material during its underground journey. Sometimes reverse osmosis (RO or desalinization) plants use this brackish water because it has less salt than seawater. It takes less energy to make this water potable, and produces fewer salt waste products.

Chapters 1, and 2 contain more information about ground water.

Procedure
Warm Up
Tell students they are about to learn how they can construct and look through a "ground water window." Explain that hydrogeologists study wells to learn what types of rock material are located below ground. Ask students to draw pictures representing what they think things

look like underground (the texture and color of rock formations), or to write brief descriptions of what happens to water after it seeps into the ground.

The Activity
Part I

1. **Hand students strips of paper numbered 2-25 and copies of the *Well Log Data Chart*—students**

Sample Strip

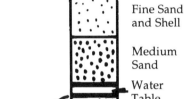

Fine Sand and Shell

Medium Sand

Water Table

Blue Colored

Course Sand

Limestone

Clay

Blue Colored

Gravel Layer

can work individually or in pairs. The length of paper represents the depth of a well that has been dug. Students will receive data about the location and types of rock materials in their wells, and will transfer this information to their strips of paper to make well logs.

2. **Demonstrate how to record the types of rock materials. Divide the strip labeled 1 into twelve one-inch sections. Show students the data from Well #1. Mark the level of the water table by drawing a double line at the appropriate point (2 inches from the top of the paper strip; this corresponds with the level found in the first column). In the second column, find the level of fine sand (0–1). Measuring from the top of the column, the first inch should be speckled with dots. From 1 inch to 2 1/2 inches, the formation is composed of medium sand. Coarse sand exists between 2 1/2 and 6 inches and so forth until the gravel layer, which fills the space between 8 and 12 inches. Complete the drawing by coloring the area between the water table and the top of the clay layer light blue. Also color the gravel layer.**

3. **Have students fill in their logs based on the number on their strips of paper (if a strip is labeled 6, the student uses data from Well # 6). Make sure students note the type of land use above their well sites.**

4. **When they have completed their well logs, ask students to answer questions based on their well logs.**

a. The horizontal scale of the cross section is 1 inch = 1 mile. The vertical scale is 1 inch = 50 feet. How many miles are horizontally represented in the cross section? How many feet are vertically represented in the cross section?

b. How many feet below the surface is the water table?

c. Ask each student to imagine a drop of water falling on the surface above his or her well. What pollutants might this drop of water pick up as it filters into the ground? (Students can refer to the land use practices above their well, but may conclude they need additional information.)

d. Have students describe the drop's movement down the column (cross section). Through which layers would it move faster? Slower?

e. Which layer might restrict the drop's movement? Explain to students that only a slight amount of water would pass through the clay. Have them speculate on the source of the water beneath the clay level (in the gravel layer).

5. Invite students to assemble their well logs in order and tape them to a wall. Distribute a copy of the *Ground Water Student Page* to each student. Compare students' well log cross sections to the chart.

a. Provide the following definitions and have students locate these parts of a ground water system on the *Well Log Ground Water Chart (Cross Section).*

• Water Table: The top of an unconfined aquifer; indicates the level below which soil and rock are saturated with water.

• Confined Aquifer: An aquifer

that is bounded above and below by impermeable layers and transmits water significantly more slowly than an unconfined aquifer. The water level in a well that taps a confined aquifer will rise above the top of the aquifer because the confined aquifer is under pressure. Also called artesian aquifer. Example: the Floridan Aquifer.

• Unconfined Aquifer: An aquifer in which the upper boundary is the water table. Example: the Biscayne Aquifer.

• Permeable Layer: The portion of aquifer that contains porous rock materials that allow water to penetrate and move freely.

• Impermeable Layer: The portion of aquifer that contains rock material that does not allow water to penetrate. Often forms the base of unconfined aquifers and the boundaries of confined aquifers. Also called an "aquiclude."

• Zone of Saturation: The part of a water-bearing formation in which all spaces between soil particles and in rock structures are filled with water.

• Zone of Aeration: The portion of an unconfined aquifer above the water table where the pore spaces among soil particles and rock formations are filled with air.

b. Ask students what direction the ground water is moving in the unconfined aquifer. (Predominantly moves from left to right.)

c. What are water sources for the unconfined aquifer? (rainfall, wetlands, canals, the river)

d. How long would it take the

water in the limestone formation to move from Well #1 to Well #15? (Assume the water moves at a constant rate and flows 100 feet per day [1 mile = 5280 feet].)

e. Now that students know about the land use above other well sites and the direction water flows, how would they answer question 4c?

f. Have students refer to the *Cone of Depression* diagram. Explain that the cone of depression results from water being drawn up the well. Ask them to locate the cone of depression on the *Well Log Ground Water Chart (Cross Section).*

g. Instruct students to refer to the *Well Log Data Chart.* What are possible sources of water in the confined aquifer? (Compare answers to 4e.)

Part II

1. Divide the class into "design teams."

2. Have the teams use the information provided (*Warm Up* and *Part I*) and the materials available to design and construct a ground water flow model. Tell each team that their model and presentation should demonstrate the following: the layering of sediments (rocks); permeability; unconfined and confined aquifers; the water table; zones of saturation and aeration; how aquifers are recharged; sources of ground water pollution; and how wells function. *NOTE:* A diagram has been provided to show one possible set-up.

3. Have the design teams designate a spokesperson or spokespersons to explain and demonstrate their model to the class.

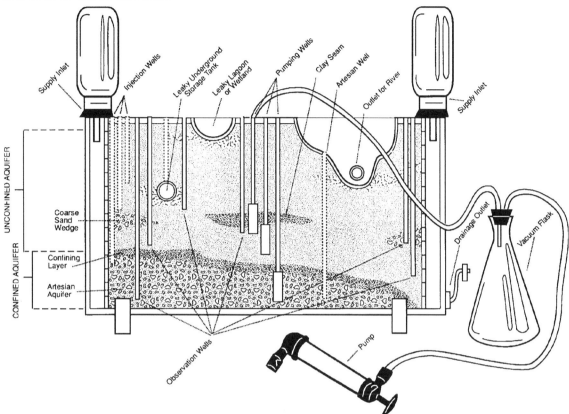

Ground water flow model.

Wrap Up

Have design teams compare their ground water flow models with the diagram of Project WET's model.

Students may be interested in learning about the rock formations beneath their community. The local water department or company might have a geologic cross section for the city or region. Students could attempt to interpret the maps.

Assessment

Have students:

• construct a well log (*Part I*, steps 2 and 3).

• analyze possible effects on ground water based on interpretations of the well logs (*Part I*, steps 4 and 5).

• determine when additional data are needed to draw valid conclusions (*Part I*, steps 4 and 5).

• identify the parts of a ground water system (*Part I*, step 5).

• compare the movement of water through diverse substrates (*Part II*, step 2).

• create a model of a ground water system (*Part II*, step 2).

Extensions

Does your school have its own well? If so, consider visiting the well site and performing a survey of possible pollution sources in the well's vicinity. What are they and where are they located? Should something be done to remove them? What are the options? The water quality of

your school's well is public information and would make an interesting study. Has your school experienced water quality problems?

The county health department environmental health section monitors drinking water quality. Many counties have environmental resource departments that work toward pollution prevention. Once students have base-level understanding of ground water, these and other resources may provide additional educational opportunities.

Share with students the diagram *Salt Water Intrusion*. Discuss how salt water can contaminate freshwater wells. When can salt water intrusion become a serious problem for coastal South Florida

Salt Water Intrusion

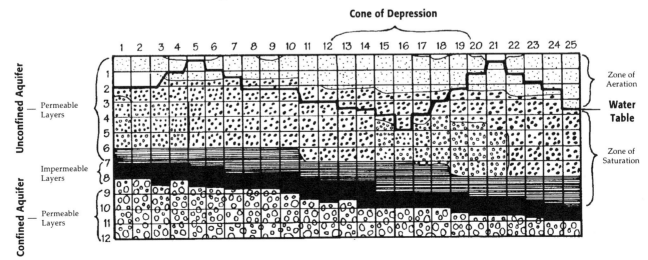

RAINFALL   **RAINFALL**

OCEAN OR GULF (Salt Water)

RUNOFF   **RUNOFF**

Mangroves

RECHARGE   **RECHARGE**

WELLS

SALT WATER   SALT WATER   SALT WATER   SALT WATER

FRESHWATER LENS

SALT WATER

Salt Water Intrusion
Caused by Overuse of Wells
and Lack of Recharge

residents? (During drought.)

Challenge students to devise a model that demonstrates a sink hole. For example, they could fill a water balloon, bury it, place model houses on top, and slowly extract the water. What happens?

Add a septic tank (using a plastic bottle with holes in it), or a surface water retention/detention pond (a shallow, unlined depres-

sion) to the ground water flow model. Observe the results. What happens?

Resources

Ground Water Flow Model: a Plexiglas sand tank model, video, and user's guide that demonstrate basic ground water principles and management concerns. Contact: Project WET, 201 Culbertson Hall, Montana State University,

Bozeman, MT 59717. (406) 994-5392.

Hoff, Mary, and Mary M. Rogers. 1991. *Our Endangered Planet: Ground Water*. Minneapolis, Minn.: Lerner.

Taylor, Carla, ed. 1985. *Ground Water: A Vital Resource*. Knoxville, Tenn.: Tennessee Valley Authority.

Well Log Ground Water Chart (Cross Section)

Cone of Depression

1 2 3 4 5 6 7 8 9 10 11 12 13 14 15 16 17 18 19 20 21 22 23 24 25

Unconfined Aquifer

Permeable Layers

Confined Aquifer

Impermeable Layers

Permeable Layers

1 2 3 4 5 6 7 8 9 10 11 12

Zone of Aeration

Water Table

Zone of Saturation

170

Well Log Data Chart

Well No.	Land Use Type	Water Table	Fine Sand and Shell	Medium Sand	Coarse Sand	Limestone	Clay Layer	Gravel Layer
				KEY Note: numbers in vertical columns are in inches				
1	farmland	2	0 - 1	1 - $2^1/_2$	$2^1/_2$ - 6	6 - 7	7 - 8	8 - 12
2	farmland	2	0 - 1	1 - 3	3 - 6	6 - 7	7 - 8	8 - 12
3	farmland	2	0 - $1^1/_2$	$1^1/_2$ - 3	3 - 6	6 - 7	7 - $8^1/_2$	$8^1/_2$ - 12
4	wetland	1	$^1/_4$ - $1^1/_2$	$1^1/_2$ - 3	3 - 6	6 - 7	7 - $8^1/_4$	$8^1/_4$ - $11^1/_2$
5	wetland	$^1/_4$	$^1/_2$ - $1^1/_2$	$1^1/_2$ - 6	—	6 - $7^1/_4$	$7^1/_4$ - $8^1/_4$	$8^1/_4$ - $11^1/_2$
6	wetland	1	$^1/_4$ - $1^3/_4$	$1^3/_4$ - 6	—	6 - $7^1/_4$	$7^1/_4$ - $8^1/_2$	$8^1/_2$ - 11
7	farmland	$1^3/_4$	0 - $1^3/_4$	$1^3/_4$ - 6	—	6 - $7^3/_4$	$7^3/_4$ - $8^3/_4$	$8^3/_4$ - 11
8	farmland	$2^1/_2$	0 - $1^3/_4$	$1^3/_4$ - 6	—	6 - $7^3/_4$	$7^3/_4$ - $8^3/_4$	$8^3/_4$ - 11
9	landfill	$2^1/_2$	$^3/_4$ - $1^3/_4$	$1^3/_4$ - 6	—	6 - $7^3/_4$	$7^3/_4$ - $8^3/_4$	$8^3/_4$ - 11
10	industry	$2^1/_2$	0 - $1^3/_4$	$1^3/_4$ - 6	—	6 - $7^3/_4$	$7^3/_4$ - 9	9 - 11
11	industry	3	0 - 2	2 - 7	—	7 - 8	8 - $9^1/_4$	$9^1/_4$ - $11^1/_2$
12	urban area	3	0 - $2^1/_4$	$2^1/_4$ - 7	—	7 - $8^1/_4$	$8^1/_4$ - $9^1/_2$	$9^1/_2$ - $11^1/_2$
13	urban area	$3^1/_2$	0 - $2^1/_4$	$2^1/_4$ - 7	—	7 - $8^1/_4$	$8^1/_4$ - $9^1/_2$	$9^1/_2$ - $11^1/_2$
14	urban area	$3^3/_4$	0 - $2^1/_4$	$2^1/_4$ - 7	—	7 - $8^1/_2$	$8^1/_2$ - $9^3/_4$	$9^3/_4$ - $11^1/_2$
15	urban area	4	0 - $2^3/_4$	$2^3/_4$ - $4^1/_2$	$4^1/_2$ - 7	7 - 9	9 - $9^3/_4$	$9^3/_4$ - 12
16	urban area	5	0 - $2^3/_4$	$2^3/_4$ - $4^1/_2$	$4^1/_2$ - 7	7 - 9	9 - $9^3/_4$	$9^3/_4$ - 12
17	farmland	4	0 - $2^3/_4$	$2^3/_4$ - $4^1/_2$	$4^1/_2$ - $7^1/_2$	$7^1/_2$ - 9	9 - 10	10 - 12
18	wastewater treatment plant	3	$^1/_4$ - $2^1/_2$	$2^1/_2$ - 4	4 - $7^1/_2$	$7^1/_2$ - 9	9 - 10	10 - 12
19	farmland	$2^1/_2$	0 - $2^1/_4$	$2^1/_4$ - $4^1/_2$	$4^1/_2$ - 8	8 - 9	9 - $10^1/_4$	$10^1/_4$ - 12
20	river	$1^1/_2$	$^1/_4$ - $2^1/_2$	$2^1/_2$ - $4^1/_2$	$4^1/_2$ - 8	8 - $9^1/_4$	$9^1/_4$ - $10^1/_2$	$10^1/_2$ - 12
21	river	$^1/_2$	1 - $2^1/_2$	$2^1/_2$ - 5	5 - 8	8 - $9^1/_4$	$9^1/_4$ - $10^1/_2$	$10^1/_2$ - 12
22	river	$1^1/_2$	$^1/_4$ - 3	3 - 8	—	8 - $9^1/_4$	$9^1/_4$ - $10^1/_2$	$10^1/_2$ - 12
23	national park	2	0 - 3	3 - 8	—	8 - $9^1/_2$	$9^1/_2$ - $10^3/_4$	$10^3/_4$ - 12
24	national park	$3^1/_4$	0 - $2^3/_4$	$2^3/_4$ - 8	—	8 - $9^3/_4$	$9^3/_4$ - 11	11 - 12
25	national park	$3^3/_4$	0 - 3	3 - 8	—	8 - 10	10 - $11^1/_4$	$11^1/_4$ - 12

Ground Water Student Page

Name:_____ Date:_____

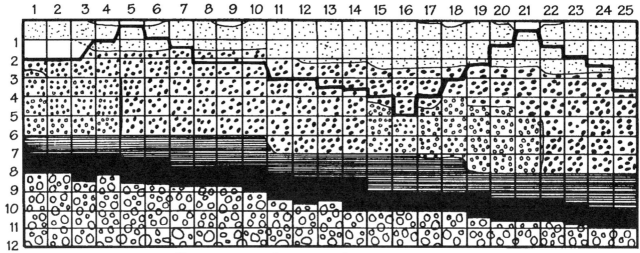

Well Log Ground Water Chart (Cross Section)

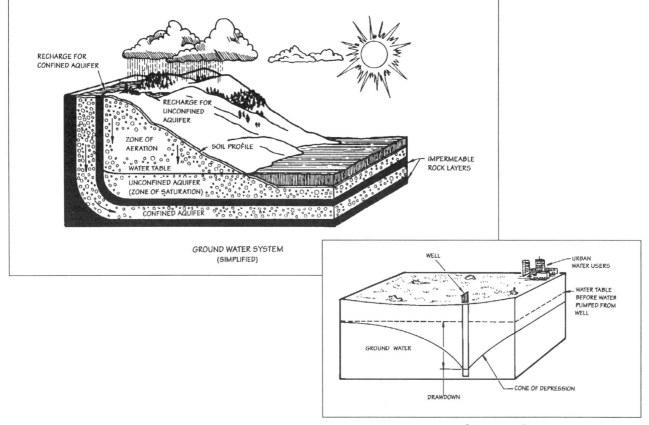

Cone of Depression

Parallels

Grade Level:
Middle School, High School

Subject Areas:
Geography, Earth Science, Ecology

Duration:
Preparation time: 50 minutes

Activity time: two 50-minute periods

Setting:
Classroom

Skills:
Gathering information; Interpreting

Vocabulary:
latitude, weather, climate

Are things that are parallel always similar?

Summary
Students trace the latitude of southern Florida around the world, comparing the weather, climate, and other environmental factors of the watershed with those of other land masses on or near the 28th parallel.

Objectives
Students will:

• identify why global locations of the same latitude have comparable or dissimilar weather patterns.

Materials
• *World atlas* (one for each group)

• *Water-soluble markers*

• *Rulers*

• *Pencils, pens*

• *Writing pads*

• *Newspaper (e.g., USA Today) showing daily or weekly world weather* (optional)

• *Earth science and geology texts* (optional)

Making Connections
Most students know that weather and climate change as one changes latitude, traveling further north or south. Differences in temperature and precipitation can cause changes in vegetation. Comparing places around the globe on the same latitude as Florida helps students comprehend how geographical features affect weather.

Background
Weather is the condition of the atmosphere at a given place and time. Climate is the long-term trend or pattern of the weather. While weather and climate are affected by elevation of land and distribution of bodies of land and water, temperature is a main variable. Because warm air holds more moisture than cold air, and because land and water heat differentially, temperature affects precipitation, and is another variable of weather and climate.

Latitude measures a location's distance above or below the equator. Because the sun is directly overhead only at the equator, latitude also indicates the sun's angle of inclination to the earth, and the daily duration and extent of solar heating. Since air, land, and water are heated mainly by the sun, latitude has a major effect on weather and climate. Prevailing currents in the atmosphere and oceans also affect weather and climate. The direction of these "invisible rivers" varies with latitude.

Because weather and climate affect the growth of plant life, latitude also has an indirect effect on the development of plant communities, which in turn, often affect the patterns of human habitation and use of a region.

Generally, locations at similar latitudes around the globe have "parallel" temperature, precipitation, vegetation, and other gross environmental similarities. Many areas at the same latitude as Florida are deserts, but the Gulf Stream moderates climate in Florida by circulating warm oceanic water along the peninsular coast. Warm water affects the regional weather, particularly the development of sea breezes, clouds, and precipitation.

Refer to chapter 3 for additional information about Florida climate.

Procedure

Warm Up
Show students pictures from Nepal and pictures from Florida. Do not tell them where the pictures are from. Where would students expect to find each place on the globe? Explain that Florida is on the same latitude as Nepal (lower elevations in Nepal do have tropical weather). Ask students if they think locations around the world at the same latitude could be expected to have

similar weather, climates, vegetation, and other environmental conditions. Have students predict which factors might be similar.

Discuss the concepts of latitude, weather, and climate, how they are interrelated, and how they affect the structure and composition of vegetative communities and other factors in the environment.

The Activity
1. **Divide the class into groups of two or three. One student will be the reporter, the rest researchers. Provide each group with a world atlas, paper, pencils, and writing pads.**

2. **Have students locate the latitudinal line that passes through Florida and trace it around the world. Each group should select a different country or part of a country on the same latitude as Florida.**

3. **Tell students to refer to the world atlas thematic maps (i.e., maps depicting climate, rainfall, natural vegetation, landforms, soils, etc.), noting similarities or differences under those topics. They should create a grid comparing Florida and the other country or place.**

4. **Ask students to determine why the southern Florida environment differs from other environments along the same parallel. They may need to refer to earth science and geology texts.** For example, Nepal is a mountainous country with elevations over 20,000 (6,000 m) feet. Increasing elevation is like moving further north on the globe. Higher elevations have fewer air molecules (gravity pulls air closer to Earth's surface). With fewer molecules striking against each other and against other surfaces, heat energy has diffi-

	Climatic region	Vegetation	Soils	Rainfall	Temperature
Florida					
Other Country					

28th parallel-Nepal

28th parallel-Florida.

culty transferring among the molecules. Therefore, the air feels colder at higher elevations. Plants and animals at higher elevations are those that can survive with less oxygen and at colder temperatures than those at lower elevations (extremely high elevations cannot support any plants and very few other organisms).

5. **Have student representatives present their group's findings to the class.**

Wrap Up

Create a class list of all the countries and weather patterns investigated. What consistencies, if any, can be found?

Have students hypothesize what environmental changes (e.g., rainfall, temperature) might cause southern Florida to become more like many of the other locations on or near the same latitude. Are those changes occurring? Are human activities accelerating them? What can be done to prevent or ameliorate those changes?

Assessment

Have students:

• locate countries and regions around the globe at the same latitude as Florida (step 2).

• identify similarities and differences among countries and regions located on the 28th parallel (step 3).

• cite reasons for varying weather patterns among countries and regions located on the 28th parallel (step 5).

• hypothesize environmental

changes that could alter southern Florida's weather patterns (*Wrap Up*).

Extensions

Have students record monthly weather data (e.g., precipitation) in a chart or log. Invite them to select locations on or near the same parallel of latitude around the world—including southern Florida. Weather data may be obtained from newspapers (e.g., *USA Today*) or from the U.S. Weather Service.

Resources

Espenshade, Edward B., Jr. 1990. *Goodes World Atlas*. Chicago, Ill.: Rand McNally. NOTE: Any reputable world atlas can be substituted.

Marsh, William M. 1987. *Earthscape: A Physical Geography*. New York, N.Y.: John Wiley & Sons.

Miller, G. Tyler, Jr. 1990. *Resource Conservation and Management*. Belmont, Calif.: Wadsworth Publishing Co.

Hurricane!

"It looked like the aftermath of an atomic blast. The center of the storm had wrapped up so tight and become so strong that its power was that of a monstrous tornado. Homestead was not just damaged; it was literally destroyed."

—John Adams, director of field operations for the South Florida Water Management District.

Summary
Students plot the path of hurricanes and predict if they will make landfall.

Objectives
Students will:

• analyze data to interpret patterns and placements of hurricanes.

• make predictions as to whether or not hurricanes will make landfall based on past observations and statistics.

Materials
• *Copies of Coordinates for Hurricanes (Parts I and II), Hurricane Plotting Map, and Hurricane Fact Sheet*

• *Pens or pencils (four different colors)*

• *Rulers*

Making Connections
Hurricanes are more frequent in southern Florida than in any other area in the United States. Because of the impact of hurri-canes on lives and property, media report heavily on these phenomena. Many students have lived through hurricanes or know someone who has. Students may also see results of hurricane action in their daily lives (de-stroyed trees, restored buildings, new growth along beaches). Learning about historic hurri-canes shows students how scientists record facts and data to prepare for future hurricanes and their impact.

Background
Hurricanes are the product of warm, open water and certain atmospheric conditions. These conditions do not occur in winter or spring, but are possible from June to November each year in the North Atlantic Ocean, Carib-bean Sea, and Gulf of Mexico.

The following hurricanes had heavy impact on the people and ecosystems of southern Florida:

The "Labor Day" Hurricane, 1935
Though small in diameter, the Labor Day Hurricane was one of the most intense hurricanes ever recorded. First sighted east and north of Turks Island (90 miles [140 k] north of the Dominican Republic), it moved toward the Florida Straits in a broad curve and hit the Florida Keys late on September 2. The storm surge at Long and Matecumbe Keys reached a height of 16.5 to 18.5

feet (5 to 5.5 m) above mean sea level. The wind velocity is believed to have been from 200 to 250 miles (320 to 400 k) per hour. After leaving the Keys, the storm continued up the west coast of Florida, passing inland at Cedar Key. Reported damage amounted to about six million dollars.

In this storm, 121 war veterans who were working on road projects at Islamorada drowned. The 11-car rescue train that had been sent for them was derailed and overturned. Ernest Hemingway, who helped in the cleanup, wrote articles condemning the federal government for not planning evacuation measures before sending the men to the Florida Keys. Throughout the Keys and Cape Sable, 376 men, women, and children were lost. A story from *A Dredgeman of Cape Sable* describes how the last people to leave Flamingo (in Everglades National Park) fared. It is the true story of Joe, a Flamingo resident, and a fisherman and his two young boys.

Recounting the story Joe said he tied the younger boy's arms around his neck and his legs around his waist. He told the father to take the older boy. Joe said that if he made it so would the boy he carried; and if they drowned they would be found together.

As he waded through the treacherous waves which rolled in from Florida Bay, Joe said he was blinded by the rain, and frequently slipped on the marl as he struggled to find the road embankment. As the wind hurled him against trees and wind-driven waves washed him off

course, he walked, swam and even crawled to make progress. And all of his efforts were accomplished in darkness.

Joe and the boy struggled three days to travel the distance of eight miles to West Lake where searchers from Homestead found them. Joe was delirious for two days in the hospital and the boy's ankles and wrists were so badly cut it took weeks for them to heal. The boy's father also survived, but the older son did not. Although Joe was a very outgoing and talkative fellow, he could seldom be persuaded to recount his personal ordeal in the hurricane of 1935.

Hurricane Donna, 1960
Donna formed near the Cape Verde Islands and traveled across the Atlantic. The eye crossed the middle Florida Keys on September 10 with the hurricane at its peak intensity. Sustained winds were 135 miles (225 k) per hour with gusts up to 174 miles (290 k) per hour. Storm surge was high in the Keys and the lower west coast of Florida.

Hurricane winds and storm surge.

After the Keys, Donna moved north and the eye went over Naples and Fort Myers. Winds of 96.6 miles (161 k) per hour with gusts to 144 miles (240 k) per hour buffeted these areas and the Everglades to the east. The effect of the hurricane on the plants and animals of the Everglades was described as follows: "After the hurricane, observers in the main storm area found a world without one green leaf, the vegetation browned as if by fire. The largest stand of big mangrove trees in the world is located near the southern tip of Florida and was 50 percent or more killed with a complete kill in some areas. [This included many trees that survived the 'Labor Day' Hurricane of 1935.] The great white heron, only found in the United States in extreme southern Florida and once in danger of extinction, suffered about a 35 to 40 percent loss but some 600 of these beautiful birds survived."

Near Daytona Beach, the storm moved into the Atlantic, strengthened over water, and later moved

up the northeastern coast of the United States with hurricane force winds.

Hurricane Camille, 1969
Camille was classified as a violent category 5 storm, with a maximum storm surge of 24.2 feet (7.4 m). It hit the coasts of Mississippi and Louisiana with such force that it leveled the Mississippi towns of Gulfport and Pass Christian. Camille took the lives of 256 people, left 10,000 homeless, and caused damages of $1,420 million. This hurricane was the only category 5 to have hit the United States in modern times.

Hurricane Hugo, September 1989
Hurricane Hugo was an immense category 4 storm. (Hurricane Andrew was also a category 4.) Hurricanes are categorized on a scale from one to five. Classification is determined by wind velocity, central pressure, and height of storm surge. Storm surge is the rise in water level on a coast as a consequence of the hurricane. Minor hurricanes rate 1; storms with severe wind velocities and low pressures rate 5. Hurricane Hugo caused extensive destruction in South Carolina. It took the lives of 49 people, left 77,000 homeless, and caused millions of dollars in damage. Hugo traveled a path typical of a major hurricane.

Hurricane Andrew, 1992
With sustained winds greater than 140 miles (87 k) per hour, Hurricane Andrew joined the ranks of Hurricanes Donna, Betsy (1965), David (1979) and 30 others whose names have been retired because they were particularly intense or destructive. Causing property damages approaching

$30 billion, Hurricane Andrew has been described as a 30-mile-wide tornado.

Refer to chapter 3 for additional information on the weather and climate of southern Florida.

Procedure
Warm Up
Ask students if they have experienced a hurricane or other major weather event. Possibly some students went through Hurricane Andrew in 1992. If so, not all of them may wish to discuss their experiences. Because of the emotional impact, all students should be respected in their desire to share or not. (If this discussion will make students uncomfortable, begin the warm up with the next paragraph.)

Discuss with students how hurricanes are formed. Review latitude, longitude, and mapping skills. Students will be plotting the progress of hurricanes—three actual and one fictional.

The Activity
1. **Divide the class into groups of three or four. Give each group a copy of the *Hurricane Plotting Map*, the *Hurricane Fact Sheet*, and *Coordinates for Hurricanes (Part I)*. Make sure they have pens or pencils of four different colors.**

2. **Tell students to plot each set of data in a different color and to use the results and information from the *Hurricane Fact Sheet* to determine if the hurricane is a historic storm and, if it was real, to predict if it made landfall.** Considering where the hurricane met land, can students guess the time of year the storm occurred? What was the probability a

hurricane would land in this part of Florida?

3. **After students have written down their predictions, give them *Coordinates for Hurricanes (Part II)* and have them plot the final points on the map.**

Wrap Up and Action
Have students discuss the reasons for their conclusions. Were they correct in identifying which hurricane was the fictional one? Why did the fourth set of coordinates not represent a real hurricane?

Which hurricanes did they think would make landfall? How did they come to this conclusion? If their conclusions were incorrect, what have they learned from their errors? Remember, although meteorologists have studied hurricanes extensively and can make predictions, nature doesn't always follow predicted pathways.

Ask if they know the names of the hurricanes or the years they actually occurred. Tell them that the three hurricanes were Camille, 1969, Hugo, 1989, and Andrew, 1992. Read the descriptions of these storms from the **Background** or other reference materials. Tell students to write the names of the storms on their tracking maps.

Remind students how dangerous these storms were to people in their path. Have students design a brochure that describes the way hurricanes are formed; the frequency and probability of hurricanes in southern Florida; and safety measures people should take in preparing for a storm. Students may select the most effective brochure and have it copied and distributed to community members or posted in local businesses.

Assessment

Have students:

• analyze facts to determine if they apply to known information about hurricanes (step 2 and *Wrap Up*).

• interpret plotted data about a hurricane's path to predict the hurricane's destination (step 2).

• evaluate accuracy of conclusions drawn (*Wrap Up*).

• write and design a brochure providing information about the development of hurricanes and safety measures people in their paths should take (*Wrap Up*).

Extensions

Discuss with students how hurricanes affect not only people but also other animals and plants. For example, Hurricane Donna devastated about 120 square miles (312 sq. km) of mangrove swamps, killing about half the trees. Also, the storm wiped out about 90 percent of epiphytes. Hurricane Andrew caused real concern that nonnative, invasive species may have spread to environments stressed by the hurricane.

Remind students that hurricanes do have beneficial effects. Hurricanes distribute seeds and introduce organisms to new areas. Tree snails may have come to southern Florida on a branch blown from a tree in the West Indies. Some people maintain that a hurricane would invigorate the Florida Bay system. Also, hurricanes bring moisture.

Hurricanes can provide issues for debate. Two scenarios follow; students can investigate and present views on them during a classroom discussion or debate.

• As research continues in the field of tropical meteorology, emphasis will be placed not only on forecasting the movement and intensity of these storms but also on controlling them. In the future, scientists may even be able to steer hurricanes. Ask students to imagine the legal and ethical questions that might arise. For example, where do you allow such a storm to strike? Do you divert a hurricane away from a land area and lose the valuable water such a storm brings?

• Florida's population growth has caused development in surge-vulnerable and other high-risk areas. This has not only affected the environment, but has placed a greater number of people in hurricane-prone areas. There has been discussion about prohibiting reconstruction of buildings within 150 feet (45 m) of the mean high tide line if they are ever destroyed by hurricanes or other forces of nature. This is controversial because hundreds of expensive buildings occupy this zone. What do you think? Consider all sides of the issue and develop positive and negative positions for each.

Resources

Douglas, Marjory Stoneman. 1976. *Hurricane.* Covington, Ga.: Mockingbird Books, Inc.

Doehring, F., I. W. Duedall and J. M. Williams. 1994. *Florida Hurricanes and Tropical Storms, 1871-1993: An Historical Survey.*

Technical paper–71. Florida Sea Grant College. Gainesville, FL.

"Hurricane Andrew's Sweep through Natural Ecosystems." *BioScience* 44(4).

Loftin, Jan P. 1993. "In the Wake of Hurricane Andrew." *Florida Water* (Winter): 3-9.

Macchio, William J. 1992. *Path of Destruction: Hurricane Andrew.* Charleston, S. C.: BD Publishing, Inc.

Will, Lawrence E. 1984. *A Dredgeman of Cape Sable.* Belle Glade, Fla.: The Glades Historical Society.

Winsberg, Morton D. 1990. *Florida Weather.* Orlando, Fla.: University of Central Florida Press.

NOTE: Most counties in southern Florida have an emergency management division. Once students have learned the basics about hurricanes, these agencies may be able to provide additional resources.

Coordinates for Hurricanes (Part I)

Coordinates for Hurricane #1
Day 1: 9.7N, 21.0W

Day 2: 10.5N, 33.3W

Day 3: 12.3N, 41.9W

Day 4: 15N, 50.0W

Day 5: 17.9N, 56.9W

Day 6: 21.7N, 60.7W

Coordinates for Hurricane #2
Day 1: 13.2N 47.8W

Day 2: 14.2N 53.3W

Day 3: 15.4N 58.4W

Day 4: 16.6N 62.5W

Coordinates for Hurricane #3
Day 0: 20.8N 83.8W
(upgraded to a hurricane on this day)

Day 1: 22.4N 84.4W

Day 2: 25.3N 87.2W

Coordinates for Hurricane #4
Day 1: 50.0N 25.1W

Day 2: 53.2N 35.1W

Day 3: 53.0 N 43.2W

Day 4: 48.1N 50.2W

Day 5: 45.5N 55.1W

Day 6: 43.0N 60.1W

- -

Coordinates for Hurricanes (Part II)

Coordinates for Hurricane #1
Day 7: 24.4N, 64.1W

Day 8: 25.8N, 68.3W

Day 9: 25.4 N, 74.1W

Day 10: 25.5N, 81.4W

Day 11: 27.2N, 88.2W

Day 12: 30.0N, 91.7W

This hurricane occurred in late August.

Coordinates for Hurricane #2
Day 5: 18.2N 65.5W

Day 6: 21.6N 68.0W

Day 7: 25.2N 71.0W

Day 8: 29.0N 76.1W

This storm was upgraded to a hurricane on September 13.

Coordinates for Hurricane #3
Day 3: 29.3N 89.0W

Day 4: Inland

This storm was upgraded to a hurricane on August 14.

Coordinates for Hurricane #4
Day 7: 40.0N 65.1W

Day 8: 35.1N 70.0W

Day 9: 33.3N 73.1W

Day 10: 30.1N 75.2W

Day 11: 27.1N 81.0W

This storm was upgraded to a hurricane on November 1.

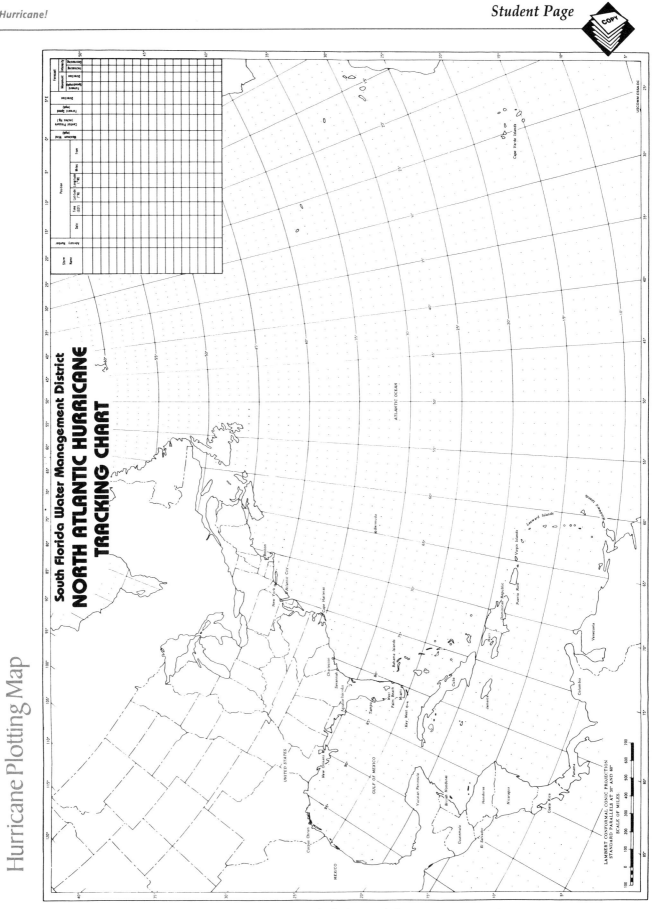

South Florida Water Management District

NORTH ATLANTIC HURRICANE TRACKING CHART

Hurricane Plotting Map

Hurricane Fact Sheet

(Consider the following information to determine if the hurricane you're tracking actually occurred and if it made landfall.)

• A storm is determined to be a hurricane if the winds are 74 miles (119 k) per hour or higher and the storm occurs in the Atlantic Ocean, Caribbean Sea, or the Gulf of Mexico in summer and fall.

• The frequency of hurricanes is greater in the Keys of southern Florida than in any other area in the United States. So many hurricanes reach Florida's southeastern shore and proceed up the east coast that this area has become known as Hurricane Alley.

• The highest risk of hurricanes is on the coasts from Florida Bay to Melbourne and from Pensacola to Panama City; there is an expected return rate of one hurricane every six to eight years. In general, hurricanes frequent southern Florida on an average of once every three years.

• The following chart indicates the annual probability (in percentage) that a tropical storm, hurricane, or great hurricane will strike in each 50-mile coastal sector (23 through 29—see map).

Tropical storm: maximum winds greater than 34 knots or 39 miles (64.7 km) per hour

Hurricanes: maximum winds greater than 65 knots or 74 miles (123 km) per hour

Great Hurricanes: sustained winds of 97 knots or 113 miles (187.6 km) per hour

Coastal Sector	23	24	25	26	27	28	29
Tropical storms (%)	12	21	19	18	16	20	20
Hurricanes (%)	5	9	13	13	12	16	15
Great Hurricanes (%)	1	2	4	2	5	7	7

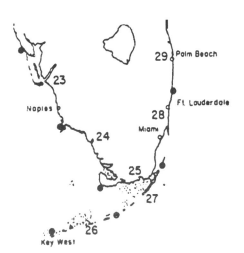

From "Hurricanes in South Florida" by R. Cecil Gentry
National Oceanic and Atmospheric Administration

Hurricane Fact Sheet (cont.)

• The peak time for hurricanes is mid-August through October, when ocean temperatures are warmest and humidity highest.

• Hurricanes that reach Florida early in the season (before June) often make landfall on the Gulf coast.

• In September, the panhandle and the southeast historically have received a large number of hurricanes. In late August and September, the most powerful hurricanes on the Atlantic are born in an area south of the Cape Verde Islands.

• Most hurricanes that have occurred in October and November have reached land in the southeast. Hurricanes late in the season may come from the Gulf of Mexico, the Caribbean Sea, or from the Atlantic Ocean. Any western Caribbean hurricane late in the season is a threat to Florida.

• Three forces contribute most of the damage caused by hurricanes: storm surge, winds, and rains. The storm surge is the most dangerous single element of a hurricane (nine out of ten people who die in a hurricane drown in the storm surge). The storm surge is the high tides and rough seas associated with the storm as it moves across a coastal area. If the ocean bottom slopes easily up to the coast, the storm surge will probably be higher than if there is deep water near the shoreline. (However, the greatest loss of life in a Florida hurricane occurred in 1928 when 2,000 people were drowned by water blown out of Lake Okeechobee.) The rains associated with a hurricane can be destructive or beneficial. The amount of rain resulting from a hurricane is determined by multiple factors. Three obvious factors are: the rate at which rain is falling in a particular area; the speed at which the storm is moving; and the size of the storm. Hurricane Andrew only averaged about eight inches of rain. Large-diameter, slow-moving storms can release as much as 20 inches (50 cm) of rain. Tornado outbreaks can also cause considerable damage and loss of life.

Survival!

Grade Level:
Middle School, High School

Subject Areas:
Life Science, Ecology, History, Language Arts

Duration:
Preparation time: Part I, 10 minutes; Part II, 10 minutes

Activity time: Part I, two 50-minute periods; Part II, up to one week

Setting:
Classroom

Skills:
Analyzing; Interpreting

Vocabulary:
wetlands, greenways

"Of the Everglades, they gave conflicting accounts . . . The sawgrass, he said, is from 5 to 10 feet tall, very thick and so stiff and sharp that it cuts like the edge of a razor; no gloves or clothes can withstand it."
—Alonzo Church, 1892

Summary
Students sharpen their survival skills as they "travel" through the plant communities of the Everglades watershed.

Objectives
Students will:

• associate dominant plants with specific communities.

• correlate elevation changes with community composition.

• identify projects to increase or enhance green space or greenways.

Materials
• *Copies of **Plant Communities Map***

• *Copies of **Survival!***

• *Plant identification and reference texts*

• *Copies of **Plant Identification Book (sample pages)***

Making Connections
When people think of Florida, they imagine palms and citrus trees throughout the state. They may not appreciate that varying conditions such as elevation and soil saturation cause some Florida soils to favor the growth of one plant species over another. Simulating an adventure through the Everglades increases students' awareness of the diversity of plant communities in southern Florida.

Background
In the book *Protecting Paradise: 300 ways to Protect Florida's Environment*, Florida's plant communities are described as "irreplaceable landscapes." Authors Cavanaugh and Spontak write, "Since 1950, Florida has lost over half of its wetlands, one-quarter of its forests, and most of its tropical hardwood hammocks, scrub, and coastal habitat."

Depending on the classification system you use, the Kissimmee-Okeechobee-Everglades watershed has over a dozen distinct plant communities. These include hardwood hammocks, pinelands (flatwoods and pine rockland), scrub or strands, dry prairies, freshwater swamps, freshwater marshes, mangrove swamps, and coastal marshes. Specific plant species (some of which overlap among communities), elevation, soil type, moisture levels, fire tolerance, and other characteristics distinguish each of these communities.

Although all communities are valuable, wetlands (including swamps, hammocks, marshes, and some prairies) are extremely so, economically and environmentally. What functions do wetlands perform? Among other things, they provide

• nursery and spawning grounds for fish and shellfish

• storage for rainwater

• a filtering system to cleanse water moving through them

• a trap for petroleum wastes, sediments, pesticides, and heavy metals

• flood and erosion control

• nesting for waterfowl

• habitat for numerous species, including many endangered animals

• rain generation (Some scientists maintain that the loss of wetlands has affected Florida's rainfall. Central and southern Florida receive 10 percent less rainfall than in historic times. There may be a link between reduced rainfall and reduced wetlands, since there is less surface water for evaporation.)

In general, plants and trees are valuable natural resources. With 314 species, Florida has greater diversity of tree species than any other state in the nation. However, since 1930, the "land of flowers" has lost 3 million acres (1,200,000 ha) of forestlands.

How important are plants? A plant species may be the primary food source or habitat for as many as 30 animals, especially insects, which are often primary consumers. Loss of the plant species may result in the loss of these animals, which may in turn affect other animal species. In short, a chain reaction upsetting

the balance of many organisms may result if a plant becomes extinct. In addition, plants absorb carbon dioxide (one forest tree takes in 26 pounds (11.7 kg) of carbon dioxide per year) and release oxygen. Plants help with temperature control. Think how much cooler it is to stand in the shade of a tree than in an open area on a hot, sunny day. Finally, plants are beautiful and inspiring. The soothing sound of wind passing through leaves and branches; the smell of newly opened flowers in spring; the many shades of color that delight our eyes; all of these add aesthetic value to our lives.

Further information about plant species and communities is found in chapters 4, and 6.

Procedure
Warm Up

Ask students to talk about natural areas they have visited in southern Florida. What plant species were dominant in these areas? Ask students to sketch five plants they associate with southern Florida. Where would students expect to find these plants? Have them indicate the areas on a map.

Inform students that some plants can be found all over Florida, while others most likely reside in only a certain community. Give each student a copy of the *Plant Communities Map*. Discuss the distribution of plant communities throughout southern Florida. Ask students if they have ever visited any of these systems. What conditions do they think create these different communities?

The Activity
Part I

1. **Divide students into groups of three or four. Ask them to elect a "watcher" who will manage the game. The other members will participate in the expedition.**

2. **Distribute a copy of *Survival!* to each group and initiate the expeditions.**

3. **When a group has completed its expedition, record the time taken and the number of points earned. Check the map to ensure all communities were visited.**

4. **Ask the winning group what strategies they used. For example, did they choose a group leader to make all decisions and therefore save time? Were they able to work efficiently as a group?**

5. **Use the following questions to assess student comprehension of the game.**

• What aspects of the plant communities did they find most interesting? Which species?

• How was elevation related to differences in plant communities?

• How were temperate and tropical species related to location within the watershed? (e.g., "Temperate species survived in southern Florida if they could get there, tropical species if they could live there.")

6. **Discuss the importance of southern Florida plant communities. Ask students to describe wetlands. What communities in the state would they classify as wetlands? Ask students to describe the functions of wetlands.**

Part II

1. **Have each group select a specific southern Florida system and research the plants, soil, elevation, humidity, and fire tolerance of their chosen plant community.**

2. **Tell each group to write one episode related to its assigned plant community. The episode will be used to create a new expedition with different options.**

3. **Compile the episodes and have the class play out their own expedition. They may also trade their expedition with other classes.**

Wrap Up and Action

Ask students to list five plants of southern Florida and identify the communities to which they belong. Compare this list with students' original list from the *Warm Up*.

Discuss the importance of plants for the health of the planet. How can students contribute to plant population stability? Mention the concept of greenways and green space. The Florida Trail currently stretches 1,000 miles (1,660 km). When completed, it will extend from the Everglades in southern Florida to Gulf Islands National Seashore in the northwest panhandle—a distance of 1,300 miles (2,158 km). Discuss how establishing a corridor system connects green spaces such as parks and allows wildlife to roam among the different areas. Such corridors help prevent inbreeding among species and aid in the dispersal of seeds. Greenways benefit not only plants and wildlife, but also humans, by providing opportunities for biking and hiking, and a

reprieve from the stresses of urban life.

Discuss the idea of creating a greenway or green space on the school grounds or within the community. Arrange a field trip to a trail or park, or suggest that students visit these areas with their families.

Assessment

Have students:

• list five southern Florida plants and the communities with which the plants are associated (*Warm Up* and *Wrap Up*).

• conduct a Survival Expedition (*Part I*, steps 1-4).

• research a southern Florida plant community and create their own expedition episode (*Part II*).

• create a school or community greenway or green space (*Wrap Up and Action*).

Extensions

To increase students' understanding of southern Florida plant communities, have them do transects in nearby plant communities. Have students extend the line about 15 feet (4.5 m) between two points and section the line into one-foot segments. At each segment, have them record the type and number of plant species that fall within the one-foot spaces. It is especially interesting to perform a transect where two different plant communities come together, thus demonstrating the "edge effect." (See activity, "Crossing the Lines.") By conducting different transects, students may compare and contrast the makeup of diverse plant communities.

Some students may also wish to identify, collect, and press leaves from different plant communities. Excellent plant books exist which can help them identify species.

Resources

Brown, Loren G. 1993. *Totch—A Life in the Everglades*. Gainesville, Fla.: University Press of Florida.

Cavanaugh, Peggy, and Margaret Spontak. 1992. *Protecting Paradise: 300 ways to Protect Florida's Environment*. Fairfield, Fla.: Phoenix Publishing.

Florida Greenways Commission. 1994. *Creating a Statewide Greenways System for People . . . for Wildlife . . . for Florida: A Report to the Governor*. Contact: Florida Greenways Commission, P.O. Box 5948, Tallahassee, FL 32314-5948.

Little, Elbert L. 1993. *The Audubon Society Field Guide to North American Trees (Eastern Region)*. New York, N.Y.: Alfred A. Knopf.

Morton, Julia. 1990. *Wild Plants for Survival in South Florida*. Miami, Fla.: Fairchild Tropical Garden.

Stevenson, George B. 1992. *Trees of Everglades National Park and the Florida Keys*. Hialeah, Fla.: Haff-Daugherty Graphics, Inc.

Stone, Calvin R. 1987. *Forty Years in the Everglades*. Tabor City, N.C.: W. Horace Carter.

Tarver, David P., John A. Rodgers, Michael J. Mahler, and Robert L. Lazor. 1979. *Aquatic and Wetland Plants of Florida*. Tallahassee, Fla.: Bureau of Aquatic Plant Research and Control, Florida Department of Environmental Protection.

Survival!

Test your knowledge of Everglades communities as you match wits with the elements, animal and plant life, and the landscape. Before you begin, make sure your group has one "watcher" and two or three travelers. Watcher, read the information below.

Watcher: Read the Directions, Introduction, and Preparation to the travelers and show them the survival inventory list. Then begin **The Game**. Read the choices, wait for the group's decision, provide the consequences of that decision, and award points. **You must read the complete text to the group—don't gloss over information to save time.**

Directions

Members of the expedition (travelers): Work together to make decisions. The objective is to move as quickly as possible through all the communities of the Everglades and accumulate points by making the right decisions. As you enter and exit each community, check it off on the *Plant Communities Map*. You are competing with other groups who are also attempting to visit all communities and exit from the Everglades with the highest score.

Introduction

You have read stories of the Calusa Indians, native people who once inhabited the Everglades and built ceremonial mounds. These mounds are found throughout the wilderness. Most people believe the Calusa are an extinct people who either died from diseases introduced by Europeans or fled to Cuba and became absorbed by other cultures. But an old Florida "cracker" has told you that he knows Calusa Indians still live deep in the Everglades. You wish to seek out this ancient culture for the answers they may hold to current dilemmas.

Preparation

Your group receives the following equipment for the expedition:

• a rough map provided by the "cracker"
• canteens (for a week's worth of water)
• a week's worth of food
• sleeping bags
• water purification tablets

In addition, your group gets 10 points to begin the game. The group may decide either to spend these points for items listed below which *may* prove useful on your expedition, or you may save these points. You are traveling in the month of January. Consider water levels and mosquitoes at that time of the year.

Survival Inventory
(Each item costs one point)

binoculars	mosquito netting
bug repellent	plant ID books
camera	animal ID books
compass	pocketknife
extra batteries	radio
first-aid kit	rain gear
flashlight	sunscreen
hat	topographic map
light rope	walking stick
matches (waterproof)	extra sneakers

Plant Identification Book

(sample pages)

You receive this if you chose "plant ID books."

Alligator flag.
Alligator flag and cattails often indicate areas of deeper water, such as alligator holes.

Courtesy: Everglades National Park

Cattails.

Courtesy: Everglades National Park

Courtesy: Everglades National Park

Cypress.

Coontie.
Highly poisonous in its natural state, the root was processed by Seminoles and white settlers to produce mash or flour.

Courtesy: Everglades National Park

Courtesy: Everglades National Park

Live oak.
Live oak generally grows on higher, dry ground such as hammocks.

Custard apple.

Saw grass. Although the leaf edges are saw-toothed, the "heart" or overlapping bases of the central leaves are edible.

Periphyton. Floating algae that is the base of the food chain in the Everglades.

Slash pine.

White stopper. A common hammock tree that exudes a skunk-like odor.

Survival!

The game!
You and your friends strike out into the Everglades and begin an adventure you will never forget . . .

1. MORNING, DAY ONE

It's January. The Glades are still wet. It's rough going since, in places, the saw grass is over five feet tall. You stop and examine this ancient plant. Upward pointing teeth on the margins and the back of the midrib cut like a razor. No animal feeds on saw grass, though ducks eat the late summer seeds. You are tired of slogging through the heavy grass and see a different type of vegetation to the right. It has a light green leaf about two feet long on a stem. You believe this area looks more open and encourage your friends to go with you. The group decides to:
a. continue in the direction of the alligator flag.
b. continue on the course they have set.

If You Chose Option:	
a.	(minus 2 points, only one point if you brought an extra pair of sneakers) You are sinking up to your necks in water and your feet are stuck in the muck of an alligator hole. Alligator flag and cattails often mark areas of deep water and frequently fringe alligator holes. Get out of the alligator hole and continue to #2.
b.	(plus 2 points) This was the best choice to complete your mission; go on to #2.

2. LATE AFTERNOON, DAY ONE

The sky is streaked orange with the setting sun. It's time to make camp. One member notes a group of live oak trees. Although it would take you a bit out of your way, she/he says you should head there. Another member warns that the island will be swampy, just like the area with the alligator flag. The group decides to:
a. make the best camp they can on the wet ground.
b. go to the group of trees.

If You Chose Option:	
a.	(minus 2 points) You would have had a miserable, wet night. Your strength and reserve would have waned, and the trip would not have been fun anymore. Fortunately, as you begin to settle down, another group of explorers passed by and informed you that the group of trees is a hammock and will be a drier place to stay. Your group packs up and proceeds to the tree island. Go to #3.
b.	(plus 3 points) You will sleep dry and fairly comfortably since hammock (tree island) vegetation grows on higher ground. In journals, Everglades travelers of the past always sought hammocks in which to make their camps. The Seminoles also used hammocks for temporary and permanent camps. In the Everglades, a change in elevation even of a few feet alters the makeup of a community. Go to #3.

3. LATE AFTERNOON, DAY ONE

As you approach the hammock, you are growing tired and impatient. It's beginning to get dark, and the hammock appears quite large. You are trying to decide the best way to enter the hammock. Should you
a. use up valuable time circling the hammock to find an animal trail through the saw palmettos that fringe it?
b. make your own path through the dense vegetation that fringes the hammock? It's getting dark; you had better get in quickly while you can still see your feet.

If You Chose Option:	
a.	(plus 3 points) Edges of hammocks are often dense with vegetation because that is where plants find the sunlight that supports growth. Also, "the edge effect" comes into play: two communities come together, each contributing species. Taking the time to find an animal trail is safer than creating your own. In addition to the danger of rattlesnakes, which frequent saw palmettos, poisonwood is a common tree species on the "edge" of hammocks. If a tree limb snaps in your face and you breathe a sigh of relief because it looks like a gumbo limbo, think twice. Poisonwood resembles the harmless gumbo limbo. Go to #4.
b.	(minus 2 points) You run the risk of stepping on a diamondback rattlesnake. The saw palmetto, with its thick, branched stem that creeps along the ground and stiff, fan-shaped leaves, provides refuge for rattlesnakes and other creatures. The plant's black, oblong fruits were an important food for Native Americans; however, early settlers who sampled them said, "We could compare the taste of them to nothing else but rotten cheese steep'd in tobacco juice." Go to #4.

4. EVENING, DAY ONE

The interior of the hammock is magical. Canopies of tall trees prevent sunlight from penetrating to the forest floor. Therefore, the inside of the hammock is open and fairly free of shrubby plants. Also, the trees that enclose you create "acoustic effects": it is very still and quiet within the hammock. As you become more aware of your surroundings, you notice a faint skunk odor. Are you sharing this hammock with a skunk? You decide to:

a. leave this hammock and, in the dark, go to a different tree island you noticed on your way in.
b. investigate the hammock to discover the source of the odor.
c. search in your plant and animal ID books for clues. *NOTE:* You can only do this if you brought a flashlight and the books!
d. ignore the smell.

If You Chose Option:	
a.	(minus 2 points) You would have faced the perils of wandering the Everglades at night. Get back in the hammock, go to bed, and then go to #5.
b.	(0 points) You run the risk of being sprayed by a skunk and disturbing other organisms. Go back to bed, then go to #5.
c.	(plus 5 points) You were able to locate information about the source of the smell. It is a tree called the white stopper, a very common hammock species. It was originally named "stopper" because it helped stop diarrhea. Go on to #5.
d.	(plus 2 points) This was a wise choice. If it was a skunk, it's best to leave it alone. Go to #5.

5. MORNING, DAY TWO

Unless you brought an extra pair of sneakers (score one point), the next day you pull on soggy sneakers (with southern Florida's high humidity, shoes do not dry overnight) and step into the tepid waters of the freshwater marsh. Before you leave the hammock, a member of your party suggests that you each search for a downed branch to use as a walking stick. Members of the group decide to

a. take the time to find suitable sticks.
b. not bother with finding walking sticks in order to save time.

If You Chose Option:	
a.	(minus 1 point) You didn't get off to an early start because you had to spend time looking for the right stick. Go to #6.
b.	(0 points) Begin your day; go to #6.

6. AFTERNOON, DAY TWO

You take a break from slogging and move onto a higher area, an area of pine flatwoods. Unlike in pine forests farther north where the soil is sandy, this ground is rough limestone, full of cavities. You recognize that the dominant tree here is slash pine.

A member of your group identifies a common plant called coontie; he thinks the root is edible, and that the Seminoles used it as a food source. He pulls up the thick underground stem and suggests that everyone take a small bite. If it is edible and tasty, it would add to food stores, which are already running low. The group decides:

a. not to eat the root, as no one is certain of its identification or edibility.
b. to take a few bites to see what it tastes like.
c. to look in the plant ID book to find out. *NOTE:* You can only exercise this option if you brought a plant ID book.

If You Chose Option:

a.	(plus 3 points) You chose well. You should never eat any wild plant unless you are with a naturalist who is positive not only of the plant's identification but also of its use.
b.	(minus 5 points) Although the plant was correctly identified and it was a food source of early Seminoles and white settlers, **in its natural state, coontie is poisonous.** Early settlers learned from the Seminoles that the rootstock had to be prepared and boiled until soft, then mashed. It was flushed with lots of water, drained, and dried in the sun. Early Miamians and other south Floridians used coontie to make flour; the Seminoles did not dry it, but cooked the mash with their sofkee stew. In its natural state, coontie is so poisonous that cattle drinking the red water from the washing process have been fatally poisoned.
c.	(plus 5 points, two of these points are for bringing the book!) By looking in the plant book, you find out coontie is poinsonous (see option b).

7. LATE AFTERNOON, DAY TWO

As you proceed across the wide expanse of the Everglades, you encounter a "solution hole." These holes, produced by the chemical weathering of the limestone cap rock, measure from a few inches to several feet deep. When the Glades is wet, water and periphyton (floating algae) may disguise the holes. What is your plan of action?
a. Wade through the water.
b. Wade through the water using your walking stick. *NOTE:* You can only exercise this option if you brought a walking stick.
c. Walk around the solution hole.

If You Chose Option:

a.	(minus 3 points) Halfway across, you're in over your head. You swim across, but your equipment is soaking wet. Take time to sort and dry your belongings, and go on to #8.
b.	(plus 3 points) With your walking sticks, you are able to locate and avoid deeper areas. Go on to #8.
c.	(minus 2 points) Walking around the solution hole takes much longer than you thought. Go to #8.

8. AFTERNOON, SEVERAL DAYS LATER

Today, wading among cypress knees, oversized ferns, prolific air plants and Spanish moss, you feel as if you have moved back in time to the Jurassic Period—to the days of dinosaurs. This is the Big Cypress, home of the black bear, panther, alligator, and cottonmouth water moccasin. As night gathers, you find yourself in the middle of a long, wide cypress strand. The water is clear and deep. You will not be able to cross the strand before dark. Some custard apple bushes are growing nearby. What are you going to do?
a. It's hopeless—panic!
b. Resolve that you will have to continue moving slowly and cautiously through the water throughout the night and make camp when you get to higher ground.
c. Take a few minutes to look around you. Discuss if there is any way to get out of the water for the night. (If you can devise something, tell the watcher; he will decide whether or not to award points.)

If You Chose Option:	
a.	(minus 5 points) Regardless of your situation, never panic. It wastes time, and panic has been known to make people do foolish things that cause injury or death.
b.	(plus 1 point) This is better than panic, but not the best. The cypress swamp is the home of alligators and cottonmouth water moccasins. Although neither species is overly aggressive, they have a definite advantage over you in the dark.
c.	(plus up to 5 points) If the watcher thinks your idea is credible, you may be awarded up to 5 points. The watcher may consult with the instructor. In addition to these points, if you brought a pocketknife, award yourself 3 points. If you brought a rope, give yourself 3 points. *HINT:* Compare your idea to that of Calvin R. Stone, the author of *Forty Years in the Everglades*, who also found himself in a cypress strand with night approaching: *"At nightfall at the end of the fourth day, I was in the middle of a wide and long cypress strand. I knew that I could not cross the strand before it got dark. I was in too far to turn back. With no hard ground to camp on, I could see it was going to be a long night. I found a thick growth of custard apple bushes and cut the tops out with a machete until I had a flat place on the top of the bushes. I cut some small cypress poles and laid them lengthwise across the bushes until they were about level. Then I cut some small branches and crisscrossed the poles to hold them together. I crawled onto this improvised bed and it put me well above water, about five feet. I slept there until daylight the next morning."*

9. LATE AFTERNOON, NEAR THE END OF YOUR ADVENTURE

The flat terrain and lack of recognizable landmarks in the Everglades and Big Cypress environments have confused even the most experienced hunters and hikers. Your group hopes to eventually make it to the prairie and mangrove coast where you have heard there are shell mounds of the Calusa. So far, you have found no signs of these ancient people. You have been wandering for about three hours, and are uncertain where you are.

> *If you brought a compass, award your group 3 points; if you brought a topographic map, give yourself 2 points. (You get a total of 5 points if you have a map and a compass.)*

10. EVENING, NEAR THE END OF YOUR ADVENTURE

Good fortune is with you as you wander into a hunting camp. An old man comes out to meet you. He seems happy to have visitors. He invites you for a supper of venison and coon stew. Sitting around a rough table after dinner, you show him the map the old "cracker" gave you. He scratches his head as he studies it. Without saying a word he folds up the map and gives it back to you.

He leans back in his chair and talks about his years in the Everglades. He loves the swamp, but he has brought enough people into it to recognize that not all people share his love. He talks about the horseflies in May that don't just bite you, but strike and leave a welt the size of a golf ball. He tells of mosquitoes that will blacken a screen and block out the light on a bright summer's day. He talks about sink holes that a man can disappear into in the wet season, and rattlers and white-mouthed water moccasins. But he also talks about the beauty of the swamp at daybreak: the sunlight broken up by the needles of giant cypress trees and reflecting off the clear blue water; fragile purple and white orchids, and tree snails with rainbow-colored shells; harmless black and golden spiders the size of your hand that build webs nine feet in diameter; a family of otters sliding down a mud chute over and over again—behavior that can only be described as play.

He looks at you and says that the Calusa Indians are extinct; that all that remains of them are the stories told through potsherds, conch shells, wooden masks, and bone ornaments—some of which are buried in wonderful mounds. The map the old "cracker'" gave you is based on legend.

Your spirits sink with disappointment. He promises to take you to a shell mound on the coast the next morning. As you climb into your sleeping bags, the old man has one last word. "Too late, we recognized the value of these Calusa people. The wisdom and experience they might have given our culture is lost forever. We can only hope that the same does not happen to the Everglades country—that its wonders are not lost to us before we recognize a wealth that cannot be bought." In the distance, a Florida panther screams, and an owl calls.

> *If you have made it this far, award yourselves 3 points. Watcher: total the points, record the time, and call the instructor to check the map. Your Everglades adventure is at an end—or maybe it's just the beginning!*

Plant Communities Map

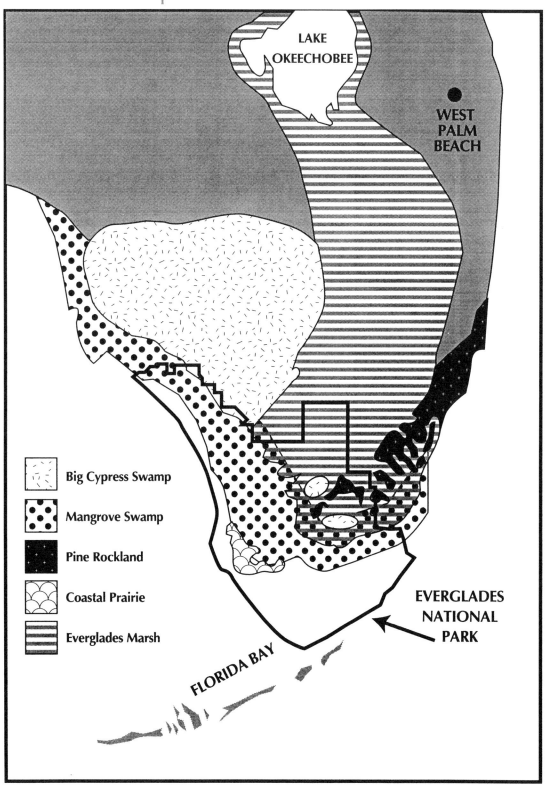

Big Cypress Swamp

Mangrove Swamp

Pine Rockland

Coastal Prairie

Everglades Marsh

LAKE OKEECHOBEE

WEST PALM BEACH

EVERGLADES NATIONAL PARK

FLORIDA BAY

Christy Burns, South Florida Water Management District

Living on the Edge

Grade Level:
Middle School

Subject Areas:
Biology, Ecology, Life Science, Geography

Duration:
Preparation time: Part I, 10 minutes; Part II, 50 minutes

Activity time: Part I, 30 minutes; Part II, two 50-minute periods

Setting:
Classroom

Skills:
Organizing; Analyzing (identifying patterns, contrasting and comparing); Evaluating (testing, critiquing); Interpreting (inferring, translating)

Vocabulary:
prop root, mangrove

Have you ever seen a walking tree?

Summary

Students gather information about different species of mangrove and the ways in which they are adapted to live at the edge of the sea. Students construct models to demonstrate how mangroves help protect shorelines and contribute to the growth of the peninsula.

Objectives

Students will:

- distinguish among the types of mangroves common to Florida and understand their zonation within the coastal community.

- describe how mangroves help stabilize the coastline and protect it from erosion and storm surge.

Materials

- *Photographs, slides, or diagrams of mangrove communities and individual species*

- **Two sets of** *Mangrove Concentration Cards* [**see instructions on** *Mangrove Concentration Cards (front)*]

- *Two large, shallow trays (at least 4" x 12" x 18"—e.g., the bottom of a tote tray, a cat litter box, roasting pan, etc.)*

- *Several sheets of Styrofoam (10 to 20 sheets, at least 1/8- to 1/2-inch thick and cut to fit into tray)*

- *Wood glue*

- *Coarse sand, washed* (enough to cover the bottoms of the trays to a depth of 1 to 3 inches)

- *Pipe cleaners* (at least 6 packages, each a different color: red, black, white, and green)

- *Two strips of Styrofoam or plastic* (cut to fit into the tray and at least as deep—i.e., 4" x 12")

- *Several small cardboard boxes* (assorted sizes, to represent buildings—e.g., condominiums, hotels, businesses, homes)

Making Connections

Most students are familiar with mangrove trees. Some students may be aware of the special adaptations that equip mangroves for survival in the stressful shoreline habitat, but few are likely to know that during heavy storms mangroves protect people who live in coastal areas, or that mangroves are "geologic agents" contributing to the growth of the Florida peninsula.

Background

Mangroves are as characteristic of southern Florida as alligators and wood storks, but their niche is the interface between land and sea—the salty, tidally washed coastline. Mangroves are among the most highly adapted organisms in the Everglades watershed. They have evolved root systems and physiological mechanisms that ideally suit them for life in their habitat.

Three species of true mangroves live in Florida—red, black, and white. A fourth tree, the buttonwood, is sometimes considered a mangrove because it is closely related to the white mangrove. But, unlike true mangroves, it is intolerant of flooding. The buttonwood is common in Florida, and is not limited to coastal mangrove swamps.

True mangroves are called "facultative halophytes"—they can use either fresh water or salt water, depending on what is available. Mangroves can grow successfully in freshwater environments, but growth of large mangrove "forests" tends to occur in saline water, where freshwater vascular plants cannot compete. Some of the largest growths of mangroves in the world fringe the southern Florida coastline, where tides and terrestrial runoff from the watershed circulate nutrients and fresh water, and flush away accumulations of salt and hydrogen sulfide (a product of submerged anaerobic soils). Intertidal zone habitat also favors the reproduction and spread of mangroves.

Among the most obvious of the mangrove's adaptations to life in water are the plants' highly modified root systems. No deep taproot anchors a mangrove, yet the roots are ideally suited to hold the tree above water and obtain the oxygen and nutrients it needs to live.

The red mangrove's shallow prop roots extend from the lower stem like arching spider legs (sometimes the red mangrove is called the "walking tree"). Drop roots hang down from branches of the upper stem. Parts of the roots that are above ground (and above water) contain small pores or lenticels that allow the roots to "breathe," taking in oxygen which moves downward to the roots through tissue called the aerenchyma. The lenticels are further adapted to prevent water (and salt) from entering during high tide. They are called "hydrophobic" because they repel water. As with all mangroves, the leaves of the red mangrove are fleshy and appear glossy or waxy. The dark green leaves are adapted to help the tree retain water. Red mangrove leaves are larger than those of the other species. The red mangrove derives its name from the reddish layer just under its thin grayish bark. The propagule, or seedling, of the red mangrove is long and cigar shaped. The red mangrove grows closest to the coast and is even found on offshore mud flats, bars, and keys.

Inland, the black mangrove replaces the red. Its system of shallow cable roots radiates outward many feet from the stem. Peglike aerial roots called pneumatophores extend upward from the cable roots. Pneumatophores contain lenticels and aerenchyma that aid the tree in oxygen exchange. Pneumatophores often extend upward a foot or so, earning the nickname "breathing tubes." The propagule of the black mangrove looks like a lima bean. The tree gets its name from its dark, blackish bark. Leaves have silvery undersides and are able to excrete salt, a quality the tree shares with the white mangrove.

The white mangrove doesn't usually have prop or cable roots; lenticels on the lower trunk aid the tree in respiration. Sometimes peg roots develop, but the white mangrove's root system is not as distinctive as those of its red and black relatives. The root surfaces exclude salt by filtering brackish water. The white mangrove is most abundant farther inland, where it replaces the black mangrove. The white mangrove is the smallest of the true mangroves. It has oval-shaped leaves and distinctive glandlike openings on the leaf stem (petiole). Its propagule is triangular.

The buttonwood occupies higher, drier sites beyond the zone of the white mangrove. It doesn't have the seedling and root adaptations of the true mangroves, but it tolerates salty soil. The buttonwood has a button-shaped propagule or seed, and the older trees have rough bark. The tree excretes salt through its leaves.

The thick growth of coastal mangroves, with their interlocking prop roots, pneumatophores, and peg roots, helps protect the fragile coastline (and human developments) from erosion by storm surge. Mangroves contribute to the growth of new land by trapping and stabilizing organic debris in their root systems. Shedding part of their leaves throughout the year, they also add to that organic buildup.

For additional information about mangroves, their ecological role, and their adaptations, refer to chapters 2, and 4.

Procedure

Warm Up
Show students slides, photographs, or diagrams depicting the mangroves of Florida. (See *Mangrove Swamp, page 62.*)

Discuss the types of mangroves common in Florida, the characteristics of each species, and their similarities and differences. Explain the zonation of mangroves from the coast inland (i.e., red mangroves, black mangroves, white mangroves, and buttonwood). Note that the buttonwood is not a true mangrove.

Ask students if they know why mangroves are suited to life on the edge of the sea. What are their special adaptations? How do they reproduce? Do mangroves build new land, or stabilize it?

The Activity

Part I

1. **Divide the class into two groups. Tell students that they will play** *Mangrove Concentration* **to gather information about Florida mangroves and the buttonwood.**

2. **Provide each group with a set of** *Mangrove Concentration Cards***. Tell them to arrange the cards randomly,** *front side up.*

3. **Tell students to turn over two cards at a time. If the cards match, players keep the cards. If not, they turn the cards back over.**

4. **When all the cards are matched up, have students present the four characteristics described on the cards for each type of mangrove.** Students can list these characteristics before making matches as well. Discuss similarities and differences among types of mangroves.

Part II

1. **Inform students that they are going to construct two models to** demonstrate the roles mangroves play in the coastal community. One model will include simulated mangroves, and the other will not. Suggestions for building the models follow. However, encourage students to contribute ideas.

• In the bottom of two trays construct shoreline "topography" out of Styrofoam. One end represents coastline, the other, inland. Add enough washed coarse sand to cover the shoreline topography to a depth of 1 to 3 inches.

Randomly place several small boxes inland to represent condos, hotels, businesses, and homes.

• On one of the models, use colored pipe cleaners to simulate the three types of mangroves, and the buttonwood. When adding the mangroves to the model, make sure they are securely inserted into the Styrofoam (black mangroves may have to be glued to the Styrofoam before adding sand).

• For red mangroves: Twist several pipe cleaners together at their midpoint to form the trunk; spread the ends of individual pipe cleaners apart to form prop roots. Add a coastal fringe of red mangroves to the model (from side to side in the tray) by interlocking the simulated prop roots and pressing them into the sand along the shoreline of the model. Another option is to use a twig, partially stripped of leaves and placed upside down, or branched end down, in the sand.

• For black mangroves: Use the same technique as for red mangroves, but spread the simulated roots apart and flatten them like the spokes of a wheel. Add pneumataphores by twisting short pieces of pipe cleaner around the flattened roots (spokes) so that they project upward. Place simulated black mangroves in a band behind the simulated red mangroves by pressing the roots into the sand so that the pneumatophores project above the surface. *NOTE:* While mangroves occur in zones, the lines between them are not exact.

• For white mangroves and buttonwoods: Push the twisted end of a bunch of pipe cleaners straight into the sand. Add a band of white mangroves behind the black mangroves, and finally, a band of simulated buttonwoods. The entire coastal fringe of simulated trees should be about 4 to 6 inches across. To simulate branches on all of the trees, simply spread apart and arrange the tops of the twisted pipe cleaners.

2. **Add water to the shoreline end of the model (to about one-third the depth of the tray). For the mangrove model, be certain the water barely covers the lower part of the prop roots of the red mangroves and covers all of the roots of the black mangroves so that only the pneumataphores project above water.**

3. **Place the small piece of Styrofoam or plastic in the water end of the tray and move it gently back and forth to simulate waves.** Push it strongly toward the "beach" to simulate storm surge. Observe, record, and discuss the effects.

Wrap Up

Have students summarize the types of mangroves that grow in

the coastal zone, their adaptations to life in a salty environment, and their distribution (be certain to emphasize that while identifiable zones do occur, intervening lines are not sharply defined). Discuss the role mangroves play in coastal protection and in the growth and stabilization of the Florida coastline. Encourage students to find other information about mangroves and apply it to the models (e.g., how leaf litter contributes energy to the estuarine food web and to growth of new land). Take students on field trips to coastlines with and without mangroves, and compare these to the models.

Assessment

Have students:

• describe characteristics of mangroves in Florida (*Part I*, step 4).

• construct models that demonstrate how mangroves protect coastal areas from erosion and from storm surge damage (*Part II*, steps 1-3).

Extensions

Conduct a field trip to the coastal zone. Photograph, make rubbings or sketches of, or collect and press representative mangrove leaves. Collect samples of propagules. Photograph or sketch special adaptive features. Develop a "Mangrove Album."

Have students research the history of Florida's mangrove pruning law.

Resources

Craighead, Frank C., Sr. 1971. *The Trees of South Florida*. Coral Gables, Fla.: University of Miami Press.

Lodge, Thomas E. 1994. *The Everglades Handbook: Understanding the Ecosystem*. Delray Beach, Fla.: St. Lucie Press.

Orr, Katherine. 1989. *The Wondrous World of the Mangrove Swamps*. Miami, Fla.: Florida Flair Books.

Mangrove Concentration Cards (front)

NOTE: **Glue this sheet to a piece of poster board and cut out cards. Cut out** *Mangrove Concentration Cards* *(back)* **and glue to the back of the front cards as follows: cards 1, 5, 9, 13 = red mangrove; cards 2, 6, 10, 14 = black mangrove; cards 3, 7, 11, 15 = white mangrove; cards 4, 8, 12, 16 = buttonwood (numbers should not be included with cards).**

1	2	3	4
mangrove largest leaf	with silvery underside of leaf	glands on petioles	salt excreted through leaf
5	**6**	**7**	**8**
prop roots	pneumatophores	smallest true mangrove	rough bark on older trees
9	**10**	**11**	**12**
salt extruder	salt extruder	salt extruder	grows in higher, less saline habitat
13	**14**	**15**	**16**
cigar-like propagule	lima bean-shaped propagule	triangular propagule	button-shaped seed

Mangrove Concentration Cards (back)

Red Mangrove	Black Mangrove	White Mangrove	Buttonwood
Red Mangrove	Black Mangrove	White Mangrove	Buttonwood
Red Mangrove	Black Mangrove	White Mangrove	Buttonwood
Red Mangrove	Black Mangrove	White Mangrove	Buttonwood

Red mangrove.

White mangrove.

Black mangrove.

Buttonwood.

Build a Perfect Beast

Grade Level:
Middle School, High School

Subject Areas:
Life Science, Ecology

Duration:
Preparation time: 30 to 50 minutes

Activity time: two 50-minute periods

Setting:
Classroom

Skills:
Organizing (matching); Analyzing (identifying components); Interpreting (summarizing); Applying

Vocabulary:
ecosystem, community, habitat, species, ecological niche, specialist, generalist, adaptation, solution hole

Have you ever received a business card from an anhinga? What might you expect to find on one?

Summary

Through a "genetic engineering" activity, students will learn about many of the special adaptations that equip native animals to live in the Kissimmee-Okeechobee-Everglades ecosystem.

Objectives

Students will:

• identify structural and behavioral adaptations that help organisms survive in their habitat.

Materials

• *Pencils*

• *Marking pens*

• *Drawing paper and/or flip charts*

• *Copies of **Habitat/Niche Cards** (one card for each group of students)*

• *Copies of **Species Cards** (one card for each group of students)*

• *Map of Kissimmee-Okeechobee-Everglades ecosystem (optional)*

• *Animal identification and guide books for the K-O-E watershed (optional)*

Making Connections

Students probably know some of the unusual animals that live in southern Florida, but they may be unaware of the animals' diverse habitats and their ecological functions. Designing organisms suited to southern Florida habitats sharpens students' awareness of behavioral and structural adaptations of animals in subtropical biomes.

Background

Many diverse animals live in the larger Everglades ecosystem, including hundreds of different kinds of mammals, birds, fish, reptiles, and amphibians, and thousands of invertebrates. The physical, biological, and/or behavioral adaptations of many of these organisms suit them to successful life in the environment(s) of southern Florida. Because much of the ecosystem is subject to recurring flood and drought, many of the animals' adaptations relate to abundance or shortage of water.

Like plants, animals are organized into *communities*, or populations of different animals living and interacting together in particular places (e.g., a freshwater marsh). A community (or group of communities) together with its nonliving environment makes an *ecosystem*. An ecosystem may be as small as a cup of water, or as large as the entire Kissimmee-Okeechobee-Everglades watershed.

To help identify organisms, scientists categorize them in groups based on their characteristics. One of the most specific classifications of organisms is *species*. Organisms of the same species have similar characteristics and produce fertile offspring. The place in the ecosystem where a species lives is called its *habitat* (e.g., an alligator hole). A species' *ecological niche* is its way of life in the community, including its diet, its nesting and feeding behavior, and other physical, chemical, or biological conditions it needs to survive and reproduce. Conditions in a habitat strongly influence the adaptations, behavior, and roles of the animals living there.

Species are either generalists or specialists, depending on whether their needs are specific or broad. Needs include habitat, diversity of food, and tolerance of variation in environmental conditions. The snail kite is a specialist. It feeds exclusively on apple snails, and it lives only in habitats where the apple snail is prevalent. The alligator, on the other hand, is a generalist. It eats a wide variety of food and ranges throughout the watershed.

Certain animals have special importance for the overall health and integrity of an ecosystem. They are called *keystone species* because they affect other organisms critically. For example, alligators excavate holes that become dry-season refuges for many other animals.

It may be helpful to think metaphorically of the organization of the natural world.

A biome (e.g., wetland, forest, desert) is like a corporation—a group of businesses or factories. An ecosystem is equivalent to a single large business or factory. Communities within ecosystems are like different departments or divisions; habitats resemble offices or workspaces in the departments; species are the workers; and ecological niches are the various jobs or occupations. Some of the workers are specialists, and others are generalists. A generic business card for a species might read as follows.

Biome—Corporation

Species—Employee name
Niche—Occupation

Address:
Habitat—Office Space
Community—Department
Ecosystem—Factory

For more information about organisms of the K-O-E watershed, refer to chapters 4, 5, and 6.

Procedure
Warm Up
Discuss the concepts of species (including keystone species), community, ecosystem, habitat, and ecological niche. Explain how various structural, biological, and/or behavioral adaptations equip certain watershed animals to survive, reproduce, and thrive in their habitats. Explain that some species are specialists or generalists, and that certain animals (keystone species) are essential to the survival of others

in a habitat. Review common southern Florida habitats.

Have students list a few southern Florida animals from each group (i.e., mammals, birds, fish, reptiles, amphibians, invertebrates).

The Activity
1. **Tell students they are going to role-play being "bioengineers" by designing an animal ideally suited biologically, structurally, and behaviorally to survive in a specific southern Florida environment. Ask students to form six equal groups or bioengineering teams.**

2. **Give each group a *Habitat/Niche Card*. Explain that each *Habitat/Niche Card* describes a specific place where an animal might live in the watershed. The cards include elements relating to ecological niche, e.g., available foods, available water, microclimatic factors.**

3. **Tell students to "design" a mammal, bird, fish, reptile, amphibian, or invertebrate. They should discuss and list the adaptations that would perfectly suit the animal to live in the assigned habitat. Among the adaptations students give their "perfect beast," they should consider:**

• physical characteristics (e.g., long legs, short curved bill, flattened tail, long claws);

• behaviors (e.g., nocturnal activity, migration, estivation); and,

• physiological processes (e.g.,

storage of water, metabolism of stored fat).

Teams can sketch or draw their animal or its special modifications (e.g., curved bill, webbed feet, long legs, etc.) to help clarify adaptations, or they may simply describe them. Teams should give their animals distinctive names. These might suggest something about appearance, where an animal lives, what it eats, etc.

4. **Each student group elects a representative to explain to the class what habitat the engineering team was assigned, what animal they came up with, and how their "perfect beast" fills an ecological niche in the assigned habitat.** If time permits, design teams could challenge another team's design, for example, "How would your animal survive if . . . ?" The team would then rebut the challenge.

5. **After students complete the presentations, show them the *Species Cards* that spotlight actual organisms in the habitats. Have students look up information about the animals listed on the *Species Cards* (using field guides) and discuss why they are suited to their habitats. Compare animals the student teams created to those on the cards.** Discuss similarities and differences. Ask students to think of and/or research other southern Florida animals (real ones) that might be found in places listed on the *Habitat/Niche Cards*.

Wrap Up
Discuss how this activity was like developing "business cards" for animals. The animal or species has a distinctive name and title; the habitat is the animal's busi-

ness or home address; and the ecological niche describes the animal's occupation or role. Students may want to create business cards for their "perfect beasts."

Discuss adaptation as a survival tool. What conditions might have led to the great diversity of communities, habitats, ecological niches, and animal life in southern Florida?

Have students discuss how people fit into the watershed ecosystems. In what communities/habitats are they found? What is their ecological niche? Are people generalists or specialists? How have people adapted to different habitats?

Assessment
Have students:

• build "perfect beasts" adapted for survival in various southern Florida habitats (step 3).

• list and discuss representative structural and behavioral adaptations among watershed animals that help them survive in southern Florida habitats (*Wrap Up*).

• identify aspects of an organism's niche related to its habitat (*Wrap Up*).

Extensions
Have students adapt this activity to southern Florida plants (i.e., "Build a Perfect Plant").

Have students "design" animals ideally suited for life in a different ecosystem (e.g., desert, rain forest), then compare them to southern Florida animals.

Have students build a "perfect beast" adapted to life on a planet

(real or imaginary) with radically different environmental conditions than those on Earth.

Resources
Fernald, Edward. A., and Donald J. Patton, eds. 1984. *Water Resources Atlas of Florida.* Tallahassee, Fla.: Florida State University.

Lodge, Thomas E. 1994. *The Everglades Handbook: Understanding the Ecosystem.* Delray Beach, Fla.: St. Lucie Press.

Miller, G. Tyler, Jr. 1990. *Resource Conservation and Management.* Belmont, Calif.: Wadsworth Publishing Co.

Niering, William A. 1984. *Wetlands: An Audubon Society Nature Guide.* New York, N.Y.: Alfred A. Knopf

Odum, E. P. 1983. *Basic Ecology.* Philadelphia, Penn.: Saunders College Publications.

Habitat/Niche Cards

Estuary or Tidal Creek

- brackish water (mixture of fresh water, terrestrial runoff, and sea water)
- water is warm and shallow
- thick growths of mangroves common along shoreline
- bottoms often covered with thick mud
- turtle grass and other marine vegetation common on bottoms
- mudflats often exposed during low tide
- tides and terrestrial runoff are rich source of nutrients
- waves, tides, and inflow from tidal creeks constantly circulate water
- creeks provide access to freshwater habitats and refuges for terrestrial species during dry season

Alligator Hole or Pond

- dug by alligators
- a source of concentrated fresh water, especially during the dry season
- occur mostly in freshwater marshes
- commonly 10 to 20 feet across and several feet deeper than surrounding wetland
- usually surrounded by a mound of mucky organic material
- center relatively free of vegetation
- floating and rooted aquatic plants common around edges
- often surrounded by low trees and shrubs
- may be occupied by more than one alligator

NOTE: Designed organism cannot be an alligator!

Hardwood Hammock

- mixture of tropical (and temperate, farther north) tree species
- ground slightly elevated above surrounding areas
- forest floor often pitted with solution holes filled with ground water
- dense foliage overhead with relatively open understory
- outer edge fringed with thick, nearly impenetrable growth of low vegetation
- interior densely shaded and several degrees cooler than surrounding area
- higher interior humidity contributes to growth of lichen on smooth-barked trees
- warmer during winter due to humidity and protection from wind

Freshwater Marsh, Wet Prairie, or Slough

- water depth during wet season seldom more than a few inches; during dry season, water collects in larger depressions
- water is warm; usually with very slight current
- subject to complete desiccation annually during dry season
- heavy growths of marsh plants including grasses and sedges
- mats of algae (periphyton) and other floating plants (e.g., bladderworts) common
- ground often covered with thick layers of marl and/or peat
- sloughs (deeper marsh communities) sometimes have water even in dry season
- marsh and wet prairie usually dotted with tree islands

Pineland

- ground slightly elevated above surrounding areas
- slash pine is dominant tree
- canopy fairly open; sunlight penetrates to forest floor
- temperature relatively warm, humidity low (compared with hammock)
- saw palmetto, cabbage palm, and other low vegetation common in understory
- hardwood hammocks sometimes occur in pinelands
- rock ridge (in rocky pineland) often pitted with solution holes which sometimes fill with water
- farther north (pine flatwoods), ground tends to be sandy soil

Vacant Lot

- bordered by asphalt parking lot, cement buildings, and a canal
- scattered tufts of grass and assorted weeds
- thin sandy soil over weathered limestone
- scattered refuse, cans, bottles, automobile tire, discarded shopping cart, cardboard boxes, assorted garbage
- partially lit at night by lights from parking lot and buildings
- many insects and other invertebrates
- noisy with nearby human activity, automobiles, etc.
- crisscrossed by several "social" trails people use as shortcuts
- edges occasionally watered by sprinkler systems of adjacent buildings

Species Cards

Estuary or Tidal Creek **Manatee**	**Alligator Hole or Pond** **Anhinga**
Hardwood Hammock **Tree Snail**	**Fresh Water Marsh,** **Wet Prairie, or Slough** **Mosquitofish**
Pineland **Corn Snake**	**Vacant Lot** **Marsh Rabbit**

Crossing the Lines

Grade Level:
Middle School, High School

Subject Areas:
Ecology, Environmental Science

Duration:
Preparation time: 50 minutes

Activity time: two 50-minute periods

Setting:
Field and classroom

Skills:
Organizing; Analyzing

Vocabulary:
community, ecotone, edge effect, peninsular effect, transect

Who goes there? Do plants and animals recognize boundaries?

Summary

Students learn about the concepts of "ecotone" and "edge effect."

Objectives

Students will:

• explain the concepts of ecotone and edge effect.

• describe how the edge effect relates to biological diversity in a watershed.

Materials

• *Rubber gloves*

• *Markers* (assorted colors)

• *Clipboards* (at least 3, one for each sampling team)

• *Grid paper* (at least 3 pads, one for each team)

• *Pencils*

• *Field guides to plants of Florida or southern Florida* (one for each team—see **Resources**)

• *Surveyor's flagging or yarn* (bright colors)

• *3 wooden stakes*

• *Heavy string* (large roll—at least 250 feet [75 m])

• *Hammer or mallet*

• *Three sampling grids* (Get these from an ecology lab or biological supply company. If necessary, see grid-making instructions.)

Making Connections

Students know that different groups of people live and interact in communities we call cities, and that the outermost edges of cities blend with undeveloped agricultural and natural areas. However, many students may not be aware that analogs to these situations exist in the natural environment. Sampling vegetation along a transect between two different biological communities—the ecotone—teaches students that, in nature, edges are not sharply delineated.

Background

The hierarchy of organization in the natural world is from the bottom up: individual organisms (plant or animal); species, or organisms with similar characteristics that can reproduce; biological communities, or populations of different species living and interacting together in specific environments; ecosystems, or the combination of communities and their physical environments; and biomes, or major terrestrial or aquatic ecosystems (e.g., deserts, forests, grasslands).

Large or small, biome or community, ecological units have indistinct boundaries. It is the nature of non-human living things to neither recognize nor honor boundaries that people draw on maps. In nature, as well as in environments people fabricate,

Coconut palm, tropical species.

communities tend to blend gradually at their margins, creating a transition zone called the "ecotone." In ecotones, species from adjoining ecological units intermingle or "cross lines."

Characteristically, species diversity, and often individual numbers of plants and animals, are greater in an ecotone than in either of the adjoining communities. This phenomenon is called the "edge effect." Sometimes, the ecotone even gives rise to unique species. It is the reason that in southern Florida, northern continental species mingle with West Indian, Caribbean, and other tropical life forms, producing the diverse mosaic of plants and animals characteristic of the watershed. Southern Florida lies in the transition area or ecotone between the temperate and tropical zones. Throughout the watershed, the edge effect operates on a smaller scale between freshwater marsh and hardwood hammock, slough and rocky pineland, and schoolyard and open field.

Of over 1,600 species of higher plants (with roots, stems, and leaves) from Lake Okeechobee south, about 60 percent are of tropical origin (mangroves, cocoplum, orchids, bromeliads, etc.), while 40 percent originated in temperate North America (red maple, bald cypress, live oak, sweet bay, and more). About 9 percent of vascular flora is unique to the southern Florida ecotone (e.g., milk pea, narrow-leaved poinsettia), and includes distantly related tropical and temperate forms.

Many of the terrestrial and freshwater animal species originated in temperate North America. Marine life forms show the strongest connection with the tropics. Animals with the ability to fly or drift on currents are a mixture of temperate and tropical forms. Animals are mobile, and move freely back and forth between communities. Temperate species include white-tailed deer, Florida panther, raccoon, river otter, gray squirrel, white pelican, bald eagle, marsh hawk, American robin, barred owl, American

alligator, diamondback rattlesnake, eastern mosquitofish, and pig frog. Tropical forms include the American crocodile, loggerhead turtle, green (Carolina) anole, brown pelican, and the Florida tree snail. The endangered Cape Sable seaside sparrow is an example of a species endemic to the ecotone. In southern Florida, people are perhaps the best example of cultures intermingling within the same species.

In its geologic history Florida was never physically connected with the West Indies. The peninsula has always been continuous with the mainland. This connection, or corridor, has served as a pathway for animals colonizing from the north. Most of the temperate fauna in the watershed came from northern parts of the peninsula that remained above water during the ice age rise and fall of the sea level. In biogeography (the study of plant and animal dispersion), this is known as the "peninsular effect."

Gray squirrel, temperate species.

River otter, temperate species.

Courtesy: Everglades National Park

Most tropical components of the watershed are botanical. Light-weight seeds of plants drift easily on ocean and atmospheric currents. The seeds of pigeon plum, saffron plum, cocoplum, Jamaica dogwood, and other tropical plants have traveled to southern Florida from the tropics in the intestinal tracts and on the feathers of migratory birds, on currents, and in strong winds during hurricanes.

Plants are fixed in their habitats and thus more easily sampled. Surveyed along a transect (a straight line or belt) between two communities and the intervening ecotone they allow students to observe the edge effect.

For additional information about southern Florida plants and animals and their ecological relationships see chapters 4, 5, and 6.

Procedure
Warm Up
Discuss the organizational hierarchy of the natural world, especially the concept of biological communities. Discuss the diversity of plants and animals in southern Florida, and the concepts of ecotone and edge effect.

A simple hand model visually demonstrates the edge effect. Mark the back of one rubber glove with dots of one color, mark the back of the other with dots of another color, and put on the gloves. Tell students that one hand represents Community A, and the other hand Community B. The dots symbolize the different species in each community. With the back of the gloves visible to students, spread your fingers open and interlock them. Tell students that the interlocked fingers represent the merging of species in the ecotone between communities.

Ask students if they can list some common southern Florida plants and animals that might have originated from temperate North America and from the tropics. How did these species colonize southern Florida?

Ask students if they can suggest ways to survey the plants (and/or animals) in differing biological communities. Tell students they will observe the edge effect by sampling plants on a transect through two adjoining natural communities.

The Activity
1. **Select an appropriate site where two different plant communities adjoin (for example, a marsh and a hardwood hammock, or a school athletic field and adjoining woods). Have students mark a transect by driving a stake into the "eco-tone" area (at the edge between the two communities). Then drive a stake into each of the bordering communities at equal distances from the first stake. Tell students to connect the stakes with heavy string.** *NOTE:* 100-150 feet (30-45 m) of string should be adequate. To make the transect clearly visible, students can tie pieces of brightly colored surveyor's flagging or yarn to each stake.

2. **Divide the class into three sampling teams—one for each community and one for the ecotone (edge). Each team should designate a recorder. Provide each team with a sampling grid, a clipboard, graph paper, and a plant guide. Instruct students to draw a small-scale replica of the sampling grid on the graph paper. The location of identified plants in the sampling grid is recorded in the comparable areas of the graph paper.**

3. **Tell each sampling team to place its grid on the ground centered over one of the three stakes.**

4. **Using the plant guides, sampling teams should identify all the plants within their grid**

and record how many of each plant are found. As plants are identified, the recorder marks their location on the grid paper. To save space, students should develop a key of plant name abbreviations. If students cannot identify the plant with the plant guide, take a sample of the plant or draw a sketch and label the plant "unidentified 1" or "U1." An example of the sample record (partially completed) follows.

This record shows that students found two plants of type y and three of type t (y and t are abbreviated plant names) in grid A1. Three plants of unidentified plant type 1 were found in grid C2.

5. **Sampling team recorders report the teams' findings to the class. Have students compare their sample plots, noting similarities and differences, and comparing diversity and quanti-** ties of different plant species.

Wrap Up

Have students discuss the significance of the edge effect for biological diversity within the watershed. What contributes to greater diversity in an ecotone? Ask students to list other aspects of the "edge effect."

Have students identify and discuss other places in the watershed where ecotones exist. Ask them if the concepts of the ecotone and edge effect apply to people. What examples can they think of?

Assessment

Have students:

• sample vegetation in grid plots in adjoining biological communities and at the communities' edges (step 4).

• compare diversity and quanti- ties of plant species found in distinct plant communities and ecotones (step 5 and *Wrap Up*).

• provide reasons why the edge effect contributes to plant diversity (*Wrap Up*).

Extensions

Students might draw a map of their transect, or create a model of it for the classroom.

Resources

Florida Department of Environmental Protection. *Classroom and Field Experiments for Florida's Environmental Resources.* Tallahassee, Fla.

Lodge, Thomas E. 1994. *The Everglades Handbook: Understanding the Ecosystem.* Delray Beach, Fla.: St. Lucie Press.

Miller, G. Tyler, Jr. 1990. *Resource Conservation and Management.* Belmont, Calif.: Wadsworth Publishing Company.

Morton, Julia. 1990. *Wild Plants for Survival in South Florida.* Miami, Florida: Fairchild Tropical Garden.

Odum, E. P. 1983. *Basic Ecology.* Philadelphia, Penn.: Saunders College Publications.

Stevenson, George B. 1992. *Trees of Everglades National Park and the Florida Keys.* Hialeah, Fla.: Haff-Daugherty Graphics, Inc.

Tarver, David P., John A. Rodgers, Michael J. Mahler, and Robert L. Lazor. 1979. *Aquatic and Wetland Plants of Florida.* Tallahassee, Fla.: Bureau of Aquatic Plant Research and Control, Florida Department of Environmental Protection.

	1	2	3	4
A	y-2 t-3			
B		y-5		
C		u1-3		
D				

Grid-Making Instructions

Below are two methods of making grids (simple and advanced). The advanced grid involves more preparation, but allows for more detailed inventories.

The simple grid requires the following:

• *A coat hanger stretched out to form a square*

• String

To make the grid, tie a piece of string to one corner of the square, stretch it, and tie the other end to the corner diagonally opposite. Repeat for the other two corners. This creates a simple grid with four quadrants.

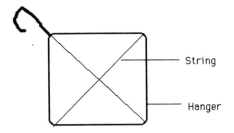

The advanced grid requires the following:

• *4 pieces of lathe, 1 inch x 0.5 inch x 1 yard (2.5 cm x 1.25 cm x .9 m)*

• *Small nails or wood screws*

• *Wood glue*

• *String*

• *Quarter-inch electric drill* (hand drill or push drill)

To make the frame, glue the four lathes together into a square, secure with nails, and allow to dry. Drill three evenly spaced holes through each side of the frame. Weave string in and out of the holes, secure with knots at either end, and repeat on other sides to create a grid, ultimately of 16 squares.

NOTE: Lathe, nails or screws, and drill may be available through the school woodworking shop. Ask the shop teacher for assistance in building the grids, if necessary. Lathe might also be available as free scrap from local cabinet or woodworking shops.

Time Frames

What can we learn from a conch shell, a brass military button, an orange, and a copy of Marjory Stoneman Douglas's The Everglades: River of Grass?

Summary

Students trace the history of southern Florida through the stories of people, past and present.

Objectives

Students will:

• identify significant people and events in southern Florida history.

• interpret artifacts and images related to the history of southern Florida, and the stories that go with them.

• recognize that specific historic events have influenced the water resources of southern Florida.

Materials

• *Teacher's artifact* (Bring an object or image that tells a story about you. If an image—a photograph or painting—it should not picture you.)

• *Students' artifacts* (objects supplied by each student that tell a story about the student)

• *The Liquid Treasure Water History Trunk, Learning From the Past* (optional, see **Resources**)

• Copies of **Southern Florida Time Frame Starter Kit**

• *Items needed to present skit*

NOTE: Listed below are materials and artifacts described in the **Starter Kit**. Encourage students to contribute additional or alternative artifacts.

• *Footlocker or other type of trunk*

• *Conch shell*

• *Object reminiscent of the military* (e.g., scrap of blue wool cloth, brass military button, old canteen)

• *Branch of an orange tree or an orange*

• *A copy of Marjory Stoneman Douglas's* The Everglades: River of Grass

• *Costumes, props, and scenery building materials* (optional)

Making Connections

You may have had the experience of searching through a drawer and coming upon a long forgotten object—a photograph, a note from a childhood friend, or a baseball signed by a once famous player. Handling or gazing upon the object brings a flood of memories. The object may belong to someone else, and you may not know the exact details of its history, but you can imagine the stories it could tell.

Artifacts and images can provide insight into past events. Young students may not have built up as many memories as adults, but

Grade Level:
Middle School, High School

Subject Areas:
History, Environmental Science

Duration:
Preparation time: 50 minutes

Activity time: two 50-minute periods

Setting:
Classroom

Skills:
Organizing; Interpreting; Presenting

Vocabulary:
artifact, Calusa, Seminole

they possess things that are special to them and that symbolize who they are. Using artifacts to interpret past events introduces students to alternative ways of studying the past.

Background

Sometimes the study of history is seen as a linear, one-dimensional memorization of dates, unpronounceable names, and boring events. But history is about people who are multidimensional and whose stories are rich and colorful, and often similar to our own.

The history of southern Florida is made up of the stories of many people (see narrative in *Southern Florida Time Frame Starter Kit*). Studying the history of southern Florida is like watching a motion picture. Thousands of individual frames compose the film of a movie, but it is the blending of those frames that creates the story.

But the stories of individuals or of communities of people do not evolve in a vacuum; often they

are created or at least influenced by events beyond the people's making or control. As with an onion, many single layers make up the whole. These layers may include individuals' ambitions and actions; the interaction of individuals and their communities; national and international political events such as wars or large migrations of people; economic events such as the Great Depression; and weather phenomena such as hurricanes, tornadoes, or freezes.

Individuals, communities, and their stories are all part of the history of the waters of southern Florida. Some of these people may no longer walk among us, but artifacts, images, and ideas they left behind can help us better understand the waters of southern Florida today.

For more information about historical events in southern Florida refer to chapters 7, 8, and 9.

Procedure

NOTE: A few days before begin-

ning this activity, ask students to bring from home an artifact or image (painting, photograph, etc.) that is significant to them (see **Warm Up**). The object or image should suggest a story or event that is important to the student. Ask students to conceal the artifacts or images in lunch bags and not to discuss them with other students.

Warm Up

Why is the study of the past important? What do students like or dislike about history? Ask students how we learn about the past. List students' answers on the board. Make sure the study of artifacts and images is one of the items in the list.

Select an artifact or image that "tells" a story about you. Explain to students how the artifact reminds you of a particular story and how that story is part of your personal history. Tell students the story; or use the one below, which is an example of how a music box tells a story.

One summer, Maria was visiting her parents' home in southern Florida. She had not visited her parents since they retired to Florida four years ago. "We still have a box of your things from your old bedroom stored in the back room," Maria's mother informed her. One quiet afternoon, Maria took time to explore the box. She inspected each item. Some were a complete mystery to her; others brought a smile. Then she came upon the music box. She remembered when she saw the music box in a store while walking with her best friend. Maria fell in love with the music box and its intricate design, but at that

Early Native Americans in southern Florida.

Courtesy: Everglades National Park

time in her life she had little money. She began to put aside a dollar or two each week for the box. Often she checked to make sure the music box had not been sold; each time moving the box out of sight at the back of the shelf. When she was halfway to her goal, she went to the store as usual to check on the box, only to find that it had been purchased. Crushed, she went home. When Maria walked into her bedroom, there was the music box on her bedside table. Her friend had purchased the music box as a special gift. Maria discovered that money is not what provides wealth in life; good friends are.

The Activity

Part I

1. **Divide students into working groups. Give each group a large grocery bag. Ask students to place the small sacks containing their artifacts in the grocery bag. Then tell students to pick a different sack from the bag.** (If a student draws his or her own sack, it should be returned and another one selected.)

2. **Have students open the small sacks and study the artifacts or objects. Each student in the group should try to identify the person the object or image represents and create a story to go with it.**

3. **After the contents of all the sacks have been considered, ask students to claim their own object and recount to the group the stories associated with it. Have students think whether political, economic, social, or environmental events played any part in the stories.** (Perhaps they experienced a hurricane,

drought, or flood. Maybe some of the students came to Florida from a different country.)

4. **Discuss how these stories are part of each individual's history. Ask if any of the students' stories contributed to or were influenced by the history of a community, a state, or a nation. Did any of the stories feature impacts on the water resources of southern Florida?**

Part II

1. **Outline the Kissimmee-Okeechobee-Everglades watershed on a map. Remind students of individuals and communities of people who have shared the waters of southern Florida.** (See *Starter Kit*.)

2. **Ask students to brainstorm a list of artifacts and images these people may have left behind that remind us of their influence. Which of these have to do with water?**

To get students started, ask them the following questions:

• What geologic events that had to do with water played a part in shaping southern Florida?

• How have people carried and transported water in the past? (gourds, skin bags, shells, etc.)

• What were people's food sources, and how was water involved? (e.g., fishing, agriculture)

• What role did water play in the regional economy?

3. **Tell students they will be creating a southern Florida history trunk (or catalogue). The trunk will contain a collection of artifacts and images, each of**

which contributes a story to the history of southern Florida's waters. A *Southern Florida Time Frame Starter Kit* (suggested script and props) has been created for the trunk. The artifacts and accompanying skit are only suggestions; encourage students to add to or change the skit in order to adapt it to their own area. Artifacts should be brought from home (with parental permission), or may be obtained from antique stores or grandparents' collections. Use a footlocker or other type of trunk to store the artifacts. This doubles as an interesting prop for performances.

4. **Divide the class into four groups. Assign or have each group choose a certain time period up through the present. If the script is used, divisions can be based on the time frames. Provide each group with the appropriate section of the script. Each group member should have a role (e.g., presenter, coordinator of artifact location, researcher, group liaison). Groups should determine what artifacts or images are appropriate for their time period and, if they want, write accompanying stories.** On a "class wish list," students may indicate artifacts or images to be acquired for the trunk. Students may want to research additional artifacts and stories, or add more time periods.

5. **Have the group liaisons organize the group presentations. One student from each group may act as narrator. Students may design simple costuming and scenery. As you follow the script, have groups present their scenarios to the**

class, school, or community group.

NOTE: In an alternative activity, students create a catalogue of historical items with descriptions and stories accompanying each object. This could be done in the style of the turn-of-the-century consumers guide: *1897 Sears, Roebuck Catalogue.*

Wrap Up
Have students discuss the effectiveness of using artifacts or images and associated stories to bring the history of an area alive. Ask students to summarize specific historical events that have influenced the water resources of southern Florida. Take students on a field trip or invite a guest speaker to show students real artifacts and to talk about their interpretation.

Assessment
Have students:

• interpret artifacts and images, identifying how these tell stories about people and events (**Part I**. steps 2-4).

• interpret artifacts and images, and how they might contribute to the history of southern Florida (**Part II**, step 4).

• organize a historical trunk they can use to present a skit about water resource use in the past (**Part II**, step 4).

• conduct a presentation that portrays significant people and events in southern Florida history (**Part II**, step 5).

• evaluate the use of characterization to educate others about the past (**Wrap Up**).

• summarize how specific histori-

cal events have influenced the water resources of southern Florida (**Wrap Up**).

Extensions
Conduct an extended study of the artifacts in the trunk. Discuss with students how political, social, economic, and environmental events originating outside of southern Florida influenced the state's history. For example, many American soldiers saw southern Florida for the first time during World War II. They were not vacationing, but training on the beaches and golf courses that were sunny year-round. More than 500 million servicemen and women trained in the region. When the war ended in 1945, soldiers and sailors went home, but many of them remembered beautiful southern Florida. Some believe this was one reason for Florida's postwar population surge.

Visit a state park such as Lake Kissimmee, where staff use "living history reenactments" to teach about the past.

Ask students how the following external events might have impacted the course of southern Florida's history and affected its natural resources:

• The Civil War

• The hurricanes of 1926, 1928, 1935, and 1992

• The Great Depression

• World War II

• Large migrations of people—particularly from Caribbean countries such as Cuba and Haiti—from 1980 to 1990.

Have students collect articles

from the newspaper that highlight stories of individuals or groups who are affecting the water resources of southern Florida. Have them discuss political, economic, and/or social events influencing these people and their actions.

Resources
Bullen, Adelaide K. *Florida Indians of Past and Present.* Gainesville, Fla.: Florida State Museum, University of Florida.

Douglas, Marjory Stoneman. 1948. *The Everglades: River of Grass.* Sarasota, Fla.: Pineapple Press.

Kesselheim, Alan S. The Watercourse, and Project WET. 1993. *The Liquid Treasure Water History Trunk, Learning From the Past.* Bozeman, Mont.: The Watercourse.

McIver, Stuart. 1988. *Glimpses of South Florida History.* Miami, Fla: Flair Books.

Oppel, Frank, and Tony Meisel. 1987. *Tales of Old Florida.* Secaucus, N. J.: Castle.

Regnier, Kathleen, Michael Gross, and Ron Zimmerman. 1992. *The Interpreter's Guidebook: Techniques for Programs and Presentations.* Stevens Point, Wisc.: UW-SP Foundation Press, Inc.

Smith, Patrick D. 1984. *A Land Remembered..* Sarasota, Fla.: Pineapple Press, Inc.Smith, Patrick D. 1984.

Tebeau, Charlton W. 1968. *Man in the Everglades: 2000 Years of Human History in the Everglades National Park.* Coral Gables, Fla.: University of Miami Press.

Southern Florida Time Frame Starter Kit

Scene: The closed trunk containing the artifacts (conch shell, military item, orange branch or orange, a copy of The Everglades: River of Grass) *is center stage.*

Narrator: Many people think of history as a long list of boring dates, unpronounceable names and places, and unrelated events. But history is about real people and their stories. In southern Florida, these real people are Calusas, Seminoles, Miccosukees and other Native Americans; Spanish explorers and adventurers; white settlers, wreckers, crackers, cowhunters—who displaced the Seminoles in the Seminole Wars; U.S. soldiers, who pursued the Seminoles, forcing them into the Everglades; early adventurers; hunters of plumes and alligator hides; artists like John James Audubon, writers like Ernest Hemingway, and musicians like Jimmy Buffet; entrepreneurs such as Henry Flagler, whose railroad not only physically but also economically connected southern Florida with northern states, and Hamilton Disston, who started the first large-scale drainage effort in southern Florida; government leaders: Governor Napoleon Bonaparte Broward, who involved government and public agencies in draining southern Florida for land reclamation, and Governor Lawton Chiles, who signed the Everglades Forever Act (1994); U.S. Army Corps engineers, and the managers, biologists, and educators of the South Florida Water Management District; Mickey Mouse; and conservationists such as Ernest Coe and Marjory Stoneman Douglas, who fought to preserve

the Everglades. (*Walks to trunk and raises the lid.*) And even though some of these people have gone away from us, they left behind artifacts, images, and written or recorded words to remind us of their stories. These stories blend and flow together to create the history of the waters of southern Florida. Some of these people have agreed to share their stories with us today.

Narrator exits and first student enters, walks to the trunk and removes a conch shell.

Calusa: I am a Calusa. My people were once very powerful. We lived on the land north of the Caloosahatchee down through the Ten Thousand Islands and all the way to Cape Sable. There were other Glades people: the Mayaimi who lived around the great central lake; the Jeaga who lived on the beaches where the sun rises; and the Tequesta who ranged from a place you call Boca Raton through the Keys.

The conch was important to my people. It gave meat, and its shell was a drinking cup, a tool, and a weapon. We knocked a hole in one side to get at the meat, then another smaller hole. We put a stick through these holes and lashed it tight with cord made from animal skin or plant material. It made a good pick for digging in the earth. We built our mounds with these picks, and dug ditches into which we drove fish and turtles.

We lived on platforms with cabbage palm roofs. The breeze passed through; it carried the mosquitoes away. But when the wind was still, we rubbed our bodies with fish oil; we sat in the smoke from the fire to escape the mosquitoes.

We had many feasts on the beach and the mounds grew from the shells, bones, and broken pots we left behind. We buried our dead in some of these mounds.

We crafted pots, carved wooden masks and hairpins from bone, and polished shells that we wore around our necks.

Food was plentiful. We did not have to grow many crops because the land and sea were good to us. But the sea brought to our shores a people who would bring the end of the Calusa. Some of us went to another place in our dugout canoes, others escaped to the Glades; but most died from the sickness these people brought. The Calusa are an extinct people, but if you are quiet, from the saw grass whispering in the breeze, the waves drumming on the shore, and the owl calling in the night, you can still hear our stories.

Calusa exits and second student enters. Second student bends over the trunk and removes an object reminiscent of the military (e.g., scrap of blue wool cloth, brass military button, old canteen).

Soldier: I am a soldier and I hate this Godforsaken land. My wool uniform is hot and scratchy. It's

· ·

either raining or the sun's burning us up. My clothes are never completely dry, my boots are always soggy, and I fear I will get foot rot. We eat cold, wet food, camp on soggy ground, and sleep with one eye open for fear a cottonmouth snake or rattler will crawl to our warmth. At night the alligators roar and thrash wildly about, and I believe the whine of the mosquitoes will drive me mad.

Lieutenant Colonel William Harney is our commanding officer. He was determined to find every last Seminole hiding in the Everglades. Frankly, I didn't have the stomach for this duty, and it would never have been necessary if the government had kept its promise. Lieutenant Colonel Harney gave his word that the Seminoles would be allowed to live on a permanent reservation if the fighting stopped. We thought that had brought an end to the Seminole Wars and we could all go home, but the Secretary of War said that the reservation was only temporary, and the Seminoles figured if they went to the reservation they'd be cornered up and shipped out west. Betrayed, the Seminoles attacked Harney, who was camped on the Caloosahatchee River, killed some of his men, and massacred the villages of Indian Key. The attack was a surprise to Harney. He didn't know his word had been broken by the Secretary of War.

Harney pursued the Seminoles into the Everglades. He captured women and children and shot and hung warriors. Chief Chekika was one he killed in this way. The Seminoles believe hanging is a very bad thing; they believe a

man's soul can't leave his body if he dies this way. Some Seminoles turned themselves in. Others just went deeper into the Glades. I guess the war is over.

Yesterday, a newspaper man asked Harney to tell him about his expedition. Harney told that fellow that if the Secretary of War, Mr. Poinsett, had been in the Everglades, he would have hung him, too. There's a rumor Harney's going to ask for an investigation of the Secretary of War. I wonder if anything will come of it. For my part, I just want to go home. I guess that's all the Seminoles ever wanted, too— just to be allowed to go home.

Soldier exits and third student enters. She goes to the trunk and removes the branch of an orange tree or an orange.

Mrs. Tuttle: I arrived at Fort Dallas on the north side of the Miami River in 1873. I came with my husband and children. On a trip north, I was fortunate enough to meet a Mr. J. E. Ingraham who represented the Plant Railroad system which had built a railroad from Jacksonville to Tampa, Florida. I told him I wanted a railroad built to Miami.

Not long after our meeting I received word that Mr. Ingraham was conducting an expedition across the Everglades from Fort Myers to Miami. They cut through the saw grass, and a few people turned back as there were so many snakes. They made progress the first few days, but one night, wildcats, panthers, and bears ate most of their food. In fact, the next day they saw a black bear that was not black at all—but white—from wallowing in their

flour. After a few weeks passed, I became very anxious. A Seminole who was a friend of mine went into the Everglades and found them. They were in very bad shape as they were down to two tablespoonfuls of grits a day to live on. But nothing was done about the railroad.

In 1894 and 1895, a terrible freeze killed almost all the orange trees and vegetables in the state. Millionaires became paupers overnight. I wrote yet another letter to a Mr. Flagler, who now worked with Mr. Ingraham. I made up a box of fruits and flowers to prove that the freeze had not hurt this part of the state.

Mr. Flagler visited me and by midnight of the first day agreed to extend his railroad to Miami in exchange for land that my husband and I owned. I remember Mr. Flagler saying, "This country has wonderful possibilities."

Mrs. Tuttle exits and the narrator enters.

Narrator: In 1896, when the railroad was extended to Miami, the city's population was 1,500 people. In a little over 100 years, the population has exploded to nearly half a million people, with 12 million visitors a year.

Henry Flagler's railroad eventually extended from Miami to Key West. Henry Flagler was never interested in Miami—frankly, he didn't care much for the city—but he was interested in Cuba. He thought that Cuba would become very prosperous and that he would ferry railroad cars from Key West to Cuba and back again loaded with goods for the northeastern United States.

In the late 1800s and 1900s, people didn't understand the value of wetlands or the hydrology of southern Florida. Wetlands were perceived as wastelands that should be drained so the land could be claimed for people.

Fortunately there were conservationists like Ernest Coe and Marjory Stoneman Douglas who, early on, saw the value of preserving the Everglades.

Narrator exits and the fourth student enters and takes from the trunk the book, The Everglades: River of Grass.

Marjory Stoneman Douglas: I was born April 7, 1890, in Minneapolis, Minnesota. I first came to Florida when I was four years old and what I remember most is the brilliant white light of the tropics. I returned to Florida when I was 25 years old and was reunited with my father after a separation of 19 years.

I began work as a reporter on my father's newspaper, *The Miami Herald,* and I discovered what I loved to do—write. I began visiting the Everglades with my friends. We would arrive at the Everglades before daybreak and build a breakfast fire and watch the sunrise.

Finally, desiring independence, I left the newspaper and began to write stories on my own. I was asked to write a book about the Miami River, but I told the editor I wanted to write about the Everglades instead. He agreed. So I wrote this book that begins, "There are no other Everglades in the world."

For twenty years, we campaigned hard to get a national park

established that would preserve a portion of the Everglades. Everglades National Park was dedicated in 1947; it was a great accomplishment. *The Everglades: River of Grass* was published the same year.

But conservationists can never rest on their laurels; there is so much work to do. In 1960, the Army Corps of Engineers decided to straighten the Kissimmee River. A system of gates, dikes, and pumps now controlled the waters of the river of grass. The water level dropped in the park; cattle waste and pesticides polluted Lake Okeechobee. As the water was drained from the wetlands, they dried up, and many species died or went away. A huge jetport was proposed for the northern boundary of the park. It would have destroyed the Everglades. It was time to organize.

We formed the Friends of the Everglades. I was 78 years old. We won the fight against the jetport; it was never finished.

But there have been many battles and there will be many more. I expect you to be leaders. There are no other Everglades in the world, and they need you.

Narrator: These are just a few of the people of southern Florida. The conch shell, the [military item], the orange branch, and the book help present their stories. Now it is your turn to contribute to the story of southern Florida. What will be your role in the fate of southern Florida's water resources? What artifacts will you leave behind to remind people in the future of what you did? Thank you.

(Players return to the stage to take a bow and to answer questions.)

Postscript (*optional*): Marjory Stoneman Douglas, physically frail but sharp of wit, celebrated her 106th birthday near Earth Day in 1996.

Melaleuca Madness

Grade Level:
Middle School

Subject Areas:
Ecology, Environmental Science, Mathematics

Duration:
Preparation time: Part I, 50 minutes; Part II, 50 minutes

Activity time: Part I, 50 minutes; Part II, 50 minutes

Setting:
Classroom, large field

Skills:
Gathering information (researching); Organizing (categorizing); Analyzing (comparing and contrasting); Interpreting (relating, drawing conclusions)

Vocabulary:
nonnative, introduced, invasive, indigenous, alien

When can uninvited guests be deadly?

Summary
Students design and participate in a variety of games to simulate the threat of invasive, exotic species into the Kissimmee-Lake Okeechobee-Everglades (K-O-E) watershed.

Objectives
Students will:

• demonstrate how the melaleuca tree outcompetes many native species.

• list characteristics of a variety of invasive, exotic species endangering the K-O-E watershed.

Materials
NOTE: Encourage students to design their own activities to demonstrate the threat of melaleuca to the K-O-E watershed.

• *"Wanted Dead, Not Alive"* *poster of melaleuca*

• *Photo of a branch from a cypress tree with cones* (except where prohibited by local or state ordinances, real branches may be used, but cypress cones may not be available year-round)

• *Photo of a branch from a melaleuca tree with pods* **(Again, a real branch may be used, but is not recommended. Volatile oils in melaleuca bark and pollen may cause respiratory distress in some people.)**

• *Calculators*

• *Marking pens and paper to create graphs*

• *Chairs, one per student*

• *Cassette tape of music or sounds from a wetland or the Everglades*

• *Paper and pen*

• *Maps of the Everglades* (optional)

Making Connections
North America has experienced the introduction of invasive, exotic species over millions of years. Humans themselves—Native Americans crossing the Bering Strait and Europeans traveling to the New World—were at one time introduced species. When students eat a kiwi fruit or an orange grown in the United States, they are consuming a once nonnative species. The starlings chattering outside their window and the praying mantis munching on insects in their yard are nonnative species. Students, especially those who live in the K-O-E watershed, may have seen posters or heard about the ongoing struggle to eliminate or contain unwanted invasive, exotic species. Understanding what enables introduced species to outcompete native species helps students appreciate the threat these organisms present to the survival of the Everglades and other parts of the watershed.

Background

"Look at that pretty black bird with the iridescent feathers! Listen to its unique song!" A novice bird watcher might get excited when he spots a starling. If he keeps watching, however, he will see another starling, and another, and another, until he realizes, "Hey, wait a minute . . . there are only starlings in this stand of trees. Where are all the other birds?"

Unfortunately, this scenario is happening in many ecosystems. Native species are threatened and endangered. The number-one cause is habitat destruction. But the next largest contributor to the decline of plants and animals is the introduction of nonnative species.

Indigenous, or native, species have adapted to each other and their habitats over long periods of time. Predator-prey relationships, reproductive life cycles, selective consumption of resources, and other ecological processes help maintain balance. When a new species invades, these long-lasting relationships may be upset.

Often, introduced species are not suited to the resources, shelter, or climate in the new habitat, and they quickly die out. But sometimes the new ecosystem lacks the predators or other factors (e.g., periods of drought, freezing weather) that controlled the introduced species' growth in its natural habitat. If the new arrival can tolerate the new conditions, has few dietary limitations, and/ or reproduces quickly and in large numbers, there may be no bounds to its consumption of resources or reproduction rate.

Introductions of nonnative species can happen accidentally or deliberately. Species may be inadvertently transported in the ballast of a ship, may be packaged in imported foods, or may escape from zoos or arboretums. Purposeful introductions occur when, for example, individuals or resource planners bring in a species for aesthetic reasons, to provide new game wildlife populations, or for pest control. In some cases, the new arrivals benefit an ecosystem and humans (e.g., the praying mantis). However, too often their impact is devastating.

Purple loosestrife, starlings, kudzu, zebra mussels. These are just a few of the species listed on "Wanted Dead, Not Alive" posters in resource management offices around the country. Sadly, the K-O-E watershed has had its share of introduced species. Florida, with its warm climate and diverse plant life, provides prime habitat for many organisms. Some of them, such as the walking catfish, feral pig, hydrilla, and water hyacinth, are quite unwelcome.

Introduced species in the K-O-E watershed have decimated resources, consumed large quantities of water, and invaded large stretches of land area. Lacking the predators and other biological controls they had at home, nonnative species are able to outcompete indigenous species, often to the point of extinction.

One nonnative species that is receiving a lot of media attention is the punk tree, also known as the paperbark tree, or the melaleuca. The melaleuca tree (*Melaleuca quinquenervia*) is one of the greatest threats to the Everglades ecosystem. It was imported from Australia as an ornamental plant and as a source of timber and ground cover. Land-use planners hoped the tree would dry up the land, and make the ground more suitable for construction.

The tree grows quickly (3 to 6 feet [.9 to 1.8 m] per year) and reproduces in high numbers. The

Melaleuca forest.

melaleuca's overwhelming growth potential leads to habitat destruction. A single seed capsule has about 200 to 250 seeds; a 30-foot (9 m) tree spreads as many as 20 million seeds. The flowers that bear the seeds resemble a bottle-brush, and appear up to five times a year. On average, melaleuca forests spread into the Everglades at the rate of 50 acres (20 ha) per day.

Estimates of how much of the Everglades is covered with forests of Melaleuca range from 500,000 acres (200,000 ha) to over 2 million acres (800,000 ha). Melaleuca have overtaken nearly 488,000 acres (195,200 ha) of remnant Everglades south of Lake Okeechobee. Native saw grass and cypress trees cannot compete with the melaleuca trees and are being squeezed out. Melaleuca forests do not provide the same kind of shelter and food supplies native animals are used to, plus the trees' dryness and oil content promote wild fires.

Everything about the melaleuca makes it virtually indestructible. Although the seeds need moist conditions to sprout, they lay dormant for up to ten years. Fire may destroy saplings, but it triggers seed release in mature trees. When older trees are felled, new growths sprout from roots and trunks.

Despite these overwhelming challenges, Everglades watershed managers are aggressively fighting the spread of this noxious plant. It is now illegal to landscape with melaleuca and developers are required to remove the tree from their sites. Extensive research is being

conducted on permanent destruction of these and other invasive plants. The most common method of eradication is called "hack-and-squirt." Workers girdle trees and then squirt them with herbicide. But this hand application costs up to $5,000 per acre ($2,000 per ha). A large-scale aerial spraying program began in the summer of 1995. Cheaper, at a cost of $266 per acre ($106 per ha), this technique only works well for dense stands of melaleuca. The South Florida Water Management District and the Florida Department of Environmental Protection have budgeted $2 million a year to eradicate melaleuca.

The pest controller's strongest ally may be education. A variety of programs inform individuals about problems associated with melaleuca and other nonnative species and about what can and should be done to remove this threat. If unchecked, growth of these deceptively beautiful trees could single-handedly (or single-seededly) destroy the Everglades ecosystem as we know it.

For more information about invasive exotic species, refer to chapters 8, and 9.

Procedure
Warm Up
Show students a copy of a "Wanted" poster for melaleuca. Ask why this plant is wanted dead, not alive. Introduce the terms "exotic," "alien," "introduced," "native," and "indigenous." Ask students to identify which terms are synonyms and to generate preliminary definitions.

Divide students into cooperative learning groups. Instruct them to

discuss and list what they know about melaleuca (including the criminal's "MO"—modus operandi—or method of operation). What questions do students have about the plant? Each group should present their findings. See if groups can answer each other's questions. If necessary, provide students with additional information, or have them research details on their own.

The Activity
Part I

Summarize characteristics of the melaleuca tree. Have students identify which characteristics help the tree outcompete native species. Challenge students to develop activities or games to demonstrate these advantages. Following are two examples that have to do with reproductive characteristics. Students can also simulate competition for light, reactions to fire, impact on other species, and so forth.

• *Melaleuca: The Next Generation (reproduction rates).*

Present a photo of a branch from a cypress tree and one from a melaleuca. With the students, count the number of pods on the melaleuca and the number of cones on the cypress branch. If each melaleuca seed pod has about 250 seeds and each cypress cone has approximately 10 seeds, how many seeds will each branch produce? Then, consider that the melaleuca flowers up to five times a year, and the cypress produces cones once a year. How many seeds per year will each branch produce? Find a picture of each type of tree. How many branches does each have? How many seeds does that mean each

	Cypress Tree (cones)	**Melaleuca Tree** (pods)
Pods/cones per branch		
Seeds per pod/cone		
Seeds per branch		
Seeds per branch per year		
Seeds per tree per year		

tree could produce per year? Create a chart or graph to compare results. What does this information say about the reproduction rate of each species?

• *Melaleuca: The Land Hog.*

This simulation is similar to musical chairs, except one student will have an advantage over the others. Tell students that they each represent different organisms that live in the Everglades ecosystem. Assign or have students research and select different plants and animals to represent. One student plays the role of the melaleuca tree. Arrange the chairs in a circle, one per student. The chairs symbolize suitable habitat for the organisms. Tell students that as with musical chairs, when the tape of wetland animal sounds or music is playing, students should circle the chairs clockwise. When the sound stops, they must find a chair. Sitting in a chair means the organism has found suitable habitat. The student who is

melaleuca circles closely around the chairs while the other organisms must stay in a larger circle, at least six feet from the chairs. When the melaleuca student sits in a chair, he or she leaves a marker, such as a paper marked with an "M." This symbolizes that the habitat is now dominated by melaleuca and is not available to other students. As the game continues, if a student cannot find a chair to sit in, he or she must leave the playing area. After the first round, one chair will be marked with an "M"; soon, all of them will be. After the game, discuss what happened. Did any of the students feel the game was unfair? Talk about how this activity symbolizes the spread of melaleuca throughout the Everglades and its implications. Challenge students to create or find a map that shows locations of dense stands of melaleuca.

Part II

1. **Assign groups of students to research four or five facts about** different introduced or nonnative species currently threatening the K-O-E watershed. Encourage groups to present their facts to the class creatively (e.g., role-playing, simulations, diagrams).

2. **Ask each group to turn in a list of the researched facts and a labeled picture of the species.** A few invasive, exotic species and their characteristics are provided on the information sheet *Steal the Exotic.*

3. **Involve students in the following game ("Steal the Exotic") to help them learn and review the facts they collected.**

• Arrange students' pictures in the center of the room.

• Divide the class in half and line the two groups up at an equal distance from the center.

• Have students in each half count off and remember their number (e.g., 1-15 for each team).

• Call out one fact about a researched organism (without giving the organism's name) and one team member's number. The two students with that number, one from each team, will race to the center of the room and look for the picture of the correct exotic. For example, "Its sap can cause skin irritation similar to that caused by its close relative, poison ivy. Number 5!" The two number-five students rush to the center of the room and look for the relevant species (in this case, the Brazilian pepper). The first student to locate it races the picture back to his or her team. The other student may try to tag the first student before he or she makes it to the other side.

NOTE: Caution students that forceful tagging terminates the game.

• Award points as follows: If the student grabs the correct exotic and returns to his or her team line untagged, the team wins two points. If the student grabs the correct exotic but is tagged by the opposing team member, each team gets one point. If the student grabs the wrong exotic and returns to the line, the team loses two points. In this case, if he or she is tagged before reaching the line, each team loses one point. The team with the most points wins!

Wrap Up and Action

Have students summarize the threats associated with introduced species. Challenge them to design posters or write stories that compare a melaleuca forest and a cypress forest.

Ask them to brainstorm techniques professionals and others could use to restrict the spread of melaleuca (or other nonnative species). Provide students with brochures or have them contact resource management agencies to learn what techniques are being used. How do these techniques compare to their ideas?

Have students put up "Wanted" posters provided by resource or pest management agencies; or, students can design their own. Posters should include a list of what individuals can do to overcome the threat of melaleuca (or another exotic). For example, some companies are producing melaleuca mulch from harvested trees. The poster could outline reasons why schools and businesses should use melaleuca mulch rather than mulch from

native trees such as the cypress. Students could work with pest management agencies to organize a melaleuca seedling removal marathon.

Assessment

Have students:

• describe characteristics of the melaleuca tree (*Warm Up*).

• design an activity or game or write a story that illustrates how introduced species such as the melaleuca challenge the survival of native species (*Part I* and *Wrap Up*).

• research and identify characteristics of exotic species endangering the K-O-E watershed (*Part II*, steps 1 and 3).

• design posters identifying how individuals can help prevent the spread of nonnative species (*Wrap Up*).

Extensions

Have students investigate how national or state parks have dealt with or are handling nonnative species. For example, in Grand Canyon National Park, and Lake Mead National Recreation Area, burros are a problem. Introduced by miners in the late 1800s, the population has increased steadily. Because burros will eat almost anything, native big horn sheep are being threatened with the loss of their food supply. In fact, park naturalists and ecologists tell the following joke: Question: Why did the burro cross the river? Answer: To eat the other side. Denuded hillsides then contribute to erosion problems that affect water quality. Eliminating trees such as melaleuca is one thing; eliminating mammals is another.

When officials initiated a burro eradication program, public outcry brought it to a halt. Later, an expensive program used helicopters to carry burros out one at time for adoption and relocation. Lake Mead is still dealing with burros, using live-removal strategies such as roundups, net gunning from helicopters, and transport to other areas.

Students can research the economic impacts of exotic species damage control. What costs are involved in controlling melaleuca populations? Students can conduct a debate: should exotic species be considered part of a natural process and be allowed to take their course, or should they be controlled? Encourage students to use multimedia approaches in their presentations. For example, a projection graph would help show the exponential growth of melaleuca populations.

Resources

Florida Department of Environmental Protection (DEP), Bureau of Aquatic Plant Management, Technical Services Section, 3917 Commonwealth Boulevard, Tallahassee, FL 32399.

Florida Exotic Pest Plant Council, 3205 College Avenue, Ft. Lauderdale, FL 33314.

Steal the Exotic

Paperbark tree (Melaleuca)

Flowers cover branch tips in a bottlebrush arrangement and pollen can cause a severe allergic reaction in many people.

Each seed capsule can have up to 200 to 250 seeds.

Invades all wetlands and surrounding areas; crowds out all other species as it spreads.

Creates a severe fire hazard in some areas and has resisted all attempts at control.

A 33 -foot tree can have as many as 20 million seeds.

Brazilian pepper

Forms impenetrable thickets and produces bright red berries in winter months.

Sap can cause skin irritation similar to poison ivy, a close relative.

Birds, raccoons, and other animals widely distribute seeds, which germinate in almost all ecosystems, smothering existing vegetation.

Water hyacinth

Clogs waterways so thoroughly that boating is impossible.

A mat of these water plants will double in size in 11 to 13 days.

Grows in water with a pH range of 4 to 10.

Common carp

A bottom feeder that degrades water quality by disturbing sediments.

Crowds out more desirable fish species through rapid population growth and the absence of natural enemies.

Grass carp

A single female may produce up to a million or more eggs.

Sterilized members of this group (fish rendered unable to produce young) have been released to control some invasive aquatic plants (especially hydrilla).

Feral pigs

Destroy native plants and displace the soil while feeding and rooting. This helps prepare the soil for invasive, exotic seeds and causes erosion.

Prey species for the Florida panther.

Popular species with hunters.

Wanted DEAD
Not Alive

illustrations provided by:
IFAS, Center for Aquatic Plants
University of Florida, Gainesville, 1990

MELALEUCA

Pond cypress cones.

Melaleuca seed pods.

Missing Pieces

Grade Level:
Middle School, High School

Subject Areas:
Government, Environmental Science

Duration:
Preparation time: 30 minutes

Activity time: 50 minutes

Setting:
Classroom

Skills:
Organizing (arranging, manipulating materials); Analyzing; Applying (planning, designing, problem solving, developing and implementing action plans)

Vocabulary:
ecosystem, restoration, watershed

Have you ever taken something apart or broken something important to you then tried to put it back together?

Summary
Students investigate the complexities of restoration projects within the Kissimmee-Okeechobee-Everglades ecosystem by piecing together a simple puzzle.

Objectives
Students will:

• describe the challenges of restoring an altered natural environment.

• develop a restoration plan for a local site.

Materials
• *Photos of altered sites*

• *News articles or reports about a restoration project (e.g., the Kissimmee River Restoration Project or the Everglades Restoration Project)*

• *Object with multiple parts (e.g., an old clock)*

• *Pattern for puzzle (select simple or more complex pattern)*

• *Old magazines*

• *Glue*

• *Scissors*

• *Ruler*

• *Drawing materials*

• *Poster board or tagboard*

Making Connections
Nearly every day, the news media report on environmental problems in southern Florida: depletion of ground water resources, eutrophication of Lake Okeechobee, the insidious spread of melaleuca, reduced populations of wood storks and snail kites, the "dead zone" in Florida Bay. All of these are symptoms of a disarticulated— or "broken"— ecosystem. Comparing restoration projects to the process of putting a puzzle back together helps students appreciate the complex challenges watershed managers face as they attempt to restore natural hydrologic conditions in the Kissimmee-Okeechobee-Everglades ecosystem.

Background
Different metaphors may be used to help explain the problems related to restoration of natural systems in southern Florida.

Many things—a clock, a radio, a bicycle, or a puzzle—can be taken apart and put back together. Other things, such as a historic watershed, may be more difficult to restore. Sometimes a thing may look the same when it is put back together, but if parts are lost, or not put back in the proper place or relationship with the other parts, neither the timepiece nor the ecosystem will work properly.

Natural systems (e.g., watersheds, ecosystems) are complex arrangements of physical factors (geology, topography, soils, climate, weather, material cycles, water, etc.) and biological components (plant and animal communities). Complexity and diversity contribute to the strength of systems when nature is unaltered, but the more parts and interrelationships a system has, the more difficult it is to restore it if parts are removed or rearranged.

Ecological processes and associations such as food chains, the ecological niche, predator-prey relationships, and various material cycles (carbon, nitrogen, sulfur, water) bind the southern Florida ecosystem together like threads in a complex web. Ultimately these processes impact global communities.

If an eggshell, like Humpty Dumpty's, breaks into many different pieces, some shell fragments may be crushed or so finely fragmented that they cannot be put back into place. When the shell is restored, the

Right: Kissimmee River before channelization.

Below: Kissimmee River restoration engineers' test fill.

loss of pieces weakens it, and damage may be irreparable if it falls again. Natural systems are like eggshells. A disrupted natural system may be even more difficult to restore if it was first altered years ago, so that knowledge about what it originally looked like and how it functioned is incomplete.

While hurricanes, fires, and floods have periodically altered the Kissimmee-Okeechobee-Everglades ecosystem over the past thousands of years, those were natural cyclic events that the system accommodated with natural resilience. Human activities—constructing canals, levees, and other flood control structures, draining wetlands, apply-

ing fertilizers and pesticides, and developing land—conducted mainly to meet the needs of growing populations, have also altered the watershed. Often, these practices occurred before people were aware of ecological consequences. Real-life consequences in southern Florida have included eutrophication of Lake Okeechobee, depletion of ground water reserves and their contamination by salt water, reductions in wading bird populations, algal blooms in Florida Bay, and more.

Times have changed, and so have people's attitudes about their environment. Altered areas, that people once thought were beyond recovery are now being restored. One of the largest such restoration projects in the world is now under way in the greater Kissimmee-Okeechobee-Everglades ecosystem.

Restoration projects in the Everglades watershed aim to remedy some of the undesirable outcomes of previous human intervention. Projects include reconnecting the Kissimmee River to some of its remnant historic channel, reclaiming associated wetlands, and restoring rain-driven sheet flow to Everglades National Park.

However, just as when "all the King's horses, and all the King's men" tried to put Humpty Dumpty back together again, restoring a river, lake, wetland, or aquifer can be a major, time-consuming, costly, and sometimes impossible undertaking.

Despite its challenges, restoration can be viewed as a way to recover the past. It offers young people in southern Florida a hopeful view of their future environment. A

Photos: South Florida Water Management District

single student, a family, a neighborhood, a class, or a school system can identify, guide, mobilize resources for, and otherwise help a restoration project. They might organize a local cleanup or replant a disturbed area. Few accomplishments can compare, especially for young people, with knowing that they helped put a piece of the system back together.

For more information about water resource issues in southern Florida, refer to chapters 1, 8, and 9.

Procedure

Warm Up
Show students pictures of altered natural sites. Discuss ways natural events (floods, hurricanes) and human activities (draining wetlands, building canals) affect natural habitats. What do students think should be done about the sites? Explain that one solution is restoration. List reasons for restoring systems (wildlife preservation, aesthetics, preservation of water quality and quantity).

Discuss a project currently under way in the South Florida Water Management District. Show students maps and plans.

Show students an old object made up of multiple parts. Ask students to speculate how easy or difficult it might be to take the object apart and put it back together again. Have them list reasons why trying to restore or replace something might be difficult, but desirable.

The Activity
1. **Divide the class into small groups. Distribute a copy of the pattern to each group. (Depend-** ing on time and students' skill level, the simple or more complex pattern may be selected.) Instruct group members to glue the pattern (facing up) onto the poster board and cut around the circle. Distribute old magazines. Have students locate natural scenes typical of southern Florida, preferably ones that include water. Tell students to cut these out and glue them to the opposite side of the poster board. An alternative is for students to draw a picture of a typical natural system (e.g., an alligator hole, the historic Kissimmee River and its floodplain, or mangrove islands in Florida Bay) on the back of poster board.

2. **Have students cut the poster board along the lines of the pattern (for more of a challenge, students can cut jagged edges). Instruct students to scatter the pieces on their desk tops. Explain that the pieces represent a natural area that has been altered. Discuss the complications of putting an ecosystem back together again.**

3. **Tell students to turn the scattered pieces facedown. Have them switch places with another group. Without turning the pieces over, the groups should try to put the puzzles together again.**

4. **Have groups tape the reconstructed puzzles together then turn the puzzles over.** Some of the pictures may be accurately reconstructed, but because of shapes that can be interchanged, and without the visual clue of a picture as a guide, some may not. This emphasizes the point that the parts of a system must fit together properly, and that incomplete knowledge of the parts can complicate restoration. Even if the puzzle has been put together properly, it is still different from the original because it has been cut apart. That is, the strength of the board has been compromised by the process of disruption and attempted restoration.

Wrap Up and Action
Discuss the relationship of the exercise to real-life restoration projects such as the Kissimmee River restoration, or the effort to restore natural water flow patterns in Everglades National Park and Florida Bay. Have students summarize what alters ecosystems and why they are difficult to restore. Do students believe that residents will choose not to further alter the southern Florida ecosystem in the future? Explain that restoration can be many times more costly than conservation or preservation. (Restoration of the Kissimmee River will be nearly ten times more expensive than construction of the C-38 Canal.)

Ask students to identify strategies for maintaining the integrity of natural systems in and around the Kissimmee-Okeechobee-Everglades watershed, while recognizing humans' need to continue using natural resources, (e.g., inventory plant and animal species, monitor water quality, employ Best Management Practices, build Stormwater Treatment Areas, etc.).

Have students identify a potential water-related restoration project near the school or in their community. In structuring their project, students might consider the following: establishing a restoration goal; formulating a restoration plan; predicting difficulties; analyzing costs; determining a time frame; projecting results (e.g., illustrating the future appearance of a restored site); maintaining restored sites. If the project proves feasible and students undertake restoration of a site, have them keep a project diary or "water log," and circulate copies to other teachers and students. Students could contact the local newspaper and ask a reporter to interview them for a feature story. Or, help students write a story about the project themselves. Send the story to the South Florida Water Management District (Office of Government and Public Affairs), to representatives at the state capitol and in Congress, and to one or more national environmental organizations (e.g., Audubon Society, National Wildlife Federation, National Parks and Conservation Association).

Assessment

Have students:

• explain or demonstrate why some altered systems cannot be restored to their original state (step 2).

• relate the challenge of assembling the pieces of an old clock, radio, puzzle, etc., to real-life restoration projects (step 4).

• develop and participate in a local restoration plan (*Wrap Up*).

Upon completing the activity, for further assessment, have students

• analyze the importance of

restoration projects and the elements that contribute to success or failure.

Extensions

Have students research other water-related restoration projects under way locally, regionally, or nationally. Contact the Environmental Protection Agency, the U.S. Army Corps of Engineers, and the Bureau of Reclamation (Washington, D.C.) for information about environmental restoration projects. Write to Everglades National Park (40001 State Road 9336, Homestead, FL 33034) and the South Florida Water Management District (P.O. Box 24680, West Palm Beach, FL 33416-4680) and request additional information about the Kissimmee River and Everglades restoration projects.

Resources

Cooke, G. Dennis, et al. 1993. *Restoration and Management of Lakes and Reservoirs*. Boca Raton, Fla.: Lewis Publishers.

Environmental Concern Inc. and The Watercourse. 1995. *WOW!: The Wonders Of Wetlands*. Published through a partnership between Environmental Concern Inc., St. Michaels, Md., and The Watercourse, Bozeman, Mont.

NOTE: Various publications related to water management and restoration issues are available from the South Florida Water Management District. Contact the Office of Government and Public Affairs at the address previously listed; or call (407) 686-8800 or FL WATS 1-800-432-2045.

Puzzle Patterns

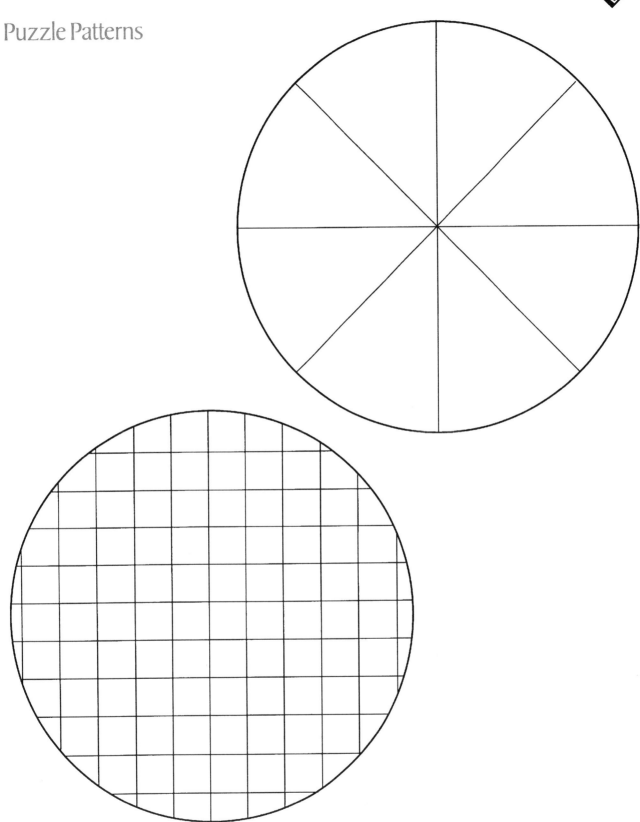

Extra! Extra!

Grade Level:
Middle School, High School

Subject Areas:
Ecology, Environmental Science

Duration:
Preparation time: 50 minutes

Activity time: one week

Setting:
Classroom

Skills:
Gathering information (researching); Applying (designing, composing, restructuring); Evaluating; Presenting (writing, drawing)

Vocabulary:
current events, water-related issue

Summary

Students assume the roles of various people on a newspaper staff and develop a special edition—an "extra"—about water in southern Florida.

Objectives

Students will:

* recognize that water is a frequent subject in the news.

* demonstrate skills necessary to publish a class newspaper that focuses on water and the watershed.

* critique the accuracy and thoroughness of student-created newspaper articles.

Materials

* *Newspapers*

* *Tabloid-sized paper* (rolls of newsprint are sometimes available from local newspapers)

* *Pens, pencils, marking pens*

* *Tape, rubber cement, or glue stick*

* *Scissors*

* *Computers and word-processing programs* (optional)

* *Computer graphics program* (optional)

Making Connections

Newspapers are one of the main sources of information about current events in our world. The bad news and the good news about water—its ebb and flow, availability, quantity, and quality—are often almost a daily subject in Florida newspapers. By creating their own special edition about water, students learn the importance of informing others about water-related subjects and issues.

Background

Newspapers are ideal vehicles for interdisciplinary exploration. They cover a diverse range of subjects, in forms ranging from want ads to in-depth special editions. In recent years, newspapers have chronicled heavy rainfall and mud slides in southern California; record snowfall and ice storms in the Northeast; the Great Flood of 1993 (Missouri and Mississippi Rivers); and the Exxon Valdez oil spill. In Florida,

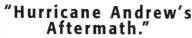

Flood Kills Deer, Other Animals in Everglades.

Group Helps Restore Lagoon for Injured Manatees.

South Florida Water Management District

newspapers often include stories, editorials, letters, and cartoons that have to do with water, and specifically with the health of the Kissimmee-Okeechobee-Everglades watershed. Numerous special editions covered Hurricane Andrew.

Newspapers juxtapose fact and opinion. They focus on current events, yet they maintain connections with the past. Editorials and letters to the editor make newspapers forums for the exchange of ideas and opinions. Newspapers are places where Americans exercise their constitutional rights to free expression. Sometimes, newspapers focus attention on issues by taking editorial stands (usually in the form of letters from the editor) in support of or against certain situations. Newspapers provide important vehicles for shaping public opinion.

In current and past newspapers, we can trace the full length of the river of history. Newspapers allow people throughout southern Florida to stand on the common ground of shared knowledge of events in the watershed, and to keep abreast of water-related issues developing in other places. Newspapers from other cities and towns in Florida and from around the country can give students different perspectives on local and regional issues.

Newspapers reflect the collective effort of many people, each with special skills and designated tasks: publishers, editors, reporters, photographers, artists, cartoonists, proofreaders, composers, typographers, and others. Most of them use computers in their work. Publishers are the

individuals or groups who own the paper and pay for its production. Reporters are at the front line. They seek out information about the events they are assigned to "cover," their "beat," as it is called. Reporters write the "copy"—the article, story, or column. Often, reporters are accompanied by photographers who capture images to illustrate the stories. Writing for newspapers differs from other forms of writing. Deadlines are short, so writing must be fast. The traditional journalistic questions of "who, what, when, where, why, and how" must be answered in an intriguing, concise style, in limited space. Reporters must be very disciplined in their writing.

Editors determine which "breaking stories"—events that are just occurring—are most important and newsworthy, and assign reporters to them. Editors also review and comment on rough drafts of stories. Composers, typographers, printers, and others are the specialists who organize, design, and produce the newspaper. Newspapers are usually divided into sections, such as classifieds, comics, editorials, markets, and entertainment. The news/features section of the paper includes most major "breaking" stories (e.g., "City Water Supply Contaminated"). An index there helps readers locate other stories. The weather section reports current and forecasted weather (e.g., "Tropical Storm Developing in Gulf"), and often, tide and lunar tables. The classified section, or "want ads" lists services, jobs, lost and found, housing sales and rentals, and more (e.g., "Water Heater For

Sale," "Plumbing Repaired," or "Swimming Instructor Needed"). Exchanges of opinion and the newspaper's stands on important issues are found in the editorial section (e.g., "*Chronicle* Supports New Water Policy"). Movie and television schedules and the "funnies" or comic strips can be found in the entertainment section (e.g., *The Ice Pirates*, matinee at 1:30 P.M.). The sports section contains information about rain delays of ball games, or stories about fishing, canoeing, or diving.

More information about water and water resource issues in southern Florida can be found in chapters 1, 8, and 9.

Procedure
Warm Up
Ask students why people read newspapers. Which section do students or their parents read first? How are newspapers important to our society? Discuss why water is "newsworthy," especially in Florida. Ask students if they can recall water-related issues in the news recently. Students should clip articles related to water from different newspapers for one week.

The Activity
1. **Provide students with a variety of local, state, and national newspapers. Ask them to list the different sections of the newspapers. Discuss the parts of the newspaper and the information each part contains.**

2. **Tell students they are going to develop a newspaper that focuses on water, primarily on topics and issues in the Kissimmee-Okeechobee-Ever-**

glades watershed. Topics and issues might include property rights, recreation, pollution in Lake Okeechobee, water uses, Kissimmee River and Everglades restoration, and storm water treatment.

3. **Discuss the different jobs involved in newspaper publishing.** Students may want to call the local newspaper office for detailed descriptions of these positions. If time allows, invite a guest speaker from the local or even the school newspaper. Arrange a tour to enhance students' understanding of the various jobs.

4. **Divide the class into groups. Each group should choose a section of the newspaper to develop.** These sections might include news/features, weather, editorial, entertainment, sports, and advertising. More than one group should choose the news/features section.

5. **Each group must have an editor and reporters. Other personnel include photographers, word processors, researchers, and artists.**

6. **Groups should brainstorm topics of interest to them and of relevance both to their part of the watershed and their section.** Editors from each group should meet to decide which subjects to pursue.

7. **Discuss how reporting differs from other types of writing.** Students will be under pressure to produce objective, researched, well written articles in a short time, that fit in limited space. Ideally, all writing should be done on computers and saved on disks or hard drives.

8. **Review interviewing techniques with students. Emphasize that newspaper articles should tell the reader who, what, when, where, how, and why. Make sure that students write or call in advance to schedule interviews. Help them design a set of questions about the topic.** Students can practice their questions with each other. They should take careful notes during the interview. If they use a tape recorder, have them ask the interviewee's permission *before* turning it on. Permission must also be obtained for any quotations used in the newspaper. A thank-you letter should follow the interview.

9. **Tell students they have a deadline of five days to complete the newspaper.** (This can be adjusted for simpler or more extensive projects.) Students have three days to research a topic (including interviews and references) and to write drafts of the articles. During the last two days, editors revise the articles and supervise the layout.

Wrap Up and Action
When students have completed the newspaper, have them evaluate their work. A set of criteria used on a scale of one to five (five being the best) will help them judge the paper. Criteria might include the following:

Accuracy

Objectivity

Readability

Interest

Success (i.e., did it increase readers' knowledge of the subject?)

Appearance

Students can also evaluate how effectively they worked together in groups; how effectively the groups coordinated completion of tasks; how dependable each group member was; etc.

Encourage students to talk about the experience of creating a special edition focusing on water. What were the rewards and frustrations of publishing a newspaper?

Depending on the desired quantity, papers can be reproduced in-house on a photocopier or taken to a printer. Post the newspaper in the classroom. Students may also want to distribute newspapers to other classrooms or around the community. Copies of student papers could be sent to the South Florida Water Management District, Office of Government and Public Affairs, P. O. Box 24680, 3301 Gun Club Road, West Palm Beach, FL 33416-4680). Papers could also be sent to representatives in the state capital and in Washington, D.C., to local and regional offices of conservation, and to resource management organizations.

Assessment
Have students:

• explain why water is a subject of interest in the news (*Warm Up*).

• work cooperatively to develop a section of a newspaper (steps 4-9).

• assume a specific task related to newspaper development (steps 5-9).

• evaluate the quality of the newspaper (*Wrap Up and Action*).

Extensions

Invite the publisher or editor of the local or county newspaper to speak to your class. The speaker should discuss the role of the newspaper in relaying information to the public.

Arrange field trips to local newspapers, or call them for free classroom materials (curriculum modules on specific subjects, videotapes, etc.). Some newspapers have a newspaper-in-education coordinator.

Have students collect photographs, articles, cartoons, editorials, and advertisements about water from local, regional, and national newspapers and put them in a "Water in the News" scrapbook.

Invite students to do a "balancing the books" activity. Students collect clippings from local, regional, or national newspapers that report on "profits" and "losses" related to water and the southern Florida environment. Clippings could be placed in the profit and loss columns of a large water "journal" kept in a school hallway.

Explain to students how water figures in other forms of writing and arts such as music, poetry, fiction, nonfiction, and television and screenplays. Ask students to think of examples (*The Everglades: River of Grass* [nonfiction book], "The Rime of the Ancient Mariner" [poem], *Wind Over the Everglades* [film], "River of Dreams" [song]).

Resources

Project WILD. 1992. Activity "Aquatic Times" from *Aquatic Project WILD*. Bethesda, Md.: Western Regional Environmental Education Council.

Your local or school newspaper.

Very good computer programs for layout and graphics include **The Writing Center**, **ClarisWorks**, **KidPix** and **KidPix Companion** (graphics), and **Aldus PageMaker**.

Water for the Future

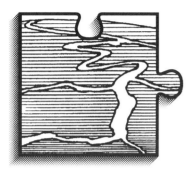

Grade Level:
Middle School, High School

Subject Areas:
Fine Arts, Mathematics, Government, Environmental Science

Duration:
Preparation time: 50 minutes

Activity time: one week

Setting:
Classroom and home

Skills:
Gathering information (observing, collecting, measuring); Analyzing (comparing); Applying; Evaluating

Vocabulary:
conservation

How is conserving water like investing in the future?

Summary
Students identify and implement water conservation habits to learn how this essential resource can be shared with other water users of today and tomorrow.

Objectives
Students will:

• analyze current water conservation plans.

• determine how water conservation practices save water.

• recognize that water conservation is important.

• identify water use habits they can change or water conservation habits they can adopt.

Materials
• *Copies of **Water Conservation Primer** (handout)*

• *Copies of **Constructing a Water Flow Cup** (student worksheet)*

• *Large paper cups (about 32 ounces [1 liter]) (2 cups per group)*

• *Heavy tape*

• *Stopwatch*

• *Pin*

• *1/16-inch-diameter (.16 cm) nail or pushpin*

Making Connections
The topic of resource conservation is coming up more and more in schools and in other facets of our society. Television and other media often present and recommend water conservation practices. Students appreciate the need for water conservation if they or someone they know has experienced a water shortage. For days after Hurricane Andrew, people in Homestead, Florida, stood in line for hours just to receive a gallon jug of potable water. By participating in simple water-saving measures, students experience ways they can positively contribute to conserving water.

Background
Earth has a finite amount of fresh, usable water. Fortunately, water is naturally recycled (collected, cleansed, and distributed) through the hydrologic cycle. Humans have developed the technology to speed this process. However, because of diverse factors (drought, flood, population growth, contamination, etc.) water supplies may not adequately meet a community's needs. Conservation of water can ensure that supplies of fresh water will be available for everyone, today and tomorrow.

Water conservation from a practical and philosophical standpoint makes sense. The idea of using only the amount of water necessary has universal appeal. However, conserving water involves changing habits. Since many of these habits have evolved over a lifetime, they can prove difficult to alter.

People can become active in conserving water by starting simply, then gradually taking more advanced steps to reduce water consumption. The simplest habits involve turning off water whenever it is not being used (while shaving or brushing teeth). When water is needed for rinsing dishes, it can be held in a sink rather than left to flow unused down the drain. An individual may simply use less water. For example, some people use a hose to "sweep" sidewalks, when a broom works well. People can shorten their shower times or reduce the amount of water they use when bathing.

Other conservation methods may initially require more effort and funds, but, in the long run, will save money and resources. For example, households can install low-flow showerheads with smaller holes that reduce water flow and increase pressure. A bottle weighted with stones takes up space in toilet tanks of older toilets, reducing the amount of water available to flush. New water-saving toilet models use as little as 1.5 gallons (9.5 l) of water compared to as much as 7 gallons (26.6 l) in older models.

Lawn care often requires large quantities of water. Water volume can be reduced by watering in the early morning or late evening, and by watering less often and more carefully (e.g., not watering sidewalks and streets). More advanced water conservation measures could include installing drip irrigation systems, and xeriscaping: landscaping with

plants that require less water. The use of an inexpensive rain switch (sensor) prevents automatic irrigation systems from running in the rain, a common occurrence in southern Florida!

If an individual acting alone can save thousands of gallons of water a year, how much can hundreds of thousands of people save? This is what is going on in many communities in southern Florida as well as in other parts of the country. Sometimes communities plan to conserve water only when water shortages threaten, or have occurred. These plans are often called emergency water demand or drought contingency plans. However, many communities are looking for ways to encourage residents to practice water conservation strategies

year-round. Using water efficiently has *economic* as well as environmental benefits. Environmentally, conserving water helps ensure the availability of ample water, and reduces wastewater treatment. Economically, water saved (or not wasted) is water that does not have to be purchased. Water conservation programs can help a municipality avoid or delay building or upgrading new drinking-water or wastewater treatment plants, potentially saving millions of dollars. Where does wastewater go in your community? (Hint: Ask the company or agency from which potable water is purchased.)

In general, a water conservation plan describes strategies the community will take to implement a water conservation

Home Water Use

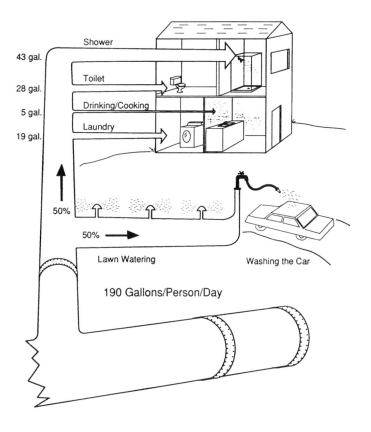

190 Gallons/Person/Day

program. The process by which a community develops its conservation plan will vary depending on the needs and demographics of the community. Most communities with successful water efficiency programs include the goals and rationale behind the plan, responsibilities and mutual benefits of those involved (community planners, water and wastewater treatment plants, energy production municipalities), and implementation procedures (i.e., how goals will be met through a combination of incentives, educational programs, efficiency strategies, and ordinances).

The key to a conservation plan's success is public acceptance and involvement. Educating citizens about the needs and benefits of water conservation is a crucial component of any plan. Youth education programs carried out in schools have proven to be effective in encouraging families to work together to conserve today's resources for tomorrow's children.

For more information about the water resources of southern Florida, refer to chapters 1, 2, 8, and 9.

Procedure

Warm Up

Have students list the ways water is used. Invite them to describe or draw pictures of situations in which they believe water is being wasted. The school facility and grounds may be a good place to begin the investigation. Has their community ever experienced a water shortage? Students can share their pictures and discuss ways they would use water more efficiently. Have them list ways water can be conserved and not wasted.

The Activity

Part I

1. **Ask students to keep track of the water they use over a one-week period (see "Home Water Audit" in** *Resources***). They can keep journals or use graphs and charts to monitor use. Have students design a chart to record their water use and the number of gallons or liters used.** Do students think they used water wisely? Did they ever waste water?

2. **Discuss reasons water should not be wasted.** Students could consider future water availability, sharing a limited resource, sustaining a resource, and cost-effectiveness.

3. **Have students research water conservation strategies and develop a set of activities they can use to conserve water at school and at home.** Their research can be supplemented with the *Water Conservation Primer* provided in this activity.

4. **Have students identify three to five water conservation habits they can individually adopt. Ask them to write these down. For the next week, they should try to practice these habits.** Instruct them to record results in their charts. Remind students that forming new habits takes time.

5. **Students can participate in one or more** *Conservation Capers* **(see side bar) while trying out their water conservation strategies. At the end of the week, ask students if their conservation practices made any difference in the amount of water used. Have students refer to their charts and** compare the amounts of water used before and after they began conservation practices. Which practices were easy to adopt? Which were more difficult? Do they hope to adopt any other conservation habits?

Part II

1. **Inform students that many communities have water conservation plans. Determine if students have seen evidence of any plan policies (restriction of time of day for watering lawns, provision of water in restaurants only upon request, retrofit programs).**

2. **What would students expect to see in a water conservation plan? Have students make a list of criteria or practices they think should be included.** They may be interested in conducting a simple survey of community members to find out what conservation measures people currently practice.

3. **Involve the students in locating and analyzing their community water conservation plan.** They can contact local utilities, water-related government agencies, and community planners. If the community has a plan, have students read the plan to identify the components. What additional strategies are included that they did not consider? Do they see evidence of the goals being met (how is the plan promoted and supported)? Invite a representative from the water utility, the municipality, or a special interest group to speak to the class about the plan, or have students interview those involved. If the community lacks a plan, or if students believe the plan needs revising, they can help

. . . .

promote a new or amended plan. If public meetings are conducted to set policy, encourage students to attend, and if appropriate, to express their views.

Wrap Up and Action

Have students summarize personal and community uses of water and why conserving water is important. If the community plan includes a water education initiative (and especially if it doesn't), students could look into becoming involved. They can encourage their families or the school to adopt water conservation procedures. Have students design posters advertising the benefits of conserving water. The posters might include a description of ongoing water conservation programs and a list of things people can do to save water.

Involve students in designing a water conservation education program to present to peers or younger students.

Assessment

Have students:

• list and illustrate ways water can be conserved (*Warm Up* and *Part I*, step 5).

• conduct a home water audit (*Part I*, step 1).

• demonstrate how water-efficient products reduce the amount of water used (*Part I*, step 5).

• compare amounts of water used before and after conservation efforts (*Part I* , step 5).

• identify criteria that should be included in a water conservation plan (*Part II*, step 2).

Upon completing the activity, for further assessment, have students

• write a paragraph or develop a TV news spot that reflects their views on the importance of water conservation.

Extensions

Contact municipalities and industries to learn how they conserve water. Visit a hardware store and compare water conservation products, paying special attention to flow rate (listed in gallons per minute or gpm). Compare the cost of the products to the amount and cost of water saved. How long would it be before the product "pays for itself"?

Have students research and compare price per gallon of water in various communities or regions. Plot this information against average consumption per person. Contact water utilities for information. What reasons other than price might explain variations (e.g., type of landscape)?

Resources

"Home Water Audit." in *Water For South Florida*. Contact: South Florida Water Management District, P. O. Box 24680, West Palm Beach, FL 33416. (407) 686-8800.

The Montana Watercourse. 1993. *A Catalogue of Water Conservation Resources*. Bozeman, Mont.: The Watercourse and National Project WET.

Water Watchers: Water Conservation Curriculum for Junior High School Science and Social Studies Classes. 1989. Contact: Massachusetts Water Resources Authority, Charlestown Navy Yard, 100 First Avenue, Boston, MA 02129. (617) 242-7110.

Water Wisdom. Contact: Massachusetts Water Resources Authority, Charlestown Navy Yard, 100 First Avenue, Boston, MA 02129. (617) 242-7110.

Conservation Capers

Conservation Caper One

Have students present a "Wasteful Water Charade." Refer to the list of wasteful water habits generated by the class in the Warm Up (e.g., leaving an unattended faucet running, flushing toilets unnecessarily, using a hose to sweep the sidewalk, allowing a faucet to leak, taking long showers). Write these on slips of paper. Divide the class into groups and give each group one of the habits. Each group should create and perform a pantomime to display the behavior written on the paper. When another group identifies the habit, this second group should create a companion pantomime to demonstrate correcting the wasteful habit.

Conservation Caper Two

Ask students if they know ways they can reduce the amount of water flowing out of their homes' faucets. Some students may be familiar with low-flow showerheads. To simulate how low-flow showerheads function, have students make water flow cups and compare the effect of flow restrictors on water quantity. (See Constructing a Water Flow Cup.)

Conservation Caper Three

Have students demonstrate the difference in amounts of water used by a toilet with a weighted water bottle in the tank (Toilet A) versus one with a full tank of water (Toilet B). For this activity, Toilet A uses three gallons (11.4 liters) of water per flush while, like most standard toilets, Toilet B uses approximately five gallons (19 liters).

Ask all students to stand in the back of the room to represent a common pool of water such as a city reservoir or ground water source. Each student represents one gallon (3.8 liters) of water. Two other students stand at either side of the room; acting like water meters, they will count the number of water students that pass by.

Indicate that the left half of the room represents a household with Toilet A and the right half represents one with Toilet B. The front of the room represents a wastewater treatment plant.

Tell students that both toilets have been flushed. Three students should move to the left and then to the front; while five move to the right, then to the front. Continue the process until all students have moved to the front.

Have students compare the number of gallons (liters) needed by each toilet. If a household was limited to a specified amount of water, which toilet would make that supply last longer? Which toilet would contribute to a higher water bill? Which would produce less wastewater?

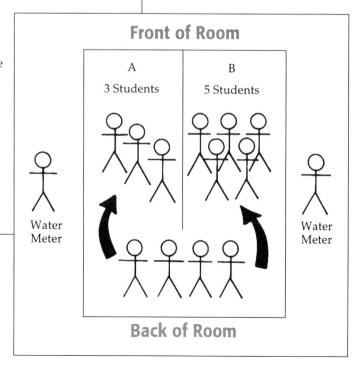

Constructing a Water Flow Cup

- Using a nail, punch five holes into the bottom of a large paper cup. Using a pin, punch five holes in a second cup. The location of the holes should be the same for each cup. Cover the holes of each cup with a piece of sturdy tape.

- Fill the cup with the large holes with water.

- With a stopwatch handy, remove the tape and have another student time how long it takes for the water to pour out of the cup. Be careful not to squeeze the cup. Repeat the procedure two more times; make sure the water level is the same for each trial. Calculate the average time.

- Repeat the procedure for the second cup (timing the flow three times and calculating the average).

- Compare the flow rates of the two cups.

- What is the difference in the drainage times of the two?

- How do the streams of water from the cups compare?

- Would one cup make a better showerhead than the other?

- How could you use the flow restrictor data from this activity to help your family save water?

Water Conservation Primer

- Turn off the water when it is not in use. Don't leave it running when brushing teeth. Turn off the water between soaps and rinses when washing hands.

- Run the dishwasher or washing machine only with a full load.

- Keep a bottle of cold drinking water in the refrigerator instead of running water until it becomes cool.

- Limit shower time to ten minutes or less.

- Take showers instead of baths. (When taking baths, limit the amount of water used.)

- Put a capped bottle of rocks or marbles in the toilet tank to reduce water use. Do not use the toilet for a trash can.

- When washing dishes by hand, use a sink full of rinse water rather than letting the water run.

- Use a broom instead of a hose to sweep sidewalks and driveways.

- When washing the car, use a hose with an on/off nozzle or use buckets of rinse water.

- Water lawns in the mornings or evenings when water will not evaporate as quickly. Make sure the water lands on vegetation and not on streets or sidewalks. If possible, save rainwater for watering lawns.

- If you need to run water before it becomes hot, store the cool running water in a bottle for future use. Unheated water can be used for rinsing dishes, and washing vegetables and hands.

- Fix leaks!

- Install a low-flow showerhead.

- Replace old toilets with low volume flush models.

In the Year 2020

Grade Level:
High School

Subject Areas:
Geography, Government,
Environmental Science

Duration:
Preparation time: Part I, 25
minutes; Part II, 25 minutes

Activity time: Part I, 50
minutes; Part II, two 50-
minute periods

Setting:
Classroom

Skills:
Analyzing; Interpreting;
Evaluating; Presenting

Vocabulary:
Atlantic Coastal Ridge,
hydroperiod, sheet flow

"When we try to pick out anything by itself, we find it hitched to everything else in the universe." How do the words of John Muir apply to the K-O-E watershed?

Summary
Given a set of parameters, students design a water management system for the K-O-E watershed that accommodates agriculture, urban development, tourism, wildlife, and natural environments. They also propose an Everglades vision statement for the year 2020.

Objectives
Students will:

• analyze water management practices and strategies in the K-O-E watershed.

• propose a vision statement for the K-O-E watershed for the year 2020.

Materials
• *The Everglades: River of Grass* by Marjory Stoneman Douglas

• *Copies or overhead of each of the following*:

• *The Greater Everglades System: Past and Present* (map)

• *Kissimmee River–Lake Okeechobee–Everglades System* (map)

• *Canal System* (map)

Making Connections
Many students are familiar with the current state of the K-O-E watershed and its related problems. Experiencing the challenges engineers faced in protecting lives and making the land suitable for development and for agriculture, students will appreciate the watershed's evolution. Projecting future views of the watershed will promote awareness of current practices and their possible impact.

Background
Water has drawn the boundaries of the South Florida Water Management District (SFWMD), and has also defined the evolution of the agency and the region. One of the largest, most complex natural ecosystems in the world, the Kissimmee-Okeechobee-Everglades (K-O-E) system, nourishes an amazing array of habitats and wildlife. Stretching 240 miles (398.4 km), from the center of the state (near Orlando) to Florida Bay, this system helps drive the life cycle of regional plants and animals and perpetuates the water cycle for people in central and southern Florida.

Historically, water from the Upper Chain of Lakes flowed gradually through the bends and curves of the Kissimmee River and over surrounding floodplains to Lake Okeechobee. The lake is a huge indentation in the system, a

730-square-mile (1,898 sq. km) shallow bowl. Before the lake was diked for flood control, water spilled over the southern rim of the bowl, or traveled via seepage or other waterways, through the saw grass marshes and tree islands of the Everglades. The water, inched southward from Lake Okeechobee in great, wide sheets, rather than in creeks and rivers; its movement is referred to as "sheet flow." The flat lowlands south of Lake Okeechobee, less than 25 feet (7.5 m) above sea level, kept the water from draining off the land.

Some water filtered down into the region's vast systems of underground storage. Some went east to the estuaries of the Atlantic Ocean or west to the Gulf of Mexico. At the coasts it became part of the subtle mix of fresh and salt water that spiny lobster, oysters, shrimp, and many other species of commercial and recreational interest thrived on.

Since the late 1800s, people have sought to control and use the K-O-E System with varying degrees of success. They drained floodplains and swamps and deepened or changed the course of waterways, always assuming their changes would be beneficial. The Everglades was altered for navigation and drainage, to encourage development; then, after the hurricanes of 1926 and 1928, flood control became the primary motivation.

In the first half of this century, nature still exerted some control over how many people could live in Florida, and over where they could live. But from 1950 to the present, advanced technology

and comprehensive changes to the landscape have made almost unlimited population growth possible. On the Atlantic Coastal Ridge, land is elevated and more suited for building. The ocean is accessible for shipping and transportation. The rich soil, the long growing season, and the infrequency of freezing temperatures make southern Florida attractive to farmers.

More people live in southern Florida now than lived in the entire state in 1960. Nearly 14 million people call the state home; 40 million more visit each year. Florida's population is projected to rise to 20 million by the year 2020. Each day, about 800 more people move to Florida, mostly to the coastal communities.

Watering lawns, washing laundry and dishes, and flushing toilets, the average urban resident in southern Florida uses about 190 gallons (722 l) of water a day. Multiply that by 365 days and millions of people, and the numbers are staggering. Agriculture, a multibillion dollar industry, consumes hundreds of thousands of gallons of water each day.

Cities and farms also generate waste and pollution that contaminate the water and other natural resources. Concrete or asphalt covers much of the land inhabited by people, and interrupts the hydrologic cycle's self-renewing movement from the skies to the ground to underground aquifers.

More than half of the state's wetlands have been lost—3.2 million acres (1,280,000 ha) have been cleared and/or drained to meet this unprecedented human

demand. Millions of acres of floodplains, coastal dunes, and uplands have also been lost.

However, several projects aim to protect or restore areas of the K-O-E watershed. These include restoring about 23 miles (38.2 km) of the Kissimmee River to its historic curves and folds; developing Stormwater Treatment Areas (STAs) to treat phosphorus-enriched agricultural runoff before it enters the Everglades; using Best Management Practices (BMPs) to reduce phosphorus loads; increasing the quantity of water to the Everglades and Florida Bay by more closely replicating the area's natural hydrology; enacting a statewide melaleuca management plan; and acquiring lands for Taylor Slough, Florida Bay, and Everglades restoration.

Additional information about management of water resources in southern Florida is found in chapters 8, and 9.

Procedure
Warm Up
Read students selections from books about the historic Everglades, such as the one below from Marjory Stoneman Douglas's *The Everglades: River of Grass*:

The Everglades begin at Lake Okeechobee . . . .Saw grass reaches up both sides of that lake in great enclosing arms, so that it is correct to say that the Everglades are there also, but south, southeast and southwest, where the lake water slopped and seeped and ran over and under the rock and soil, the greatest mass of the saw grass begins. It stretches as it always has stretched, in one thick enormous curving river of grass, to the very end. This is the Everglades.

It reaches one hundred miles from Lake Okeechobee to the Gulf of Mexico, fifty, sixty, even seventy miles wide. No one has ever fought his way along its full length. Few have ever crossed the northern wilderness of nothing but grass. Down that almost invisible slope the water moves. The grass stands. Where the grass and the water are there is the heart, the current, the meaning of the Everglades.

Ask students if this description applies to the Everglades now. What might have been the objectives of engineers who altered the Everglades from its original natural and historical state? List possible objectives on the board. The list should include some of the following:

• to provide access from Lake Okeechobee to the Atlantic Ocean and the Gulf of Mexico (navigation/transportation).

• to make land suitable for development. (This and navigation were the original reasons the Everglades was altered.)

• to carry water away from populated areas and farms during major storms and hurricanes (flood control).

• to contain the water within Lake Okeechobee for water supply, and to release it from the lake during times of high water such as hurricanes. (The great hurricane of 1928 caused 1,836 deaths, 1,870 injuries, and $287 million worth of damage.)

• to add water to underground water supplies for urban use, and to carry water to agricultural areas.

• to carry fresh water to the lower east coast, and to hold back ocean water, thus preventing saltwater contamination of underground water supplies.

• to provide for the water needs of a growing population.

The Activity
Part I

1. **Divide students into small "engineering" groups. Give them the map,** *The Greater Everglades System: Past and Present,* **and have them compare and contrast natural, agricultural, and urban areas in the historical and fragmented ecosystem. Discuss patterns of development (consider soil type, elevation, and shipping and transportation), reasons why people come to Florida, and reasons why the state is appealing to farmers.** Lead students to understand that on the Atlantic Coastal Ridge, land is elevated and more suitable for building. Rich soil, a long growing season, and infrequent freezing temperatures make southern Florida attractive to farmers.

2. **Provide students with maps of southern Florida that depict the Kissimmee River-Lake Okeechobee-Everglades System. Refer to the list students developed in the** *Warm Up;* **tell them they will design a water management system that accomplishes each of those objectives.**

3. **Tell students they may use any methods they can imagine to accomplish the objectives. Encourage them to be creative.** You may want to provide the following information: Canals can be dredged to drain water from the land and shunt it to the ocean.

Large areas can be set aside as storage for water for urban and agricultural use. Water will flow on its own down gradients and pumps can be installed to accelerate the water's movement or to back-pump water (such as in Lake Okeechobee). Dikes can be constructed to contain water. Lift locks can raise or lower boats from one water level to another, for example, when they enter or leave Lake Okeechobee and the Okeechobee waterway or the Kissimmee River.

4. **Have students mark the maps. They should indicate canals, dikes, or other structures they would use to contain Lake Okeechobee and manipulate the original sheet flow of the Everglades to satisfy their objectives.**

5. **When students have completed their maps, distribute the map** *Canal System* **to each group. Have students compare their water management systems with the canal system designed by the Army Corps of Engineers.** Of the objectives students listed, how many have to do with the needs of humans? How many are intended to protect wildlife and the environment?

6. **Read the following statement to students from the SFWMD Annual Report of 1993:**

This region was created by the state in 1949 and charged with providing flood protection and water supply, preventing salt water intrusion, encouraging agricultural and urban development, and preserving fish and wildlife. During the first twenty years of its existence, this challenge centered on protecting human interests. That began to change in the 1970's as Floridians started to realize that human development was endangering the unique ecosystems of the Kissimmee-Okeechobee-Everglades system.

Tell students that through Florida's Everglades Forever Act (1994), the District has committed to a plan to restore a major portion of the remaining Everglades ecosystem through construction projects, research, and regulation. The District's goal is to implement solutions for issues of water quality and water quantity, hydropattern, and the invasion of exotic plants and animals.

Part II

1. **Tell students that the canal system developed by the Army Corps of Engineers to alleviate past problems actually created complex new dilemmas. Have students re-form into their original "engineering" groups.**

2. **Assign each group one of the following areas of the K-O-E-watershed: Upper Chain of Lakes, Kissimmee River, Lake Okeechobee, Everglades Agricultural Area, a Water Conservation Area, Everglades National Park, Big Cypress National Preserve, and Florida Bay.**

3. **Have students research their assigned area and prepare a presentation regarding:**

• water quality

• water quantity

• hydroperiod

• the effect of population increase and urban development on water quality and quantity and the hydroperiod

• the effect of agricultural activities on water quality and quantity and the hydroperiod

• proposed solutions to water quality and quantity and hydroperiod issues. (For example, construction of STAs in the Everglades Agricultural Area to reduce the phosphorus load of waters.)

4. **After students have heard all the presentations, involve the class in envisioning the K-O-E watershed in the year 2020.** Remind students to consider the information they learned from the presentations and to think about the spectrum of possibilities for the Everglades. Their vision might range from returning the Everglades to its natural state of about 150 years ago, to allowing the complete development of southern Florida. Tell students to consider the current problems facing the K-O-E watershed and problems with proposed solutions. Do students believe it is possible to return the area to the condition it was in 1845? Do they believe most Americans and visitors from around the world would allow development in the Everglades, including Everglades National Park?

5. **In determining their vision for the Everglades, have students consider the following questions:**

• Is it possible that water and other resources will become a limiting factor for future growth in southern Florida?

• Is it likely that some people will argue that human use of water in southern Florida is a priority?

• How does water "cycle" or

move through southern Florida? If natural areas continue to be developed and "paved over," will it affect the hydrologic cycle and reduce moisture in southern Florida?

• If natural areas continue to be developed, how will it affect the recreational and tourist industries of southern Florida?

6. **In developing their vision for the Everglades, ask students to react to the following quotation from 1994-1995 chairperson Valerie Boyd of the SFWMD Governing Board:**

As a fifth generation Floridian, I feel obligated to restore the Everglades, and to preserve the ecological heritage and bounty of this state for future generations. At the same time, I also believe we must recognize the tremendous inherent value of agricultural and urban development in our region— because this human development bolsters Florida's economy, and also contributes to the rest of the country and the world. There must be ways to preserve both the natural wonders of Florida's Everglades and the vigor and productivity of our cities and farms.

Wrap Up and Action

Ask students if their vision of the Everglades achieves a balance among natural, urban, and agricultural environments.

"When we try to pick out anything by itself, we find it hitched to everything else in the universe." Have students discuss how John Muir's words apply to the K-O-E watershed. Have students present their vision of the Everglades to other students or a community group. They may wish to incorporate drama, art, or music into their presentation.

Assessment:

Have students

• create a water management system for southern Florida based on a set of objectives (*Part I*, steps 2-4).

• compare and contrast their system with the current canal system of southern Florida (*Part I*, step 5).

• develop a vision statement for southern Florida for the year 2020 (*Part II*, steps 4-7).

Extensions

Have students research the Central & Southern Florida Project Comprehensive Review Study (U.S. Army Corps of Engineers Restudy).

Hold mock hearings on management priorities for the Everglades watershed. Have students research and represent special interest groups including farmers, developers, urban residents, businesses, and conservation groups.

Have students attend a public meeting of the South Florida Water Management District and compare their visions of the Everglades with that of the SFWMD. Request a copy of the water management district's vision for 2010 (for water supply) and for 2050 (for the entire watershed). What do students think of these visions?

Brainstorm and then research careers associated with Everglades ecosystem restoration from science to engineering and public communications to environmental law.

Resources

Blake, Nelson M. 1980. *Water Into Land, Land Into Water*. Tallahassee, Fla.: University Presses of Florida.

Cavanaugh, Peggy, and Margaret Spontak. 1992. *Protecting Paradise*. Fairfield, Fla.: Phoenix Publishing.

Douglas, Marjory Stoneman. 1947. *The Everglades: River of Grass*. Sarasota, Fla.: Pineapple Press.

Fernald, Edward. A., and Donald J. Patton, eds. 1984. *Water Resources Atlas of Florida*. Tallahassee, Fla.: Florida State University.

Fernald, Edward A., and Elizabeth D. Purdum, eds. 1992. *Atlas of Florida*. Tallahassee, Fla.: University Presses of Florida.

Huser, Tom. 1989. *Into the Fifth Decade, The First Forty Years of the South Florida Water Management District 1949-1989*. South Florida Water Management District.

Office of the Governor. Environmental Affairs. *Save our Everglades Annual Report*. Tallahassee, Fla.

South Florida Water Management District. *Everglades, Annual Report*.

South Florida Water Management District. *How Much . . . How Good? The Story of South Florida's Water*.

· ·

The Greater Everglades System: Past and Present

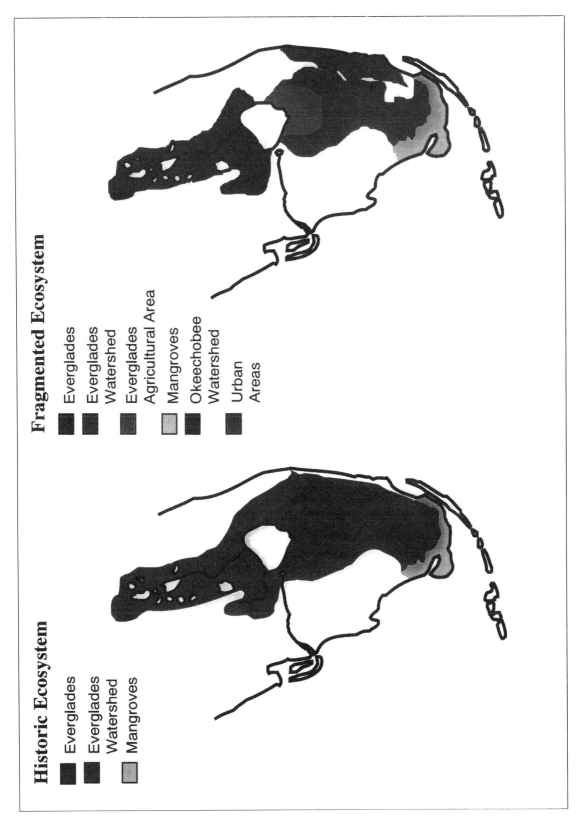

Historic Ecosystem

- Everglades
- Everglades Watershed
- Mangroves

Fragmented Ecosystem

- Everglades
- Everglades Watershed
- Everglades Agricultural Area
- Mangroves
- Okeechobee Watershed
- Urban Areas

Kissimmee River-Lake Okeechobee-Everglades System

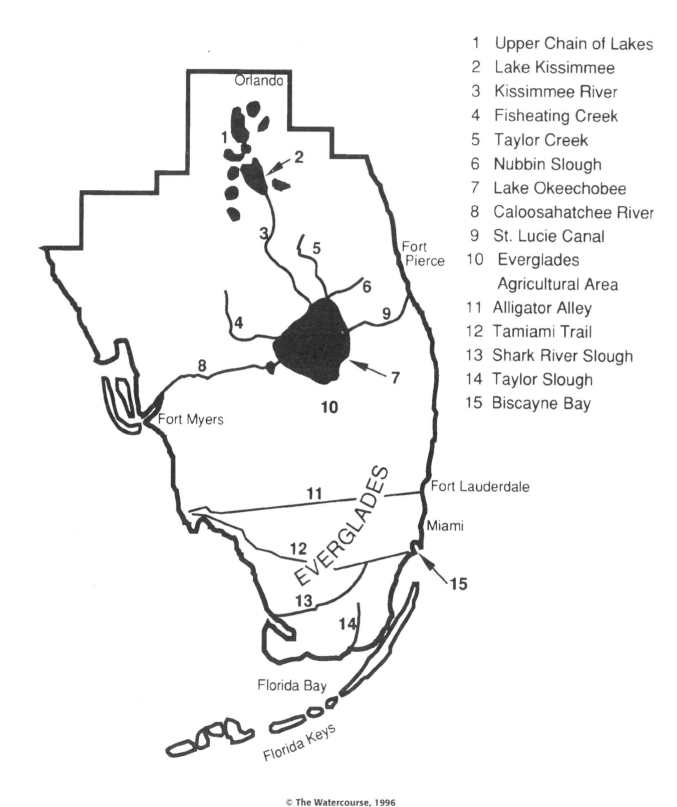

1   Upper Chain of Lakes
2   Lake Kissimmee
3   Kissimmee River
4   Fisheating Creek
5   Taylor Creek
6   Nubbin Slough
7   Lake Okeechobee
8   Caloosahatchee River
9   St. Lucie Canal
10   Everglades
      Agricultural Area
11   Alligator Alley
12   Tamiami Trail
13   Shark River Slough
14   Taylor Slough
15   Biscayne Bay

Canal System

1. Upper Chain of Lakes
2. Lake Kissimmee
3. Kissimmee River
4. Fisheating Creek
5. Taylor Creek
6. Nubbin Slough
7. Lake Okeechobee
8. Caloosahatchee River
9. St. Lucie Canal
10. Everglades Agricultural Area
11. Alligator Alley
12. Tamiami Trail
13. Shark River Slough
14. Taylor Slough
15. Biscayne Bay

Orlando

1

2

3

5

Fort Pierce

6

9

4

7

8

Fort Myers

10

Altered water flow

EVERGLADES

11

Fort Lauderdale

Miami

12

15

13

14

Water flow reduction

Saline water may be a factor in the decline of the delicate coral reefs.

Florida Bay

Florida Keys

HAWKS CHANNEL

List of Species

Common plants and animals referred to in the text.

Plants

alligator flag	*Thalia geniculata*
bald cypress	*Taxodium distichum*
beak rushes	*Rhynchospora megalocarpa*
black mangrove	*Avicennia germinians*
black needlerush	*Juncus roemerianus*
bluestem or dwarf palmetto	*Sabal minor*
Brazilian pepper	*Schinus terebinthifolius*
butterfly orchid	*Encyclia tampensis*
buttonwood	*Conocarpus erectus*
cattail	*Typha latifolia*
cocoplum	*Chrysobalanus icaco*
coontie	*Zamia floridana*
devil's claw	*Pisonia aculeata*
dwarf huckleberry	*Gaylussacia dumosa*
dwarf live oak	*Quercus minima*
epidendrum	*Epidendrum nocturnum*
fetterbush	*Lyonia lucida*
Florida rosemary	*Ceratiola ericoides*
gallberry	*Ilex glabra*
gumbo limbo	*Bursera simaruba*
highbush blueberry	*Vaccinium corymbosum*
hydrilla	*Hydrilla verticillata*
Jamaica dogwood	*Piscidia piscipula*
live oak	*Quercus virginiana*

longleaf pine	*Pinus palustris*
melaleuca	*Melaleuca quinquenervia*
mahogany	*Swietenia mahogani*
maidencane	*Panicum hemitomon*
manatee grass	*Syringodium filiforme*
mastic	*Mastichodendron foetidissimum*
milk pea	*Galactia* spp.
moonflower	*Ipomoea alba*
muhly grass	*Muhlenbergia capillaris*
pickerelweed	*Pontederia lanceolata*
pigeon plum	*Coccoloba diversifolia*
poisonwood	*Metopium toxiferum*
pond apple	*Annona glabra*
pond cypress	*Taxodium ascendens*
pond pine	*Pinus serotina*
purple bladderwort	*Utricularia purpurea*
red bay	*Persea borbonia*
red mangrove	*Rhizophora mangle*
red maple	*Acer rubrum*
red mulberry	*Morus rubra*
resurrection fern	*Polypodium polypodioides*
saffron plum	*Bumelia celastrina*
sand pine	*Pinus clausus*
satinleaf	*Chyrsophyllum oliviforme*
saw grass	*Cladium jamaicense*
saw palmetto	*Serenoa repens*
sea grape	*Coccoloba uvifera*
sea oxeye	*Borrichia arborescens*
sea purslane	*Sesuvium portulacastrum*
sedge	*Fimbristylis caroliniana*
silver palm	*Coccothrinax argentata*
slash pine	*Pinus elliottii*
smooth cordgrass	*Spartina alterniflora*
southern Florida slash pine	*Pinus elliottii densa*

Spanish moss	*Tillandsia usneoides*
spike rush	*Eleocharis elongata*
staggerbush	*Lyonia fruticosa*
strangler fig	*Ficus aurea*
turkey oak	*Quercus laevis*
turtle grass	*Thalassia testudinum*
water hyacinth	*Eichhornia crassipes*
wax myrtle	*Myrica cerifera*
white mangrove	*Laguncularia racemosa*
white stopper	*Eugenia axillaris*
white water lily	*Nymphaea odorata*
white-topped sedge	*Dichromena colorata*
wiregrass	*Aristida stricta*
woody glasswort	*Salicornia virginica*

Crustaceans, Mollusks, Insects, and other Invertebrates

blue crab	*Callinectes sapidus*
crayfish	*Procambarus alleni*
ghost crab	*Ocypode albicans*
grass shrimp	*Palaemonetes* spp.
mud crab (fiddler crab)	*Uca* spp.
panaeid shrimp	*Panaeus* spp.
pink shrimp	*Penaeus duorarum*
spiny lobster	*Panulirus argus*
stone crab	*Menippe mercenaria*
apple snail	*Pomacea paludosus*
queen conch	*Strombus gigas*
Florida tree snail	*Liguus fasciatus*
oyster	*Crassostrea virginica*
zebra butterfly	*Heliconius charitonius*
Schaus' swallowtail butterfly	*Papilio aristodemus ponceanus*
mosquito (more than 40	*Aedes taeniorhynchus*
species in 12 genera)	*Anopheles* spp.
	Culex spp.

golden orb weaver spider	*Nephila clavipes*
cockroach (palmetto bug)	*Periplaneta americana*

Fish

American flagfish	*Jordanella floridae*
bluefin killifish	*Lucania goodei*
bluespotted sunfish	*Enneacanthus gloriosus*
bowfin	*Amia calva*
golden topminnow	*Fundulus chrysotus*
greater amberjack	*Seriola dumerili*
Florida gar	*Lepisosteus platyrchinchus*
Florida largemouth bass	*Micropterus salmoides floridanus*
least killifish	*Heterandria formosa*
mangrove snapper	*Lutjanus griseus*
mosquitofish	*Gambusia affinis*
mullet	*Mugil cephalus*
rainwater killifish	*Lucania parva*
red drum	*Sciaenops ocellatus*
red snapper	*Lutjanus campechanus*
snook	*Centropomus undecimalis*
southern bluegill	*Lepomis macrochirus mystacalis*
speckled perch (black crappie)	*Pomoxis nigromaculatus*
spotted seatrout	*Cynoscion nebulosus*
tarpon	*Megalops atlanticus*
yellow bullhead	*Ictalurus natalis*

Reptiles and Amphibians

American alligator	*Alligator mississippiensis*
American crocodile	*Crocodylus acutus*
black racer	*Coluber constrictor*
brown anole	*Anolis sagrei*
box turtle	*Terrapene carolina*
bullfrog	*Rana catesbeiana*
corn snake	*Elaphe guttata*
diamondback terrapin	*Malaclemys terrapin*

dusky pigmy rattlesnake	*Sistrurus miliarius barbouri*
dwarf salamander	*Eurycea quadridigitata*
eastern coral snake	*Micrurus fulvius fulvius*
eastern diamondback rattlesnake	*Crotalus adamanteus*
eastern indigo snake	*Drymarchon corais cooperi*
Florida chorus frog	*Pseudacris nigrita*
Florida cottonmouth	*Agkistrodon piscivorus conanti*
Florida reef gecko	*Schaerodactylus notatus*
Florida softshell turtle	*Apalone ferox*
greater siren	*Siren lacertina*
green anole	*Anolis caroliniensis*
hognose snake	*Heterodon platyrhinos*
king snake	*Lampropeltis getulus*
loggerhead turtle	*Caretta caretta*
marine toad	*Bufo marinus*
peninsula newt	*Notophthalmus viridescens*
pig frog	*Rana grylio*
rough green snake	*Opheodrys aestivus*
scarlet kingsnake	*Lampropeltis triangulum elapsoides*
southern toad	*Bufo terrestris*
southeastern five-lined skink	*Eumeces inexpectatus*
squirrel treefrog	*Hyla squirella*

Birds

American crow	*Corvus brachyrhynchos*
American robin	*Turdus migratorius*
American white pelican	*Pelecanus erythrorhynchos*
anhinga	*Anhinga anhinga*
bald eagle	*Haliaeetus leucocephalus*
barred owl	*Strix varia*
belted kingfisher	*Ceryle alcyon*
black-crowned night heron	*Nycticorax nycticorax*
bluejay	*Cyanocitta cristata*
boat-tailed grackle	*Quiscalus major*

brown pelican	*Pelecanus accidentalis*
Cape Sable seaside sparrow	*Ammodramus maritimus mirabilis*
cardinal	*Cardinalis cardinalis*
cattle egret	*Bubulcus ibis*
double-crested cormorant	*Phalacrocorax auritus*
glossy ibis	*Plegadis falcinellus*
great blue heron	*Ardea herodias*
great egret	*Casmerodius albus*
greater flamingo	*Phoenicopterus ruber*
least tern	*Sterna albifrons*
limpkin	*Aramus guarauna*
marsh wren	*Cistothorus platensis*
northern harrier (marsh hawk)	*Circus cyaneus*
osprey	*Pandion haliaetus*
pine warbler	*Dendroica pinus*
red-cockaded woodpecker	*Picoides borealis*
red-bellied woodpecker	*Melanerpes carolinus*
red-shouldered hawk	*Buteo lineatus*
roseate spoonbill	*Ajaja ajaja*
seaside sparrow	*Ammodramus maritimus*
snail kite	*Rostrahamus sociabilis*
snowy egret	*Egretta thula*
white ibis	*Eudocimus albus*
wood stork ("iron head")	*Mycteria americana*
yellow-crowned night heron	*Nycticorax violaceus*

Mammals

Atlantic bottlenose dolphin	*Tursiops truncatus*
black bear	*Ursus americanus*
bobcat	*Lynx rufus*
feral hog (wild boar)	*Sus scrofa*
Everglades mink	*Mustela vison*
Florida panther	*Felis concolor coryi*
fox squirrel	*Sciurus niger*

gray fox	*Urocyon cineroargenteus*
gray squirrel	*Sciurus carolinensis*
Key deer	*Odocoileus virginianus clavium*
marsh rabbit	*Sylvilagus palustris*
nine-banded armadillo	*Dasypus novemcinctus*
opossum	*Didelphis marsupialis*
porpoise	*Phocoena phocoena*
raccoon	*Procyon lotor*
river otter	*Lutra canadensis*
West Indian manatee	*Trichechus manatus*
white-tailed deer	*Odocoileus virginianus*

Resources

. . . .

Agency Documents

Center for Occupational Research and Development. 1991. *Teacher's Guide: Applied Biology/ Chemistry—Water.* Waco, Tex.

Cox, James, Randy Kautz, Maureen MacLaughlin, and Terry Gilbert. 1994. *Closing The Gaps In Florida's Wildlife Habitat Conservation System.* Florida Game and Freshwater Fish Commission.

Department of the Interior, National Park Service. 1991. *Superintendent's Annual Narrative Report.* Homestead, Fla.

Everglades Coalition, The. 1992. *Everglades in the 21st Century: The Water Management Future.*

Florida Department of Environmental Protection. *Classroom and Field Experiments for Florida's Environmental Resources.* Tallahassee, Fla.

Florida Department of Environmental Protection. 1988. *Aquatic and Wetland Plants of Florida.* (4th edition). Tallahassee, Fla.

Florida Greenways Commission. 1994. *Creating a Statewide Greenways System for People . . . for Wildlife . . . for Florida: A Report to the Governor.* Contact: Florida Greenways Commission, P.O. Box 5948, Tallahassee, FL 32314-5948.

Governor's Commission, The. *Governor's Commission for a Sustainable South Florida 1995.* Final Report. Tallahassee, Fla.

Huser, Tom. 1989. *Into the Fifth Decade, The First Forty Years of the South Florida Water Management District 1949-1989.* South Florida Water Management District.

Montana Watercourse, The. 1993. *A Catalogue of Water Conservation Resources.* Bozeman, Mont.: The Watercourse and National Project WET.

National Geographic Society. 1993. "Water—The Power, Promise, and Turmoil of North America's Fresh Water," *National Geographic* (Special Edition). Washington, D.C.

National Geographic Society. 1994. "The Everglades, Dying for Help," *National Geographic.* Washington, D.C.

National Wildlife Federation, The. 1987. *Status Report on Our Nation's Wetlands.*

North American Association for Environmental Education. 1992. *The Wetlands Issue: What Should We Do With Our Bogs, Swamps and Marshes?* Troy, Oh.

Office of the Governor. Environmental Affairs. *Save our Everglades Annual Report.* Tallahassee, Fla.

South Florida Management and Coordination Working Group 1993, The. The Science Sub-Group. *Federal Objectives for The South Florida Restoration* (report).

South Florida Management District. *Everglades, Annual Report.*

South Florida Water Management District 1994. *Strategic Plan for the 1990s: Partnerships in Water Management: The Vision for the Future.*

South Florida Water Management District 1994. *District Water Management Plan,* Vol. 2.: Integrated Plans.

South Florida Water Management District "Home Water Audit," *Water For South Florida.*

South Florida Water Management District. *How Much . . . How Good? The Story of South Florida's Water.*

State of Florida Department of Environmental Protection. 1992. "A Geological Overview of Florida," Thomas M. Scott. Open File Report No. 50, Florida Geological Survey.

Wilderness Society, The. *Ten Most Endangered National Parks.* May 24, 1988.

World Watch Institute. 1993. "Facing Water Scarcity," *State of the World.* New York, N.Y.: W. W. Norton & Company.

. . . .

Books

Abbott, Edwin A. 1952. *Flatland.* 6th ed. New York, N.Y.: Dover Publications, Inc.

Albright, Horace Marden. 1985. *The Birth of the National Park Service: The Founding Years, 1913-33.* Salt Lake City, Utah: Howe Brothers.

Bell, C. Ritchie, and Bryan J. Taylor. 1982. *Florida Wildflowers and Roadside Plants.* Chapel Hill, N.C.: Laurel Hill Press.

Blake, Nelson M. 1980. *Water Into Land, Land Into Water.* Tallahassee, Fla.: University Presses of Florida.

Brookfield, Charles M., and Oliver Griswold. 1985. *They All Called it Tropical.* 9th ed. Miami, Fla.: Historical Association of Southern Florida.

Brown, Loren G. "Totch". 1994. *Totch: A Life in the Everglades.* Gainesville, Fla.: University of Florida Press.

Bullen, Adelaide K. *Florida Indians of Past and Present.* Gainesville, Fla.: Florida State Museum, University of Florida.

Caduto, Michael J. 1985. *Pond and Brook: A Guide to Nature Study in Freshwater Environments.* Englewood Cliffs, N.J.: Prentice Hall, Inc.

Campbell, Gayla, and Steve Wildberger. 1992. *The Monitor's Handbook.* Chestertown, Md.: LaMotte Company.

Carmichael, Pete, and Winston Williams. 1991. *Florida's Fabulous Reptiles and Amphibians.* Tampa, Fla.: World Publications.

Carr, Archie. 1973. *The Everglades.* New York, N.Y.: Time-Life Books.

Carter, Elizabeth F. 1987. *A Hiking Guide to the Trails of Florida.* Birmingham, Ala.: Menasha Ridge Press.

Cavanaugh, Peggy, and Margaret Spontak. 1992. *Protecting Paradise: 300 Ways To Protect Florida's Environment.* Fairfield, Fla.: Phoenix Publishing.

Coble, Charles, et al. 1988. *Prentice Hall Earth Science.* Englewood Cliffs, N.J.: Prentice Hall, Inc.

Cooke, G. Dennis, et al. 1993. *Restoration and Management of Lakes and Reservoirs.* Boca Raton, Fla.: Lewis Publishers.

Corson, Walter H., ed. 1990. *The Global Ecology Handbook: What You Can Do About the Environmental Crisis.* Boston, Mass.: Beacon Press.

Craighead, Frank C. Sr. 1972. *The Trees of South Florida.* Vol. I. Coral Gables, Fla.: University of Miami Press.

Davis, Steven M., and John C. Ogden, eds. 1994. *Everglades: The Ecosystem and Its Restoration.* Delray Beach, Fla.: St. Lucie Press.

de Golia, Jack. 1978. *Everglades: The Story Behind the Scenery.* Las Vegas, Nev.: KC Publications.

Doppelt, Bob, Mary Scurlock, Chris Frissell, and James Karr. 1993. *Entering the Watershed: A New Approach to Save America's River Ecosystems.* Washington, D.C.: Island Press.

Douglas, Marjory Stoneman. 1976. *Hurricane.* Revised ed. Atlanta, Ga.: Mockingbird Books.

Douglas, Marjory Stoneman. 1987. *Voice of the River.* Sarasota, Fla.: Pineapple Press, Inc.

Douglas, Marjory Stoneman. 1988. *The Everglades: River of Grass.* Sarasota, Fla.: Pineapple Press.

Espenshade, Edward B., Jr. 1990. *Goodes World Atlas.* Chicago, Ill.: Rand McNally.

Fernald, Edward. A., and Donald J. Patton, eds. 1984. *Water Resources Atlas of Florida.* Tallahassee, Fla.: Florida State University.

Fernald, Edward A., and Elizabeth D. Purdum, eds. 1992. *Atlas of Florida.* Tallahassee, Fla.: University Presses of Florida.

Garbarino, Merwyn S., and Frank W. Porter, ed. 1989. *The Seminole.* New York, N.Y.: Chelsea House Publishers.

Gato, Jeannette, ed. 1991. *The Monroe County Environmental Story.* Big Pine Key, Fla.: The Monroe County Environmental Education Task Force.

George, Jean Craighead. 1988. *Everglades Wildguide.* Washington, D.C.: U.S. Department of the Interior.

Gill, Joan E., and Beth R. Read, eds. 1975. *Born of the Sun.* Hollywood, Fla.: Worth International Communications Corp.

Glaros, Lou, and Doug Sphar. 1987. *A Canoeing and Kayaking Guide to the Streams of Florida.* Volume II: Central and South Peninsula. Birmingham, Ala.: Menasha Ridge Press.

Glasgow, Vaughn L. 1991. *A Social History of the American Alligator.* New York, N.Y.: St. Martin's Press.

Grow, Gerald. 1987. *Florida Parks, A Guide to Camping in Nature.* Tallahassee, Fla.: Longleaf Publications.

Harris, Bill. 1985. *The Everglades: A Timeless Wilderness.* New York, N.Y.: Crescent Books.

Haynes, Sande, Dennis M. Ross, and Joseph E. Dodge, Jr. Eds. 1991. *The Dade County Environmental Story.* Miami Springs, Fla.: Friends of the Everglades.

Hoff, Mary, and Mary M. Rogers. 1991. *Our Endangered Planet: Ground Water.* Minneapolis, Minn.: Lerner.

Humphrey, Stephen R. ed. 1992. *Rare and Endangered Biota of Florida,* (4 vols.). Gainesville, Fla.: University Presses of Florida.

Jacobson, Cliff. 1991. *Water, Water Everywhere.* (3 vols.). Loveland, Col.: Hach Company.

Kersey, Harry A. Jr. 1987. *The Seminole and Miccosukee Tribes: A Critical Bibliography.* Bloomington. Ind.: Indiana University Press.

Kersey, Harry A. Jr., and Voncile Mallory. 1982. *The Seminole World of Tommy Tiger.* Tallahassee, Fla.: Division of Archives, History and Records Management, Florida Department of State, The Capitol.

Kesselheim, Alan S., The Watercourse, and Project WET. 1993. *The Liquid Treasure Water History Trunk, Learning From the Past.* Bozeman, Mont.: The Watercourse.

Lazell, James D. Jr. 1989. *Wildlife of the Florida Keys: A Natural History.* Washington, D.C.: Island Press.

Little, Elbert L. 1993. *The Audubon Society Field Guide to North American Trees (Eastern Region).* New York, N.Y.: Alfred A. Knopf.

Lodge, Thomas E. 1994. *The Everglades Handbook: Understanding the Ecosystem.* Delray Beach, Fla.: St. Lucie Press.

Macchio, William J. 1992. *Path of Destruction: Hurricane Andrew.* Charleston, S.C.: BD Publishing, Inc.

Marsh, William M. 1987. *Earthscape: A Physical Geography.* New York, N.Y.: John Wiley & Sons.

Matthiessen, Peter. 1990. *Killing Mister Watson.* New York, N.Y.: Random House.

McCarthy, Kevin M., ed. 1990. *Nine Stories by Marjory Stoneman Douglas.* Gainesville, Fla.: University Presses of Florida.

McIver, Stuart. 1988. *Glimpses of South Florida History.* Miami, Fla.: Flair Books.

McIver, Stuart. 1991. *True Tales of the Everglades.* Miami, Fla.: Florida Flair Books.

Miller, Tyler G. Jr. 1990. *Resource Conservation and Management.* Belmont, Calif.: Wadsworth Publishing Company.

Morton, Julia F. 1971. *Plants Poisonous to People in Florida and Other Warm Areas.* Miami, Fla.: Hurricane House.

Morton, Julia F. 1990. *Wild Plants for Survival in South Florida.* Miami, Fla.: Fairchild Tropical Garden.

Myers Ronald L., and John J. Ewel eds. 1990. *Ecosystems of Florida.* 1991. Orlando, Fla.: University of Central Florida Press.

Neil, Wilfred T. 1956. *Florida's Seminole Indians* 2nd ed. St. Petersburg, Fla.: Great Outdoors Publishing Co.

Newell, David M. 1974. *If Nothin' Don't Happen.* New York, N.Y.: Alfred A. Knopf.

Niering, William A. 1984. *Wetlands: An Audubon Society Nature Guide.* New York, N.Y.: Alfred A. Knopf

Odum, E. P. 1983. *Basic Ecology.* Philadelphia, Penn.: Saunders College Publications.

Odum, Eugene P. 1989. *Ecology and our Endangered Life-Support Systems.* Sunderland, Mass.: Sinauer Associates, Inc.

Oppel, Frank, and Tony Meisel. 1987. *Tales of Old Florida.* Secaucus, N.J.: Castle.

Orr, Katherine. 1989. *The Wonderous World of the Mangrove Swamps of the Everglades and Florida Keys.* Miami, Fla.: Florida Flair Books.

Regnier, Kathleen, Michael Gross, and Ron Zimmerman. 1992. *The Interpreter's Guidebook: Techniques for Programs and Presentations.* Stevens Point, Wisc.: UW-SP Foundation Press, Inc.

Robertson, William B. Jr. 1989. *Everglades: The Park Story.* 2nd ed. Homestead, Fla.: Florida National Parks and Monuments Association, Inc.

Robson, Lucia St. Clair. 1988. *Light a Distant Fire.* New York, N.Y.: Ballantine Books.

Ross, Sande. 1990. *The Nature of Dade County, A Hometown Handbook.* Miami Springs, Fla.: Friends of the Everglades.

Smiley, Nixon. 1977. *Florida: Land of Images.* Miami, Fla.: E. A. Seemann Publishing, Inc.

Smith, Patrick D. 1984. *A Land Remembered..* Sarasota, Fla.: Pineapple Press, Inc.

Smith, Patrick D. 1987. *Forever Island and Allapattah: A Patrick Smith Reader.* Sarasota, Fla.: Pineapple Press, Inc.

Stevenson, George B. 1969. *Trees of Everglades National Park and the Florida Keys.* Homestead Fla.: Florida National Parks & Monuments Association, Inc.

Stone, Calvin, R. 1979. *Forty Years in the Everglades.* Tabor City, N.C.: Atlantic Publishing Co.

Tarver, David P., et al. 1979. *Aquatic and Wetland Plants of Florida.* Tallahassee, Fla.: Florida Department of Natural Resources.

Taylor, Carla, ed. 1985. *Ground Water: A Vital Resource.* Knoxville, Tenn.: Tennessee Valley Authority.

Tebeau, Charlton W. 1968. *Man in the Everglades: 2000 Years of Human History in the Everglades National Park.* Coral Gables, Fla.: University of Miami Press.

Tebeau, Charlton W. 1991. *The Story of the Chokoloskee Bay Country.* Miami, Fla.: Florida Flair Books.

Toops, Connie, and Willard E. Dilley. 1986. *Birds of South Florida: An Interpretive Guide.* Conway, Ark.: River Road Press.

Toops, Connie. 1988. *The Alligator: Monarch of the Marsh.* Homestead, Fla.: Florida National Parks and Monuments Association, Inc.

Truitt, John O., and Louis D. Ober. 1971. *A Guide to the Lizards of South Florida.* Miami, Fla.: Hurricane House Publishers, Inc.

Unterbrink, Mary. 1984. *Manatees: Gentle Giants in Peril.* St. Petersburg, Fla.: Great Outdoors Publishing Co.

Van Meter, Victoria B. 1992. *Florida's Sea Turtles.* Florida Power and Light Co.

Weber, Jeff. 1986. *A Visitor's Guide to the Everglades.* Miami, Fla.: Florida Flair Books.

Whitehead, Charles E. 1991. *The Camp-fires of the Everglades or Wild Sport in the South.* Gainesville, Fla.: University of Florida Press.

Will, Lawrence E. 1984. *A Dredgeman of Cape Sable.* Belle Glade, Fla.: The Glades Historical Society.

Winsberg, Morton D. 1990. *Florida Weather.* Orlando, Fla.: University of Central Florida Press.

Zim, Herbert S., and Alexander C. Martin. Rev. Ed. 1987. *Trees.* New York, N.Y.: Golden Press.

Water Watchers: Water Conservation Curriculum for Junior High School Science and Social Studies Classes. 1989. Boston, Ma.: Massachusetts Water Resources Authority.

Water Wisdom. Boston, Ma.: Massachusetts Water Resources Authority.

WOW!: The Wonders Of Wetlands. 1995. Published through a partnership between Environmental Concern Inc., St. Michaels, Md., and The Watercourse, Bozeman, Mont.

Journals, Reports, and Reprints

Dahm, Clifford N., editor. 1995. "Kissimmee River Restoration," *Restoration Ecology,* September 1995, 145-238.

Doehring, F., I. W. Duedall, and J. M. Williams. 1994. *Florida Hurricanes and Tropical Storms, 1871-1993: An Historical Survey.* Technical Paper 71. Florida Sea Grant College.

Duplaix, Nicole. "South Florida Water: Paying the Price," *National Geographic,* July, 1990, 89-101.

Hillis, D. M., M. T. Dixon and A. L. Jones, "Minimal Genetic Variation in a Morphologically Diverse Species (Florida Tree Snail, *Liguus fasciatus*)," *Journal of Heredity* 82 (1991) 282-286.

Holloway, Marguerite. 1994. "Nurturing Nature: Trends in Biological Restoration." *Scientific American.* April, 99-108.

Jones, Archie L., "Descriptions of Six New Forms of Florida Tree Snails, *Liguus fasciatus*," *Nautilus* 94 (1979) 153-159.

Loope, Lloyd, et al. "Hurricane Impact on Uplands and Freshwater Swamp Forest," *BioScience,* April 1994, 238-246.

Pierce, Charles William. 1962. "The Cruise of the Bonton," *Tequesta, The Journal of the Historical Association of Southern Florida,* Number XXII. Miami, Fla.: University of Miami Press.

Pimm, Stuart L., et al. "Hurricane Andrew," *BioScience,* April 1994, 224-229.

Roman, Charles T., et al. "Hurricane Andrew's Impact on Freshwater Resources," *BioScience,* April 1994, 247-255.

Smith III, Thomas J., et al. "Mangroves, Hurricanes, and Lightning Strikes," *BioScience,* April 1994, 256-262.

Taylor, Dale L. 1981. *Fire History and Fire Records for Everglades National Park 1948-1979.* Homestead, Fla.: National Park Service, South Florida Research Center, Everglades National Park.

Tilmant, James T., et al. "Hurricane Andrew's Effects on Marine Resources," *BioScience,* April 1994, 230-237.

White, William A. 1970. *The Geomorphology of the Florida Peninsula.* Tallahassee, Fla.: State of Florida Department of Natural Resources.

Magazines

Hardy, John T. "Where the Sea Meets the Sky," *Natural History,* May 1991, 59-65.

Loftin, Jan P. 1993. "In the Wake of Hurricane Andrew." *Florida Water* (Winter): 3-9.

McGivney, Annette. "Mother Nature's Theme Park," *Backpacker,* April 1994, 52-59.

Monks, Vicki. "Engineering the Everglades: the Army Corps Begins to Undo Its Own Damage," *National Parks,* September-October 1990, 32-36; 44.

Postel, Sandra. "The Not-For-Everglades?" *World Watch,* March-April 1991, 34.

Ross, Kevlin. "Army Corps' Change of Heart: Florida's Kissimmee River to Meander Once More," *Currents,* July-August 1990, 22-24.

Toner, Mike. "Fixing A Broken River," *National Wildlife,* April-May 1991, 19-20.

Underwood, Ellen P., and Jan P. Loftin. "The Everglades: Back to the Future," *Florida Water,* winter 1995, 14-18.

Williams, Joy. "The Imaginary Everglades," *Outside,* January 1994, 38-43; 90-95.

Wray, Phoebe. "Manatees Slide Toward Extinction," *E Magazine,* July-August 1990, 10-11.

"The Everglades In the 21st Century: The Water Management Future," *Florida Naturalist,* spring 1993, 10-11.

"Wetlands" *Buzzworm,* November-December 1991, 57.

Miscellaneous

Ground Water Flow Model: a Plexiglas sand tank model, video, and user's guide that demonstrate basic ground water principles and management concerns. Contact: Project WET, 201 Culbertson Hall, Montana State University, Bozeman, MT 59717. (406) 994-5392.

Florida Department of Environmental Protection (DEP), 3900 Commonwealth Boulevard, Tallahassee, FL 32399.

Florida Exotic Pest Plant Council, 3205 College Avenue, Ft. Lauderdale, FL 33314.

Florida Water. (biennial). Contact: South Florida Water Management District, West Palm Beach, FL.

Bureau of Aquatic Plant Management, Technical Services Section, 3917 Commonwealth Boulevard, Tallahassee, FL 32399.

Major Watersheds

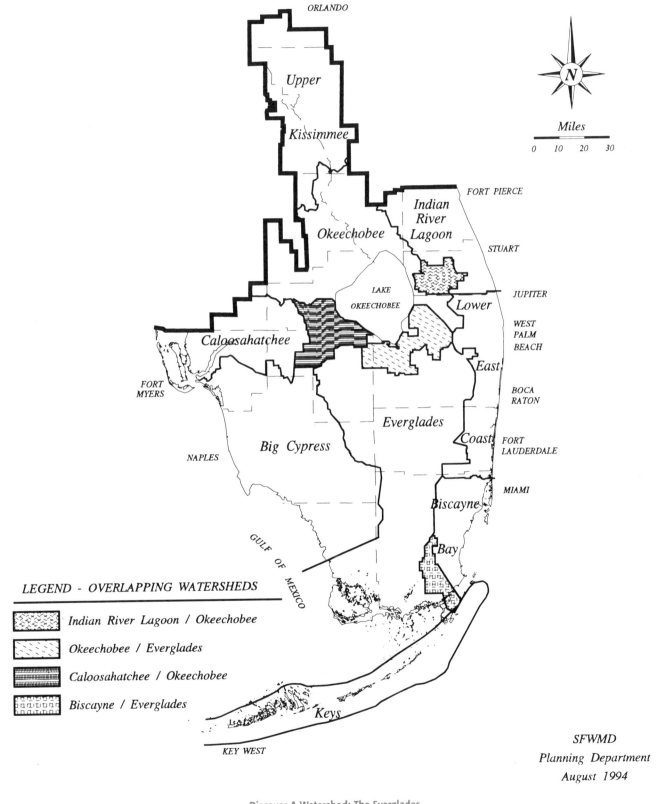

ORLANDO

Upper

Kissimmee

Okeechobee

Indian River Lagoon

FORT PIERCE

STUART

LAKE OKEECHOBEE

JUPITER

Lower

WEST PALM BEACH

Caloosahatchee

East

BOCA RATON

FORT MYERS

Everglades

Coast

FORT LAUDERDALE

NAPLES

Big Cypress

MIAMI

Biscayne

Bay

GULF OF MEXICO

Keys

KEY WEST

LEGEND - OVERLAPPING WATERSHEDS

Indian River Lagoon / Okeechobee

Okeechobee / Everglades

Caloosahatchee / Okeechobee

Biscayne / Everglades

Miles

0   10   20   30

SFWMD
Planning Department
August 1994

C&SF Flood Control System

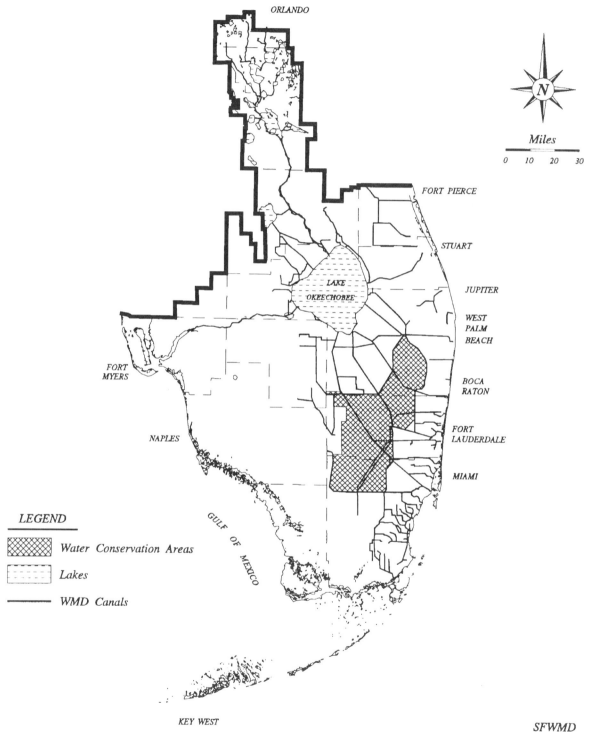

ORLANDO

FORT PIERCE

STUART

JUPITER

WEST
PALM
BEACH

LAKE
OKEECHOBEE

BOCA
RATON

FORT
MYERS

FORT
LAUDERDALE

NAPLES

MIAMI

GULF OF MEXICO

LEGEND

Water Conservation Areas

Lakes

WMD Canals

KEY WEST

Miles

0 10 20 30

SFWMD
Planning Department
March 1994

Ground Water Supply

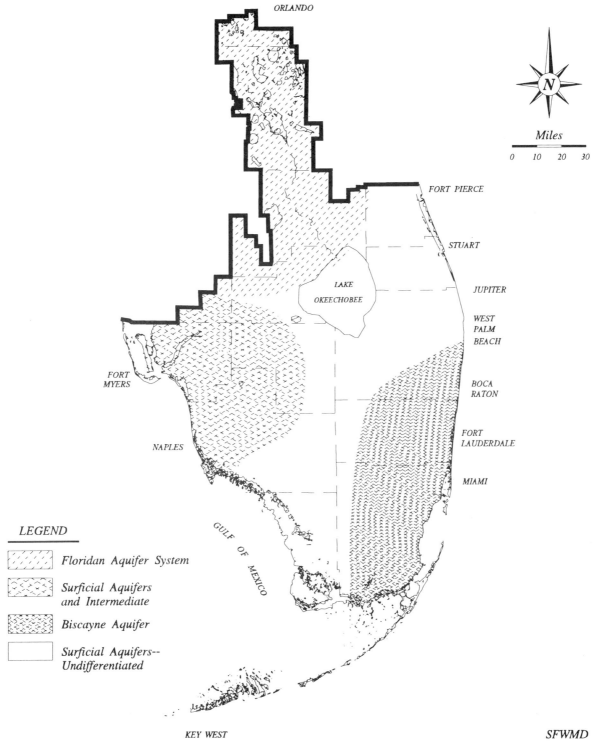

ORLANDO

FORT PIERCE

STUART

JUPITER

LAKE
OKEECHOBEE

WEST
PALM
BEACH

BOCA
RATON

FORT
MYERS

FORT
LAUDERDALE

MIAMI

NAPLES

GULF OF MEXICO

Miles

0   10   20   30

N

LEGEND

Floridan Aquifer System

Surficial Aquifers
and Intermediate

Biscayne Aquifer

Surficial Aquifers--
Undifferentiated

KEY WEST

SFWMD
Planning Department
March 1994

STA's (Stormwater Treatment Areas)

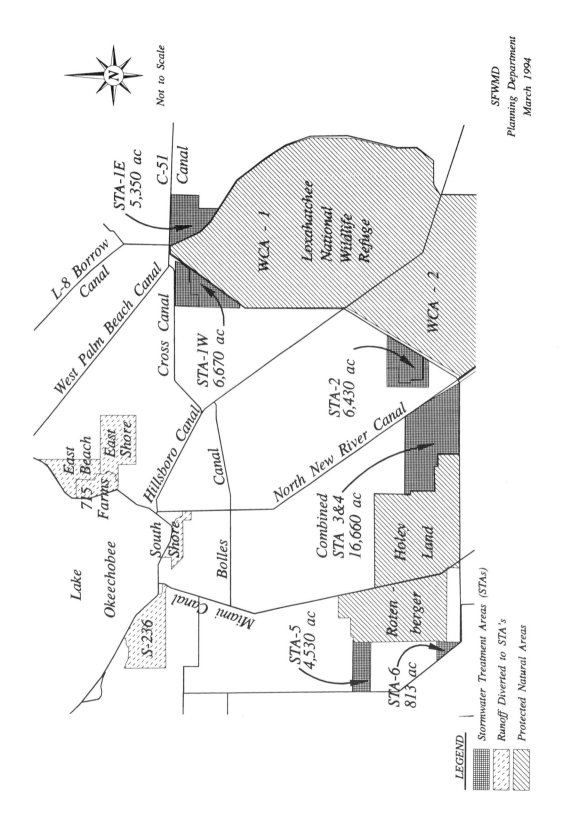

LEGEND

Stormwater Treatment Areas (STAs)

Runoff Diverted to STA's

Protected Natural Areas

STA-1E 5,350 ac

C-51 Canal

L-8 Borrow Canal

West Palm Beach Canal

Cross Canal

STA-1W 6,670 ac

WCA - 1

Loxahatchee National Wildlife Refuge

WCA - 2

STA-2 6,430 ac

Hillsboro Canal

North New River Canal

Combined STA 3&4 16,660 ac

East Beach 755

East Shore

South Shore

Bolles Canal

Lake Okeechobee

Miami Canal

S-236

STA-5 4,530 ac

STA-6 813 ac

Holey Land

Roten - berger Land

Not to Scale

N

SFWMD
Planning Department
March 1994

Evolution of the Canal and Levee System

West Palm Beach Canal

North New River Canal

Hillsboro Canal

Miami Canal

1920

Caloosahatchee River Canal

St. Lucie Canal

Herbert Hoover Dike around Lake Okeechobee

Tamiami Trail Canal

1930

1950

Lake Istokpoga

1960

C-38 Canal

L-67

L-28

Alligator Alley Canal

1970

Present

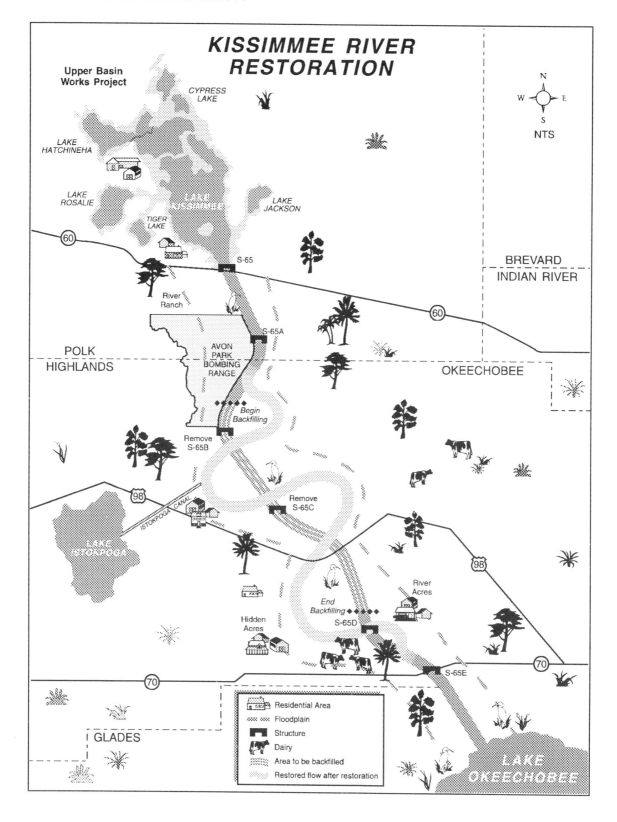

KISSIMMEE RIVER RESTORATION

Upper Basin Works Project

CYPRESS LAKE

LAKE HATCHINEHA

LAKE ROSALIE

TIGER LAKE

LAKE JACKSON

N
W E
S
NTS

(60)

BREVARD
INDIAN RIVER

S-65

River Ranch

S-65A

(60)

POLK
HIGHLANDS

AVON PARK BOMBING RANGE

OKEECHOBEE

Begin Backfilling

Remove S-65B

(98)

ISTOKPOGA CANAL

Remove S-65C

LAKE ISTOKPOGA

(98)

River Acres

End Backfilling

S-65D

Hidden Acres

S-65E

(70)

(70)

Residential Area
Floodplain
Structure
Dairy
Area to be backfilled
Restored flow after restoration

GLADES

LAKE OKEECHOBEE

© The Watercourse, 1996

268

2050 VISION

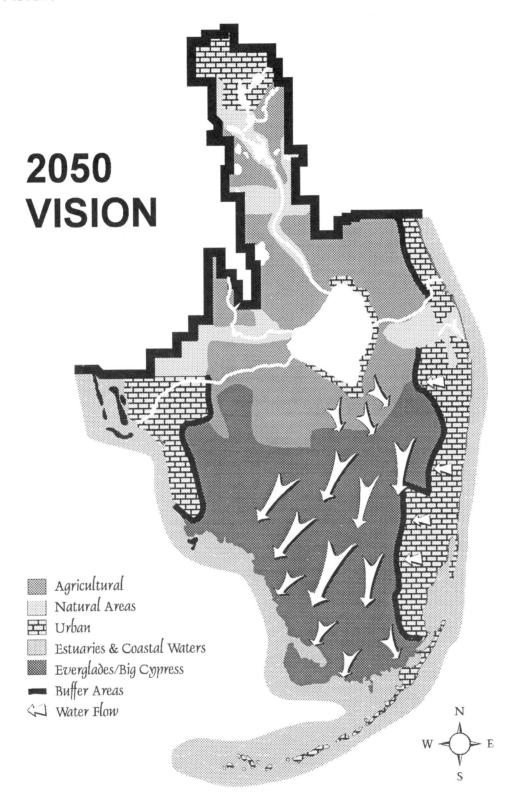

Agricultural
Natural Areas
Urban
Estuaries & Coastal Waters
Everglades/Big Cypress
Buffer Areas
Water Flow

Index

depression, cone of 168, 170, 172

depressions, tropical 40, 41

desiccation 16, 205

detritus 28-29, 64-65, 67, 95

devil's claw 55, 251

diatoms 5, 95, 99

discharge 12, 38, 76, 166

Disston, Hamilton 118, 122, 216

District, Central and Southern Florida Flood Control 118, 122-123

District, South Florida Water Management 48, 75, 83, 116, 118, 123-125, 127-130, 132-138, 140, 146, 163, 176, 216, 221, 229-230, 234-235, 239, 242, 246

diversity 16, 44, 56-57, 68, 70, 88, 91, 96, 99, 122, 132, 142-143, 145, 147, 184-185, 203-204, 207-210, 228

divide, drainage 161

dogwood, Jamaica 68, 88, 209, 251

dolphin, Atlantic bottle-nosed 81, 83

dome, cypress 44

Donna, Hurricane 39, 44, 46, 64, 177, 179

Dorn, J. K. 111

Douglas, Marjory Stoneman 19, 102, 109, 179, 212, 215-216, 218, 242-243, 246

drought 12, 15, 35, 47-48, 50, 57, 62, 69-70, 74, 92, 94-95, 97, 122, 125, 129, 144, 169, 202, 214, 220, 236-237

drum, red 65, 254

Duane, J. E. 46

eagle, bald 87, 208, 255

ecosystem 5, 10, 17, 19, 29, 34-35, 37, 68, 70, 74, 80-81, 88, 90-96, 98-101, 121, 124, 126, 128, 130, 130-131, 134, 136-137, 139-140, 142-143, 145-148, 198, 202-204, 210, 220-222, 227-229, 244-245

ecotone 88, 90, 121, 207-210

effect, Coriolis 37, 40-41

effect, edge 55, 88, 96, 186, 190, 207-210

effect, peninsular 88, 207-208

effects, cumulative 125, 128

egret, cattle 84-85, 256

egret, great 84, 86, 256

egret, snowy 84, 86, 256

endemic 77, 81, 85, 90, 208

enrichment, nutrient 141

energy, maintenance 99-100

Engineers, U. S. Army Corps of 83, 118, 122, 127, 129, 146, 230

ephemeral (streams) 12

Epidendrum 58, 251

epiphytes 53, 56-57, 179

Epoch, Eocene 24

Epoch, Miocene 24

Epoch, Oligocene 24

Epoch, Paleocene 24

Epoch, Pleistocene 21, 24, 30

Epoch, Pliocene 24

equation, hydrologic 12

equator 20, 35, 37, 40, 173

erosion 12, 15, 18, 20, 22, 27, 30-31, 97, 101, 143, 163, 185, 195-196, 198, 223-224

estivation 95, 203

estuaries, effects on 145

estuary 5, 8, 10, 14, 16, 65, 95, 127, 142, 145, 154-156, 163, 205-206

eutrophication 13, 160, 162, 227-228

evaporation 9-10, 12, 25, 36, 48, 59, 129-130, 153-154, 162, 185

evapotranspiration 12, 48, 125, 154

events, current 232-233

extinction 10, 17, 71, 93, 117, 177, 220

eyewall 39, 42-43

facies 25

fern, resurrection 57, 252

ferns 10, 49, 53, 57, 61, 71, 88, 192

fetterbush 51-53, 251

fig, strangler 55, 67, 253

fire 34, 47, 50-54, 59-60, 79, 91, 96-99, 101-102, 110, 113, 117, 125, 145, 177, 184, 186, 216, 218, 221, 224

fire, changes in the role of 145

fire-dependent 96, 98

fish 5, 10, 30, 41, 44, 48, 60-61, 64-65, 68-71, 76, 79, 82, 84-85, 90-95, 101, 103, 112, 114-115, 123, 134-135, 142, 144, 146, 185, 202-203, 216, 224, 244, 254

fish, commercial 10, 70

fish, peripheral freshwater 69

fish, primary freshwater 69

fish, secondary freshwater 69

flag, alligator 61, 188, 190, 251

flagfish 69, 95, 254

Flagler, Henry 111, 118, 216-217

Flamingo 64, 85, 95, 110-111, 113-115, 177, 256

flatwoods, pine 7, 50-53, 191, 205

flood 10, 12, 35, 41, 44, 46, 48, 50, 66, 75, 83, 95, 98, 118, 122-123, 125-127, 130, 133-135, 137, 140, 185, 202, 212, 214, 228, 232, 236, 243-244

floodplain 7, 134-135, 156, 229

floor, forest 55, 96-97, 191, 205

flow, base 12, 143

Florida, Miccosukee Tribe of Indians of (Native Americans) 108

flow, channel 12

flow, ground water 12, 168-170, 266

flow, overland 12

flow, sheet 7, 13, 123, 129, 142-143, 147, 161-162, 228, 242-244

flow, storm 12

Fontaneda, Escalante de 103, 109

foraminifera 27

Formation, Anastasia 24, 26, 28, 32

Formation, Avon Park 24

Formation, Cedar Keys 24, 33

Formation, Cypresshead 24, 32

Formation, Fort Thompson 24, 32

Lagoon, Indian River 66, 137

Lagoon, Lake worth 66

Lake, Cypress 11

Lake, Turkey 7, 11, 131

Lakes, Upper Chain of 7, 11, 18, 121, 137, 242, 245

landfall 39-41, 43-44, 176, 178, 182-183

latitude 8, 16, 31, 35, 37, 39-40, 43, 50, 173-176, 178

Latitudes, Horse 43

layer, impermeable 15, 165, 168

layers, permeable 170

leaf, satin 88

lenticels 63, 196

Leon, Juan Ponce de 109

lifting, atmospheric 36

lightning 9, 38, 77, 79, 96, 101

lily, white water 61, 253

limbo, gumbo 56, 67, 88, 190, 251

limestone 13-14, 20-22, 24-28, 30-34, 50, 53, 59, 61, 127, 154, 166-168, 171, 191-192, 205

Limestone, Miami 22, 24-28, 30-31

Limestone, Ocala 24, 32

Limestone, Oldsmar 24

limestone, oolitic 26

Limestone, Suwanee 24, 32

Limestone, Tamiami 14, 24

limpkin 94, 256

lobster, spiny 10-11, 64, 66-67, 243, 253

log, well 165-172

longitude 40, 176, 178

mahogany 252

maidencane 61, 252

mammals 60, 65, 68, 76, 81-82, 94-95, 97, 202-203, 223, 256

manatee 53, 66, 81-83, 145, 206, 252, 257

mangrove 7, 16, 21, 28-29, 41, 43-44, 50, 59, 62-67, 74-78, 81-83, 96, 100, 109-110, 113-114, 121, 129, 177, 179, 184, 193, 195-201, 229, 251-254

mangrove, black 63-64, 196, 199-201, 251

mangrove, red 62-64, 196, 199-201, 252

mangrove, white 63-64, 196, 199-201, 253

maple, red 208, 252

maritime 34, 37, 56

marl 5, 14, 19-22, 24, 60-61, 91, 123, 177, 205

Marl, Caloosahatchee 24

marsh, salt 16, 65, 78, 95, 128

marshes 6-7, 12, 16, 21, 36, 48, 50, 52, 58-60, 65, 68, 70-71, 77, 99-100, 106, 121, 128, 135-136, 184, 205, 243

marshes, coastal 50, 65, 184

marshes, freshwater 7, 50, 52, 59, 71, 77, 121, 128, 184, 205

Marshall, Art 134

mastic 88, 252

melaleuca 125-126, 144, 219-227, 243, 252

mercury 142

Miccosukee (Native Amercians) 105-109

Miami 7, 11, 22, 24-28, 30-32, 110-112, 118, 129, 186, 198, 210, 215, 217-218

microclimate 19, 96

microflora 92, 132

mink, Everglades 81, 256

Model, Everglades Landscape 140

Model, Natural System 140

Model, South Florida Regional Simulation 140

Model, Wetlands Water Quality 140

mollusks 27-28, 65-66, 253

moonflower 34, 66, 252

mosaics, vegetative 44, 98-99

mosquitofish 8, 69, 71, 91-95, 206, 208, 254

mosquitoes 92, 95, 253

moss, Spanish 57, 102-103, 189, 192, 253

mulberry, red 252

mullet 64-65, 67, 69, 112-113, 129, 254

myrtle, wax 51, 55, 253

needlerush, black 65, 251

nesting 29, 31, 41, 48, 60, 65-66, 71, 73-76, 78-80, 90-91, 93, 114, 123-124, 127, 129, 143-144, 185, 203

newt, eastern 70

niche, ecological 90, 202-204, 228

nitrogen 34, 100-101, 131, 133, 228

nocturnal 70, 78-79, 203

nutrients 7, 10, 12-14, 56, 60, 62, 91, 96-97, 100-101, 125, 129-133, 142, 147, 162, 196, 205

nutrients, recycling of 96

oak, dwarf live 51, 251

oak, live 51, 55, 57, 188, 190, 208, 251

oak, turkey 53, 253

Okeechobee, Lake 7-8, 11, 18, 21, 24, 36, 40, 46-49, 52, 59, 70, 102-103, 118, 121-122, 128, 131, 133-135, 137, 141-143, 147, 154-155, 160-163, 183, 208, 218, 221, 227-228, 234, 242-245

oligotrophy 101

omnivorous 91, 94

ooids 24-25

oolite 19, 25, 27

opossum 54, 257

orchid, butterfly 57-58, 251

orchids 10, 53, 55, 57-58, 67, 88, 115, 124, 193, 208

osmosis, reverse 32, 137, 167

Osceola 105, 107

ospreys 67, 85, 129

otter, river 82, 100, 208, 257

outcropping 25

overstory 52, 97

owl, barred 86, 208, 255

oxeye, sea 65, 252

Ridge, Central Florida 7, 15, 161

rise, sea level 28-29, 33, 128

River, Caloosahatchee 11, 217

River, Kissimmee 7-8, 11, 121, 134-135, 137, 142, 153-156, 161-162, 215, 218, 227-230, 234, 242-245

River, Shark 13, 28, 61, 82, 92, 129-130

River, Saint Lucie 8, 11

robin 208, 255

rock, pinnacle 18-19, 25-26, 61, 67, 99

rock, sedimentary 19-20, 22, 31

rockland, South Florida 53

rockplowing 126-127

roots, cable 63, 196

roots, drop 62, 196

roots, peg 63, 196

roots, prop 28, 62, 66-67, 79, 196-199

rosemary, Florida 52, 251

runoff 7, 12, 16, 62, 127, 131, 137, 144-145, 154, 160, 162, 166, 196, 205, 243

runoff, subsurface 12

runoff, surface 12

rush, spike 61, 253

rushes 251

salamander, dwarf 70, 255

salinity 25, 44, 65, 69, 129-130, 145, 162-163

Sanctuary, Corkscrew Swamp 58

Sand, Pamlico 22

sand, quartz 22, 24, 26, 29

sandstone 20, 22, 24, 32

saturation, zone of 165, 168, 170

Schinus (Brazilian pepper) 126, 251

scrub 7, 50, 52-53, 99, 184

sedge 34, 61, 252-253

sedge, white-topped 253

sediment 7, 20-22, 26-29, 62, 65, 131-132, 162-163, 166

sediments, undifferentiated 32

Seminole (Native Americans) 11, 78, 82, 98, 102, 105-111, 135, 190-191, 212, 216-217

serotinous 96

shrimp, grass 68, 253

shrimp, pink 11, 64, 67-68, 145, 253

silica 28

siren, greater 70, 255

siren, lesser 70

skink, southeastern five-lined 80, 255

slough 7-8, 13, 58-59, 61, 82, 90, 92, 116, 129-130, 144, 156, 205-206, 208, 243

Slough, Nubbin 8

Slough, Shark River 13, 61, 82, 92, 129-130

Slough, Taylor 13, 61, 116, 129-130, 144, 243

sloughs 7-8, 12-13, 16, 28, 59, 61, 68, 70, 72-73, 76, 78, 82, 205

snails, apple 82, 90, 94-95, 146, 203

snails, tree 44, 68-69, 89, 95, 115, 124, 138-139, 179, 193

snake, corn 139, 206, 254

snake, eastern coral 76-77, 255

snake, eastern hognose 78

snake, eastern indigo 77-78, 255

snake, Everglades rat 78

snake, king 116, 255

snake, mangrove salt marsh 78

snake, rough green 54, 78, 255

snake, yellow rat 78

snapper, mangrove 64, 129, 254

snapper, red 70, 254

snook 64-65, 67, 69-70, 129, 254

sofkee 54, 191

sparrow, Cape Sable seaside 84, 90, 136, 208, 256

specialist 90, 202-203

species 90, 207

species, alien 70, 144

species, introduced 70, 127, 142, 144, 219-220, 223

species, indigenous 220

species, invasive 144, 179

species, keystone 90, 203

species, nonnative 41, 51, 127, 136, 144, 219-221, 223

spider, golden orb weaver 68, 139, 254

spoonbill, roseate 85-86, 256

squirrel, gray 208, 257

squirrels, fox 81

stages, seral 97

staggerbush 52, 253

stomata 63, 101, 154

stopper, white 56, 189, 191, 253

stork, wood 90, 92-93, 95, 124, 155, 256

storm, tropical 40-42, 182, 233

storms, Cape Verde 40

storms, convection 37, 39

storms, low-pressure 34, 38

strands, cypress 52, 59, 142

Stream, Gulf 7, 25, 34, 36-37, 81, 174

Stream, Polar Jet 34, 38

subsidence, soil 137

subsidy, energy 100

substrate 30, 50, 60, 75, 98, 127

succession, plant 97-98

succession, primary 98

succession, secondary 98

succulent 63, 65, 95

sugar cane 6, 60, 112, 114, 131, 133

sulfur 34, 100-101, 228

sunfish 69, 94, 100, 254

sunfish, bluespotted 69, 254

surge, storm 41-42, 44, 176-178, 183, 195-196, 198

Swamp, Big Cypress 58-59, 147

Other Watercourse Publications

. . . .

The Watercourse has produced a number of publications that explore diverse water and natural resource topics. The *Project WET Curriculum and Activity Guide* contains over 90 innovative water activities and is available from State Project WET coordinators at locally-sponsored workshops. *WOW! The Wonders Of Wetlands* has over 70 pages of new background material followed by more than 40 proven activities from the original publication produced by Environmental Concern Inc. *Water Conservation Module for Educators* is designed for middle-school and secondary educators, and presents information and activities aimed at using water more efficiently, in a format to encourage individual and group participation.

The *WETnet Newsletter* provides readers news on water and environmental education trends, grant information and fundraising strategies, and the experience of over 38 state Project WET coordinators. *Science Activities* is a collection of seven selected Project WET activities. *The Liquid Treasure Water History Trunk: Learning From the Past* contains stories, activities and information for procuring artifacts needed to assemble a water history trunk. *A Landowner's Guide to Western*

Water Rights is an informative reference to a confusing and often sensitive issue. *Water Celebration! A Handbook* provides everything you need to know about putting on your own water festival.

Getting to Know the Waters of Yellowstone, produced in cooperation with the National Park Service, celebrates the park's water resources, its geothermal features, rivers and waterfalls and relates how plants and animals adapt to Yellowstone's unique water environments. *Water, a Gift of Nature* explores the many facets of water through beautiful full-color photographs and interpretive text. *The Rainstick, A Fable* features a story based in West Africa, factual information, and directions for building an ancient instrument, the rainstick, through which contemporary people find a connection with their environment. *The Water Story* is a 16-page booklet for upper elementary and middle-school-aged students that tells the story of water through creative, hands-on activities, projects, games and a poster.

The Ground Water Flow Model Package includes a model, users guide and video, and everything needed to conduct a ground water education class or workshop.

For further information contact:

The Watercourse
201 Culbertson Hall
Montana State University
Bozeman, Montana 59717.
OR phone (406) 994-5392
or fax (406) 994-1919

. . . .